Praise for the first edition:

"Pastor has occupied one of the more illuminating vantage points for examining Washington's vexing relations with its southern neighbors. . . . [His] goal is to help construct a new United States policy, shifting away from reflexive, sometimes covert interventions and from economic handouts. . . . He prefers a policy based on free trade and multinational efforts by groups like the Organization of American States to guarantee democracy."

—**CLIFFORD KRAUSS,**
NEW YORK TIMES

"A magnificent contribution to understanding U.S.–Latin America relations and for offering a provocative vision of the relationship in the 21st century."

—**RAUL ALFONSÍN,**
PRESIDENT OF ARGENTINA
(1983–89)

"Pastor sweeps us through 200 years of U.S. relations with Latin America . . . probing, knowledgeable, insightful, he identifies key issues and suggests answers."

—**PIERO GLEIJESES,**
WASHINGTON POST

"As we move into the post-Cold War phase of international relations, the analysis and policy recommendations contained in this excellent, timely book will help all of us who are trying to think through the implications of this new period for U.S. national security."

—**SAM NUNN,**
FORMER CHAIRMAN,
SENATE COMMITTEE ON ARMED SERVICES

"An impressive volume . . . a significant contribution to rethinking U.S. relations with our closest neighbors."

—**ABRAHAM F. LOWENTHAL,**
FOREIGN AFFAIRS

"Robert Pastor has written yet another brilliant book on the United States and Latin America. Again, he interprets the future against the background of the past. His proposals for future policy are creative, imaginative and intellectually sound. This book is required reading for everyone concerned with U.S.–Latin American policy in the years ahead. He is right on target."

—**THEODORE M. HESBURGH, C.S.C.,**
PRESIDENT EMERITUS,
UNIVERSITY OF NOTRE DAME

"Dr. Pastor's book provides important insights into the complex historical relationship between the United States and Latin America and the Caribbean. By isolating the excessive weight of the ideological elements that dominated inter-American links during the Cold War, Dr. Pastor allows us to see in a fresh light the pattern of hope and error in our cyclical and unequal agenda."

—**JAVIER PÉREZ DE CUÉLLAR,**
FORMER SECRETARY GENERAL
OF THE UNITED NATIONS

"How will U.S. relations with Latin America change after the Cold War? Robert Pastor brings years of experience as a scholar and practitioner to the question, and comes up with provocative and innovative answers."

—**JOSEPH S. NYE, JR.,**
DEAN, JOHN F. KENNEDY
SCHOOL OF GOVERNMENT,
HARVARD UNIVERSITY

EXITING THE WHIRLPOOL

OTHER BOOKS BY ROBERT A. PASTOR

A Century's Journey: How the Great Powers Shape the World (editor, 1999)

The Controversial Pivot: The U.S. Congress and North America (edited with Rafael Fernandez de Castro, 1998)

Collective Responses to Regional Problems: The Case of Latin America and the Caribbean (coedited with Carl Kaysen and Laura Reed, 1994)

Democracy in the Caribbean: Political, Economic, and Social Perspectives (coedited with Jorge Dominguez and Delisle Worrel, 1993)

Integration with Mexico: Options for U.S. Policy (1993)

Whirlpool: U.S. Foreign Policy Toward Latin America and the Caribbean (1992) (First edition published by Princeton University Press) *(El Remolino: Politica Exterior de Estados Unidos Hacia America Latina y el Caribe,* 1995)

Democracy in the Americas: Stopping the Pendulum (editor, 1989)

Condemned to Repetition: The United States and Nicaragua (1987; with new epilogue, 1988)

Limits to Friendship: The United States and Mexico (with Jorge G. Castañeda, 1988) (*Limites en la Amistad: Mexico y Estados Unidos*)

Latin America's Debt Crisis: Adjusting to the Past or Planning for the Future? (editor, 1987)

Migration and Development in the Caribbean: The Unexplored Connection (editor, 1985)

Congress and the Politics of U.S. Foreign Economic Policy (1980)

EXITING THE WHIRLPOOL

U.S. Foreign Policy Toward Latin America and the Caribbean

Second Edition

ROBERT A. PASTOR

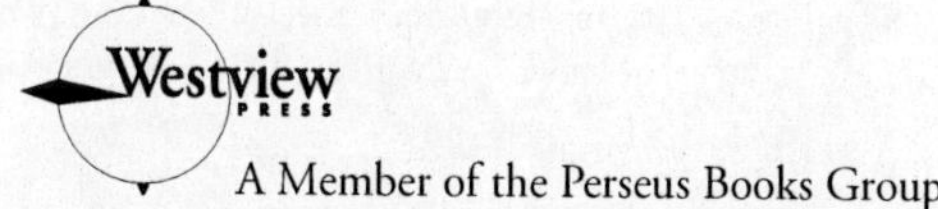

A Member of the Perseus Books Group

Published in 2001 in the United States of America by Westview Press, 5500 Central Avenue, Boulder, Colorado 80301-2877, and in the United Kingdom by Westview Press, 12 Hid's Copse Road, Cumnor Hill, Oxford OX2 9JJ

Find us on the World Wide Web at www.westviewpress.com

Library of Congress Cataloging-in-Publication Data
Pastor, Robert A.
Exiting the whirlpool : U.S. foreign policy toward Latin America and the Caribbean / Robert A. Pastor. — Rev. and expanded 2nd. ed.
p. cm.
Rev. and expanded 2nd. ed. of: Whirlpool. 1992.
Includes bibliographical references and index.
ISBN 0-8133-3811-5
1. Latin America—Foreign relations—United States. 2. United States—Foreign relations—Latin America. 3. Caribbean Area—Foreign relations—United States. 4. United States—Foreign relations—Caribbean Area. 5. United States—Foreign relations—1945–1989. 6. United States—Foreign relations—1989–1993. 7. United States—Foreign relations—1993– I. Pastor, Robert A. Whirlpool. II. Title.
F1418.P365 2001
327.308—dc21 00-049529

The paper used in this publication meets the requirements of the American National Standard for Permanence of Paper for Printed Library Materials Z39.48-1984.

10 9 8 7

To
Margy, Tiffin, and Kip

Whirlpool: *an eddy or vortex of water that moves rapidly in a circle so as to produce a depression in the center, into which floating objects may be drawn.*

—**WEBSTER'S NEW COLLEGIATE DICTIONARY**

It has happened in twenty places, twenty countries, islands, colonies, territories—these words with which we play, thinking they are interchangeable and that the use of a particular one alters the truth. I cannot see our predicament as unique. . . . The pace of events . . . is not more than the pace of a chaos on which strict limits have been imposed. I speak of territories . . . set adrift yet not altogether abandoned, where this controlled chaos approximates in the end, after the heady speeches and token deportations, to a continuing order. The chaos lies all within.

—***V. S. NAIPAUL*, THE MIMIC MEN**

CONTENTS

TABLES AND FIGURES

Tables

Figures

PREFACE TO THE SECOND EDITION

I finished writing the first edition of this book in early 1992. The Soviet Union had just disappeared, and the Cold War, which had shaped U.S.–Latin American relations for forty-five years, was over. The book sought to explain U.S. policy toward the region in the twentieth century, although it focused primarily on the past three decades. To crystallize the American predicament, I used the metaphor of a whirlpool, a perilous eddy that draws the United States into its center where small countries like Cuba or Nicaragua become major obsessions and then, just as suddenly, releases the United States to drift to the rim, where Americans* forget the region and deal with other matters. At the end of the Cold War, as at the end of the two world wars, the United States drifted to the edge of the whirlpool, but it did not escape. My thesis was that the Cold War's end would be less important in shaping the future of U.S.–Latin American relations than two other phenomena: the consolidation of democracy and the expansion of freer trade. Subsequent developments have confirmed this thesis and have led me to modify the title to permit readers to realize that a permanent exit from the whirlpool is now possible. An entirely new relationship—a modern and respectful one—is now within reach.

The first edition was received very positively, and many colleagues, who used it in courses in inter-American relations, asked if I would write a new edition. This is what I have done. For teachers and others familiar with the first edition, I have added a chapter on the Clinton administration's policies toward the Americas and have updated the material, omit-

*For lack of a suitable alternative, I use *American* to refer to the citizens of the United States, even though the term ought to apply to all of the people of the Americas. In the past, Latin Americans sometimes referred to U.S. citizens as "Norteamericanos," but after the North American Free Trade Agreement (NAFTA), that term should refer to Canadians and Mexicans as well.

ted some details, and tightened the arguments. I have also reduced and rewritten the concluding section on strategies for exiting the whirlpool to illuminate the issues that face the hemisphere in the twenty-first century.

For Chapter 9 on revolutionary change, I have incorporated some startling new revelations based on interviews that I had in January 2000 in Grenada with senior revolutionary and military figures, who are serving sentences of life in prison. In October 1983, the United States invaded that island soon after the execution of Prime Minister Maurice Bishop and several of his ministers by the hard-line faction led by Deputy Prime Minister Bernard Coard. At the time, the administration claimed that the invasion was aimed to prevent Cuba from joining with Coard to seize the island. Through interviews with Coard and many others, including the colonel who ordered Bishop's arrest and the man who killed him, I learned that the probable motive for the murder was that Coard and the others feared that Bishop was about to invite Cuban military forces to intervene *against them.* Fidel Castro warned Coard not to hurt Bishop and, after his murder, refused to defend the regime.

Because of the asymmetry in power and wealth between the United States and Latin America, many books on the subject see the United States as the actor and Latin America as the dependent, defenseless object. It is true that the imbalance of power has pervasive effects on the relationship, but the premise of this book is that Latin Americans are also actors with more space to define and pursue their interests than the dependency paradigm would grant, or than they have used.

This interactive approach stands in sharp contrast to the more prevalent perspectives. Peter Smith, professor at the University of California, San Diego, suggests that a study of inter-American relations requires only a "meditation on the character and conduct of the United States" and how it has exercised "its perennial predominance." The title of his book, *Talons of the Eagle*, evokes a rapacious and unforgiving America.[1] Another respected scholar, Lars Schoultz of the University of North Carolina, weaves virtually every instance of American duplicity, arrogance, and interventionism into a seamless tapestry that is captured by the title of his book: *Beneath the United States: A History of U.S. Policy Toward Latin America.*[2] To understand U.S. policy, writes Schoultz, one should start with Thucydides' insight: "Large nations do what they wish, while small nations accept what they must." In Shoultz's view, the United States was motivated by a combination of "self-interest" and a belief in Latin America's inferiority.

Of course, all countries and people act out of "self-interest"; the hard questions are how each defines and pursues its interests. There have been times, as we shall see, when the United States defined its interests in narrow, military terms, as the Kennedy administration did in launching the Bay of Pigs invasion of Cuba in 1961, and there have been moments when it defined its interests in a far-sighted and cooperative manner, as the same administration did with the Alliance for Progress. That the United States is capable of both policies suggests that its image as a malevolent hegemone is, at the least, inadequate for explaining its policies. It also suggests that the process of defining interests and constructing strategies to pursue them is as significant, and perhaps as elusive, as the objective interest itself.

There are two other problems with the dependency paradigm. First, it does not help one enter the minds of U.S. policymakers to understand how they view their choices and how they define the national interest. This book aims to do that. Second, the other approach often conveys a sense of fatalism, that because Latin America is weak it is predestined to lose any collision with the "northern colossus." This has led to defiance or passivity. This book analyzes that unproductive interaction to find a means to escape it; it tries to explain the choices that are available to both sides so that both the United States and Latin America can discover more effective paths to pursue their respective interests.

It would be presumptuous to think that this book affected U.S. policy in the 1990s, but at least some satisfaction can be derived from the fact that inter-American relations moved in the direction that the first edition proposed. At the two Summits of the Americas in 1994 and 1998, the democratic leaders talked about a "hemispheric community of democracies" and a free trade area for the Americas, using the words and the themes sketched in Chapter 15 of the first edition.

Whether or not the book had any influence on policy, it certainly had an effect on me. After my nomination by President Clinton to be ambassador to Panama, the chapter on General Omar Torrijos was widely debated in Panama. Friends of Torrijos, Panama's ruler from 1968 to his death in 1981, liked the chapter, despite my criticism of his dictatorship; Torrijos's enemies overlooked my censure and were upset with the humorous anecdotes that made the general seem something other than an ogre. Several of them approached U.S. Senator Jesse Helms and expressed concern that if I were confirmed I might favor the military, only to realize that Helms opposed me for the opposite reason and, more simply, because I supported the Panama Canal Treaties.

The old battles fade away slowly. This book tries to understand them and to explain the choices and constraints of the presidents and Congress from Carter through Clinton, but mostly, this book is pointed toward the new opportunities in the Americas. At the beginning of the twenty-first century, the Americas can construct a unique region, one that integrates industrialized and developing countries in a democratic and peaceful framework. Understanding the past is the best preparation for charting the future.

In addition to all the people who reviewed the book in its first incarnation, let me also mention the following people, who offered useful comments to help me revise the book: Richard Bloomfield, Javier Corrales, Juan del Aguila, Jorge Dominguez, Richard Feinberg, Charles Hankla, and Joseph Tulchin. I also want to express my gratitude to Charles Hankla, Aaron Siegler, and Benjamin Goodrich for research assistance, and Sharon DeJohn for copyediting the manuscript. Karl Yambert, my editor at Westview, encouraged me to go forward with this project, and I am grateful to him for that. I owe my greatest debt to my wife, Margy, and my two children, Tiffin and Robert Kiplin, for giving me a compelling reason to exit the whirlpool. Readers of the previous book join me in thanking Kip for his masterful design of the original cover when he was just nine years old.

Robert Pastor

Notes

1. Peter H. Smith, *Talons of the Eagle: Dynamics of U.S.–Latin American Relations*, 2d ed. (New York: Oxford University Press, 2000), p. 4.

2. Lars Schoultz, *Beneath the United States: A History of U.S. Policy toward Latin America* (Cambridge, Mass.: Harvard University Press, 1998).

PREFACE TO THE FIRST EDITION

"The Panama Canal is ours. We bought it, and we should keep it!" In 1978, opponents of new Panama Canal Treaties pounded into the American consciousness the reasons why the United States should not give the Canal to Panama. In the heat of the debate, *New Yorker* magazine published a cartoon of a man coming home from work after a hard day. He takes off his trench coat and tells his wife: "Last year, I didn't even know we had a Panama Canal. Today, I can't do without it."

Through the 1980s, small countries like Panama and Nicaragua preoccupied Americans. By the 1990s, these countries had disappeared from our newspapers and consciousness. This book is an inquiry into a Latin American whirlpool that alternately incenses or somnambulates the American public. With the end of the Cold War, some Americans thought they had escaped the whirlpool, but the invasion of Panama on December 20, 1989, and of Haiti four years later, suggests that the vortex retains its pull.

This book seeks to explain why the United States has kept returning to the same questions in inter-American relations and why the answers, which also bear the weight of history, have failed to solve the problems. My thesis, in brief, is that the end of the Cold War changed inter-American relations in important ways, but it did not solve the hemisphere's recurring problems. What the end of the Cold War offers is time to learn from past mistakes and to use new opportunities presented by the more important trends of democracy and freer trade.

This book is about U.S. policy toward all of Latin America, but like U.S. policy, it devotes a disproportionate amount of time to the Caribbean Basin. Some analysts argue that a wiser policy would concentrate more on Brazil than on Nicaragua, but I believe that such a wish will remain unfulfilled until Washington comes to terms with the whirlpool that draws it back to the nearer region.

In the opening two chapters, I introduce the book's main themes through the bloodshot eyes of Omar Torrijos, an unusual man who embodied many of the contradictions of the Latin American dilemma and its complicated relationship with the United States. The chapters of Part I analyze the policies of Presidents Jimmy Carter, Ronald Reagan, George Bush, and Bill Clinton, and the distinctive role played by Congress in the making of U.S. foreign policy.

Part II examines how U.S. policymakers have addressed four recurring problems in inter-American relations throughout the twentieth century. The first issue is how to deal with succession crises involving long-standing dictators who have cooperated with the United States but have alienated their people. The second is how to deal with revolutionary regimes. Succession crises and revolutions have proven so problematic that Americans have demanded that their government formulate longer-term economic and political strategies to preclude revolution. Chapter 10 discusses the "Marshall Plan reflex," the pattern of U.S. economic responses to crises and the region's economic problems, and Chapter 11 analyzes America's periodic and often inconsistent efforts to promote democracy in the region.*

In Part III, I map the exit from the whirlpool and develop a new approach to the region. Among the multiple causes of the difficult relationship between the United States and Latin America is the disparity in wealth and power, but the inter-American relationship does not have to await a significant narrowing of that gap before improvement is possible. The first step is to disentangle the convoluted psychology of the relationship, and I try to do that by using the Puerto Rican case, which seems unique but actually contains in its economic success and its political disabilities all the ingredients of the Latin American dilemma. Collective action in the hemisphere on behalf of democracy and freer trade has been impeded by the interaction of U.S. interventionism and Latin America's defense of sovereignty. In Chapter 13, I show how the redefinition of the traditional concept of political and economic sovereignty has offered the roadmap to the exit by the international community. Specifically, Nicaragua's invitation to the international community to observe and mediate its elections and Mexico's proposal for a free trade area with the United States are two precedent-shattering cases that have

---

*With regard to describing the organization of the book, I have revised the Preface to the First Edition to correspond to the new ordering of the chapters.

made possible a new approach to inter-American relations. In the final chapter, I propose specific policies for the United States, the Summit leaders of the Americas, and the Organization of American States to achieve the hemisphere's hopes for peace, democracy, and development.

My style in this book is to integrate the perspective of the policymaker with the eye of the scholar, searching for patterns in the crevices of collective decisions. In Washington, policymakers are often described as inept and their policies as incoherent or inconsistent. I have long believed that those characterizations are veils that critics use to disguise disagreements on policy. I will not conceal my differences on specific policies, but I will always try to describe those policies fairly and objectively. I have worked with Jimmy Carter in different roles for twenty-five years, including as his national security advisor for Latin America when he was president. I invited his comments on drafts of the chapter on his administration and the one on Reagan's. On the Carter chapter, he scribbled: "Too harsh on him." On the Reagan chapter, he wrote: "Too easy on him." From this, I conclude that I achieved a certain measure of balance.

I am not interested in formulating an abstract theory that provides few lessons for the real world. It is that world which this book seeks to affect. In *Condemned to Repetition: The United States and Nicaragua*, after years of researching and rethinking past policy mistakes, I reached some conclusions as to why the United States and Nicaragua had shared such a tragic history. Fortunately, I was able to test these ideas when I was invited to organize the Carter Center's mission to observe the elections in Nicaragua in 1989–1990. Whereas the Carter administration had failed to mediate the Nicaraguan crisis in 1978–1979, Carter and I, as representatives of a nongovernmental organization, succeeded a decade later in mediating the rules of an electoral contest. For the first time in Nicaragua's history, all Nicaraguans, including the Sandinistas who lost, took pride in the fact that they had participated in an election that was judged free and fair by everyone inside and out of the country (see Chapter 13).

In the course of writing numerous drafts, I have incurred many debts. First, I especially appreciate the efforts of Richard Ullman, Douglas Chalmers, David Carroll, and Abraham Lowenthal, who waded through the entire manuscript and offered exceptionally constructive comments, and to Gretchen Oberfranc, whose editorial skills made the manuscript more readable. I am also grateful to the following people for their critiques of individual chapters: Ernst Haas, Jennifer McCoy, Peter Vaky,

Juan Manuel Garcia-Passalacqua, Ambler Moss, Robert S. McNamara, W. Anthony Lake, James Blight, Jay Taylor, and Steven Hochman. During the past four years, Frank Boyd, Jennifer Cannady, and Svetlana Savranskaya provided helpful research assistance. Emory University and the Carter Center offered a genial environment and a few cherished moments for writing, and Felicia Agudelo helped me make best use of that time. Finally, the book would not have been possible without the encouragement of Walter Lippincott.

The departure of the Cold War and the arrival of democracy and freer trade in the western hemisphere demand a new language but also an understanding of history. That is the dual purpose of this book: to review the past and chart a path toward a new hemispheric community based on the values and ideals that the peoples of the Americas have frequently invoked but rarely fulfilled.

R.A.P.

1

THE LESSONS AND LEGACY OF OMAR TORRIJOS

You call us Latin Americans because you won't look deep enough inside yourselves—where you would find us too.

—OMAR TORRIJOS

Located in the center of the western hemisphere, Panama has always lured American presidents into devoting more attention to it than its size would seem to warrant. Jimmy Carter spent more time on the Panama Canal Treaties than on any other issue in his first two years in office. Ronald Reagan rode his opposition to the treaties to the White House, and George Bush rid himself of the "wimp" image by invading the country. The United States has had a substantial impact on Panama; the question is whether it has learned anything from its involvement.

Reagan's secretary of state, Alexander Haig, apparently had not. In February 1981 he sent a strongly worded message to General Omar Torrijos, the head of the National Guard of Panama and the country's leader. Instructed to deliver the message immediately, U.S. Ambassador Ambler Moss flew by helicopter to the military barracks at Farallon. He found Torrijos in a hammock, swinging and meditating and savoring every puff of a Cuban cigar, a Cohiba, a gift from Fidel. Torrijos had not heard from Ronald Reagan since the latter had called him a "tinhorn Marxist dictator" during the debates on the Canal treaties.

"General," Moss said in Spanish, "I have a message for you from Secretary of State Haig." He then read the message. Haig let Torrijos know that the flabbiness in U.S. foreign policy had been firmed up; no longer would Washington tolerate Torrijos's adventures with leftist guerrillas or Cubans. Torrijos would have to shape up, or else.

Torrijos listened without displaying any emotion—except that he began puffing more rapidly on his Cohiba. When Moss was finished, the general lifted himself out of the hammock and asked if the ambassador would mind writing down his response. Moss took out his pad and pencil, and Torrijos dictated: "Señor Haig, I cannot acknowledge receipt of this message. It was obviously sent to the wrong address. It should have gone to Puerto Rico. Omar Torrijos."[1]

Torrijos was not well-educated, but his life and career provide a kind of guide to the complicated relationship between the United States and Latin America and valuable lessons for both. Torrijos could be flip, as when he replied to Haig with a parody of a post office message, or he could be deep, as when he conveyed the point that times had changed: The United States could still give instructions to Central America, but it should no longer expect them to be followed. The influence of the United States in Latin America had diminished, not because of the decline of U.S. power or a lack of will on the part of its leaders, but because of the deepening of nationalism in the region. In 1954 the CIA overthrew the government of Guatemala with a force of 150. Thirty years later, the CIA could not dislodge the Sandinista regime with an army of more than 20,000 contras. Torrijos had tried to tell President Reagan that it was no longer easy to depose small governments, but Reagan had to learn the hard way.

Panama under Torrijos had recovered its pride and identity with the Canal treaties, and part of that identity was being a "bridge" between oceans, continents, and ideologies. Torrijos was not about to change that. Indeed, what he liked most about his job was directing traffic across the isthmus.

Born into a middle-class family in 1929, Omar Torrijos Herrera decided to pursue his ambition in the military. After graduating from a Salvadoran military academy, he entered Panama's National Guard and climbed the ranks. He was a lieutenant colonel in 1968 when Arnulfo Arias, a conservative, nationalistic politician, was elected president for the third time.

Prior to his election, Arias made a deal with the leader of the Guard. If he supported Arias's election and allowed him to replace the Guard's top leadership, Arias promised not to alter the command structure. After his election, however, Arias fired numerous officers, and on October 11,

1968, the Guard overthrew him. Torrijos was one of the officers who led the coup, and from then until he died in a plane crash on July 31, 1981, Torrijos was Panama's "Maximum Leader."[2]

In his attempt to shape a new and modern Panama while keeping one foot planted in the *caudillo* (strongman) tradition of Latin America's past, Torrijos embodied all the contradictions, the dependent psychology, the insecurities, and the assertiveness that often characterize the way leaders of the region view themselves and the United States.

In one remote alcove of his brain, Torrijos believed that the United States controlled his destiny and his country's. But he never let that thought interfere with what he wanted to do. Few leaders in the region acted more independently than he did, and none was better at handling the United States. His views of the United States were hardly straightforward. While admiring the United States, he also resented its power. While trusting Jimmy Carter, he also delighted in trying to fool Carter's administration. While often trying to manipulate the United States, he liked to conduct secret missions on behalf of the U.S. president, such as when he tried to convince the Sandinistas in June 1979 to accept Carter's plan for a transitional government.[3] When Carter called him in September 1978 to seek his support for a U.S. resolution in the Organization of American States (OAS) to mediate the Nicaraguan conflict, Torrijos tried to persuade Carter to see the problem differently: "The crisis in Nicaragua can be described as a simple problem: a mentally deranged man [Anastasio Somoza] with an army of criminals is attacking a defenseless population. . . . This is not a problem for the OAS; what we need is a psychiatrist."

Like many Latin Americans of his generation, particularly those with a romantic bent, Torrijos admired Castro for the social successes of the revolution and for his courage in defying the United States. But Torrijos's practical side had seen Cuba, and he did not want it to be Panama's future.

Senator Howard Metzenbaum, who had traveled all the way to Panama in the fall of 1978 to meet Torrijos, did not mince words when he spoke with him: "General Torrijos, I must tell you in all candor that neither I nor my constituents like dictators." Torrijos blew a circle of cigar smoke at the distinguished senator, paused, and then replied: "Neither do I."

When his daughter returned from school and told him that other students had made fun of her and called her father a dictator, he consoled her. In telling the story later, he winked and said of the students: "They were right." Later, Torrijos confided to me that he was not a dictator. And he wasn't. And he was. And that was true of a lot of things people said about him.

But he was no opportunist. Torrijos had a clear vision of the purposes of his politics, and he was among the first to see that Central America was passing through a dangerous transition from an authoritarian, elitist past to a more popularly based, nonaligned future. The shape of the future would depend on whether effective answers could be devised to meet four challenges: the development of a national identity that would be independent of, but not antagonistic to, the United States; the expansion of each nation's social and economic base and the opening of channels of power to the talented children of the lower middle class; the establishment of a civilian, democratic political framework; and the related but distinct task of removing the military from politics. (In Central America, only Costa Rica faced a different set of challenges.)

Torrijos did *not* have a clear idea of these four challenges when he first seized power in 1968, nor would he ever have articulated them in this way, but his programs reflected an intuitive grasp of these core issues. He had a reformist impulse, and over time his views of Panama's problems matured and his solutions became more practical. By the time he died in 1981, he had succeeded in navigating his nation through the first two challenges, and he had made some progress on the last two. But he failed to complete his task because of his premature death and the personal contradiction of being a populist in a military uniform, of believing in social justice but not democracy.

The Zone of Panama's Identity

Torrijos's consuming mission was to unite Panama, to erase the ten-mile-wide strip of North America that had divided his country in half since independence in 1903. Like the Argentines on the Malvinas, the Panamanians were united in their determination to retrieve their self-respect and sovereignty over the Panama Canal and Canal Zone; unlike the Argentines, who went to war and lost the islands, Torrijos won the Canal and developed a closer relationship with the United States at the same time.

Before approaching the prize, Torrijos first sought international support. Panama sent special envoys to neighboring countries and joined the Non-Aligned Movement to try to steer it toward endorsing Panama's goals. In 1973 Torrijos invited the United Nations Security

Council to hold its annual meeting in Panama. When the representatives arrived, the Panamanian foreign minister introduced a resolution calling for new treaties. The United States, unprepared and embarrassed, vetoed the resolution.

The U.S. State Department denounced Torrijos for his theatrics, but Secretary of State Henry Kissinger acknowledged his effectiveness by negotiating a joint statement of principles in February 1974. This document was to be the framework of new Canal treaties; however, before real negotiations began, President Gerald Ford found himself under assault from the right wing of his party. Ronald Reagan used Panama very effectively on the campaign trail, and Ford put the negotiations in the freezer.

Torrijos used the time to lobby his neighbors, and his efforts paid off. After the U.S. presidential elections in November, eight presidents in the area—led by the democratic presidents from Venezuela, Costa Rica, and Colombia—wrote to President-elect Carter urging him to make the Canal treaties his highest priority in inter-American relations. Torrijos himself announced that "Panama's patience machine only has fuel for six more months. . . . [1977 was the year when the United States] would run out of excuses and Panama would run out of patience."

The quixotic side of Torrijos wanted to liberate the Zone. He later said that this was the path he would have followed if Ronald Reagan had won the nomination and election in 1976. He expected that Reagan would have blocked real negotiations and that violent incidents would have been impossible to prevent. The extreme left, he knew, would exploit the violence. "They will start their own fires to gain their own goals," he said. "Three hundred thousand Latin Americans would be raising the anti-Yankee banner as they raised it when the Americans went in to fight Sandino. . . . If I had historical vanity, I would have gone more for Sandino's place than for the real solution of our problem."

But Torrijos never let his romantic side carry him away. "I do not delude myself. . . . Through a war . . . there would be mourning in Panamanian homes. And hate, a profound feeling of hate for the United States. The truth is that in our country, the extreme left and the extreme right live off the problem, not off its solution." With Jimmy Carter, he chose the road of negotiation and compromise. The leftists in Panama wanted the U.S. military out immediately. Torrijos accepted the year 2000, a nice round number, as the date when the United States would formally transfer full authority for the operation and defense of the Canal. "I am satisfied," Torrijos said on the eve of the signing ceremony in September 1977. "We now have to walk for twenty-three years with a pebble in our shoes, but that's the price we have to pay for getting the dagger out of our heart. I did not concede any more than I can sell to my people." In fact, the treaties narrowly received approval by the necessary two-thirds of Panamanian voters.

Torrijos used Castro's support for the Canal treaties to undermine Panamanian leftists who complained that Torrijos had given away too much to the gringos. He also used the United States to try to neutralize rightist opposition, which was based primarily on the fear that the treaties would guarantee Torrijos's tenure in perpetuity.

Just as the United States was unaware of Torrijos's political problems, so too had he underestimated the challenge facing Carter to secure ratification. Deeply ingrained in the American spirit was the feeling that the Panama Canal was not Panamanian but U.S. territory. To relinquish the Canal was a statement that Americans had reached, in the words of one author, "a turning point in our growth as a nation."[4]

In the United States, members of the "new right" understood this feeling. Gary Jarmin of the American Conservative Union saw the Canal issue as "an excellent opportunity for conservatives to seize control of the Republican Party" and to put Ronald Reagan in a position where he could capture the nomination in 1980.[5] Richard Viguerie called it "a cutting issue" and used it to expand his mailing list of conservative contributors:

> It's an issue the conservatives can't lose on. If we lose the vote in the Senate, we will have had the issue for 8 or 9 months. We will have rallied many new people to our cause. . . . The left has had . . . their civil rights causes and their Vietnam war protests and ecology. . . . Now conservatives can get excited about the Panama Canal give-away and they can go to the polls, look for a person's name on the ballot who favored the treaties and vote against him.[6]

Ronald Reagan was the point man for the treaty opponents. In a debate against William F. Buckley Jr., Reagan insisted that if the United States yielded to Panama's "unreasonable demands . . . we would become a laughing stock. . . . And by doing so, I think we cloak weakness in the suit of virtue." Reagan argued that the Panamanians could not run the Canal and should not, because "we bought it. We paid for it. It's ours. And we should keep it." Carter's response was tempered: "We don't have to show our strength as a nation by running over a small nation. . . . I don't see the treaties as a withdrawal. We are retaining permanent rights to defend the Canal." Carter argued that the prestige of the United States would be diminished by not recognizing Panama's legitimate claim.

Torrijos tried to help the pro-treaty forces, in his own style. He enlisted John Wayne, a friend of his, a frequent visitor to Panama, and also, in Torrijos's words, "a helluva lot better actor than Reagan." The Duke tried to persuade his old friend, but when Reagan ignored the advice, Wayne sent him a letter, showing "point-by-God-damn-point in the Treaty where you are misinforming people." With ideas and information that arrived at his California home via a circuitous route from my office through mutual friends in Panama, Wayne put the thoughts in his own words in a letter to "Ronnie":

> I went to a lot of trouble and I brought in people to prove to you that the alarming things you are saying are untruths. You have lost a great and unique "appointment with history." If you had given time and thought on this issue, your attitude would have gained you the image of leadership that I wished for you, rather than, in the long run, a realization by the public that you are merely making statements for political expediency.[7]

Wayne also sent a long letter to the Senate and to leaders all over the country, explaining his support for the treaties and rebutting the arguments of opponents. Many senators said that Wayne's was the most crucial endorsement for the treaties.

Torrijos sent businessman Gabriel Lewis to the United States as Panama's ambassador. No Latin American has understood the U.S. political process better or has used his influence more effectively in Washington. In addition to educating the Senate about Panama, Lewis schooled Torrijos on the arguments that struck the most responsive chords in Americans. Torrijos soon found himself telling senators that he needed the Canal treaties "to recover the climate of confidence for investors that we used to have."

When he met Carter on the day of the treaty-signing ceremony, September 7, 1977, Torrijos said: "Remember, we are selling the same product to two different audiences." Carter agreed that they should use two different sales campaigns, but they needed to be sure that the messages were not inconsistent.

At Lewis's suggestion, Torrijos hosted visits by forty-four U.S. senators. Many treated Torrijos as a hostile witness before one of their committees rather than as a head of government. He said that he was "deeply offended" by the interrogation but viewed it as "necessary, and I controlled myself in order to bear it. I had to start from the premise that I am a dictator, which doesn't please me because I know I am not a dictator."

Torrijos did more than just bear it. With candor and his unusual wit, he won over some senators; but for all of them, he demolished their image of him as a stereotypical Latin dictator. Torrijos complimented a senator who had distinguished himself in the Watergate hearings for administering "a moral laxative to the machinery of the U.S. government." One legislator goaded him, "General, are you a communist?" Torrijos produced a response that could have saved some Hollywood careers in the 1950s: "I have never declared that I am *not* a communist, and I will not. Nor, by the same token, do I have to declare that I am not a homosexual or a son-of-a-bitch."

Torrijos later told U.S. Ambassador Moss that while listening to the translation of the Senate debate on Panamanian radio, he broke hundreds of transistor radios. The speech that caused him to break the most radios was given by Dennis DeConcini. The senator from Arizona offered an amendment to the first treaty that declared war against the very purpose of the treaty by demanding a unilateral and unrestricted right to intervene in Panama's internal affairs. DeConcini insisted that the United States needed that provision to deal with labor strikes or other problems.

"Listening to DeConcini," Torrijos mused, "I ask myself the question: Have we by any chance lost a war? The United States didn't demand as much from Japan." Carter liked the amendment no better, but he was persuaded by his political advisers that the first treaty, assuring the neutrality of the Canal and the right of the United States and Panama to defend it, could not be approved without it, so he acquiesced. That treaty passed on March 16, 1978, by one vote, 68 to 32. Torrijos sent instructions to Lewis to meet with Carter, who received the ambassador that evening in his residence. Lewis told Carter that Panama would not accept the treaty unless the DeConcini amendment was repealed. Carter said that he would try to have it neutralized in the second treaty.

Lewis negotiated new language with Senators Frank Church and Robert Byrd. After many difficult sessions aimed at bringing the amendment into alignment with the spirit of the treaties, Senator Byrd asked Lewis to check the new language with Torrijos. Lewis phoned, and the reply was vintage Torrijos: "If Byrd, as captain of the ship, can bring it safely into port, I will make sure that the pier will be in the right place to meet it."

Because Carter and the Senate recognized the justice of Panama's claim, the practical side of Omar Torrijos prevailed. Had the Senate confused legitimate accommodation with appeasement and rejected the treaties, the Canal would have been sabotaged. Instead, on April 18, 1978, the Senate ratified the second Panama Canal Treaty, the one that erased the Zone and would transfer the Canal in the year 2000.

Torrijos never let himself become too filled with his own importance, however. In reminiscing about his big night as the guest of honor at a state dinner in the East Room in September 1977, he recalled: "There I was. Sitting between Rosalynn and Jimmy. And I thought to myself, 'Sancho, we have stumbled onto the White House.'"

The two very different leaders grew close. Their relationship started when they were about to go on stage at the OAS and sign the Panama Canal Treaties in the presence of eighteen presidents and international television. Suddenly, Torrijos grabbed Carter, gave him a warm embrace, and this tough military leader started to cry. Brushing away the tears, Torrijos said that he had doubted that the United States would ever recognize the justice of Panama's demands. Carter had restored Torrijos's faith in the United States.

Carter had made a friend. When the Mexican president denied the Shah of Iran reentry into Mexico after his operation in the United States and other governments shied away, Carter asked his Panamanian friend for a favor. Torrijos never hesitated. He volunteered Lewis's home on Contadora and met the Shah at Panama's airport. "Imagine that," he mused as he watched the Shah descend the steps of his plane, "2,500 years of the Persian Empire reduced to ten people and two dogs."

The Other Three Challenges

Cumplido. That one word, meaning "mission accomplished," was printed on billboards all over Panama soon after the Panama Canal Treaties were ratified. Torrijos had succeeded in persuading the United States to acknowledge Panama as a partner, not just as *its* Canal. In doing so, he had given his nation pride and a new identity.

Of the other three challenges—incorporate the poor, establish democracy, and remove the military from politics—Torrijos was only interested in the first. From the moment he took power, he tried to reorient a very narrowly based government to respond to the economic, health, and especially educational needs of Panama's poor in urban and rural areas. To direct this effort, he recruited a team of young and able technocrats, including Nicolas Ardito-Barletta, who would later become the senior vice president for Latin America at the World Bank. To obtain the revenues needed for a social revolution, Torrijos provided a framework that would give businessmen confidence and attract capital. Before 1968 there were a few small banks in Panama. Torrijos and Ardito-Barletta revised Panamanian laws and invited the major world banks to move to Panama. Within a decade, Panama had become one of the largest banking centers in the hemisphere.

Torrijos also recruited young Marxists to help in his social revolution because they were idealistic and motivated. When one of them returned from graduate study in Italy, Torrijos dispatched him to take charge of a rural development project in a remote part of Panama. After a year on the job, the young leader complained to Torrijos that none of his theories seemed to be working. "Then, you had better change your theories," Torrijos told him. Torrijos approached the social and economic problems of his country with zeal, but without ideology. The son of schoolteachers, Torrijos was fond of saying that he believed in the classroom struggle, not the class struggle.

The general brought the least enthusiasm to the third and fourth challenges. Indeed, during most of his first decade as chief of government he moved in the opposite direction, bringing the military into government and trying to take politics out of Panama. Torrijos had little patience or use for democratic government, which he viewed as too decentralized and cumbersome. He also viewed the old political party system as corrupt and elitist. To clarify some remarks he had made about the old order, he told the press that, although "it is not exactly correct that the political parties make me feel like vomiting," as he was alleged to have said, nevertheless, "decisions on the country's fate should not be confused with the private interests of these groups."

The original declaration announcing the coup in 1968 pledged "the removal of the National Guard from politics," but this apparently did not reflect Torrijos's views. He defined an important role for the Guard in the 1972 constitution, which also provided him with emergency powers for six years. At the same time, Congress was replaced with a Legislative Assembly of 505 representatives that was biased in favor of the rural areas and against the traditional political parties. The press remained censored, and many political leaders were exiled.

When Carter and several U.S. senators encouraged Torrijos to hold elections, he initially resisted and then toyed with the idea of running himself. He finally decided to support the candidacy of Aristides Royo, the co-negotiator for the Canal treaties. Before doing so, he permitted exiles to return, political parties to organize, and the Inter-American Commission on Human Rights to review the state of human rights in the country. Their report was positive. The political process was opened at an important moment. Torrijos then returned to the barracks and pledged to keep the military out of the government and give it a new role "as guardian of the process and supporters of the National Development Plan."

But he was half-hearted in his support of the new democracy. Although insisting that Royo should be treated as the real leader, he remained the ultimate source of power in Panama. I visited Torrijos in early June 1979, at President Carter's request, to ask him to pledge to Carter that he would stop shipping arms to the Sandinistas. Torrijos countered that a letter on that subject should come from Royo, not him. I could hardly disagree with the importance of reinforcing the civilian government, although we both knew that was a fiction. The truth was that Torrijos let Royo run most of the government, but Royo could not prevent Torrijos from making policy or from conducting his special operations, such as aiding the Sandinistas.

After Torrijos died, the military followed his example, not his instructions. His failure to institutionalize a transfer of power to civilians proved to be his most tragic legacy. One of his officers, then Colonel Manuel Antonio Noriega, the keeper of the secrets as head of G-2 (military intelligence), was able to abuse Torrijos's system of indirect military rule for perverse and corrupt ends. Noriega tried to imitate Torrijos and his adventures. He would fly to Havana one day and to Washington the next, selling secrets to both places. But unlike Torrijos, he was greedy and lacked moral purpose. And in the end, he undermined or destroyed almost everything that Torrijos tried to create. Torrijos's last mission—to reform the Guard and keep it out of politics—failed abysmally.

Torrijos's Lessons

The Panama Canal Treaties were a watershed event. The United States recognized that the protection of U.S. interests in an open, efficient Canal required a change in U.S. strategy and a new partnership based on respect rather than a relationship of dominance based on power. By displaying a readiness to negotiate and compromise without threats, the United States encouraged the pragmatic side of Torrijos and Panama to prevail over the defiant, nationalistic side, which in much of Latin America often teeters on the tightrope of anti-Americanism.

Opponents of the treaties said that Torrijos was a Marxist, that if Carter gave up the Canal the general would turn Panama into another Cuba and give the Canal to the Soviets. Their vision was narrow and wrong. But if the treaties had been rejected, their predictions might have come true.

After the ratification of the treaties, however, Panama's politics and economic policy moved to the center. The left lost the only issue it could use to broaden its base and tilt the country. The Communist party, which had been a force in the early 1970s, had faded by the end of the decade. Until Torrijos's death, and for a time afterward, Panama was a nation with an identity, a major banking center of Latin America, and an island of stability in a turbulent Central America. Noriega, who emerged from Torrijos's incomplete legacy, almost shattered that. Ronald Reagan had another chance to test his strategy of confronting tinhorn dictators rather than negotiating with them. He fought Noriega and Daniel Ortega, and the results were disastrous in both countries.

Three lessons can be drawn from Torrijos's career, one for Latin America, one for the United States, and one for all. First, both Latin America and the United States should realize that Torrijos's accomplishments were jeopardized by his failure to establish a democratic political system that would permit peaceful change and hold the government accountable. Noriega's abuses and the sanctions imposed by the Reagan and Bush administrations fractured the country's economy and morale so badly that the U.S. invasion of December 20, 1989, was almost a relief. Arguments that democracy should wait until a state reduces illiteracy, improves the economy, or completes a major task like the Canal treaties are not only self-serving; they jeopardize the accomplishment of these or any objective. A decade of democracy, however, restored sufficient confidence to Panama to assure a peaceful transfer of the Canal in 2000.

The other two lessons are more encouraging. Torrijos's most significant legacy was that he proved that Latin Americans could achieve goals in the United States by understanding the way Washington works. Panama implemented a very sophisticated strategy to achieve a nearly impossible mission. If Latin Americans understood the importance of this lesson, they would have studied Panama's tactics. Alas, it is hard to find a single important study from the entire region on how and why Panama secured the Canal treaties.

The reason is that Panama's success can be understood only if one abandons the region's stereotypes of the United States. Few observers realize that an effective policy by a small nation can influence a nation as powerful as the United States. But a simple comparison of the strategies of Noriega and Daniel Ortega on the one hand and those of two Jamaican prime ministers and Omar Torrijos on the other leads to the inescapable conclusion that the size of the nation is less important than its leader's approach. Noriega's objective was actually the simplest of the five—to prevent a U.S. invasion—but his conduct provoked the one thing he wanted to avoid. Ortega's goal was to prevent the United States from interfering in Nicaragua, but he also took actions that made it easier for President Reagan to gain funds for the contras.

In contrast, Edward Seaga persuaded Reagan to adopt the Caribbean Basin Initiative (CBI), a one-way free trade arrangement; Michael Manley persuaded Bush to relieve Latin America's debt to the U.S. government; and Torrijos helped to persuade two-thirds of the U.S. Senate to give away the Canal. These were all very difficult goals to achieve, with many Americans opposed to them. It is too easy to view Ortega and Noriega as victims of U.S. aggression; *the issue for Latin America is why Noriega and Ortega brought out the worst in the United States whereas Torrijos and the two Jamaicans brought out the best.*

Torrijos's lesson for Latin America is: Engage Washington. It is psychologically and politically easier for a Latin populist to rant at the Northern Colossus or to dismiss a "Washington strategy" as something that tyrants like Anastasio Somoza and Rafael Trujillo pursued. But the influence of those two in Washington was always grossly exaggerated. Neither secured any real support, as became evident when their regimes faltered. In contrast, Torrijos and his ambassador engaged in an open debate on a task that was more daunting. The lesson for the region was more profound because they succeeded while enhancing their nation's dignity. Fifteen years later, Mexico finally adopted a similar approach and succeeded in persuading Congress to accept the North American Free Trade Agreement (NAFTA).

The third lesson is for North Americans, but is similar to the second: Look below the uniforms of Latin America, listen to the silence rather than the passion, and hesitate before labeling leaders "tinhorn dictators." In an address to the Panamanian Assembly after the treaties were signed, Torrijos said that negotiations were less satisfying but ultimately more rewarding than liberation. He explained that he chose talks because he sensed that Carter's team was willing to listen:

> [Carter's team gives] added weight to questions of morality. These men know and believe that there is no code of law which can legalize a colonial enclave. They have struck a balance between the strength of a large nation and that of a small nation, not because the former has become militarily weak and the latter militarily strong, but because conscience, honor, and morality have created an equality through which we have reached an understanding.

It is rare that one can test alternative policies in the real world. The world is not a laboratory that will remain fixed while a social scientist changes a single variable to see whether the results will be different. But Panama offers a good test because Torrijos described what he would have done if the path toward real negotiations had been blocked, as Reagan had recommended. On the day of the ratification of the second Canal treaty, Torrijos told a crowd in Panama that he had a secret operation that would have demolished the locks in the Canal. "No son potables" ("the water is not drinkable") was the code phrase that would have set the operation in motion and closed the Canal.[8] This was not bluff or bluster; it was frustration and desperation. Distrust would have bred belligerence, just as it did in Nicaragua and has done for more than forty years in Cuba.

Torrijos had his unique qualities, but he shared with many Latin leaders an acute sensitivity to the way they are treated by Americans. A demonstration of trust can yield dividends, and the slightest sign of disrespect can provoke outrage. Torrijos's lesson to the United States is that respect for legitimate Latin American concerns produces better results than threats, force, or lack of interest.

On a sweltering August day in Panama in 1981, hundreds of thousands of Panamanians and a most unusual collection of world leaders—

among them General David Jones, chairman of the U.S. Joint Chiefs of Staff, and Cuban Vice President Carlos Rafael Rodriguez—came to pay their last respects to Omar Torrijos. As dignitaries filed past the coffin, journalists asked them for their thoughts on the man. President Reagan's ambassador, Ambler Moss, said: "Torrijos was beginning to come around to see things in Central America as we do." A few moments later, Rodriguez said that Torrijos's views continued to coincide with those of the Cuban government. Some observers might conclude that Torrijos had been fooling the United States, and others that he had been deceiving Cuba. The truth is that both governments were right to trust him to follow his nation's interests as he saw them. "Well-intentioned" was the way Fidel Castro described him to me, with the same measure of uncertainty as when I tried to describe Torrijos to him.

Torrijos once put it this way: "In politics as in gynecology, things either are, or they aren't. No one can be slightly pregnant." No one except for Omar Torrijos.

One of the conservative arguments against the Canal treaties was that if the United States gave in to Panamanian demands for the Zone, the demands would escalate, and soon Panama would try to throw out the U.S. military. The opposite happened. Military cooperation became so close that in August 1980 Torrijos accepted a parachute exercise seventy miles west of the Canal by the 82d Airborne. He set only one condition: reciprocity. And so the same day, a Panamanian airborne company parachuted into Fort Bragg, North Carolina. "It was," Torrijos said with evident pride, "the first time Latin Americans ever practiced an invasion of the United States."

Fidel Castro could only dream of doing that. Torrijos did it.

Notes

1. Most of the quotations and anecdotes in this chapter come from the author's personal experiences with Omar Torrijos. Some are from press conferences; others are from "Meditaciones," a long report dictated by Torrijos on November 25, 1977. He sent me the tape and copies of his correspondence and reports of conversations with other leaders. I am also grateful to numerous friends of the general, and especially to the late Gabriel Lewis Galindo and Ambler Moss, for their reminiscences. Torrijos spoke and wrote in Spanish. Translations are by me or by those who conveyed the story. For other work on Torrijos, see William Jorden, *Panama Odyssey* (Austin: University of Texas Press, 1984);

Graham Greene, *Getting to Know the General* (New York: Simon & Schuster, 1984); Rómulo Escobar Bethancourt, *Torrijos: ¡Colonia Americana, No!* (Bogotá: Carlos Valencia Editores, 1981); and a profile by Karen DeYoung, "Torrijos, Who Won Canal, Dies in Air Crash," *Washington Post,* August 2, 1981, pp. A1, 12.

2. The agreement between Arias and the Guard was published soon after the coup. For this and an introduction to Panama's politics, see Steve Ropp, *Panamanian Politics: From Guarded Nation to National Guard* (New York: Praeger, 1982), pp. 37–38.

3. See Robert A. Pastor, *Condemned to Repetition: The United States and Nicaragua* (Princeton: Princeton University Press, 1987), chap. 9.

4. David McCullough, "Ceding the Canal Slowly," *Time,* August 22, 1977, p. 13.

5. Quoted in William J. Lanouette, "The Panama Canal Treaties—Playing in Peoria and in the Senate," *National Journal,* October 8, 1977, pp. 1556–1562.

6. On Viguerie's claim, see *San Francisco Chronicle,* April 23, 1978, p. 19.

7. This is a quotation from Wayne's letter to Reagan. The Panamanians provided me with copies of the correspondence.

8. "Operación Potable" is described in Escobar Bethancourt, *Torrijos,* chap. 1. Destruction of the locks would have emptied the lakes that are used to move ships through the Canal. Two years of rain would be needed to refill the lakes.

2

WHIRLPOOL

In 1909, the United States took a bear by the tail, and it has never been able to let it go. Once in, [the United States] found that it could not get out. It tried to get out, and disaster struck Nicaragua, and dragged it in again.[1]

—HAROLD NORMAN DENNY, 1929

In 1933, exhausted by the costly Nicaraguan intervention, the United States withdrew its marines and swam to the rim of the whirlpool. It remained there, focusing on other matters for forty-five years, when it was dragged in again.

Like all nations and peoples, the United States is moved by fears and, to a lesser degree, by hopes. The fear in the early part of the twentieth century that Germany would gain a foothold in Hispaniola led U.S. policymakers to invade the island. "Though [the United States] did not need and it did not want such a coaling station [in Haiti], it could not permit a European government to secure one," wrote a former secretary of state to a Senate committee investigating the U.S. intervention. "The indications were that Germany intended to obtain one unless she was prevented from doing so by the United States."[2] After World War II, the United States feared that a Latin American nation would align with the Soviet Union and, when that fear came true, that one would align with Cuba. Such fears led the United States to send its own forces into the Dominican Republic and Grenada and to intervene with proxies in Guatemala, Cuba, and Nicaragua.

There is a rhythm in the way Americans respond to crises in Latin America, and the way U.S. presidents react to criticism. In early 1927, after President Calvin Coolidge sent the marines back to Nicaragua, the criticism from Congress and newspapers was deafening. The most constructive came from William Borah, chairman of the Senate Foreign Relations Committee, who proposed that U.S. forces supervise an election. No U.S. president can resist the promotion of elections as a strategy to cope with instability, and Coolidge modified his policy accordingly.

A second criticism is the failure to deal with the roots of the problem. "We should have learnt [sic] by now that the enforcement of peace from outside does not resolve the basic causes which make men resort to revolution," wrote Norman H. Davis in 1931.[3] Each crisis has generated both reactive and long-term proposals. John F. Kennedy responded to Cuba with the Bay of Pigs and the Alliance for Progress. Ronald Reagan sought to stymie Nicaragua with the contras but also with the Caribbean Basin Initiative.

Eventually, when the crisis passes, so too do U.S. resources and interest. It took about fifteen years for the United States to withdraw from the region after World War I. It took almost ten years after Castro's rise provoked a spasm of aid to Latin America before attention and money shifted to other parts of the world. After a decade of frustrations in Central America and the end of the Cold War, Washington again lost sight of the region, until the drug war replaced the Cold War. This alternating cycle of fixation and inattention is a central characteristic of the whirlpool.

Another attribute is that all the actors in the crisis tend to stereotype one another or project motives. Some view the United States as Satan, others as a savior, but few as an actor snared by circumstances. The United States is similarly confused about the purposes of other actors. Former U.S. Ambassador John Bartlow Martin once complained: "If we pursue our relationships with them, they accuse us of intervention; if we ignore them, they accuse us of caring less about our neighbors than about Bangladesh."[4]

Why has the world's most powerful nation been unable either to calm the whirlpool or to escape from it? Policymakers have not stopped to answer that or other questions that are posed with each pull toward U.S. involvement or push toward disengagement—questions of whether the United States ought to have a "special relationship" with the region and what that means, of how to preclude instability, discourage foreign penetration, promote peaceful political change, encourage economic development, defend human rights, reinforce democracy, maintain good relations with our neighbors, and gain respect for U.S. investment, the American flag, and U.S. citizens. Answers to these questions have differed from one administration to the next, and particularly when there is a change in the party in power. But the differences have never been as wide as they appear at the time, or as large as the administration claims at its beginning, or as narrow as it suggests when its power is waning or its policy is wanting and it seeks strength by asserting continuity or bipartisanship.

In this book, by identifying the continuity in policies between different presidents, I try to explain the constraints that have limited the choices for American presidents; by identifying the changes in policies, I illustrate the choices that presidents have made. The two most different presidents, Carter and Reagan, agreed in their opposition to the leftist insurgency in El Salvador, but Carter conditioned aid to the government on improvements in human rights, whereas Reagan's support was unequivocal. Truman and Carter tried but failed to encourage two different Somozas to give up power, whereas Eisenhower and Nixon sent to Managua ambassadors who considered U.S. interests to be identical with the Somozas'. Their choices have shaped U.S. policy.

The Caribbean Basin and South America

In the beginning, and almost always in its rhetoric, the United States has spoken of Latin America and the Caribbean as a single region. James Monroe's message to Congress in 1823, warning Europe against interference, referred to all of "our southern brethren" in the "American continents." In 1889, the invitation to an inter-American conference in Washington was extended to all of the nations of the region. This was also true of the Rio Pact, the Organization of American States, and the Alliance for Progress. Yet, in reality, the United States has always approached Latin America as if there were two distinct regions—the Caribbean Basin and South America—with different problems and histories.

Caribbean Basin is a relatively new term for a region—the nations and dependencies in and around the Caribbean Sea—that the United States has long considered as a unit. Historically, U.S. foreign policy textbooks have defined the entire area as "Middle America" or simply "the Caribbean."[5] Since the 1960s, however, the number of independent islands in the Caribbean has increased from three to thirteen; the new English-speaking nations have become a critical mass, distinct from the old Latin Caribbean and intent on appropriating the term *Caribbean* to apply to their community. Thus, when U.S. attention returned to the region in the late 1970s, a new term was needed to recognize that Central America and the Caribbean are different, with few connections and less affinity, but posing similar strategic problems for the United States because of their proximity, vulnerability, and chronic instability. Ergo, the Caribbean Basin.[6]

These three characteristics—proximity, vulnerability, and instability—make the region of special concern to the United States. To fathom that concern, one must understand the thirty-three nations and dependencies in Central America and the Caribbean. They are diverse politically, economically, culturally, and linguistically. All are small in size and population and have limited markets and resources. They rely on trade, aid, tourism, and foreign investment from the United States for a large proportion of their domestic product. Together, these characteristics mean that the major forces that shape these nations' destinies originate abroad, whether as fluctuating prices of sugar and oil, interest rates charged by U.S. banks, or the unpredictable devastation of hurricanes.

Openness and vulnerability have shaped the nations' choices and their leaders' views of the world. After his first two terms in office, Michael Manley, Jamaica's eloquent prime minister, wrote *Struggle in the Periphery,* the story of the great colossus preying on a small nation's independence. United States presidents would enjoy exercising even a small percentage of the influence that leaders in these nations are certain they possess.

The practical effect of vulnerability, however, is that sustained development has proven elusive. This is one reason for the prevalence of utopian revolutionaries and millenary rhetoric. Nonetheless, partly because of the proximity to the U.S. market, the nations of the region are ranked in the middle, or higher, among developing countries in terms of per capita income, education, and life expectancy. Indeed, Barbados has long been in the top rank of the United Nations "Human Development Index."[7] The region's advantages and disadvantages both stem from its proximity to the United States, which is the principal destination for the region's products and a highly unequal competitor for its skilled population.

The United States is, therefore, both a solution and a problem, a source of aid and a rival, an outlet for unskilled labor and a magnet for the region's talent. Caribbean Basin nations all confront a vexing strategic dilemma: how to retain autonomy while seeking regional integration, how to elude the dominance of the United States while securing improved access to its market.

Three oil-producing nations—Mexico, Venezuela, and Colombia—touch the Caribbean and share with their smaller neighbors a high degree of dependence on the U.S. market. Mexico is a North American nation with an exceedingly complicated relationship with the United States. Venezuela and Colombia are part of the Caribbean Basin and South America at the same time.

The nations of South America are generally larger, more stable, and more integrated than those in the Caribbean Basin. Their economic and political relations with Europe are almost as extensive and, in some cases, more extensive than their ties with the United States. The principal geopolitical concerns of Argentina, Brazil, Chile, Bolivia, Peru, Ecuador, Uruguay, and Paraguay are with each other. Many have fought each other; some have lost territory in the course of these wars.

The United States has always pursued policies toward the Caribbean Basin that are different from those it has formulated for South America. When Great Britain violated the Monroe Doctrine by seizing the Falkland Islands off Argentina in 1833, the United States hardly paid any attention. The contrast between that relaxed response and the U.S. threat to use force if Spain and France did not withdraw from the Dominican Republic and Mexico three decades later is a function of geography and a symbol of the different ways the United States has approached the two regions. The United States sent troops to the Caribbean Basin more than twenty times, but not once to South America. Theodore Roosevelt made a clear distinction:

> The great and prosperous civilized commonwealths, such as the Argentine, Brazil, and Chile, in the southern half of South America have advanced so far that they no longer stand in any position of tutelage toward the United States. Their friendship is the friendship of equals for equals. My view was that as regards these nations there was no more necessity for asserting the Monroe Doctrine than there was to assert it for Canada.[8]

Equally clear was the justification for active engagement in the Caribbean Basin. Philander C. Knox, secretary of state under William Howard Taft, explained: "The logic of political geography and of strategy and now our tremendous national interest created by the Panama Canal make the safety, the peace, and the prosperity of Central America and the zone of the Caribbean of paramount importance to the government of the United States."[9]

Besides proximity, the United States is now tied to the Caribbean Basin in a new way. The region has been the largest source of legal and illegal immigration since the Immigration Act of 1965. Since 1970, more than 20 million legal immigrants have come to the United States, and about half of those came from Latin America. The largest source of immigrants—40 percent of the total—have come from the Caribbean Basin, and Mexico has accounted for the lion's share of that. (see Table 2.1). In the long term, these transnational human bonds may prove more influential in shaping inter-American relations than have strategic concerns.

Perhaps as much as 90 percent of the time that senior U.S. policymakers have given to Latin America has been devoted to the Caribbean Basin, and more than 80 percent of the cases addressed by the OAS originated in the region.[10] Even though this book is concerned with all of Latin America, its principal aim is to explore U.S. policy, so it follows the preoccupation of U.S. policymakers in giving most attention to the recurring policy quandaries that have arisen in the Caribbean Basin. My purpose, however, is not to write a book about U.S. policy toward the Caribbean Basin but to understand the causes of the periodic obsessions with that closer region so that future policy reflects a longer-term definition of U.S. interests and a more balanced approach to all of Latin America and the Caribbean. In the last chapter, I explore the role of Brazil in the new economic geography of the Americas.

National Security

No country in Latin America has the capacity to threaten the United States directly, but it is precisely those countries that are its smallest, poorest, and least stable that are the most tempting targets for U.S. adversaries. National security managers have remained alert to the possibility that an unfriendly neighbor might seek to defend itself by providing a base or a platform for a hostile rival of the United States. Still, Americans have had difficulty understanding why the smaller nations could pose the larger problems.

Few important terms are used more often and loosely and in such different contexts than *national security.* After the Soviet Union launched *Sputnik,* President Eisenhower judged that U.S. national security de-

TABLE 2.1 Latin American and Caribbean Immigration into the United States, 1820–1998

	Region of Last Residence								
	All Countries	*Mexico*	*Caribbean*	*Central America*	*Caribbean Basin Subtotal*	*South America*	*Caribbean Basin as % of All Latin American Immigration*	*Latin America and Caribbean Basin as % of All Immigration*	*Europe as % of All Immigration*
1820–1860	5,062,414	17,766	40,487	968	59,221	6,201	90.5	1.3	91.9
1861–1900	14,061,192	10,237	85,111	1,205	96,553	5,904	94.2	0.7	89.8
1901–1920	14,532,297	268,646	230,972	25,351	524,969	59,179	89.9	4.0	85.0
1921–1930	4,107,209	459,287	74,899	15,769	549,955	42,215	92.9	14.4	60.0
1931–1940	528,431	22,319	15,502	5,861	46,283	7,803	85.6	10.2	66.0
1941–1950	1,035,039	60,589	49,725	25,665	135,979	21,831	86.2	15.2	60.0
1951–1960	2,515,479	299,811	123,091	44,751	467,653	91,628	83.6	22.2	53.0
1961–1970	3,321,677	453,937	470,213	101,330	1,025,480	257,954	79.9	38.6	34.0
1971–1980	4,493,314	640,294	741,126	134,640	1,516,060	295,741	83.7	40.3	18.0
1981–1990	7,338,062	1,655,843	872,051	468,088	2,995,982	461,847	86.6	47.1	10.4
1991–1998	7,605,068	1,932,151	825,099	423,077	3,180,327	443,662	87.8	47.7	15.0
Total									
1820–1998	64,600,182	5,820,880	3,528,276	1,246,705	10,598,462	1,693,965	86.2	19.0	65.1

SOURCE: U.S. Department of Justice, Immigration and Naturalization Service, 1998 Statistical Yearbook (Washington, D.C.: Government Printing Office, 1999). U.S. Department of Justice, Immigration and Naturalization Service, Annual Report 1998 (available online: http://www.ins.gov/graphics/publicaffairs/newsrels/98Legal.pdf)

pended on educating a new generation of Americans in science, and Congress passed the National Defense Education Act. President Kennedy implored Congress to pass the Trade Expansion Act of 1962 in the name of national security. President Johnson sent Americans to fight in Vietnam in the interest of U.S. national security, and President Nixon withdrew them for the same reason. Nixon first used national security as a defense against the Watergate scandal; Carter used it to advance his national energy program. President Reagan frequently invoked the term to persuade Congress to give aid to the contras. Any term used to guide the United States through so many different mazes should raise eyebrows, if not questions.

The simplest definition of *national security* is the "defense of a nation's interests and values." There are three levels of defense: (1) the unity of the state, (2) the protection of borders, and (3) the defense of other interests and values. In the eighteenth and nineteenth centuries, the United States was most concerned about the first two levels. In the twentieth century, Washington was preoccupied with the third level, which, in turn, begs three sets of questions:

- *Which interests and values?* A list includes strategic interests in defending the United States against nuclear missiles, geopolitical interests in maintaining alliances, the political interests of the president, the economic interests of large or small businesses, the overseas property of American corporations, the human rights of another nation's citizens, the nation's ideals, the environmental interests of the Sierra Club or of the nation, and the interests of future generations. Which of these interests count, and how do you count them?
- *Who decides which interests should be given priority?* Nations seldom, if ever, pursue all their interests at the same time. Decisions need to be made about which interests should be pursued (trade-offs) and which come first (priorities). Who makes such decisions? The U.S. president is commander-in-chief, but Congress shares with him most of the powers to make foreign policy. In the executive branch, the secretaries of state and defense and the national security adviser all "make policy." How can one recognize a foreign policy if each says something different, or if Congress passes a law contradicting them?

- *What is the best defense of a nation, and when?* When does a potential threat require a response? Should force be a first option or a last resort in dealing with a particular threat to national security? Do troops on the border provide the best defense, or is the best defense, as a football coach once said, a good offense?

The history of the United States has not provided a single set of answers to these three basic questions of national security. Rather, U.S. national security policy is replete with examples of diverse interests, shifting priorities, different decisionmakers, and widely varying responses. Over time, however, and with some variations, one can discern a steady expansion of America's conception of its national security. In the nineteenth century the United States, by and large, ignored the chronic instability in Latin America. In the twentieth century, as U.S. power and wealth expanded, the nation's interest in its neighbors' internal affairs grew as well. The construction of the Panama Canal—with an investment equivalent to one-third of the U.S. budget in 1914—was a sign of U.S. strength and a motive for widening the arc of defense. Presidents became preoccupied with protecting this strategic asset from the region's instability and other foreign powers—to such an extent that some historians referred to the entire policy toward the Caribbean Basin as "the Panama policy."[11]

Still, there were many different ways to defend the Canal and U.S. interests in Latin America during the twentieth century. Theodore Roosevelt and his secretary of state, Elihu Root, tried to preclude instability and revolution by multilateral negotiations leading to international treaties. William Howard Taft used marines, dollars, and customs receiverships to help the countries remain solvent and stable. Woodrow Wilson replaced "dollar diplomacy" with the promotion of freedom, but he continued to use the marines. Franklin D. Roosevelt, Harry Truman, Jimmy Carter, and Bill Clinton pledged nonintervention and meant it. Dwight D. Eisenhower, John F. Kennedy, Lyndon Johnson, Richard Nixon, Ronald Reagan, and George Bush violated their pledges of nonintervention because they perceived serious threats to U.S. security. Presidents defined U.S. interests differently and chose different means to defend them.

In his search for a definition of national security, Arnold Wolfers concluded that it is little more than an "ambiguous symbol" used by presidents to build support for a particular program.[12] Rather than a guide, national security is a concept that is subjective, relative, and dynamic. It is subjective because it depends on the personality and bureaucratic role of the definer. A conservative president is more likely to interpret threats to the United States as more serious than a liberal one would, and the Pentagon will always describe threats in more ominous terms than the Department of State. The White House definition will be more sensitive to the public mood, reflecting the president's political interest. A nation will calculate threats differently if there is a war abroad or a depression at home.

The concept of national security is also relative. How a country's leaders define security depends on the size, power, and self-concept of the country. Small, poor, divided countries are more likely to be preoccupied with internal threats. As states become richer, their concept of national security expands. When oil revenues multiplied in the 1970s, Venezuela and Mexico began to play more active roles in Central America; when their oil profits declined in the 1980s, they withdrew. Threats to these governments had not changed, but their resources and capabilities had shrunk.

Finally, the concept of national security is dynamic. The history of the United States illustrates how its definition of national security expanded with its economy and power. Richer people in exclusive neighborhoods are not threatened more by crime than are poor people in ghettos. The rich have more locks on their doors because they can afford more and have more to lose.

As states change and their relationships evolve, their leaders will change their concept of security. In the first decade of the twentieth century the United States needed exclusive control of the Panama Canal to protect it; by the 1970s, exclusive control had become a threat to the Canal. Access to raw materials was a strategic interest of the United States for many years, but today Americans are more concerned about access to markets and new interests related to drugs, terrorism, trade, and the environment.

There is, in brief, no single or simple formula for defining a nation's security or judging when it is at risk. The Soviet installation of nuclear missiles in Cuba in 1962 constituted the most serious threat to the United States since World War II; yet, even then, President Kennedy's advisers disagreed not only on the appropriate response but also on the nature of the threat. The Joint Chiefs of Staff believed that the missiles altered the balance of power; Secretary of Defense Robert McNamara and President Kennedy believed that they affected only the world's *perception* of the balance.[13] Although Kennedy's decision to compel the Soviets to withdraw the missiles brought the world to the brink of nuclear holocaust, his decision was based not on an *objective* threat but on a *subjective* judgment about how others would perceive U.S. actions. If U.S. policymakers could not agree that the missiles constituted an objective threat, it is not at all surprising that the nature and intensity of other "threats" in the hemisphere have been subject to vigorous debate.

The point is that there is no formula for distinguishing between objective and subjective threats to U.S. security in Latin America. If there were such a formula, national security policy could be made by computer, and judgment would not be necessary. Without a formula, one must assess the nature and immediacy of a threat and decide on a proper response. On this, people naturally differ. The end of the Cold War has reduced significantly the sense of international threat, although some view the menace of drugs and terrorism as constituting an almost equivalent threat.

In the United States, everyone is entitled to an opinion, but the Constitution gives the authority for aggregating these opinions to the president and, to a lesser degree, Congress. In assessing a threat and proposing a response, the president knows that he must pass two tests: first, the democratic test of gaining the acquiescence, if not the support, of Congress and the American people; and second, the empirical test of achieving the objectives that he defines. A president rarely concludes that U.S. national security is directly threatened without being reasonably certain that his policy will pass both tests. These tests represent the bond of democratic accountability. If a president fails these tests, the people will exercise their power to replace him or his party's nominee at the next election.

Lenses

We have established that there is no guide for assessing a threat to the national security and prescribing a response, and yet the most important debates on U.S. policy toward Latin America have revolved around these questions. How are we to understand and judge that debate? Scholars have generated literally a "thicket of theories" to explain how and why the U.S. government assesses threats and makes policy.[14] These theories locate the explanatory variables in geopolitics (realism), institutions (the president, the bureaucracy, Congress, interest groups), democratic politics, or the decisionmaking process. For the sake of simplicity, I use just two "lenses" to interpret developments in Latin America, assess threats, and propose policies. For want of better terms, I refer to them as the "conservative" and "liberal" lenses. Two debates on U.S. policy toward Central America roughly sixty years apart offer a basis for explaining them.

In 1928 *Foreign Affairs* published two views on "Our Foreign Policy," one by Ogden Mills and one by Franklin D. Roosevelt. The essence of Mills's conservative and Republican argument was that U.S. foreign policy should remain *independent and separate* from Europe or any group of nations. He criticized Democrats for their "high-sounding phrases or promises" and advocated dealing with diplomatic problems in a *businesslike* way. The Monroe Doctrine was the "cornerstone" of U.S. foreign policy toward Latin America. The United States should respect Latin American governments, "but sovereignty carries with it certain *obligations*"—such as protecting American citizens and property. When these were violated in Nicaragua, "we could not do less than to *send troops* there."[15]

Roosevelt extracted a different lesson from American history. "The real American spirit," he argued, is to try to be a *model* that other nations would want to emulate, not to be "selfish" or arrogantly try to impose that model by force. He criticized conservative Republicans who "placed money leadership ahead of *moral leadership.*" He praised Woodrow Wilson for restoring "high moral purpose" to U.S. policy and for *collaborating* with Latin Americans to *mediate* disputes. Roosevelt defended Wilson's interventions in the Dominican Republic and Haiti because they restored order, built roads and schools, and improved health conditions, but he acknowledged that Latin American condemnation of the interventions had caused him to rethink his position. "*By what right,* they say, other than the right of main force, does the United States arrogate unto itself the privilege of intervening alone in the internal affairs of another sovereign Republic?"

The main difference between the conservative lens and the liberal one was that the former tended to see threats more intensely and the latter tried to understand and be more responsive to the Latin Americans. "We are exceedingly jealous of our own sovereignty," Roosevelt wrote, "and it is only right that we should respect a similar feeling among other nations." He continued:

> It is not the right or the duty of the United States to intervene alone. It is rather the duty of the United States to associate with itself other American

> Republics, to give intelligent joint study to the problem, and, if the conditions warrant, to offer the helping hand or hands in the name of the Americas. Single-handed intervention by us in the internal affairs of other nations must end; with the cooperation of others we shall have more order in this hemisphere and less dislike.[16]

During the foreign policy debate in the 1980s, President Reagan described the origin of Central America's crisis as "a Soviet-Cuban power play—pure and simple." The interests of the United States were viewed as commensurate with the nature and the intensity of the threat: "The national security of all the Americas is at stake in Central America." The region is vital because of its proximity, its potential use as a Soviet base, its sea lanes (two-thirds of all U.S. foreign trade and petroleum pass through the region), and its migration ("a tidal wave of refugees"). To make the national security argument compelling, President Reagan connected developments in a small, poor region with those in the principal geopolitical arena: "If we cannot defend ourselves [in the Caribbean Basin], we cannot expect to prevail elsewhere. Our credibility would collapse, our alliances would crumble, and the safety of our homeland would be put in jeopardy."[17]

Senator Christopher Dodd, chairman of the Senate Foreign Relations Subcommittee on Western Hemisphere Affairs, offered the Democratic response. He stressed his party's agreement with Reagan's anti-Soviet and anti-Marxist security goals. His principal criticisms were that Reagan "fundamentally misunderstands the causes of conflict" and that military solutions are counterproductive. Dodd argued that the origin of the crisis was the region's poverty and injustice and that the United States ought to stress diplomacy and human rights and work with Latin American governments "to move with the tide of history rather than stand against it."[18]

These two debates occurred sixty years apart, but the arguments had barely changed. Conservatives focus on a relatively narrower idea of U.S. interests and a military-based definition of power. They believe that the United States should approach problems unilaterally and in a practical and forceful problem-solving manner. Liberals give higher priority to the moral dimension and to what Joseph S. Nye calls co-optive or "soft power," which derives from the American model.[19] They look at the social and economic causes of the crisis, try to understand the issues from the other's perspective, and rely on multilateral, diplomatic approaches.

It is not that conservatives do not care about morality or Latin American views, or that liberals do not care about order or protecting U.S. interests, sometimes by force. It is simply that each perspective listens to a different Latin American voice and gives different emphasis to each U.S. interest. The differences are clear in the memoirs of Richard Nixon and former Speaker of the House Jim Wright. Nixon heard Latin Americans fearful of communism and desirous of U.S. investment, whereas Wright listened to concerns about poverty and social justice and to yearnings for U.S. respect for Latin American sovereignty.[20] The United States has had to make choices among interests and strategies, and in the twentieth century the core of the Republican and Democratic Parties tended to make different choices. There have been, of course, important exceptions to this generalization: conservative Democrats who voted with Republicans, and liberal Republicans who aligned with Democrats. And there have been Republicans, notably Ronald Reagan, who were zealous on behalf of ideology.

Beyond these two lenses, which are dominant in the debate on policy, are a radical lens, which is influential in the literature on the region, and an interactive lens, which I use in this book. The radical lens has as many variations and names as authors; it has influenced the language of the debate more than the policy. It sees the origins of the region's crisis in a system of exploitation imposed by the United States, mainly for economic reasons. Some radical authors recognize the significance of strategic motives but see these as less important than the overarching need to maintain a capitalistic system for the benefit of U.S. business. Prescriptions for U.S. policy vary. One author argues that "the only choice" for U.S. policymakers is either to "work with revolutionaries to achieve a more orderly and equitable society, or . . . try to cap the upheavals until the pressure builds . . . to blow the societies apart with even greater force."[21]

The liberal and conservative lenses disagree on which U.S. policy will solve Latin America's problems. The radical lens offers a useful antidote to this debate but takes the argument too far in suggesting that the United States is the problem. Despite their differences, the liberal, conservative, and radical lenses share the premise that most developments in the region should be interpreted as the result of external decisions by the United States: Because of the disparity in size, power, and wealth, it is logical that the United States should simply work its will. But that premise is flawed. Presidents have often failed to achieve their goals in the region, as Reagan's effort to overthrow the Sandinistas demonstrated.

An interactive lens is needed to compensate for the undue weight given to U.S. policy. This lens is not new,[22] but its importance has increased. It presumes that the region is composed of actors—nations, groups, leaders—that try to influence the United States even as they are influenced by it. Of course, all actors are not equal. The interactive perspective recognizes the vast disparity in power that separates the United States from the region, but it does not assume that such power automatically translates into influence or control.[23] Indeed, such power is reversible, with leaders or groups in the region trying to use the United States to further their own political or economic ends.

Some observers have found this role reversal difficult to interpret. For example, in summarizing U.S.-Nicaraguan relations over a forty-year period, Walter LaFeber concludes: "As every President after Hoover knew, [the] Somozas did as they were told."[24] It is true that, to strengthen their internal position, the Somozas cultivated the myth that they were working for the United States, but the Somozas were no one's fools or servants. They cooperated with the United States only when it was in their interest. They were eager to help the United States overthrow Guatemalan President Jacobo Arbenz in 1954 and Cuban President Fidel Castro in 1961, but they also wanted to eliminate Costa Rican President José Figueres and desisted only after Secretary of State John Foster Dulles threatened them.[25]

The United States applied considerable pressure, unsuccessfully, on Anastasio Somoza Garcia in 1936 and 1945–1947 to discourage him from running for the presidency.[26] Efforts by Carter to pressure the son, Anastasio Somoza Debayle, to accept a democratic transition in 1978–1979 also failed. Eventually, as the Nicaraguan state developed, Somoza's myth backfired, antagonizing the nationalistic sensibilities of Nicaraguans and the rest of Latin America. Indeed, the Sandinistas found it useful to employ the opposite of Somoza's myth—the United States as a hostile rival—to establish their nationalist credentials and to mobilize youthful support. But that myth also came back to haunt them in the 1990 election. Nicaraguans, in brief, have been able to puncture myths perpetrated by their leaders better than some scholars of U.S.-Nicaraguan relations. The lesson is that to understand U.S. policy toward the region, one should start by looking at the region on its own terms.

If we reverse the conventional perspective and examine the region from the inside rather than from the notion of superpowers exploiting targets of opportunity, we see a region struggling with underdevelopment and chronic political instability, determined to widen its scope for self-determination and cultural affirmation. Surveying the history, Venezuelan journalist Carlos Rangel noted that "peace and democracy have been fragile curiosities; our norms are tyranny or civil war."[27] Poverty and recurring political crises were pervasive before the United States turned its attention and power to the area.

Yet, if one cannot understand political change in the region by looking only at U.S. policy, neither can one focus on the region alone. One must also understand the interaction. Leaders from small, open countries sometimes believe that their nations' destinies are controlled by others, whereas many observers in the United States think that underdevelopment has more to do with a "state of mind" than with the international system.[28] An accurate reading of the interaction needs to integrate these two seemingly contradictory perspectives.

The interactive perspective also helps to explain how and why an internal crisis becomes internationalized. Conservatives argued that the Soviet Union orchestrated crises; radicals suggested that the United States injected the East-West conflict to mask its rejection of change. In small, open nations, local groups often reach outside for funding or political support, particularly when the regime blocks their path to power. Businessmen reach out to chambers of commerce; some unions relate to the AFL-CIO, others to communist unions; leftists seek help from Cuba, rightists from military governments. Outsiders provide help to local groups as part of their own competitions.

Because the nations are smaller than the United States, it is natural to view the direction of influence as coming from the north. There is no disputing the large influence of the United States on the region's politics, but one should not underestimate the guile or the manipulative skills of local actors, the strengths of some institutions, such as the military, and the pride and intransigence of local leaders in resisting too intimate an encroachment by the United States. Moreover, local actors have a powerful equalizer: They are playing on their own turf.

The issue is not whether local or external actors are more important or purer, but rather how they interact to confound each other. Studies that focus on either the hegemonic impulse of the United States or the recalcitrance of Latin America are necessarily one-sided; they fail to see that both sides have been caught in neurotic webs that have brought out the worst in both.

Motives Vivendi

The United States policy toward Latin America is often described as fluctuating between neglect of the region and panic when events seem to veer in an adverse direction.[29] This cycle is consistent with the view that U.S. motives are primarily strategic rather than economic or political: The United States seeks not to impose political systems or to exploit economies but rather to *avoid* the possible emergence of hostile governments or policies. For this reason, the United States does not act until the situation becomes grave.

The characterization of the policy as a neglect-panic cycle also says something about the psychology of U.S.–Latin American relations. "Neglect" presumes a certain tutelary responsibility. This is obviously inconsistent with the region's demands for autonomy, but it is characteristic of the region's ambivalence toward the United States. Latin leaders want independence, but they have also wanted to rely on the United States. They want aid from the United States, but they also resent the dependence this represents.

The United States, too, is a prisoner of this self-contradictory psychology. Washington does not want to dominate, but it cannot remain passive for too long either to instability or to radicalism. It is caught, as it has been since the end of the nineteenth century, between the Teller Amendment, pledging not to annex Cuba, and the Platt Amendment, permitting U.S. intervention in Cuba's affairs. The United States might not want to control, but it also does not want to allow events to get *out* of its control. (The distinction between controlling in an imperial manner and reacting from fear is clear cut during peacetime but less evident during a prolonged period of instability when civil conflict connects with foreign intervention.) If one adds these matching contradictions to the gap in power and wealth, one has begun to understand U.S. policy toward the region.

Because the terrain is a developing area, and because the connection between local political crisis and U.S. national security is indirect, the task for U.S. policymakers is often how to influence political change in a sensitive developing country. The United States can no longer do this effectively by itself because its policies often provoke from local nationalists a reaction that is the opposite of what it seeks.

To influence political change, normalize and balance U.S.–Latin American relations, and escape the whirlpool that has trapped the hemisphere in unproductive cycles, the United States must adapt its objectives to take into account other national perspectives. Instead of confrontation with nationalism in pursuit of a unilateral objective, a more effective path is the pursuit of a modified multilateral objective. The best evidence of the comparative effectiveness of the indirect, multilateral strategy is that the Sandinistas survived Reagan's frontal assault but could not prevail when Bush retreated and the arena shifted from the battlefield to the ballot box. For this new approach to work, however, Latin America must also take risks and modify a defensive, narrow conception of sovereignty. The goal is to establish a peaceful, democratic, and prosperous community of nations. The unprecedented wave of democratization in Latin America provides a promising foundation for achieving this goal.

Notes

1. Harold Norman Denny, *Dollars for Bullets: The Story of American Rule in Nicaragua* (New York: Dial Press, 1929), p. 7.

2. Letter from Robert Lansing, former secretary of state, to Senator Medill McCormick, chairman of the U.S. Senate Select Committee on Haiti and Santo Domingo, May 4, 1922, in James W. Gantenbein, ed., *The Evolution of Our Latin American Policy: A Documentary Record* (New York: Octagon Books, 1971), p. 636.

3. Norman H. Davis, "Wanted: A Consistent Latin American Policy," *Foreign Affairs* 9 (July 1931): 558.

4. John Bartlow Martin, *U.S. Policy on the Caribbean* (Boulder, Colo.: Westview Press, 1978), p. 9.

5. See, for example, Wilfrid Hardy Callcott, *The Caribbean Policy of the United States, 1890–1920* (Baltimore: Johns Hopkins University Press, 1942); Dexter Perkins, *The United States and the Caribbean* (Cambridge, Mass.: Harvard University Press, 1947); and Dana G. Munro, *The United States and the Caribbean Republics, 1921–1933* (Princeton: Princeton University Press, 1974). All three books cover Central America as well as the Caribbean.

6. For a discussion of the concept of a Caribbean Basin and the similarities and differences among the nations of the region, see Robert Pastor, "Sinking in the Caribbean Basin," *Foreign Affairs* 60 (Summer 1982): 1038–1058.

7. United Nations Development Programme, *Human Development Report, 1991* (New York: Oxford University Press, 1991), p. 16; and *Human Development Report 2000,* www.undp.org/hdr2000/english/presskit/hdi.pdf.

8. *The Autobiography of Theodore Roosevelt* (New York: Charles Scribner's Sons, 1919), p. 270.

9. Quoted in Denny, *Dollars for Bullets,* pp. 46–47.

10. Ronald Scheman, *The Inter-American Dilemma* (New York: Praeger, 1988), p. 15.

11. See, for example, Samuel F. Bemis, *The Latin American Policy of the United States* (New York: Harcourt, Brace & Co., 1943), pp. 185–189.

12. Arnold Wolfers, "National Security as an Ambiguous Symbol," in Arnold Wolfers, ed., *Discord and Collaboration* (Baltimore: Johns Hopkins University Press, 1962).

13. James G. Blight and David A. Welch, *On the Brink: Americans and Soviets Reexamine the Cuban Missile Crisis* (New York: Farrar, Straus & Giroux, 1990). President Kennedy said that the missiles would not have changed the balance of power, but they "would have appeared to—and appearances contribute to reality." *Public Papers of the Presidents of the United States: John F. Kennedy, 1962* (Washington, D.C.: Government Printing Office, 1963), p. 898.

14. The phrase "thicket of theories" is James Kurth's. See his essay, "A Widening Gyre: The Logic of American Weapons Procurement," in G. John Ikenberry, ed., *American Foreign Policy: Theoretical Essays* (Boston: Scott, Foresman, 1989).

15. Ogden L. Mills, "Our Foreign Policy: A Republican View," *Foreign Affairs* 6 (July 1928): 555–572. Roosevelt's is in the same issue, "Our Foreign Policy: A Democratic View," pp. 573–586.

16. Roosevelt, "Our Foreign Policy," pp. 584–585.

17. Presidential address, *The New York Times,* April 28, 1983; Lou Cannon, "A Latin Axis Could Take Central America, Reagan Says," *Washington Post,* July 21, 1983, p. A1; Reagan press conference, *The New York Times,* July 27, 1983, p. A10; Francis X. Clines, "Reagan Calls Salvador Aid Foes Naive," *The New York Times,* March 20, 1984, p. A3.

18. The transcript of Dodd's address is reprinted in the *The New York Times,* April 28, 1983, p. A12.

19. Joseph S. Nye Jr., *Bound To Lead: The Changing Nature of American Power* (New York: Basic Books, 1990).

20. Richard Nixon, *RN: The Memoirs of Richard Nixon* (New York: Grosset & Dunlap, 1978), pp. 186–192, 283; and Jim Wright, *Balance of Power: Presidents and Congress from the Era of McCarthy to the Age of Gingrich* (Atlanta, Ga.: Turner Publishing, 1996), pp. 293–297, 412–438.

21. Walter LaFeber, *Inevitable Revolutions* (New York: W. W. Norton, 1983), pp. 16–17. For other radical interpretations, see William A. Williams, *Empire as a Way of Life* (Oxford: Oxford University Press, 1980); Karl Bermann, *Under the Big Stick* (Boston: South End Press, 1986); and two literature reviews that in-

clude discussion of the radical and other perspectives: Jorge Dominguez, "Consensus and Divergence: The State of the Literature on Inter-American Relations," *Latin American Research Review* 13 (1978): 87–126; and Robert Pastor, "Explaining U.S. Policy toward the Caribbean Basin: Fixed and Emerging Images," *World Politics* 38 (April 1986): 483–515.

22. See, for example, Cole Blasier, *The Hovering Giant: U.S. Responses to Revolutionary Change in Latin America* (Pittsburgh: University of Pittsburgh Press, 1985); Abraham F. Lowenthal, *Partners in Conflict* (Baltimore: Johns Hopkins University Press, 1987); and Richard E. Welch Jr., *Response to Revolution: The United States and the Cuban Revolution, 1959–1961* (Chapel Hill: University of North Carolina Press, 1985).

23. The interactive perspective builds on the concept of asymmetric interdependence developed by Robert Keohane and Joseph S. Nye, *Power and Interdependence: World Politics in Transition* (Boston: Little, Brown, 1977).

24. LaFeber, *Inevitable Revolutions,* p. 230.

25. U.S. Department of State, *Foreign Relations of the United States, 1952–54* (Washington, D.C.: Government Printing Office, 1983), pp. 1387–1390.

26. Richard Millet, *Guardians of the Dynasty: A History of the U.S.-Created Guardia Nacional de Nicaragua and the Somoza Family* (Maryknoll, N.Y.: Orbis Books, 1977), pp. 210–215.

27. Carlos Rangel, "Is Democracy Possible in Latin America?" in *Democracy and Dictatorship in Latin America* (New York: Foundation for the Study of Independent Social Ideas, n.d.), p. 73.

28. Compare, for example, Michael Manley, *Jamaica: Struggle in the Periphery* (London: Third World Media Limited, 1982), with Lawrence Harrison, *Underdevelopment Is a State of Mind: The Latin American Case* (Washington, D.C.: University Press of America, 1985).

29. See Lowenthal, *Partners in Conflict.* For another succinct summary of this cycle, see Virginia R. Dominguez and Jorge I. Dominguez, *The Caribbean* (New York: Foreign Policy Association Headline Series 253, 1981), pp. 64–77.

Part 1

THE QUEST FOR THE NATIONAL INTEREST

The question—what is national interest?—can be answered, if at all, only by exploring the use of the formula by responsible statesmen.

—CHARLES A. BEARD, 1934

There are no natural points to divide a nation's foreign policy. Sometimes, the crucial turning points have coincided with a specific domestic or foreign event, such as the Depression or the Cuban revolution. Sometimes the policy of a particular president differs so much from his predecessor's or his successor's as to justify a separate designation in the history books. More often, a president leaves an imprint, often a slogan, on his policy that will permit historians to distinguish it from that of others.

To understand where the United States is headed, we begin by examining the policies of the four most recent administrations. Jimmy Carter, Ronald Reagan, George Bush, and Bill Clinton all accepted the same panoply of U.S. interests in the region: national security, human rights, democracy, and economic development. But the four presidents differed greatly on which interests should get priority and how these should be defined and pursued. Carter employed a liberal lens, focusing on the moral issues, trying to be responsive to Latin America's concerns; Reagan employed a conservative lens, concentrating on the security problems, acting forcefully and unilaterally; and Bush and Clinton represented pragmatic compromises. Chapters 3–6 describe the views of each of these presidents and their senior advisers as they took office, the agendas they faced, their major policies, Latin America's reactions to them, and their legacies.

As U.S. presidents changed, so did the hemisphere's landscape, although for different reasons. In the mid-1970s, Latin America was governed mostly by authoritarian military regimes. Many Latin leaders reached beyond the hemisphere to assume leadership roles in the Third World. In the 1980s, the hemispheric agenda split, with the United States focusing on Central America and communism and with Latin America concerned with debt and democracy. In the 1990s Latin America had become democratic, and it was anxious to collaborate with the United States on establishing a hemispheric free trade area and securing its democratic gains.

The ricochet in the debate on policy from one president to the next is not as stark as it seems. Nor should apparent shifts obscure the continuity of policy or the effect of broader societal forces, often channeled through Congress. Latin Americans tend to look for a president's signature, but U.S. foreign policy cannot be understood without examining Congress's role and the dialectic by which the two branches make foreign policy. Chapter 7 explains how "interbranch politics" places new issues and values on the foreign policy agenda and compensates for presidential emphases.

3

THE CARTER ADMINISTRATION: A TEST OF PRINCIPLE

Our sharing of history and our sharing of a common purpose has always bound us together. The Mexican people know what Yankee imperialism means, and being from Georgia, I have also heard the same phrase used.

—JIMMY CARTER

Within a single year, two events unprecedented in the history of the United States shook the nation's confidence in itself as the moral leader of the free world. In August 1974 President Richard M. Nixon resigned under a pall of scandal. Eight months later, the United States suffered the humiliation of military defeat as it watched the U.S. ambassador to Vietnam flee his post by helicopter.

Latin America was far from the nation's eye, but the region had used the previous decade to assert itself internationally, progress economically, and regress politically with a series of military coups. Old problems in Panama and Cuba festered; new concerns related to human rights and North-South economic issues awaited the attention of the next U.S. president. Washington, however, was absorbed in a constitutional crisis and its first defeat in war.

In the presidential campaign of 1976, Americans yearned for a moral rebirth and a replenishment of virtue. No candidate better captured and articulated this need than Jimmy Carter. The United States wanted an "outsider," someone untainted by Lyndon Johnson's war, Richard Nixon's cover-up, or Gerald Ford's pardon. Of all the candidates, Carter was the most removed from Washington. A former governor of Georgia, Carter lived in his hometown of some six hundred people in a remote part of the state. A born-again Christian, Carter promised that he would never lie, that government would be "as good as its people," and that the United States would once again shine as a beacon for human rights and idealism. The times suited his message, and within a year Carter went from relative political obscurity to the White House. His mission was to restore faith in the United States at home and abroad:

> In the aftermath of Vietnam and Watergate and the C.I.A. revelations, our nation's reputation was soiled. Many Americans turned away from our own Government, and said: "It embarrasses me." The vision, the ideals, the commitments that were there 200 years ago when our Nation was formed, have somehow been lost. One of the great responsibilities that I share with you is to restore that vision and that degree of cleanness and decency and honesty and truth and principle to our country.[1]

Carter's approach held special promise for Latin America, which had suffered a decade of repression. In the first two years of his term, Carter addressed an agenda of interdependence and formulated a new approach to the region. By the end of 1978, the administration had implemented most of the initiatives begun the previous year. In its last two years, however, the administration was compelled to address a more traditional security agenda as the old world of superpower competition and balance-of-power geopolitics returned. It focused on the Caribbean Basin and managed crises, putting to the test the principles that Carter had outlined at the beginning of his term.

Background

Jimmy Carter had a deeper interest in Latin America and the Caribbean than either of his two principal foreign policy advisers, Secretary of State Cyrus Vance and National Security Adviser Zbigniew Brzezinski. This was partly because Carter had much less experience in other areas of the world than they had, but also because he spoke some Spanish—the first president to do so since Thomas Jefferson—and he had traveled privately or as governor to Mexico, Brazil, Colombia, Argentina, and Costa Rica.

Carter's emphasis on human rights was a central element of his policy toward Latin America, not only because of a deep personal commitment, but also because of his concern about the massive human rights violations in the region and the lack of interest by the Nixon and Ford administrations. Even before his election, Carter had shaped this concern for human rights into a framework for policy:

> I do not say to you that we can remake the world in our own image. I recognize the limits on our power, but the present administration—our government—has been so obsessed with balance of power politics that it has often ignored basic American values and a common and proper concern for human rights.
>
> Ours is a great and a powerful nation, committed to certain enduring ideals, and those ideals must be reflected not only in our domestic policy but also in our foreign policy. There are practical, effective ways in which our power can be used to alleviate human suffering around the world. We should begin by having it understood that if any nation . . . deprives its own people of basic human rights, that fact will help shape our own people's attitude toward that nation's repressive government. . . . Now we must be realistic . . . we do not and should not insist on identical standards. . . . We can live with diversity in governmental systems, but we cannot look away when a government tortures people or jails them for their beliefs.[2]

Vance and Brzezinski entered the administration with almost the same substantive agenda and no important differences on the key issues of U.S. policy toward Latin America.[3] However, the two men differed markedly in personality, temperament, and background, and their new positions reinforced those differences. Vance, the respected corporate lawyer, was a careful and skilled negotiator. He was almost everyone's candidate, including Brzezinski's, to be secretary of state. As national security adviser and as a professor of Soviet politics, Brzezinski was more apt than Vance to evaluate an event in terms of its implications for U.S.-Soviet relations, and he was generally more conservative, although not on all issues. Brzezinski's Polish background led him to view some events in anti-Soviet terms, but it also made him more sensitive to Latin American nationalism and the region's view of the United States, which bore some similarities to Poland's view of Russia.

The differences that separated Vance and Brzezinski in 1979 on the best way to approach the Soviet Union, Iran, and China ironically promoted agreement in some other areas, including Latin America, as both tried to preserve their overall relationship. A second reason why the rivalry rarely spilled over into Latin American policy was that Vance delegated most work in this area to his deputy, Warren Christopher.

In converting its predisposition into a policy, the new administration had the benefit of the work done by two private commissions. Carter, Vance, and Brzezinski were members of the Trilateral Commission, which provided a conceptual framework for collaboration among the industrialized countries in approaching the full gamut of international issues. With regard to Latin America, the most important influence on the Carter administration was the Commission on U.S.–Latin American Relations, chaired by Sol M. Linowitz, a former ambassador to the Organization of American States (OAS). A private, bipartisan group of twenty distinguished leaders, the Linowitz Commission was established in 1974 and during the following two years issued two reports recommending a new U.S. policy that would take into account "an increasingly interdependent world in which Latin American nations seek to be active and independent participants."[4] The reports helped the administration define a new relationship with Latin America, and twenty-seven of the twenty-eight recommendations in the second report were adopted as policy. Sol Linowitz became Carter's co-negotiator with Ellsworth Bunker for new Panama Canal treaties. Michael Blumenthal, another member, became secretary of the treasury. Commission staff were appointed to key positions in the government. I moved from staff director of the commission to director of Latin American affairs on the National Security Council (NSC).

Carter's Preferred Agenda

Because of Watergate and the transition from Nixon to Ford, a multitude of difficult issues had accumulated by 1977. Carter, a man who delighted in trying to accomplish more than anyone thought possible, was also averse to setting priorities. He decided to tackle virtually all of the issues at once. He also took pride in not taking into account the political dimension of the issues; the consequence was that he unintentionally facilitated a coalescing of opponents of each of his policies.[5]

On Latin American issues, Carter decided that the first issue for the NSC would be Panama. On January 27, 1977, the Policy Review Committee (PRC), one of two committees of the NSC, held its first meeting and recommended to the president that Vance inform the Panamanian foreign minister of the U.S. intention to negotiate a new treaty in good faith and rapidly.[6] New treaties were needed because the old paternalistic relationship treated Panamanians as second-class citizens in their own country. Nationalistic grievances led to riots in 1964, and many observers feared that a second round of violence could destroy the Canal. Ronald Reagan called this blackmail and insisted that the United States not retreat one step. Carter argued that the old treaty endangered the Canal and that a new one would protect it; he described the treaties as a sign of "confidence in ourselves now and in the future."[7] The administration's public relations problem stemmed from the fact that its central argument was counterintuitive, that the United States could defend the Canal better if it gave up control and made Panama a partner.

Within six months after negotiations began, the two sides agreed to two treaties. The basic Panama Canal Treaty required the United States to eliminate the Canal Zone and gradually transfer property and responsibilities for operation of the Canal to Panama until the year 2000, when Panama would become solely responsible for administering it. The Treaty on the Permanent Neutrality of the Canal granted the United States and Panama rights to defend a neutral Canal beyond the year 2000. Carter and Omar Torrijos signed the treaties at the OAS on September 7, 1977.

To describe the treaties as unpopular is an understatement, and Carter had to invest considerable prestige and political capital to get them ratified. In the spring of 1978, after the second-longest treaty debate in history, the Senate ratified both treaties by a single vote.

By that time, Carter had articulated a new approach to the region in a Pan American Day speech on April 14, 1977: "As nations of the 'New World,' we once believed that we could prosper in isolation from the 'Old World.' But . . . all of us have taken such vital roles in the world community that isolation would now be harmful to our own best interests and to other countries." Carter proposed to open the hemispheric envelope; instead of excluding global issues from the region, he encouraged the leaders of the region to help define a new relationship between developing and industrialized nations.[8]

The speech was the culmination of a three-month NSC study and a PRC meeting on March 24, 1977, to debate the issues and make recommendations to the president on the entire gamut of inter-American issues, including Cuba, human rights, Mexico, and arms control. The main conceptual issue was whether the United States should assert the traditional "special relationship" with Latin America or accept a global policy for the developing world that could be adapted to the unique characteristics of the region's past relationship with the United States, as the Linowitz Commission had recommended. Carter accepted the latter recommendation: to focus on global North-South economic issues but, at the same time, to give greater attention to Latin America within that framework.

The PRC also discussed the principle of nonintervention. Carter had said that he opposed intervention in the internal affairs of other countries *unless* U.S. security interests were directly threatened.[9] Building on that statement, the PRC proposed a multilateral approach in which U.S. policy would depend to an important degree on the views of Latin America, particularly the democracies.

Carter accepted this and other recommendations and developed them in his speech. Whereas Nixon and Ford had been equivocal or hostile toward a North-South dialogue, Carter supported it and encouraged the Latin Americans to take the lead. Instead of defending U.S. corporations or demanding that Latin America improve its investment climate, he asked U.S. businesses to be flexible and adapt to the region's needs. Human rights, of course, was the center of his message, and he pledged to condition U.S. relations on how a government treated its people: "You will find the United States eager to stand beside those nations which respect human rights and which promote democratic ideals." He promised to sign the American Convention on Human Rights and urged other governments to join the United States in increasing support for the Inter-American Commission on Human Rights and for assistance to political refugees.

Finally, on the security agenda, Carter expressed his desire to improve relations with Cuba "on a measured and reciprocal basis." He said that the United States would show restraint in its own arms sales, and promised to sign Protocol I of the Treaty of Tlatelolco, which banned the placement of nuclear weapons in Latin America.

Although encouraged by Carter's energy and ideas, many Latin leaders were skeptical that the United States would really consult them on key economic issues. To try to dispel this uncertainty, Carter invited ambassadors from five major sugar-producing countries in the hemisphere to discuss decisions that he needed to make on sugar. As a result of the meeting, he rejected the International Trade Commission's recommendations for import quotas on sugar and a farm group's petition to drop sugar from U.S. tariff preferences. He also decided that the United States would negotiate an international sugar agreement.[10]

At the meeting, the president announced that he would send his wife to seven nations in Latin America and the Caribbean for consultations. In her travels from May 30 to June 12, Rosalynn Carter used her public statements and private conversations to repeat and expand the main themes in Carter's Pan American Day speech. She also asked each leader to sign or ratify the Treaty of Tlatelolco and the American Convention on Human Rights and to encourage others to do so. In Jamaica, she assured Michael Manley, who thought that previous administrations had tried to destabilize him, that Carter was prepared to support a social democratic experiment. In Peru and Ecuador, she used every opportunity to reinforce the democratization process promised by the military governments. She sought the same objective in Brazil, although more delicately.

On her return, Rosalynn Carter briefed the president and Secretary of State Vance, who then departed for the OAS General Assembly. That meeting was dominated by the human rights issue, marking, as a *Washington Post* reporter put it, "a new phase in U.S.–Latin American relations."[11] Instead of a lack of interest or a resistance to Latin American resolutions, the United States assumed joint leadership with its democratic friends. One OAS diplomat said it was "the first time a U.S. representative was both positive and publicly and privately consistent." The United States joined with Venezuela, Costa Rica, and the Caribbean to pass narrowly a resolution that strengthened the Inter-American Commission on Human Rights and affirmed that "there are no circumstances that justify torture, summary execution, or prolonged detention without trial contrary to law." When the military governments of the southern cone tried to change the resolution to justify violations against terrorism, their amendment was rejected.[12]

The president of Venezuela, Carlos Andres Perez, was probably the most energetic and determined democratic leader in the region. Carter deliberately cultivated a close relationship with him, much as President John F. Kennedy had with Pérez's mentor, Rómulo Betancourt. Carter encouraged Pérez to be an interlocutor with Torrijos during the Canal negotiations. He wrote to him regularly and met with him in June and September 1977 in Washington and in March 1978 in Caracas. Together, they developed common or similar positions on the entire inter-American agenda, including human rights, North-South economic issues, arms control, and nonproliferation. The relationship paid off. In February 1978, when the Uruguayan military government tried to obtain the thirteen votes in the OAS needed to host the next General Assembly,

Venezuela joined the United States to block that effort. This decision contrasted with the acquiescence by the United States and Latin America to Chile's initiative in 1976 to host the General Assembly.[13]

Carter's policies on human rights and democratization came to dominate the public's perception of his approach to Latin America. Arthur Schlesinger Jr. commented that "nothing the Carter Administration has done has excited more hope," but he also noted that the policy generated considerable confusion as well.[14] By and large, the confusion was in the United States, where critics found the policy punitive, too soft, or simply inconsistent. Most Third World dictators pretended to be confused, but in their complaints about being singled out for criticism, they unwittingly acknowledged that they understood Carter was serious. Haitian president Jean-Claude Duvalier, to take one example, released political prisoners and improved the atrocious conditions in his jails shortly after the election of Carter, and he re-arrested opponents in late November 1980 after Carter's defeat.[15]

An NSC directive established an interagency committee chaired by Deputy Secretary of State Warren Christopher to ensure that human rights criteria were incorporated into U.S. foreign policy and foreign aid decisions. One of the administration's first decisions was to modify the Ford budget for the 1977 fiscal year by reducing aid to three countries for human rights reasons. Four Latin military governments protested the new policy by ending their military assistance agreements with the United States. Such actions aroused some Americans, including Ronald Reagan, who wrote: "Little wonder that friendly nations such as Argentina, Brazil, Chile, Nicaragua, Guatemala, and El Salvador have been dismayed by Carter's policies."[16] Each of these governments was then a military dictatorship.

Carter also sought opportunities to strengthen the trend toward democracy in the hemisphere. High-level meetings were arranged with Chilean opposition leaders. In May 1978 Carter called on Dominican President Joaquín Balaguer to permit a free election or lose aid. The election went forward, and Balaguer lost.[17] Through letters and special envoys, Carter also reinforced the democratization process in Ecuador, Peru, and other countries. On a visit to Venezuela and Brazil in March 1978, he stressed the need for the developing world to participate more fully in decisions that shaped the global economy: "The United States is eager to work with you, as we have in the past, to shape a more just international economic and political order."[18] But it was difficult to translate this principle into a specific program, partly because of a lack of funds, but mostly because of a lack of international consensus and a paucity of formulas for changing the terms of trade or the voting of international institutions.

An initiative in the Caribbean proved easier to implement. Based on Andrew Young's visit there and an NSC study, Carter established a Caribbean Group under World Bank auspices to coordinate the region's economic development. By 1980, the group had coordinated and quadrupled foreign aid to a level of $1 billion.

The culmination of Carter's efforts to seek a multilateral consensus on his goals occurred appropriately enough in Panama in mid-June 1978, on the occasion of the exchange of the Canal treaties. Omar Torrijos and Carter invited the presidents of Venezuela, Colombia, and Costa Rica and the prime minister of Jamaica. They signed a "Joint Declaration of Panama," which identified specific steps that the leaders pledged to take and would urge others to take to resolve conflict in the hemisphere, promote human rights, and develop a more just and equitable international economy. The statement was as clear an affirmation of U.S. policy as one is likely to find in inter-American relations in the postwar period, and it was endorsed by the most important Latin and Caribbean democratic leaders and also by Torrijos.

Four days after returning from Panama, Carter addressed the OAS General Assembly in Washington and encouraged the leaders to tackle the outstanding territorial disputes in the hemisphere, much as the United States and Panama had done: "I pledge today my government's willingness to join in the effort to find peaceful and just solutions to other problems."[19] Unanticipated crises in the next two years, however, prevented the fulfillment of this pledge.

Expectations Unfulfilled in Mexico and Cuba

One month before Carter's inauguration, José López Portillo took office as president of a country whose financial and political situation was fragile. Carter recognized the importance of Mexico's political stability and development for the United States, and one of his purposes in inviting the new president as his first state visitor was to help restore the financial community's confidence in Mexico. The conversations went well, and the two presidents established a U.S.-Mexican consultative mechanism to ensure that the numerous issues in the relationship would receive high-level attention.

Kind words by Carter did less to restore the confidence of the international financial community than did major oil discoveries in Mexico. López Portillo decided to build a gas pipeline to the United States, and his government began discussions to sell gas to several U.S. companies. Officials in the United States informed the Mexicans that they needed to negotiate an agreement with the U.S. government *before* talking to the gas companies because U.S. regulatory agencies would not approve an agreement if the price were too high. The companies did not mind paying a high price for gas because that would permit them to raise their domestically regulated price. López Portillo ignored the warnings: Either he did not understand the issue (a conclusion that emerges from his memoirs) or he or his energy minister was convinced—perhaps with some material inducements—by the gas companies that Carter would have to accept the contract they signed in August 1977.[20] But, as forewarned, the U.S. agencies did not approve the contract.

During Carter's visit to Mexico in February 1979, negotiations on gas were put back on track, and a new agreement was reached in the fall of 1980. Nevertheless, López Portillo did not forgive Carter for his failure to approve the gas deal in 1977. Two years later, when presented with an opportunity to throw sand in Carter's face, he did so by breaking a promise and denying the shah of Iran reentry into Mexico after his operation in New York. Carter "was outraged," and their relationship never recovered.[21]

The Carter administration did not have the same high expectations for Cuba that it had for Mexico, but it was just as ready to take the initiative and a risk. In his confirmation hearings before the Senate Foreign Relations Committee, Vance signaled to Castro: "If Cuba is willing to live within the international system, then we ought to seek ways to find whether we can eliminate the impediments which exist between us and try to move toward normalization."[22] The PRC discussed Cuba on March 9 and recommended an approach along the lines that Carter had sketched during a telephone call-in program moderated by Walter Cronkite:

> I would like to do what I can to ease tensions with Cuba. . . . *Before any full normalization of relationships can take place,* though, Cuba would have to make some fairly substantial changes in their attitude. *I would like to insist,*

> for instance, that they not interfere in the internal affairs of countries in this hemisphere, and *that they decrease their military involvement in Africa,* and that they reinforce a commitment to human rights by releasing political prisoners that have been in jail now in Cuba for 17 or 18 years, things of that kind. But I think before we can reach that point, we'll have to have discussions with them.[23]

Cronkite pursued Carter, asking whether his concerns were preconditions to discussions. "No," said Carter, breaking with the position of the Ford administration, which had suspended talks with Cuba after its intervention in Angola. "The preconditions that I describe would be prior to full normalization of relations."[24]

Talks produced a quick agreement on fisheries and maritime boundaries, followed by the establishment of Interests Sections in lieu of embassies, which would have signified diplomatic relations. Both sides took several other steps, but on the central issue of Cuban support for revolutionary movements in Africa, Fidel Castro was unyielding: "These issues are not matters for negotiation. . . . We will not make any concessions on matters of principle in order to improve relations with the United States."[25]

By the fall of 1977, there were reports of more Cuban troops and military advisers in Africa. In November, Carter blasted Cuba: "The Cubans have, in effect, taken on the colonial aspect that the Portuguese gave up in months gone by. . . . [They] are now spreading into other countries in Africa, like Mozambique. Recently, they are building up their so-called advisers in Ethiopia. We consider this to be a threat to the permanent peace in Africa."[26] At that time, there were four hundred Cuban military advisers in Ethiopia; by April 1978 there were seventeen thousand Cuban troops there, serving under a Soviet general. Carter's hopes for normal relations with Cuba were dashed, and he said so publicly: "There is no possibility that we would see any substantial improvement in our relationship with Cuba as long as he's committed to this military intrusion policy in the internal affairs of African people. There is no doubt in my mind that Cuba is used by the Soviet Union as surrogates in several places in Africa."[27]

Wayne Smith, who was then State Department Cuban desk officer, argues that normalization ended because Brzezinski publicized the Cuban military presence in Africa,[28] but this assessment ignores Carter's statements and the real cause: The United States viewed Cuban-Soviet expansionism in Africa as contrary to its national interest, and Castro valued his role in Africa more than he did normalization.

Castro might have thought he could still change Carter's mind on normalization if he changed his policy on political prisoners. In the summer of 1978, in secret negotiations, Castro's representatives informed U.S. officials that he was prepared to release as many as 3,900 political prisoners to the United States. (He released about 3,600; 1,000 immigrated to the United States.) During the next year he also released all U.S. political and criminal prisoners and people with dual citizenship. This represented a reversal from a position he had taken in an interview with Barbara Walters one year before.[29] Both governments continued to cooperate on some matters, such as search-and-rescue and antidrug efforts, but on the crucial security issues no progress occurred despite several secret talks with Castro by Peter Tarnoff, Vance's executive secretary, and me in Havana.

The Old World Revisited

Cuban-Soviet military activities in Africa were one reason why the international landscape, which had seemed so bright in 1977, had darkened two years later. The ominous trends affected America's view of the world and of the hemisphere. A symptom of this change in mood was that in 1979 Congress, for the first time in a decade, increased the administration's defense budget by 10 percent. In its last two years the Carter administration devoted an increasing share of its energy to managing crises in Nicaragua, Grenada, Cuba (the Soviet brigade and the Mariel boatlift), and El Salvador.

The administration anticipated the crisis in Nicaragua, and between September 1978 and July 1979 the NSC met twenty-five times to develop a strategy to deal with a country struggling to rid itself of the oppressive Somoza dynasty.[30] There was a consensus that if the United States did nothing, Somoza would try to repress the popular movement against him, the country would polarize even further, and the Sandinista National Liberation Front (FSLN) would eventually win a military victory. Although the Carter administration recognized that the Sandinistas had broadened their base of support, it viewed the key leaders as Marxist-Leninists who saw Cuba and the Soviet Union as allies and the United States as an enemy. Caught between a dictator it refused to defend and a guerrilla movement that it would not support, the administration tried to facilitate a democratic transition in Nicaragua, subject to two conditions. First, Carter would not ask a sitting president to step down, nor would he try to overthrow him. Second, the president insisted that U.S. policy should not be unilateral. A solution would have to emerge from a cooperative effort involving the United States and democratic governments in Latin America.

The OAS dispatched a team to mediate a transition agreement between the opposition and the Somoza government. The group recommended a plebiscite on Somoza's tenure, but Somoza rejected the conditions that would have permitted it to be fair. The United States had warned Somoza that it would impose sanctions against his regime if he blocked the plebiscite, and on February 8, 1979, the United States reduced its embassy by half, ended the small economic aid program, and terminated its AID and military missions.

Somoza responded by doubling the size of the National Guard. But by May 1979, with Castro's help, the three Sandinista factions had united and established a secure and ample arms flow from Cuba through Panama and Costa Rica. The United States was unaware of the magnitude of the arms transfer, nor did it have conclusive evidence of the involvement of Panama, Costa Rica, or Cuba. In early June the FSLN launched a military offensive and, supported by Mexico, Panama, Costa Rica, and the Andean Pact, mounted a political initiative to strip Somoza of formal legitimacy and transfer it to themselves.

The United States called a meeting of the OAS and proposed a cease-fire between the FSLN and the National Guard that would coincide with Somoza's departure and then lead toward a negotiated coalition government. An inter-American force would oversee the cease-fire and facilitate the integration of the armed forces. Nicaraguan moderates failed to see this proposal as a way to strengthen their position and so rejected it. The Sandinistas correctly saw it as an attempt to deny them exclusive power, and with the help of Panama, Costa Rica, Mexico, and Venezuela they blocked the U.S. proposal. With democratic friends in the region so opposed, Carter rejected unilateral action. On July 17, 1979, Somoza fled Nicaragua for Miami, and the Sandinistas received a joyous welcome in Managua two days later.

The United States was determined to avoid with Nicaragua the mutual hostility that had characterized early U.S.-Cuban relations and had led to a break. At some political cost, Carter met with three members of the Sandinista junta in the White House and subsequently asked Congress for $75 million for the new government. Because of the growing conservative mood in Congress and the Sandinistas' anti-American rhetoric, the issue of aid to Nicaragua was debated at great length and with considerable heat. After a long delay, Congress approved the funding with many conditions, the most important being that the president would have to end aid if he received conclusive evidence that the Nicaraguan government was assisting a foreign insurgency.

Both Congress and the president were concerned about the Nicaraguan revolution's impact on Central America and the Caribbean, and with good reason. As a result of the revolution, leftist guerrillas became emboldened; the military and the right, more intransigent; and the middle, more precarious. A key U.S. security interest was to try to prevent the FSLN from pouring gasoline on its increasingly combustible neighbors.

The administration concluded that the status quo in Central America was neither defensible nor sustainable; the only way to avoid violent revolution, which the United States judged to be contrary to both its and Central America's best interest, was to encourage the opening up of the political process. Honduras seemed ready for elections, so the administration decided to put its aid and support there as an example to the other countries. Because Guatemala and El Salvador were moving in the opposite direction, Assistant Secretary of State Viron Vaky informed the military leaders there that the United States shared their concerns about revolution but would not support them until they ended repression and permitted a genuine political opening.

Vaky's message had no discernible impact on the Guatemalan regime, but on October 15, 1979, the Salvadoran political door began to creak open. A group of young army officers seized power and invited several moderate and leftist civilians to help them implement serious social, economic, and political reforms. The coup appeared to be a breakthrough, but Carter personally decided that U.S. support would depend on the new government's progress in implementing the reforms, particularly agrarian reform, and stopping repression.

In 1979 revolution also came to the Caribbean. On March 13, forty-five members of the New Jewel Movement (NJM) seized power in a nearly bloodless coup on the small island of Grenada. It was the first unconstitutional change of government in the English-speaking Caribbean, and it unsettled the region. The leaders of other Caribbean governments held an emergency meeting in Barbados, but after receiving assurances from the NJM that it would hold elections soon, they accepted the new regime and advised the United States to do the same. Washington agreed and sent its ambassador to Barbados (also accredited to Grenada) to meet the NJM leaders and discuss aid programs and a possible Peace Corps project.

Within two weeks, however, the new regime invited Cuba to help build a people's revolutionary army, and it postponed elections indefinitely. After the U.S. ambassador expressed concern to Prime Minister Maurice Bishop about Grenada's growing military relations with Cuba, Bishop publicly denounced the United States, and relations deteriorated. The administration adopted a strategy toward Grenada different from that toward Nicaragua, although, paradoxically, for the same reasons. In both cases the administration placed great weight on the views of friendly democratic neighbors. The Latin Americans advised Carter to support the revolutionary regime in Nicaragua to prevent it from being seized by Marxists. Caribbean democracies encouraged the United States to help the other islands instead of Grenada, arguing that aid to Grenada might unintentionally encourage local radicals on other islands to replicate the NJM coup. Therefore, the main thrust of U.S. policy in the Caribbean was to help other governments.

When Fidel Castro hosted the summit of the Non-Aligned Movement (NAM) in September 1979, he was flanked by the leaders of the revolutionary governments of Nicaragua and Grenada. Together, the three boldly tried to steer the NAM toward an illogical "natural alliance" with the Soviet Union. The Carter administration took the NAM seriously and encouraged moderate Third World leaders to resist Cuba's efforts to seize control of the movement. Whether U.S. consultations helped or not, the moderates were decisive in preventing Cuba from shifting the NAM's direction. To the American public, however, the overall impression of the summit was one of numerous leaders journeying to Havana to condemn the United States.

The NAM summit coincided with the "discovery" by Washington of a Soviet brigade in Cuba. Castro thought the United States had concocted the incident to embarrass him, but it was more embarrassing to the Carter administration. As with previous collisions in Cuba, the Soviet brigade issue had less to do with Cuba than with the perceived balance of power between the Soviet Union and the United States.

Six months before the brigade's discovery by the CIA, Presidents Carter and Brezhnev had signed the second Strategic Arms Limitation

Treaty (SALT II). The deepening conservative mood in the United States made many senators nervous about ratifying the treaty. Several pressed the administration to take a harder line against the Soviet Union, and one asked about reports that the Soviets had sent soldiers to Cuba. Based on intelligence reports, Vance denied any evidence of this, but the administration promised to conduct more extensive surveillance, and in August it detected a Soviet combat unit. At the time, most senior officials were on vacation, and the information leaked to the press before the government was able to ascertain the nature and origin of the reported brigade or to try to negotiate privately with the Soviets. Upon learning of the report, Frank Church, chairman of the Senate Foreign Relations Committee, announced that SALT II would not pass the Senate unless the brigade was withdrawn.

A genuine crisis would have united the administration, but the brigade issue was a political dilemma. As such, it exacerbated the growing division between Vance and Brzezinski. Neither wanted the brigade issue to interfere with ratification of SALT. Vance thought prospects for ratification would be improved if the United States played down the brigade, which, the CIA later learned, had been in Cuba since the 1960s. Senate Majority Leader Robert Byrd agreed. Brzezinski, on the other hand, saw SALT as only one element in a wider strategic relationship; he thought the brigade issue should be used to "stress Cuban adventurism worldwide on behalf of the Soviet Union."[31] On October 1, 1979, Carter explained to the nation that Brezhnev had assured him that the so-called brigade was a training unit (a lie that upset Castro[32]) and that the Soviets would not change its structure. He argued for the ratification of SALT II by playing down the brigade as Vance and Byrd recommended, but also by criticizing Soviet-Cuban adventurism as Brzezinski suggested. He also established a new Caribbean Joint Task Force in Florida.

There is a special poignancy in the fact that Carter delivered this speech on the same day that the Panama Canal Treaties came into force. Vice President Walter Mondale was in Panama at that moment with several democratic presidents from the region to celebrate the passing of an old era in inter-American relations, and yet Carter's speech served as a powerful reminder that the old era was not entirely history. The administration's internal debate also prevented it from consulting with these governments before announcing the Caribbean Task Force. One of the Latin presidents commented to Mondale about the unfortunate symbolism.

If the domestic or global political environment had been sunny, these regional events—the Nicaraguan and Grenadian revolutions, the Havana summit, the Soviet brigade—would have been less troubling. In fact, the opposite was the case. In July 1979, at the moment that the Sandinistas were coming to power in Managua, the full effect of the shah's fall hit the United States with the second oil shock. The price of gas soared, supply declined, and the nation waited in long lines of cars for gas. Carter's popularity fell below that of Nixon's in the two months before he resigned. Carter went to Camp David for two weeks to assess the state of his presidency.

The climate continued to deteriorate through the year and into 1980. Inflation climbed to double digits. In November 1979, the U.S. embassy staff in Teheran was taken hostage, and one month later, Soviet troops marched into Afghanistan. The administration's perspective on Latin America focused on security issues in the Caribbean Basin. The aid program was increased significantly, and the administration began to explore ways to widen the Caribbean Group to include Central America or encourage the formation of a parallel group. In April 1980, drawing from personal experience, Carter also proposed a new people-to-people program, Caribbean/Central American Action, to reduce misunderstanding and promote good relationships among people and groups in the region.

In El Salvador, the war worsened. With all the leverage the United States and Venezuela could muster, the military accepted a coalition government with the Christian Democratic party, led by José Napoleón Duarte, and that government finally implemented an agrarian reform. But, as if responding to a Newtonian principle of political violence, each positive reformist step by the government precipitated grotesque murders by right-wing death squads. After the land reform, Archbishop Oscar Romero was murdered. The killing of four U.S. religious workers in November 1980 finally compelled Carter to suspend all economic and military aid in support of the ultimatum that Duarte gave to the military. A major leftist attack was expected in January 1981, but Carter did not release any aid until the military agreed to investigate the murders, dismiss several officers from the security forces, and strengthen Duarte's position. Most of these steps were implemented.[33]

In November 1980 the Salvadoran guerrillas persuaded the Sandinistas to support their final offensive in January. This proved a major error for both. The offensive was a fiasco, and the evidence of Nicaraguan support for it was conclusive, destroying the relationship that the Carter administration had been trying to nurture and providing an additional reason for the Reagan administration to confront the Sandinistas.

Central America was unsettled by the Nicaraguan revolution, but democracy in the eastern Caribbean was strengthened after the Grenadian revolution as the people became more wary of radicals in their midst. Elections occurred on schedule in six countries, and moderates defeated radicals by large margins. The only country in the Caribbean to experience instability in 1980 was Cuba. As a result of Carter's dismantling of the embargo on travel between the United States and Cuba, more than 110,000 Cuban-Americans visited the island in 1979. They brought money and success stories, and left the first visible signs of discontent that Cuba had seen in a generation. In a speech in December 1979, Castro acknowledged the discontent and its link to the more open relationship developed during the previous two years:

> Nowadays, the counter-revolution . . . has begun to appear. . . . [Why?] Is it because we let down our guard? . . . Is it because the absence of the enemy has caused us to lose our faculties? Is it because we have felt . . . too much at ease? Perhaps, in a certain way, we have needed an enemy; because when we have a clearly defined enemy, engaged in hard-fought combat, we are more united, energetic, stimulated.[34]

In late 1979 Cubans began breaking into Latin American embassies in Havana, seeking asylum. After a violent incident at the Peruvian embassy in April 1980, Castro decided to teach Peru a lesson by removing the guard from the embassy and informing the people of Havana that they were free to go there if they wished. Within twenty-four hours, more than ten thousand Cubans crowded into the small embassy compound of a nation poorer than Cuba. Castro, surprised and embarrassed, tried to redefine the issue in U.S.-Cuban terms by inviting Cuban-Americans to Mariel Harbor outside Havana to pick up their relatives. The Carter administration tried but failed to discourage the Cuban-Americans from going, but the Coast Guard feared a major loss of life if they stopped the boats. Castro allowed a few relatives to leave but filled the boats with criminals and mental patients. By the time the boatlift halted on September 25, 1980, more than 125,000 Cubans had arrived in Florida.[35]

An Assessment

One could say that in a symbolic way the Carter administration arrived pursuing the Panama Canal and left escaping from Mariel. It began with a preferred agenda that reflected a vision of inter-American relations and contained those issues that the administration judged most important: the Canal treaties, human rights, democratization, a North-South dialogue, nonproliferation, and arms control. Carter also chose to pursue these ends differently than most of his predecessors had done: Instead of unilateral or covert actions, he insisted on openness and multilateral cooperation. Yet in its last two years, the administration addressed a traditional security agenda: war, revolution, instability in the Caribbean Basin, and Soviet-Cuban expansion. This was an uncomfortable set of issues for the administration, and there was no consensus on how to deal with these issues.

The seeds of Carter's unpopularity were sown in the fact that the Soviet Union and its allies did not reciprocate the new tolerance embodied in Carter's policies. Instead, the Soviets seemed to try to take advantage of the United States by modernizing and expanding intermediate missiles in Europe, intervening with Cuba in the Horn of Africa, and, finally, invading Afghanistan. In addition, by 1979, the rise of a fundamentalist Iran and the surge in oil prices had reinforced the impression that Carter was losing control of events. The global environment that initially made Carter's moral message so pertinent and his new policies so necessary had changed.

Carter was faced with a choice: shift his emphasis to defense and containment or continue to stress human rights and cooperative multilateralism. He adapted to the changes in the world even while retaining his original emphasis, but the human rights image that carried him into the White House was not suited for a cold world of realpolitik, and the disjunction caused some public discomfort. Conservatives felt he remained too wedded to human rights; liberals feared his increased defense budget reflected abandonment of his principles.

Still, much was accomplished in the four years. Carter's two greatest achievements were the Panama Canal Treaties and the promotion of human rights. He paid a heavy political price for both initiatives; the benefits accrued to the United States and, ironically, to his successor. If the United States had not ratified new Canal treaties, the Canal might have been closed, and Central America's crises in the 1980s would have been much worse.

What was the impact of the Carter human rights policy? First, the consciousness of the world was raised against violations of human rights, and leaders recognized an international cost for repression and a corresponding benefit for those governments that respected human rights. Second, international norms and institutions were strengthened. In large part because of the Carter administration's lobbying, the American Convention on Human Rights was transformed from a moribund treaty that only two nations had ratified by 1977 to one that came into force with fourteen ratifications by 1980. (The administration had more success in persuading other governments to ratify the treaty than it had with the U.S. Senate.) The budget and staff of the Inter-American Commission on Human Rights quadrupled, and its activities expanded. Third, violations of the most basic human rights—the "integrity of the person"—declined sharply throughout the hemisphere. Disappearances in Argentina dropped from five hundred in 1978 to fewer than fifty in 1979; and there were no confirmed disappearances in Chile or Uruguay after 1978. Political prisoners were released in substantial numbers in many countries, including 3,900 from Cuba and all those held in Paraguay.

By the end of the Carter years, many observers continued to criticize the administration for its inconsistency, and some still doubted its impact, but no one questioned its commitment. William F. Buckley Jr., who had criticized Carter's policy, later reviewed the trials of Argentine military leaders in 1985 and admitted he had been wrong: Carter's policy "had concrete results. Pressure was felt by the criminal abductors. The man scheduled for execution was, often, merely kept in jail."[36] Similarly, Carter's reinforcement of democracy helped push the pendulum in a positive direction in Peru, Ecuador, Bolivia, Brazil, Honduras, and, decisively, in the Dominican Republic. Bolivian General Hugo Banzer, whose regime ended with a free election in 1978, later commented bitterly: "Mr. Carter didn't send me a letter ordering elections, but we could feel the pressure."[37]

The Carter administration's decision to set U.S. policies in a global context was significant theoretically but was unknown to the general public. The administration prided itself on not having a slogan, but in retrospect this was probably a handicap, depriving the public of a handle to understand the policy. Without a slogan, the administration's approach became known not by its principles but by its salient features: human rights and democracy by those who were sympathetic to Carter, and the revolutions in Nicaragua and Grenada and Cuban refugees by those who were not.

The Carter administration did not achieve as much on a North-South agenda as it had hoped, but it accomplished more than Congress would support. The United States negotiated an agreement on a common fund, replenishment of the international development banks, and new cooperative programs in science and technology. Carter established a North-South fellowship program, named after the late Senator Hubert H. Humphrey, for young professionals from the developing world to come to the United States for one year of postgraduate study. Congress, however, passed only a single foreign aid bill during the four years, and that was in 1977; the other bills were approved as continuing resolutions. Interest in the Third World declined in the industrialized world, and by the end of Carter's term the North-South dialogue was virtually mute.

Despite the rise in oil prices, the late 1970s witnessed economic growth for most of Latin America, averaging about 5.5 percent.[38] Although Americans answered "no" to Ronald Reagan's famous question—Are you better off in 1980 than you were in 1976?—most people in Latin America would have answered positively.

The Carter administration broke new ground on arms control and non-proliferation policies but, as with any complicated edifice, it would take a favorable international climate and more than one term to complete the structure. Carter's arms control initiatives probably restrained some arms purchases in Latin America, but they also accelerated the degree to which the region turned to the Soviet Union and Europe for arms.[39] Washington pursued a conventional arms control agreement in the region, but without support from other countries, it could not succeed.

Carter's decision to sign Protocol I of the Treaty of Tlatelolco, Latin America's nonproliferation treaty, on May 26, 1977, gave the treaty a boost, but the overall nonproliferation policy caused tensions in U.S. relations with Argentina and Brazil. Much later, Carter's concerns were proven legitimate and Brazil's statement that it was not trying to build a nuclear weapon was proven a lie.[40] But at the time, the administration's efforts provoked a backlash.

Jeane Kirkpatrick criticized Carter's policies for creating security problems in the hemisphere, by weakening conservative governments.[41] The problem with her argument is that it distracts from the main issue. People in repressive societies—whether Nicaragua, Argentina, or Cuba—were encouraged by Carter's human rights policy and made new demands on their governments. In my view, this is a credit to the United States. The issue, which Kirkpatrick sidesteps, is whether the United States should pressure or defend the dictators. The Carter administration believed that dictators were the problem and that human rights was the solution, whereas Kirkpatrick's argument implies the opposite is the case.

Others were critical of Carter for retreating under pressure to the traditional Cold War agenda in his last two years.[42] This implies that the United States should have been unconcerned about Soviet-Cuban expansion, and that is an unrealistic premise. It is true that as the administration tried to adjust to a changing agenda, Carter's commitment to his principles was tested.

To review some of his more difficult decisions, in Nicaragua, when democratic governments in the region decided to support the Sandinistas instead of backing the U.S. strategy of seeking a moderate alternative, Carter decided against unilateral intervention. In the case of El Salvador, although the left grew stronger and the prospects for revolution seemed more real, Carter resisted pressures to support the government unconditionally. The United States, he said, would provide economic and military aid *only if* the government implemented land reform and took steps to ease repression. Even his final decision in January 1981 to approve $5 million in military aid to El Salvador was taken because the military had responded to most of the specific demands made by Duarte and backed by Carter. Carter did not hesitate to suspend aid to the Sandinistas when the administration obtained conclusive proof that they were transferring weapons to the Salvadoran guerrillas. If the judgment on Carter's policy during these crises depends on whether he adhered to his three principles—human rights, nonintervention, and multilateral cooperation—he passed the test.

Despite continuous consultations, the administration's effort to forge a coalition of like-minded democracies to pursue a common policy in the Caribbean Basin did not bear fruit. The authoritarian military regimes were under assault by Carter's human rights policies and thus had no reason to cooperate. Democratic governments in the region were nervous that alignment with the United States would hurt them on the left or that opposition would hurt them on the right. With both sets of governments reluctant to collaborate with the United States, multilateral approaches were impossible. Time was necessary to bring together their conceptions of national security and for democracy to spread. Carter believed it was worth the time and the investment, even though the benefits would accrue to future generations and administrations.

If one accepts Carter's goal to work most closely with America's democratic friends in the region, then perhaps the final judgment on his policy should come from them. Henry Forde, the foreign minister of Barbados, offered one such judgment at the OAS General Assembly in

Washington on November 19, 1980, after Carter's loss to Reagan. Forde listed the many criticisms leveled at Carter's human rights policy, and then he said: "It is our view that it has been the single most creative act of policy in the hemisphere in many a long year. It has raised the consciousness and stirred the consciences of many a leader in this region; it has given hope to many an oppressed citizen; it has helped, perhaps more than any other element of policy, to correct the image of the United States as an unfeeling giant, casting its shadow over its neighbors."[43]

Notes

1. "Address to a Democratic Party Campaign Luncheon, 20 September 1978," in *Public Papers of the Presidents of the United States: Jimmy Carter, 1978,* (Washington, D.C.: Government Printing Office, 1979), vol. 2, p. 1554 (hereafter cited as *Public Papers, Carter*).

2. This speech is reprinted in Jimmy Carter, *A Government as Good as Its People* (New York: Simon & Schuster, 1977), pp. 166–171.

3. Both Vance and Brzezinski had read and agreed with the Linowitz Commission's reports. See Vance's memorandum to Carter in October 1976, reprinted in his *Hard Choices: Critical Years in America's Foreign Policy* (New York: Simon & Schuster, 1983), pp. 444, 451–453. Brzezinski had developed some of these ideas in *Between Two Ages: America's Role in the Technetronic Era* (New York: Viking Press, 1970), p. 288.

4. Commission on U.S.-Latin American Relations, *The Americas in a Changing World,* October 1974; and *The United States and Latin America: Next Steps,* December 20, 1976. Both were published by the Center for Inter-American Relations in New York.

5. Erwin Hargrove, "Jimmy Carter: The Politics of Public Goods," in Fred I. Greenstein, ed., *Leadership in the Modern Presidency* (Cambridge, Mass.: Harvard University Press, 1988), p. 231; Charles O. Jones, *The Trusteeship Presidency: Jimmy Carter and the United States Congress* (Baton Rouge: Louisiana State University Press, 1988). The two authors write that Carter deliberately ignored the political dimension of his policies at the beginning.

6. See William J. Jorden, *Panama Odyssey* (Austin: University of Texas Press, 1984); and George D. Moffett III, *The Limits of Victory: The Ratification of the Panama Canal Treaties* (Ithaca: Cornell University Press, 1985).

7. For Reagan's comments, see William J. Lanouette, "The Panama Canal Treaties—Playing in Peoria and in the Senate," *National Journal,* October 8, 1977, pp. 1556–1562. For Carter's, see *Public Papers, Carter, 1977,* vol. 2, pp. 1889–1890.

8. For the Pan American Day speech, see *Public Papers, Carter, 1977,* vol. 1, pp. 611–616.

9. Carter: "We don't have any inclination to be involved in the internal affairs of another country unless our security should be directly threatened." *Public Papers, Carter, 1978,* vol. 2, p. 2019.

10. He also instructed the secretary of agriculture to institute an income support program for sugar farmers. *Public Papers, Carter, 1977,* vol. 1, pp. 797–801.

11. Karen DeYoung, "Human Rights Motion Passes, Underlines Divisions in O.A.S.," *Washington Post,* June 23, 1977, p. A20.

12. Fourteen governments—one more than necessary—voted for the U.S. resolution, eight abstained, and three were absent. DeYoung, "Human Rights Motion Passes," p. A20.

13. Lewis Diuguid, "O.A.S. Refuses to Meet in Uruguay," *Washington Post,* February 3, 1978, p. A23.

14. Arthur M. Schlesinger Jr., "Human Rights and the American Tradition," *Foreign Affairs: America and the World* 57, no. 3 (1978): 503.

15. See Patrick Lemoine and Erich Goode, "Living Hell in Haiti," *Inquiry,* March 3, 1980, pp. 12–19. In late 1976 the treatment of political prisoners improved, according to Lemoine, who was arrested in 1971 and released in February 1977. By September 1977, after a visit to the island by Andrew Young, all 104 political prisoners had been released and granted amnesty. U.S. Ambassador Ernest Preeg later wrote that the political opening begun in November 1976 closed on November 28, 1980, because Duvalier expected Reagan to give "a lower priority to human rights." Preeg, *Haiti and the CBI: A Time of Change and Opportunity* (Miami: University of Miami Graduate School of International Studies, 1985), pp. 17–21.

16. Ronald Reagan, "The Canal as Opportunity: A New Relationship with Latin America," *Orbis* 21 (Fall 1977): 560.

17. See Michael J. Kryzanek, "The 1978 Election in the Dominican Republic: Opposition Politics, Intervention, and the Carter Administration," *Caribbean Studies* 19 (April–July 1979): 51–73.

18. Jimmy Carter, "A Just International Order," *Department of State News Release,* March 29, 1978.

19. For the Panama declaration and Carter's address at the OAS, see *Public Papers, Carter, 1978,* vol. 1, pp. 1123–1125, 1141–1146.

20. José López Portillo, *Mis Tiempos* (Mexico: Fernandez Editores, 1988), pp. 603, 681, 758, 811–815. For a more complete description of this event—and of both U.S. and Mexican interpretations—see George Grayson, "The U.S.-Mexi-

can Natural Gas Deal and What We Can Learn from It," *Orbis* 24 (Fall 1980). López Portillo's administration is viewed as the most corrupt in Mexican history, and his oil minister went to jail on charges of corruption.

21. Jimmy Carter, *Keeping Faith: Memoirs of a President* (New York: Bantam, 1982), p. 468.

22. U.S. Senate, Committee on Foreign Relations, *Nomination of Hon. Cyrus R. Vance To Be Secretary of State,* January 11, 1977, p. 17.

23. *Public Papers, Carter, 1977,* vol. 1, pp. 293–294 (emphasis added).

24. See his interviews on April 15 and May 30, 1977, *Public Papers, Carter, 1977,* vol. 1, pp. 647–648, 1042–1043.

25. Castro's statement in Tanzania on March 21, 1977, is cited in Edward Gonzalez, "Institutionalization, Political Elites, and Foreign Policies," in Cole Blasier and Carmelo Mesa-Lago, eds., *Cuba in the World* (Pittsburgh: University of Pittsburgh Press, 1979), p. 29.

26. *Public Papers, Carter, 1977,* vol. 2, p. 2011.

27. *Public Papers, Carter, 1978,* vol. 1, pp. 903–909.

28. Five days after Carter's statement on November 11, 1977, Brzezinski released a chart detailing the number of Cubans in African countries and said, on background, that a Cuban buildup would make normalization of relations impossible. Wayne Smith wrote that Brzezinski's comment actually increased the likelihood of a Cuban buildup. Smith, *The Closest of Enemies* (New York: W. W. Norton, 1987), pp. 122–127.

29. Castro had said that he would not take any of these human rights steps until the United States freed all of its prisoners, because they were all victims of capitalism. He also said he would not release U.S. political prisoners because "some of them are important C.I.A. agents." Excerpts from Barbara Walters's interview with Castro in May 1977, in *Foreign Policy* 28 (Fall 1977): 929.

30. See Robert A. Pastor, *Condemned to Repetition: The United States and Nicaragua* (Princeton: Princeton University Press, 1987); and Anthony Lake, *Somoza Falling* (Boston: Houghton Mifflin, 1989).

31. This section reflects my own perceptions as a participant in the decisionmaking process at the time, but it also borrows from the memoirs of Vance, Brzezinski, and Carter. See Vance, *Hard Choices,* pp. 358–364; Zbigniew Brzezinski, *Power and Principle: Memoirs of the National Security Adviser, 1977–1981* (New York: Farrar, Straus & Giroux, 1983), pp. 346–352; and Carter, *Keeping Faith,* pp. 262–264.

32. At a meeting I attended in Havana on January 11, 1992, Castro said the Soviet unit was a brigade, not a training center, and he was disturbed that the Soviets had described it in that way.

33. For a description of the steps taken at that time, see Robert Pastor, "Continuity and Change in U.S. Foreign Policy: Carter and Reagan on El Salvador," *Journal of Policy Analysis and Management* 3 (Winter 1984): 179–180.

34. Fidel Castro, "Address to the National People's Government Assembly," December 27, 1979, mimeographed, pp. 49–55.

35. Alex Larzelere, *The 1980 Cuban Boatlift: Castro's Ploy, America's Dilemma* (Washington, D.C.: National Defense University Press, 1988).

36. William F. Buckley Jr., "Lessons from Argentina," *Washington Post*, June 9, 1985, p. D7.

37. Quoted in Ray Bonner, "Bolivia Becomes a Battleground," *Los Angeles Times*, August 31, 1980.

38. Inter-American Development Bank, *Economic and Social Progress in Latin America, 1982* (Washington, D.C., 1982), p. xv.

39. French and Soviet sales grew faster and surpassed U.S. arms sales agreements from 1978 to 1980. "Multilateral Arms Transfer Trends in the Third World," report printed in U.S. Senate Committee on Foreign Relations, *Proposed Sale of F–16s to Venezuela*, 97th Cong., 2d sess., February 5, 1982, pp. 26–27.

40. James Brooke, "Brazil Uncovers Plan by Military to Build Atom Bomb and Stops It," *The New York Times*, October 9, 1990, pp. 1, 4. The project had begun in 1975; when President Fernando Collor de Mello learned of it in September 1990, he stopped it.

41. Jeane Kirkpatrick, "U.S. Security and Latin America," *Commentary* 71 (January 1981).

42. See, for example, William LeoGrande, "The Revolution in Nicaragua: Another Cuba?" *Foreign Affairs* 58 (Fall 1979): 28–50; and Abraham Lowenthal, "Jimmy Carter and Latin America" in Kenneth Oye, Donald Rothschild, and Robert Lieber, eds., *Eagle Entangled: U.S. Foreign Policy in a Complex World* (New York: Little, Brown, 1979).

43. Address to the OAS General Assembly by the Hon. Henry de B. Forde of Barbados, November 19, 1980, Washington, D.C.

4

THE REAGAN ADMINISTRATION: A TEST OF STRENGTH

Suppose we put a blockade around that island [Cuba] and said [to the USSR], "Now buster, we'll lift it when you take your forces out of Afghanistan."[1]

—RONALD REAGAN, 1980

To some Americans, the establishment of a Soviet presence in Cuba in 1961 was not just a violation of the hallowed Monroe Doctrine; it was the first of a series of humiliating reverses. Next came the agonizing defeat of the United States by a small Asian nation, anti-American revolutions in Iran and Nicaragua, and the manipulation of oil prices by weaker nations. These and other events left Americans feeling frustrated with the world and impatient with their leaders.

Ronald Reagan tapped that frustration and impatience effectively in 1980. His campaign was a ringing declaration that the United States could once again take charge of its destiny and the world's, and the American people were ready for Reagan's message. Two public opinion analysts described the nation as feeling "bullied by OPEC, humiliated by the Ayatollah Khomeni, tricked by Castro, out-traded by Japan, and outgunned by the Russians. By the time of the 1980 Presidential election, fearing that America was losing control over its foreign affairs, voters were more than ready to exorcise the ghost of Vietnam and replace it with a new posture of American assertiveness."[2]

Ronald Reagan offered a vision of the world that was not cluttered with complexity. All one needed to know was that the United States was engaged in a global struggle against Soviet communism. "The inescapable truth," Reagan stated, "is that we are at war, and we are losing that war simply because we don't or won't realize we are in it . . . [and] there can only be one end. . . . War ends in victory or defeat."[3] During a war, leaders do not have to make difficult trade-offs between competing values because victory is the single goal. For Reagan, events were interpreted and became significant only through this organizing prism: Terrorism was manipulated by a single source, the Soviet Union;[4] human rights was a fight against communism; economic development could succeed only if Marxists were removed and the state reduced.

In no region was Reagan's worldview applied with more clarity, consistency, and vigor than in what he called America's "backyard." To Reagan, the Monroe Doctrine was a living guide of almost spiritual importance: "These two great continents [North and South America] were placed here—you can call it mystical if you want—but were placed here between the oceans to be found by people who had a love for freedom, a courage, and there was a divine purpose in that."[5]

With seven national security advisers in eight years and a management style that was diffuse at best, Reagan did not easily translate his ideology into a single policy. Each department, and the National Security Council (NSC), made and implemented its own policy according to its bureaucratic mission and its leader's preference. On Central America, the Pentagon conducted military exercises, the CIA undertook covert actions, the State Department negotiated, and the NSC had its own operation. A second problem was the gap between Reagan's perception and the Latin American reality. The region's leaders rejected the crystalline vision of a bipolar world in favor of one in which they pursued their economic interests independent of the superpowers. The question was which would be compelled to adapt: Latin America to Reagan's vision, or Reagan to Latin America's new realities.

Unlike his five predecessors, Ronald Reagan had two full terms to achieve his goals. He used direct force only once in the region, in Grenada in 1983, but the center of his policy was Central America, where he employed threats, indirect force, and a military presence. It was there that the Reagan administration proclaimed it was involved in a test of American strength.

Background

During the 1980 presidential campaign, Reagan's positions on Latin America offered a stark contrast to Carter's. In addition to his fervent opposition to the Canal treaties, Reagan defended both Augusto Pinochet's Chilean government and the Argentine military regime in its war against "a well-equipped force of 15,000 terrorists." He criticized Carter's policies on human rights, arms control, and nonproliferation for antagonizing friendly military dictators.[6]

Jeane Kirkpatrick, who would become Reagan's ambassador to the United Nations based on her criticisms of Carter, wrote that the Democratic president had "contributed . . . to the alienation of major nations, the growth of neutralism, the destabilization of friendly governments, the spread of Cuban influence, and the decline of U.S. power in the region."[7] She did not offer an alternative prescription, except by implication. In her censure of Carter's policy toward military regimes and her distinction between authoritarian and totalitarian governments, she implied that U.S. policy should be determined solely by a regime's friendliness. No matter how tenuous its legitimacy or how repressive its actions, a friendly regime should receive U.S. support because the alternative is uncertain or worse.

The 1980 Republican party platform adopted a similar stance. It deplored "the Marxist Sandinista takeover of Nicaragua" and demanded an end to aid to the regime. The principal message of the platform and of Reagan's campaign was that Soviet-Cuban power was advancing in the world and that the United States must devote all its energies to stopping it and rolling it back.[8]

The Centrality of Central America

"The morning of an Administration," Alexander Haig noted in his memoirs about being Reagan's secretary of state for eighteen months, "is the best time to send signals." Haig wanted to send just two:

> Our signal to the Soviets had to be a plain warning that their time of unresisted adventuring in the Third World was over, and that America's capacity to tolerate the mischief of Moscow's proxies, Cuba and Libya, had been exceeded. Our signal to other nations must be equally simple and believ-

able: once again, a relationship with the United States brings dividends, not just risks.[9]

The administration sent the Soviets the first signal by drawing a line in Central America, and the second by embracing the military governments of South America.

On February 23, 1981, the State Department issued a White Paper presenting "definitive evidence of the clandestine military support given by the Soviet Union, Cuba, and their communist allies to Marxist-Leninist guerrillas" trying to overthrow the Salvadoran government. Alexander Haig described the issue as "externally-managed and orchestrated interventionism" and promised "to deal with it at the source." The administration increased military aid and advisers to El Salvador.

Haig also proposed a blockade and other military actions against Cuba in three meetings of the NSC in June and November 1981 and February 1982. His proposal was rejected because Secretary of Defense Caspar Weinberger feared another Vietnam, and the military worried that the Soviets might respond forcefully in another part of the world. Others in the administration doubted that Congress or the public would accept such action without a Cuban provocation, and White House political staff did not want to divert the president and the public from domestic economic issues, especially a tax cut. Haig, by his own admission, was "virtually alone" in arguing for the blockade that Reagan himself had advocated during the campaign.[10]

Whatever effect the administration's signals may have had on the Soviet Union, the initial impact on El Salvador was counterproductive. The struggle in that country was not, at that time, between the Marxist guerrillas and the government; the Marxists had been defeated soundly in their January 1981 offensive. Rather, the struggle was between the government and rightist elements, and the latter interpreted statements by the president and Haig as indicating support for them in their battle against José Napoleón Duarte, the leader of the Christian Democrats and Salvador's junta.[11]

The administration's highest priority was to defeat the insurgency by modernizing Salvador's military. The head of the U.S. military team undermined Duarte by negotiating an aid program directly with the military.[12] One month later, Salvadoran rightist leader Roberto D'Aubuisson told the press that based on his meetings with "members of Reagan's group [Roger Fontaine of the NSC] . . . the Reagan administration would not be bothered by a takeover" that eliminated the Christian Democrats from the government. Recognizing the seriousness of D'Aubuisson's threat, the State Department endorsed Duarte and warned against a coup. The White House, however, equivocated: "We just don't have a view on that."[13]

The Salvadoran guerrillas (FMLN) grew stronger. Instead of changing its strategy, however, the Reagan administration blamed the Sandinista government. Carter had suspended aid to Nicaragua in January 1981 because of evidence that it was sending arms to the FMLN.[14] U.S. Ambassador Lawrence Pezzullo used the possibility of renewing aid as leverage in negotiating with the Sandinistas, but despite an apparent halt in arms transfers, Reagan terminated the aid program on April 1, 1981.[15] Assistant Secretary of State Thomas Enders then discussed an agreement with the Sandinistas to reduce their military relations with the Soviet Union and Cuba and prevent any future arms transfers to the FMLN. But instead of negotiating seriously, each side preferred to display examples of why the other was not serious.

Having "tried" negotiations, the administration decided on a more confrontational approach. An NSC meeting on November 16, 1981, made the pivotal decision—formalized in Directive No. 17 and signed the next day by President Reagan—to fund and direct a secret anti-Sandinista guerrilla force, which later became known as the contras, or counterrevolutionaries. In briefing the congressional intelligence committees in December, CIA Director William Casey described the proposal as a $19 million program to set up a five-hundred-man force aimed at the "Cuban infrastructure" in Nicaragua that was allegedly training and supplying arms to the Salvadoran guerrillas. The House Intelligence Committee approved of interdicting arms from Nicaragua but was skeptical about whether that was Reagan's objective.[16]

In March 1982 the contras destroyed two bridges in Nicaragua. The Sandinista government condemned the United States and declared a state of emergency. Thus began a downward spiral in which the political space in Nicaragua was systematically reduced, the government grew more militarized and dependent on the Soviet Union, and the United States found itself locked in indirect combat with a small nation.

Repairing Relationships for the Common Struggle

The Reagan administration's anticommunism and its decision to distance itself from its predecessor led it to embrace military governments in Latin America that the Carter administration had treated coolly because of human rights violations. As Reagan's first Latin American visitor, Argentine General Roberto Viola underscored the break with the past. The effect of Reagan's campaign against Carter had already been felt in Argentina. Carlos Saul Menem, who would be elected Argentina's president in 1989, said: "I was in jail when Reagan won, and those who held me captive jumped for joy." On the eve of Viola's visit, his government arrested three Argentine human rights activists. Instead of criticizing Argentine repression, State Department spokesman William Dyess took aim at Carter's policy: "We want good relations with Argentina. Any abnormality in relations is due to a large extent to the public position this country took regarding human rights practices in the country." The administration viewed its policy as a success when Argentina agreed to help the contras.[17]

On March 1 the administration also improved relations with Chile by restoring Export-Import Bank financing and inviting the government to participate in joint naval exercises. In the international development banks, it stopped voting against loans to the military governments of Argentina, Chile, Uruguay, and Paraguay. Jeane Kirkpatrick visited Chile in August 1981 and said that the United States intended "to normalize completely its relations with Chile in order to work together in a pleasant way." She would not meet with several human rights activists, and they were arrested after her departure.[18]

Whereas the Carter administration had sought ways to be responsive to the Third World, the Reagan administration described the "so-called Third World" as "a myth—and a dangerous one."[19] Reagan also reversed his predecessors' efforts to curb arms sales and nuclear proliferation. During its first two years, the Reagan administration sold more than twice as many arms (in dollars) as were sold during Carter's four years.[20] In 1982, overturning Carter's decision, Reagan authorized the export of 143 tons of heavy water and a computer system for Argentina's nuclear program, without demanding safeguards. The administration claimed that the sale would permit it to influence Argentina to stop completion of an enrichment plant; however, as it turned out, the sale facilitated completion of the plant one year later.[21]

In his memoirs, President Reagan wrote that "one of the greatest frustrations during those eight years was my inability to communicate to the American people and to Congress the seriousness of the threat we faced in Central America."[22] It was not for want of trying. The "great communicator" gave more speeches on the region than on any other foreign policy issue. His purpose was to obtain aid for the contras and the Salvadoran government, and his language was unequivocal. Central America, Reagan argued, "is simply too close, and the strategic stakes are too high, for us to ignore the danger of governments seizing power there with ideological and military ties to the Soviet Union."[23] While warning Congress of the consequences of not supporting him, Reagan also tried to secure support by responding to some of the criticism of his program. To counter the impression that he viewed the region's problems solely in East-West military terms, Reagan proposed an innovative one-way free trade agreement called the Caribbean Basin Initiative (CBI); he toned down his criticism of Carter's human rights policy; and he established the National Endowment for Democracy to promote freedom.

Many members of Congress supported these initiatives, but fewer accepted Reagan's policies toward Nicaragua and El Salvador. In addition, in January 1983, foreign ministers from Venezuela, Colombia, Mexico, and Panama met on Contadora Island in Panama to explore alternatives for ending the East-West conflict in Central America. Reagan did not cease trying to overcome both the congressional and the Contadora constraints.

While attention was focused on Central America, Reagan's first and only use of direct U.S. force in the region occurred on the small island of Grenada. In mid-October 1983 a faction of the Marxist regime killed Prime Minister Maurice Bishop and several of his colleagues. The English-speaking Caribbean, one of the few genuinely democratic regions in the developing world, was shocked by the violence, and six neighboring governments invited the United States to join them to remove the regime. The bombing of the marine barracks in Lebanon two days before was probably more influential in Reagan's decision than was the safety of the American medical students on Grenada, who were endangered more by the invasion than by the fight between the regime's factions.[24] Although U.S. forces met little resistance on an island the size of Martha's Vineyard, Reagan viewed the invasion as a triumph and a vindication of his campaign theme: "Our days of weakness are over. Our military forces are back on their feet and standing tall."[25] The invasion was condemned by most states in the OAS and the UN, but it was popular in Grenada and the Caribbean, and this reinforced the support for it in the United States.

In an attempt to obtain a bipartisan boost to increase aid to Central America, Reagan asked Henry Kissinger to chair a commission and issue a report in January 1984. Its analysis of the indigenous causes of the regional crisis differed from the administration's, as did its conclusion that local revolutions posed no threat to the United States.[26] The administration, however, deftly chose to agree with its other conclusion, that Soviet-Cuban involvement required a strong U.S. response. On February 3, claiming bipartisan support, Reagan asked Congress to fund a five-year, $8 billion aid program to Central America.

In an election year and with a widening budget deficit, many members of Congress wanted to avoid the aid issue. But the president would not let up until the spring, when his effort was jeopardized by the disclosure of CIA involvement in the mining of Nicaragua's harbors.[27] A second reason Reagan could not persuade Congress was that few members believed he was genuinely interested in negotiations. Reagan tried to allay that suspicion by sending Secretary of State George Shultz, who had replaced Haig in 1982, to Managua for talks in June. But evidence disclosed later during the Iran-Contra hearings confirmed that Congress's skepticism was justified. In a secret NSC meeting on June 25, 1984, Reagan said that the purpose of Shultz's trip was to deceive Congress, not to negotiate: "If we are just talking about negotiations with Nicaragua, that is too far-fetched to imagine that a Communist government like that would make any reasonable deal with us, but if it is to get Congress to support the anti-Sandinistas, then that can be helpful."[28]

With the economy improving, public opinion surveys suggested that the only issue standing in the way of Reagan's reelection was peace. He therefore stopped pressing for contra aid, and Congress passed a bill with an amendment sponsored by Representative Edward Boland that barred funds for the contras. Boland said the amendment "clearly ends U.S. support for the war in Nicaragua."[29] Reagan signed the law on October 12, 1984, but he also told Robert McFarlane, his national security adviser, to "assure the contras of continuing administration support [and]—to help them hold body and soul together—until the time when Congress would again agree to support them."[30] This was the mission assigned to NSC staff member Oliver North. The CIA withdrew its aid to the contras, but Director Casey personally advised North on setting up a covert operation outside the government to provide funds and supplies to the contras. North's operation began when the law said it should stop, and it continued until aid was approved in the fall of 1986 and his operation was disclosed.

None of this was known during the election campaign of 1984. Reagan was then talking peace and negotiations, defusing the argument made by Democratic presidential candidate Walter Mondale that Reagan's reelection would mean a deeper war in Central America. In the end, Central America played a small part in the voters' calculations, and President Reagan won by a landslide.

Reagan's Liberation Strategy and North's Compass

Reagan used his 1985 State of the Union message to dress up his contra program into a doctrine on wars of national liberation: "We must not break faith with those who are risking their lives on every continent from Afghanistan to Nicaragua to defy Soviet-supported aggression and secure rights which have been ours from birth. . . . Support for freedom-fighters is self-defense." On February 21 Reagan candidly described his goal as seeing the Sandinista government "removed in the sense of its present structure," and he said he would not quit until the Sandinistas "say uncle."[31] After some members of Congress insisted that other steps, such as an embargo, should be tried before overthrowing the government, Reagan obliged, decreeing an embargo on May 1.

The next month, after President Daniel Ortega visited Moscow, the administration found the votes to approve $27 million in nonlethal humanitarian aid for the contras. This was the first time that Congress openly debated and affirmed support for a movement whose aim was to overthrow a government with which the United States had diplomatic relations. The U.S. actions provoked the Soviets to increase their aid to Nicaragua. By the end of 1985, the Nicaraguan army was using sophisticated military equipment to suppress the contras, and Reagan decided to ratchet up the arms race. In the summer of 1986, Congress approved $100 million for the contras, 75 percent of it military aid.

While the United States concentrated on Central America, the rest of Latin America was undergoing a profound transformation. Democracy, which had begun to replace military regimes in the late 1970s, continued its sweep. In 1985, competitive elections were held in Brazil, Uruguay, Guatemala, and Grenada, and power was transferred peacefully from one civilian government to another in Bolivia and Peru, the first time in forty years for the latter. Two long-standing Caribbean dictators also fell, raising hopes that democracy might emerge from the ruins. Forbes Burnham, who had ruled Guyana for twenty years, died in 1985; and Jean-

Claude Duvalier, whose family had controlled Haiti for almost thirty years, fled the country on February 7, 1986. The United States stopped aid to Duvalier in the closing moments of his regime, but Reagan denied that the United States had forced Duvalier to leave.[32]

Many of the new democratic governments feared that Reagan's contra war could polarize their countries and divert the United States from the debt crisis. Foreign ministers from four new democratic governments—Argentina, Brazil, Uruguay, and Peru—joined the original Contadora countries in a meeting with Shultz on February 10, 1986, to request that the United States open talks with the Sandinistas and stop funding the contras. Reagan ignored their request and refused to meet them. The newly elected presidents in Central America tried again. Guatemalan President Vinicio Cerezo invited his Central American colleagues to a summit meeting in Esquipulas, Guatemala, on May 25, 1986, to discuss peace in the region and the idea of a Central American parliament.

The administration tried to block these efforts and displayed little interest in the debt crisis, although this was probably the most serious cause of fragility for democracies in the region. Enders dismissed the debt crisis in 1982 as "basically a question between borrowing governments and the markets themselves."[33] But by 1985, Latin America owed $368 billion, and it was impossible to ignore the crisis or view it as strictly a private matter. Annual debt service payments consumed nearly 44 percent of the region's foreign exchange. In just four years (1982–1985) Latin America transferred $106.7 billion of capital to the United States and other industrialized countries to service its debt, making it a larger exporter of capital to the United States in this short period than the United States was to Latin America during the entire decade of the Alliance for Progress.[34] Only when the region threatened a debtors' cartel in the fall of 1985 did Secretary of the Treasury James Baker offer a plan. He proposed that both private and development banks increase funding to the major debtor countries if they adopted market-oriented reforms.

The Latin Americans welcomed the plan but said it was not enough. They wanted more loans and reduced interest rates. In an important shift from previous calls for a new international economic order, most governments recognized that they needed to change their economic policies. Argentina instituted a severe austerity program in June 1985, and Brazil followed seven months later with a similar plan. The decline in oil prices at the time also compelled Mexico and Venezuela to accept market-oriented reforms and trade liberalization.

The other issue that engaged the United States and Latin America was the expanding trade in cocaine. The Drug Enforcement Administration estimated that the amount of cocaine imported into the country increased nearly twenty-fold between 1981 and 1987. The administration preferred an enforcement strategy to cut off supplies and prosecute traffickers, whereas the Latin Americans insisted that the only effective approach was to reduce demand. Thus, drugs too became a cause for increased tension rather than collaboration in inter-American relations.

Oliver North's operation to provide arms to the contras using funds from the profits of arms sales to Iran was exposed in October 1986. Ironically, North and National Security Adviser John Poindexter were dismissed at the moment when congressionally approved military aid to the contras began to flow. One year later, the congressional committees that investigated the affair issued their report. They found the president ultimately responsible, although not legally culpable. Reagan had the Hobbesian choice of either admitting to a crime or appearing to be out of touch with his own administration. If the former were true, he might have been impeached; the smart strategy was to look stupid. During the congressional hearings, Poindexter said that he hid the key decisions from Reagan, thus saving his presidency. (At his trial, after Reagan left office, Poindexter admitted that Reagan knew. Reagan testified but could recall little.[35])

Even during the investigations, Reagan never ceased trying to win support for the contras. His main adversary was not the scandal but the peace plan arranged by Costa Rican President Oscar Arias and signed in August 1987 in Esquipulas by the five Central American presidents. The plan called for democratization through national reconciliation and an end to outside support for insurgencies. All five presidents asked Reagan to end aid to the contras, but Reagan called the plan "fatally flawed" and reaffirmed his request for military aid as the only way to bring democracy to Nicaragua. In a chilling confrontation with Reagan at the White House, Arias told him: "We agree on the ends but we disagree on the means. You want democracy in Central America by imposing it with bullets. I want democracy by imposing it with votes."[36]

Reagan insisted that the Sandinistas would negotiate and hold free elections only if the United States gave military aid to the contras. Congress disagreed. It rejected aid and was proven right when negotiations in March 1988 between the Sandinistas and the contras yielded a cease-fire.

Nicaraguans could not negotiate under the continuing pressure of Reagan's approach.

Another negative product of the administration's obsession with the contras was the relationship it cultivated with General Manuel Antonio Noriega, the commander of Panama's army. Noriega had long been a CIA "intelligence asset," but his value was enhanced in 1983 when he became head of the army. From then until at least 1986, Noriega helped the contras and coordinated attacks against the Sandinistas in exchange for at least $300,000 and an understanding by the Reagan administration that it would overlook his corruption and control of Panama's politics.[37]

This deal came unstuck in June 1987, when a senior Panamanian military officer accused Noriega of killing a political leader, manipulating the election of 1984, and skimming profits from drug traffickers. This revelation generated a powerful civic reaction in Panama.[38] Noriega arrested the leaders of the opposition. The Reagan administration suspended aid and encouraged President Arturo Delvalle to fire Noriega in February 1988, shortly after he had been indicted in Miami and Tampa for drug trafficking. Instead, Noriega fired Delvalle. Washington then imposed economic sanctions and withheld money for the Canal. This strategy brought the Panamanian economy to its knees while Noriega reveled in his defiance of the United States.

The Legacy of Ronald Reagan

On assuming the presidency in 1981, Ronald Reagan believed he had a mandate in Latin America to confront and defeat Communists and reassure "friendly" military governments that had been alienated by the Carter administration's policies. Reagan defended El Salvador, destabilized Nicaragua, invaded Grenada, and dismantled Carter's policies on human rights and arms control. In his second term, Reagan's approach broadened: He professed a commitment to human rights, democracy, and negotiations and implemented a one-way free trade plan for the Caribbean Basin; and his secretary of the treasury proposed a plan for the international development banks to address the debt issue. Yet the evolution in his policy should not obscure the tenacity with which he held to his initial and central objective: to change the Sandinista regime.

Latin America also changed in the 1980s. The assertiveness of many Latin American governments appeared a permanent fixture in international relations in the late 1970s, but a decade later, it was replaced by national preoccupation. This change was less the result of American policy than of internal pressure from debt and democratic transition. Concerned about reelection and coping daily with financial crises, Latin America's leaders became more moderate and realistic.

The United States did not convince Latin America or impose its vision on the region. Nor did the Reagan administration, so certain of its position, adapt to the region's concerns. Instead, Latin America and the United States each concentrated on its own priorities. This does not mean that Latin America had no influence. The CBI was Jamaican Prime Minister Edward Seaga's idea. Contadora diplomacy constrained the Reagan administration from undertaking more forceful actions in Central America, and even the Caribbean exercised a kind of silent veto on Reagan's actions against Grenada until the regime self-destructed.

Ronald Reagan deliberately cultivated an image of detachment from the daily work of government, and in evaluating his presidency, one must distinguish between the man and his administration. Reagan's aloofness served him well when he faced the Iran-Contra questions, but the puzzling side of his leadership is that he tried to affect a Churchillian style while seeming unaware of his administration's policies.

In his memoirs, Constantine Menges, who worked at the CIA and then the NSC under Reagan, describes himself as the guardian of Reagan's Central American policy against the maneuvers of Shultz and other senior administration officials.[39] Menges could never explain why the president consistently allowed Shultz and others to hijack his policy. Like Oliver North, Menges was fired from the NSC yet continued to refer to himself as one of Reagan's very few loyal followers. In Menges's memoirs, as well as in those of Haig, North, and even Frank McNeil, a State Department official who worked on Central America during the 1980s but opposed the contra policy, Reagan's *name* is constantly invoked for contradictory policies but Reagan's *person* is absent. Edmund Morris, the biographer who watched Reagan up close for the last three years of his presidency, confessed to being baffled by the man. Morris's only relief was in learning that "everybody else who had ever known him, including his wife, is equally bewildered."[40] Oliver North captured that quality when he wrote that Reagan was "almost always scripted" and that he "didn't always know what he knew."[41]

One needs to understand how Reagan used language before one can decide whether there is more or less there than meets the eye. Trained as an actor, but having an intuitive grasp of power, Reagan never permitted anyone to upstage him. He used words to project sincerity and yet did not really mean what he said, so his words were not as dangerous as his critics feared or as true as his followers hoped. When Reagan said the national security of all the Americas was at stake in Central America, his critics feared he was going to war, and his supporters hoped he would. Both were wrong. All Reagan was doing was trying to scare Congress into supporting his program. In his memoirs, he wrote that he never intended to send troops to Central America, and that is probably true.

In the end, Reagan seemed more committed to certain policies than almost any other politician, and yet he was actually less committed. That explains why he ran so hard against the Panama Canal Treaties and then dropped the issue entirely when he became president. It explains why he publicly committed his soul to supporting the contras and then did not utter a word when his successor abandoned them in the bipartisan accord of 1989. And yet he was such a good actor, with such a gift for simplifying reality, that he retained a devoted following regardless of what he said.

To evaluate his administration's policy, one can start with his own objectives. How successful was Reagan in undermining communism in the Caribbean Basin? There is no disputing his success in replacing a Marxist regime with a democratic government in Grenada. Reagan vividly recalls the invasion as "one of the highest of the high points of my eight years,"[42] a curious comment considering the size and significance of that island.

Beyond that, the record is either mixed or poor. If one judges the contra strategy by whether U.S. interests and concerns in Nicaragua were better or worse off at the end than at the beginning of Reagan's term, the policy faltered. There were fewer moderate leaders and less tolerance for political dissent in Nicaragua; the Sandinistas were much more militarized and dependent on the Soviet Union and Cuba; the human toll was tragic for such a poor country; and the war and the embargo severely weakened the economy and lowered the morale of the civic opposition, who felt that the United States cared only about the contras. Even with this high cost, some analysts might see the contra policy vindicated by the defeat of the Sandinistas in the February 1990 election, except that Reagan himself said that the Sandinistas would never permit a free election unless Congress approved military aid to the contras. Congress rejected both the aid and Reagan's argument, and Congress was proven right.[43]

In the United States itself, the cost of the contras was also high. No single incident stained Ronald Reagan's presidency as much as the Iran-Contra affair. Although Reagan was popular when he left office, a majority of the American people judged him a liar on the Iran-Contra issue, a conclusion that even his devoted acolyte North reached in his memoirs.[44] Several senior administration officials were convicted of criminal charges stemming from that scandal. The congressional investigation concluded: "Enough is clear to demonstrate beyond doubt that fundamental processes of governance were disregarded, and the rule of law was subverted."[45]

One could argue that the Salvadoran military became more professional, but its war against the left failed in part because Washington stymied negotiations with the left and failed to exert sufficient pressure on the military to stop the death squads. In Panama, the administration found itself stuck in a hole that it had dug itself, with no prospect of pulling Noriega out.

How does the administration fare using criteria weighted in favor of human rights? In every authoritarian Central American country except Nicaragua, the main struggle for democracy in the last decades has been against the right. The Reagan administration refused to fight that war, fearful of dividing the noncommunist forces. Only for one moment, in El Salvador in December 1983, did the administration deliver a critial message to the right.

The administration's efforts to improve U.S. relations with military regimes miscarried, ironically because many were replaced by democracies. Although Reagan changed direction in his second term and tried to take credit for the new democracies, most of the newly elected presidents in South America risked his displeasure by acknowledging the contribution of his predecessor.[46] The administration does deserve some credit for bringing democracy to Argentina, but by a convoluted route. The Argentine generals thought that if they helped the United States in Nicaragua, then Washington would help or, at least, acquiesce when Argentina seized its strategic prize, the Malvinas, in April 1982. But the United States first negotiated as a neutral and then supported the British, leaving the generals feeling betrayed.[47] Their disastrous defeat finally forced the military to give up power to civilians in a free election. For his part, Reagan admits in his memoirs that he tried to dissuade English Prime Minister Margaret Thatcher from an unconditional victory for fear that it would lead to a violent overthrow of the military dictatorship in Buenos Aires "by leftist guerrillas."[48] This was an utterly implausible scenario, and Thatcher was unmoved by Reagan's appeal.

In justifying its confrontation with Nicaragua, the administration discovered and then elaborated a commitment to democracy. Most important, it informed the military throughout Latin America that U.S. support for them depended on their acceptance of civilian, democratically elected governments. Even though the administration disliked the radical approach of Peruvian President Alan Garcia, it was careful not to antagonize him or give a green light to the military to overthrow him. This was the first time that conservative Republicans had been willing to coexist with social democrats in Latin America in preference to stable military regimes. Therefore, although the administration did not facilitate transitions toward democracy in the region and failed to use its influence to help consolidate the new regimes, it deserves credit for preventing the new democracies from being overthrown.

The Reagan administration's approach remained unilateral without apologies, in the evident belief that leadership on moral issues requires strength, not compromise. It listened to its friends less and sought to divide regional efforts more than any other administration in the postwar period. The administration showed a blatant disregard for international law and organizations. Instead of bringing evidence of Nicaraguan subversion to the OAS, the Reagan administration released it as a White Paper. Instead of bringing Nicaragua to the World Court, the administration was dragged there by Nicaragua and then refused to accept the court's jurisdiction. By 1985, the administration stopped pretending to seek a multilateral approach to the region's problems, and the assistant secretary of state began defending unilateralism:

> We can't abdicate our responsibility to protect our interests to a committee of Latin American countries. . . . The notion that if we have interests at stake we should ask Latin Americans what to do about it is wrong. . . . They want to know what we are going to do. They want to know if we have the guts to protect our interests, and if we don't, then they are going to walk away, and that is the way it should be.[49]

The Reagan administration is unlikely to be remembered for its foreign economic policies because it sidestepped the debt issue. It did initially improve relations with Mexico by helping that country reschedule its debts, but by the end of Reagan's second term that relationship had been strained by differences on Central America. The CBI was a positive program, but it did not compensate the region for the adverse effect of Washington's reduction of sugar quotas. Overall during the Reagan years, the gross domestic product of Latin America and the Caribbean declined by 8.3 percent.

President Reagan's legacy in Latin America and the Caribbean is an ironic one. He accomplished least in the area where he tried the hardest—Central America—and most in the area where he tried the least—democracy. He fought communism in the region, but he did so by polarizing the debate in the United States. He sought democracy in Central America but presided over a constitutional scandal that brought his presidency to the brink of disaster. He was proud and optimistic about democracy's progress in South America at a time when the region grew increasingly pessimistic about its social and economic prospects.

Perhaps the most intriguing irony of the Reagan administration was that its strategy toward Nicaragua gradually came to resemble the communist strategy against which it was directed. The "Reagan Doctrine" was a replica of the Communists' support of national liberation movements. The administration's role in organizing, training, and supplying the contras was the same role it accused Nicaragua of playing with Salvadoran guerrillas. The administration's reliance on propaganda, covert actions, and deceit was modeled on the Soviet Union's activities. The obsession with overthrowing the Sandinistas led Reagan to ally with Manuel Noriega and threaten Oscar Arias, a Nobel Peace Prize winner.

To be sure, the United States had supported coups in Latin America before, but it had never publicly acknowledged its support for an army of insurgents dedicated to overthrowing a government with which it had diplomatic relations. Nor had it ever supported as large an insurgency for so long or incorporated that policy into presidential doctrine. In many ways, the administration forged a policy that reflected the revolutionary style of Cuba more than that of previous U.S. administrations.

That may be Reagan's tragic legacy: At a moment of unprecedented opportunities for inter-American cooperation among democracies, the United States chose to pursue its war against Nicaragua alone. To defeat Communists, Reagan adopted their tactics and jettisoned America's purpose: respect for the rule of law. The strength of the United States was never questioned, but its effectiveness and judgment were tested and found wanting.

Notes

1. He made that statement during the presidential campaign of 1980. Quoted in Ronnie Dugger, *On Reagan: The Man and His Presidency* (New York: McGraw-Hill, 1983), p. 360.

2. Daniel Yankovich and Larry Kaagan, "Assertive America," *Foreign Affairs: America and the World* 59 (1980): 696.

3. Quoted in Dugger, *On Reagan,* p. 351.

4. In an interview with the *Wall Street Journal* in 1980, Reagan stated this view without reservations: "The Soviet Union underlies all the unrest that is going on. If they weren't engaged in this game of dominoes, there wouldn't be any hotspots in the world." Quoted in Dugger, *On Reagan,* p. 353.

5. "Briefing: Reagan's Religious 'We,'" *The New York Times,* February 17, 1984, p. B16.

6. See Dugger, *On Reagan,* pp. 382–383; and Ronald Reagan, "The Canal as Opportunity: A New Relationship with Latin America," *Orbis* 21 (Fall 1977): 551–561.

7. Jeane Kirkpatrick, "U.S. Security and Latin America," *Commentary* 71 (January 1981): 29. Her other article was "Dictatorships and Double Standards," *Commentary* 68 (November 1979).

8. Republican National Convention, *Republican Platform* (Detroit, July 14, 1980), pp. 68–69.

9. Alexander M. Haig Jr., *Caveat: Realism, Reagan and Foreign Policy* (New York: Macmillan, 1984), pp. 96–97.

10. The principal source for this summary of the debate within the administration is Haig, *Caveat,* pp. 98–100, 117–140, but two other articles cast light on the positions of others: Don Obendorfer, "Applying Pressure in Central America," *Washington Post,* November 23, 1983; and Leslie H. Gelb, "Haig Is Said to Press for Military Options for Salvadoran Action," *The New York Times,* November 5, 1981.

11. In an interview with *Time* on January 5, 1981, Reagan suggested postponing the land and banking reforms in El Salvador, and the right in El Salvador rejoiced. An article by Viera Altamirano in Salvador's *El Diario de Hoy* the same day praised Reagan for rejecting "a policy of appeasement toward Communism" in favor of a confrontational approach.

12. Interview with José Napoleón Duarte, July 26–27, 1983, San José, Costa Rica.

13. Juan de Onis, "Haig Opposes a Coup by Salvador's Right," *The New York Times,* March 5, 1981, p. A9.

14. Some of this evidence was released in the White Paper in February 1981, but the most credible and important proof was not released until September 1985. See U.S. Department of State, *Revolution Beyond Our Borders,* Special Report No. 132, September 1985, pp. 7–10.

15. Interview with Lawrence Pezzullo, July 30, 1985, New York City.

16. For a chronology of the Reagan administration's covert decisions on Nicaragua, see U.S. Senate and House Select Committees on Secret Military Assistance to Iran and the Nicaraguan Opposition, *Report of the Congressional Committees Investigating the Iran-Contra Affair,* 100th Cong., 1st sess., November 17, 1987 (hereafter cited as Congress, *Iran-Contra Report*).

17. I am indebted to Mick Anderson's *Dossier Secreto* for bringing Menem's observation to my attention. It can be found in Alfredo Leveo and José Antonio Diaz, *El Heredero de Peron* (Buenos Aires: Planeta, 1989), p. 147. Jackson Diehl, "State Department Official Sees Role for Argentina in Central America," *Washington Post,* March 10, 1982, p. A18; March 12, 1981, p. A16.

18. John Dinges, "Kirkpatrick Trip Upsets Opposition in Chile," *Washington Post,* August 13, 1981, p. A25; Raymond Bonner, "Chilean Exiles Appeal to Mrs. Kirkpatrick for Help," *The New York Times,* September 22, 1981, p. A16.

19. This was Haig's characterization. See also Reagan's speech on developing countries, *The New York Times,* October 16, 1981, p. A12.

20. Sam Dillon, "U.S. Arms Sales to Latin America Skyrocket," *Miami Herald,* November 28, 1982.

21. Milton R. Benjamin, "U.S. Is Allowing Argentina to Buy Critical A-System," *Washington Post,* July 19, 1982, pp. A1, 4; "Argentina's Blow to U.S. Nonproliferation Policy," letter by John Buell to *The New York Times,* November 29, 1983, p. A30.

22. Ronald Reagan, *An American Life* (New York: Simon & Schuster, 1990), p. 471.

23. Department of State, President Reagan's Address to the National Association of Manufacturers, March 10, 1983.

24. For an analysis of the justifications for the invasion, see Robert Pastor, "The Invasion of Grenada: A Pre- and Post-Mortem," in Scott B. MacDonald, Harald M. Sandstrom, and Paul B. Goodwin, eds., *The Caribbean after Grenada: Revolution, Conflict, and Democracy* (New York: Praeger, 1988).

25. Juan Williams, "President Defends Using Force," *Washington Post,* December 13, 1983, p. 1.

26. *The Report of the President's National Bipartisan Commission on Central America* (New York: Macmillan, 1984).

27. "Senate, 84–12, Acts to Oppose Mining Nicaragua's Ports; Rebuke to Reagan," *The New York Times,* April 11, 1984, p. 1. For a full account of what the CIA did, see David Rogers and David Ignatius, "How CIA-Aided Raids in Nicaragua in '84 Led Congress to End Funds," and "CIA Internal Report Details U.S. Role in Contra Raids in Nicaragua Last Year," *Wall Street Journal,* March 6, 1985.

28. Excerpts of the document were reprinted in the *The New York Times* (April 14, 1989, p. 9) during the trial of Oliver North and later declassified. In the meeting, National Security Adviser Robert McFarlane criticized Nicaragua and other "Marxist-Leninist regimes" for using negotiations as "tactical exercises," but Reagan did precisely that (p. 10).

29. Congress, *Iran-Contra Report,* p. 41.

30. Ibid., p. 4.

31. Cited in Loretta Tofani, "'Contra' Cause Is Just, Reagan Says," *Washington Post,* March 31, 1985, p. A22.

32. "President Reagan's Press Conference," *The New York Times,* February 12, 1986, p. 10.

33. Thomas Enders, Address to the Inter-American Press Association, Chicago, September 30, 1982, printed by U.S. Department of State.

34. UN Economic Commission for Latin America and the Caribbean (ECLAC), *Economic Survey of Latin America and the Caribbean, 1985* (Mexico City, 1986), table 1, p. 23.

35. Poindexter told Congress: "The buck stops here with me. I made the decision." At Poindexter's trial, his lawyer argued that "the President was the driving engine behind his [Poindexter's] actions" and that his client was a victim of "a frame-up." David Johnston, "Poindexter Is Found Guilty of All Five Criminal Charges for Iran-Contra Cover-Up," *The New York Times,* April 8, 1990, p. 1.

36. Cited in *Foreign Broadcast Information Service* (hereafter cited as *FBIS*), October 29, 1987, pp. 6–7.

37. See David Lyons, "Noriega Was Spy, U.S. Concedes," *Miami Herald,* May 31, 1991. Also see a document submitted by the U.S. government to the U.S. District Court of the District of Columbia in *U.S.* v. *Oliver North* (No. 88–0080), especially pp. 40–42.

38. For two balanced assessments of these events, see Margaret E. Scranton, *The Noriega Years* (Boulder, Colo.: Lynne Rienner, 1991); and John Dinges, *Our Man in Panama* (New York: Random House, 1990).

39. Constantine C. Menges, *Inside the National Security Council: The True Story of the Making and Unmaking of Reagan's Foreign Policy* (New York: Simon & Schuster, 1988).

40. See Edward Morris, *Dutch: A Memoir of Ronald Reagan* (New York: Random House, 1999); and "Official Biographer Puzzled by Reagan Persona," in the newsletter of the Miller Center of the University of Virginia, Spring 1991, pp. 3–4. Frank McNeil, *War and Peace in Central America* (New York: Charles Scribner's Sons, 1988).

41. Oliver North, *Under Fire* (New York: HarperCollins, 1991), pp. 14, 17.

42. Reagan, *An American Life*, p. 458.

43. Reagan expressed his "disappointment that the House voted to remove the pressure of the democratic resistance on the Sandinista regime," saying that the Sandinistas would never negotiate seriously and permit a free election without such pressure. *The New York Times*, February 25, 1988, p. 8.

44. North, *Under Fire*, pp. 11–14. A *New York Times*/CBS News poll from January 12–15, 1989 (p. 14), found that 52 percent of the American people believed that President Reagan was "lying when he said he did not know that the money from the Iranian arms sales was going to help the contras"; 33 percent said he was telling the truth.

45. Congress, *Iran-Contra Report*, p. 11.

46. For example, Uruguayan President Julio Sanguinetti described Carter's efforts as "very important," particularly as compared with Reagan's policy. "We Fought in a Great Silence: Interview with Sanguinetti," *Newsweek*, December 10, 1984, p. 17.

47. General Galtieri described the "excellent" rapport established with Reagan and the "deception . . . bitterness . . . [and] betrayal" he felt when Reagan failed to support him. Oriana Fallaci's interview, *Washington Post*, June 13, 1982, p. C5.

48. Reagan, *An American Life*, p. 360.

49. Interview with Elliot Abrams, "Big Sticks and Good Neighbors," *Detroit News*, September 12, 1985.

5

THE BUSH ADMINISTRATION: A TEST OF PRAGMATISM

Pragmatism? Is that all you have to offer?

—TOM STOPPARD, *ROSENCRANTZ AND GUILDENSTERN ARE DEAD*

For Latin America, the 1980s was a decade of debt-induced depression that compelled leaders to face two unpleasant facts: The region was becoming marginalized globally, and, despite heroic efforts to diversify, it remained more dependent on the United States than on any other country. Latin America's new democratic leaders reluctantly concluded that both their fate and their opportunity remained in the western hemisphere, but President Reagan was too preoccupied with Central America to respond to this agenda. They welcomed George Bush, particularly because he lacked his predecessor's ideological intensity. Together, the region's presidents grappled pragmatically with debt, democratic transitions, and drug trafficking, seeking new ways to relate the hemisphere to a rapidly changing world.

The United States was hampered by a chronic deficit and diminished resources, but Bush did not need aid to make a difference in the region. What he needed were new initiatives on debt and trade, and he fashioned those. Although Europe and Japan had increased their economic power relative to the United States, they were also less interested in Latin America. Thus, the hemispheric importance of the United States actually increased even as its global economic position appeared to decline.

Global trends and a proliferation of pragmatists combined to make possible a dramatic reshaping of regional and global politics. Carlos Salinas, the president of Mexico, initiated the process in the spring of 1990 with his proposal for a free trade area with the United States, and the rush of change that followed his decision marked it as a watershed. The proposal was all the more remarkable because Salinas presided over the nation in Latin America where the scars of U.S. intervention were the deepest and where nationalism was the most defensive. Although Bush did not have a plan, Salinas gave him one brimming with geopolitical purpose: bilateral integration that could become a platform for a global competitive edge. Salinas also catalyzed a change among Latin American leaders that led them to request admission to this new club.

The Setting

The agenda that Bush inherited upon taking office was divided much as the hemisphere had been. The United States aimed to contain leftist revolution in Central America, topple Noriega in Panama, and prevent drugs from entering the United States. The Latin Americans were mainly concerned about reducing their debts and consolidating their new democracies.

The changes within the Soviet Union and in its relations with the United States were the pivotal geopolitical facts of the late 1980s, and these also affected the inter-American agenda. In 1981 the Soviet Union was Reagan's "evil empire," and the United States was the last, best hope to stop Soviet-Cuban expansionism. Eight years later, in his Senate confirmation hearings, Secretary of State-designate James Baker acknowledged the changes in the Soviet Union, although then and throughout the year he called on Mikhail Gorbachev to prove his "new thinking" by resolving regional conflicts, including those in Central America. As late as December 1989, at a summit meeting in Malta, Bush accused Gorbachev of stoking the flames of revolution in El Salvador. Gorbachev apparently persuaded Bush that the Soviet Union was not responsible for sending surface-to-air missiles to the Salvadoran rebels, so Bush blamed the Sandinistas for not telling the truth "to our Soviet *friends*."[1] A small nation in Central America had replaced the Soviet Union as America's biggest problem in its neighborhood. Malta had turned upside down the central tenet of U.S. foreign policy toward Latin America: to keep the Soviets out of the hemisphere.

The main issue in Latin America continued to be the economy. By 1989, the region's per capita domestic product had dropped 8 percent below its 1981 level. As a whole, the region suffered an average of 758 percent inflation in 1988. Latin America's total external debt exceeded $400 billion, and its *net* transfer of capital due to debt service from 1982 through 1988 amounted to about $180 billion.[2] Banks in the United States wanted to reduce their exposure and leave. Lacking new investment, Latin America's economy declined. Debt remained the region's albatross. During the 1980s, leaders of Latin American democracies had offered proposals on debt, but Reagan blocked these and seemed allergic to meeting with more than one Latin American leader at a time. The Bush team was ready to listen.

The senior triumvirate of foreign policymakers—Bush, Baker, and National Security Adviser Brent Scowcroft—had substantial foreign policy experience, though little or none in Latin America. Baker had managed Bush's two presidential campaigns in 1980 and 1988, and their relationship was closer than between any previous president and secretary of state. In confirmation hearings, Baker defined his political orientation as conservative but activist:

> Some have described my philosophy as "pragmatic." . . . I am actually a Texas Republican, *all* of whom are conservative. I will admit to pragmatism, however, if by that you mean being realistic about the world and appreciating the importance of getting things done. . . . My purpose is not to understand this world in order to accept it but to understand it in order to change it where necessary—sometimes by large steps, often of necessity by small steps, yet always pressing forward. And the only sure guide for such change is the compass of American ideals and values.[3]

Bush's team was ready to consult with allies and negotiate with all adversaries except Sandinista Nicaragua. The first lesson they drew from the past was that negotiations were unlikely to succeed unless the United States demonstrated its strength and was prepared to employ force, if necessary. Baker attributed some of the positive changes in U.S.-Soviet relations "to the policy of peace through strength pursued over the last eight years." Baker's second lesson was that "we must have bipartisanship to succeed."

Bernard Aronson, a Democratic consultant who lobbied Capitol Hill on domestic and foreign issues, was appointed assistant secretary of state for inter-American affairs. He had helped the Reagan administration persuade "swing" Democratic members of Congress to vote for aid to the contras. Aronson had little knowledge of or experience in Latin America, but he was a quick study. His expertise was as a political broker who could work with both parties, even in a polarized environment, and who had the adeptness and intelligence to use these political skills with Latin American leaders as well. His appointment was a clear sign that Baker saw the Latin American problem as primarily a domestic political one and that he preferred a pragmatic political operator to a person of committed ideology. The transition from Reagan to Bush was smooth, as one would expect. Yet there was a subtle but real shift in Latin American policy, illustrated by the departure on inauguration day of Elliott Abrams, Reagan's acerbic, hard-line assistant secretary, even before Aronson had been appointed.

The two main foreign policy actors in the Bush administration were the State Department and the White House, but Baker's relationship with the president and Scowcroft's "passion for anonymity" meant that the competition between State and the NSC that had bedeviled the Nixon and Carter administrations was muted. Aronson was the captain, although his ability to manage the overall policy was constrained by the president's own active involvement and an agenda that included domestic issues such as drugs and trade. Congress played an important role, particularly in matters of aid and trade. This, then, was the geopolitical context, the old agenda and the new opportunities, and the people who would manage the policy. The Bush administration's openness to new ideas and people with different views was evident from the beginning. Instead of fighting or stiff-arming Democrats in and out of Congress, Bush's team consulted and often worked with them.

Smoothing or Removing the Inherited Agenda

The first step out of Central America was to make peace on Capitol Hill. On November 18, barely two weeks after his election, Bush visited Speaker of the House Jim Wright for a private lunch. Wright brought up Central America. "This has been the most implacable issue of the last eight years. Also the most politically polarizing and personally divisive," said Wright. Without hesitation, Bush agreed. Then, Bush asked: "Would you be willing to work with Jim Baker in trying to search out the ingredients of a common policy?" It was Wright's turn to agree.[4]

The bipartisan accord that Baker and Wright negotiated and announced on March 24 typified the Bush approach to Latin America. The accord removed the controversial contra issue from the foreign policy agenda by offering something to both sides. For conservative Republicans, Bush obtained $49.7 million in humanitarian aid for the contras, and he promised not to abandon them. For Wright and the liberal Democrats, Bush pledged his support for the Arias Plan and vowed not to seek military aid for the contras before the Nicaraguan elections. In other words, Bush said he would neither support nor abandon the contras—a scintillating pragmatic compromise, a recognition that both sides had half a point.

Many in the administration doubted that Daniel Ortega would hold a free election in February 1990, but they decided to use the elections anyway as the device for avoiding a collision with Congress on contra aid. This was the first step toward a political escape for the administration from the morass of Nicaragua, but it was hardly a solution. A solution required delicate negotiations between the Sandinistas and the internal opposition in Managua, not between Democrats and Republicans in Washington or, for that matter, between the U.S. and Soviet governments in Moscow.

Instead of going to Managua to negotiate or to Latin America to consult, Aronson's first trip abroad as assistant secretary of state was to Moscow. The administration later claimed that its secret partnership with the Soviets was "behind the Sandinistas' stunning election loss" in February 1990.[5] This was either an indication of the degree to which the administration misunderstood the political dynamics in Nicaragua or an after-the-fact attempt to take credit for the election outcome. If there was a secret understanding, it is hard to explain why the administration devoted so much time during the electoral process to criticizing the Soviet Union and the Sandinistas for supplying arms to the Salvadoran guerrillas (FMLN) and denying a fair and equal playing field for the opposition. In December 1989, on the eve of the Malta Summit with Gorbachev, Secretary Baker was so upset by Soviet policy that he publicly warned: "Soviet behavior in Central America remains the biggest obstacle to an across-the-board improvement in United States–Soviet relations."[6] Frustration, not satisfaction, over the Soviets' failure to deliver on these two key issues characterized the administration's view of the Soviets *before* the election.

Nonetheless, increasing cooperation between the superpowers eliminated a complicating factor in the Nicaraguan election and probably contributed to a favorable climate there. The Soviets supported free elections, and Cuba did not oppose them. Bush chose to encourage the coalition of opposition parties (UNO) to participate in the elections—an important change from Reagan's policy in 1984—but he refused to negotiate with the Sandinistas directly. Instead, by default more than by choice, he stepped back from Nicaragua and allowed others to negotiate a bridge and the rules of the game between the Sandinistas and UNO (see Chapter 13).

Vice President Dan Quayle believed the election would be "a sham," and the State Department maintained a constant drumbeat of criticism against the Sandinistas for tilting the playing field against UNO.[7] When Jimmy Carter phoned Baker at 4 A.M. on February 26, 1990, with the news that Violeta de Chamorro had defeated Ortega in a landslide and that Ortega had accepted defeat, Baker was delighted.

The administration also made significant progress on the debt problem. On March 10, 1989, Treasury Secretary Brady offered a plan that encouraged the private banks to reduce the value of their debt in exchange for guarantees from the international development banks and market-oriented reforms by the debtor countries. Second, he shifted the balance of power to the debtor nations and away from the private banks by indicating that the International Monetary Fund should disburse its loans *before* the banks reach agreement with the debtor nations.

The debt proposal was congruent with the emerging U.S. strategy of combining U.S. political leadership with Japanese financing. For the $30 billion needed to fund the Brady Plan, the United States asked the World Bank and the IMF each to contribute $12 billion and Japan, $6 billion.

One of the reasons for developing a new debt plan was to assist the new Mexican government of Carlos Salinas in reducing its debt as a basis for economic recovery. Bush and Baker understood the consequences for their state of Texas if Mexico failed in its delicate transition from a closed political and economic system to a more modern, competitive one. In their first meeting in November 1988, Salinas impressed on Bush the importance of debt relief, and Mexico was the first country to negotiate an arrangement under the Brady Plan's provisions, although it took nearly a year to complete the final agreement. Costa Rica and Venezuela followed after that.

The Bush administration, like its predecessor, initially preferred to address its agenda by itself or on a bilateral basis where U.S. leverage was greatest. When Jimmy Carter and Gerald Ford invited Baker to a meeting with a group of Latin American leaders in March 1989, Baker was initially reluctant to attend, fearful of a possible confrontation. But he decided to come, and in the first address on Latin America in the Bush administration, Baker looked back to the Cold War, asking Latin Americans to join with the United States to send a clear signal to the Soviet Union that "this is simply not a dumping ground for their arms and their failed ideologies." His principal message, however, was forward-looking: "We need each other now. . . . Latin America's democratic leaders are reaching out to the United States to offer a new partnership. . . . I am here on behalf of a new President . . . with our answer: We are reaching back to you." Baker spoke of "the democratic wave sweeping Latin America today," of the movement toward freer markets and less state intervention in the economy, of the need for cooperation on drugs, debt, and Central America. "We are committed to work with Latin and Central American democratic leaders to translate the bright promise of the Esquipulas agreement into concrete realities on the ground."[8] In all, the speech reflected a much-welcomed interest in consulting the region.

Panamanian elections were scheduled for May 7, 1989, but General Manuel Noriega was persecuting the opposition, restricting the press and observers, and manipulating the electoral council. On behalf of Carter, I visited Panama one month before the election and persuaded a very reluctant and belligerent Noriega to invite Carter and the Council of Freely-Elected Heads of Government to observe the elections. In his memoir, he later blamed me for pressuring him to accept observers.[9] Some Bush administration officials opposed such a mission, fearing that Carter's commitment to the Canal Treaties might affect his judgment of the election. In fact, Carter's announcement, based on a 3 to 1 victory by the opposition in a "quick count," and his denunciation of the fraud, made it impossible for Noriega to claim victory. This left his government without legitimacy and opened the way for condemnation by the OAS on May 17, 1989. The OAS then dispatched the foreign ministers of Ecuador, Trinidad and Tobago, and Guatemala to try to negotiate a peaceful transfer of power. Noriega blamed the United States and was unresponsive to the OAS mission, which failed to use its potential leverage effectively against him. The United States, which had increased its troop levels in the Canal area after the election debacle, began to step up the pressure.

On October 3 several officers in the Panamanian Defense Forces (PDF) tried to overthrow Noriega. They held him captive for a few hours while the United States tried to determine who they were and whether to support them. Before either question could be answered, Noriega's supporters counterattacked, freed him, and murdered the coup plotters. The confusion surrounding the coup attempt rebounded badly against Bush. Republicans and many Democrats charged him with timidity and indecisiveness, suggesting that a quicker reaction would have displaced Noriega.[10] Bush undoubtedly felt the pressure, although, typically, he tried to deny it: "Those doves that now become instant hawks on Capitol Hill; they don't bother me one bit because the American people supported me by over two to one, and I think I sent a strong signal . . . that we are not going to imprudently use the force of the United States."[11]

The one "Latin American issue" that had a continuing and expanding hold on the American public was drugs. In September 1989, after a major speech by President Bush in which he called drugs the country's "gravest domestic threat," 64 percent of the American people identified drugs as the nation's number-one problem.[12] Latin American countries cultivated and shipped all of the cocaine that entered the United States. As vice president, George Bush had been in charge of the Reagan administration's efforts to stop the flow. He saw firsthand their failure. Each year the price of cocaine declined and the purity increased, meaning that more drugs entered the country.

By 1988, the United States and Latin America realized that they shared both the causes and the negative consequences of the drug problem. The Omnibus Drug Act of 1988 emphasized the importance of the demand side of the drug problem by increasing federal funding for education and health programs.[13] In September 1989 President Bush launched his own antidrug program, which included a proposal to work with the Andean countries to help eradicate coca, destroy cocaine-processing centers, and provide development aid for peasants to grow alternative crops. Aware of the corrupting power of the drug cartel, many of the leaders in the region were ready to cooperate if Washington showed some respect, and Bush was prepared to do that.

Progress had been made in the first year on virtually every issue on the inter-American agenda: Nicaragua, debt, drugs, and U.S.-Mexican relations. Bush consulted often with Latin American presidents and had begun to forge new bonds. All of these developments augured well for U.S.–Latin American relations, except that Bush was haunted by his one failure, Panama. Taunted by Noriega and mocked by congressional leaders of both parties, Bush's personal prestige became the issue.

Panama's Liberation of Bush

The OAS mediation in Panama failed to persuade Noriega to leave, and the Latin American governments would not consider imposing sanctions against him, although at the Nineteenth OAS General Assembly in November the Inter-American Human Rights Commission issued a report that called Noriega's government "devoid of constitutional legitimacy."[14] Several days later, officials in the Bush administration leaked details of a $3 million covert action plan by the United States to unseat Noriega.[15] According to U.S. intelligence, Noriega had plans to take American hostages and fight guerrilla-style in the mountains in the event of a U.S. invasion. Because of these reports, General Fred Woerner, in charge of Southern Command in Panama, opposed an invasion, but on October 1, 1989, he was replaced by General Maxwell Thurman. Together with Colin Powell, the new chairman of the Joint Chiefs of Staff, Thurman developed a contingency plan for a massive, rapid invasion. Beginning in November, U.S. troops and military equipment were gradually and secretly moved into Panama for possible use.[16]

On Friday, December 15, 1989, the Noriega-controlled National Assembly in Panama declared that a "state of war" with the United States existed, and it named Noriega chief of government. The next day, with tensions running high, members of the Panama Defense Force (PDF) opened fire on a car carrying four U.S. military officers when it did not stop at a roadblock. One officer was killed, a second was injured, and a third who witnessed the event was detained and beaten.

This was hardly the first incident against American forces. During the previous eighteen months, Noriega's thugs had been responsible for hundreds of unprovoked attacks against American soldiers and their families. But the incident of December 15 apparently caused Bush to cross his Rubicon. He called it "an enormous outrage," and two days later he approved an invasion for 1 A.M. on Wednesday, December 20. At that moment, 10,000 U.S. troops, backed by helicopter gunships and fighter-bombers, flew into Panama and joined about 13,000 soldiers already at U.S. bases in the Canal area. Their objectives were to capture Noriega, install the government of Guillermo Endara, who was elected on May 7, and protect American citizens. Although Noriega had often accused the United States of planning an invasion, he was surprised, and no Americans were taken hostage.

The Air Force rained 422 bombs on Panama in thirteen hours, and U.S. forces secured control of the country within five days. Less planning was given to the political side of the invasion. The U.S. government informed Endara and his two vice presidents, Ricardo Arias Calderon and Guillermo Ford, only three hours before the invasion. "We had an alternative, the most difficult in our political careers," Arias later recalled. "Either cross our arms and let the country suffer not only a military invasion by the United States but also have an occupation government imposed, *or* take over the government to which the people elected us on May 7 and attempt, upon the foundation of popular sovereignty, to rescue the nation's sovereignty."[17] Needless to say, they chose to take the reins of government and to rely on U.S. military forces to disarm the Panamanian army and help establish a new police force. Noriega escaped the U.S. grip by seeking asylum at the Papal Nuncio, but on January 4 he surrendered and was flown to Miami, where he was arraigned on charges of drug trafficking.

From Chile to Mexico, the reaction to the first unilateral U.S. invasion in Latin America in more than sixty years was swift and negative. Bush had not bothered to consult any Latin leaders beforehand. On December 22 the OAS passed a resolution that "deeply regrets the military intervention in Panama" and urged the withdrawal of U.S. troops. Twenty nations voted for the resolution, seven abstained, and the United States was alone in opposing it. The UN General Assembly passed a stronger resolution, condemning the intervention with a vote of 75–20–40.[18] Some days after the invasion, interviews with President Bush and his closest advisers suggested that personal motives were not insignificant. "We suspected that the President felt after the [October failed] coup that sooner or later we would have to do this," said one senior White House adviser. Another said that Bush felt Noriega "was thumbing his nose at him." And Bush himself admitted publicly just before the invasion: "I've been frustrated that he's been in power so long, extraordinarily frustrated."[19]

The invasion was criticized throughout the world, but it was judged a success then in Panama and in the United States. A CBS News poll in Panama in early January found that 92 percent of Panamanian adults approved of the sending of troops, and 76 percent wished the United States had sent them during the coup in October.[20] The American people also approved of the invasion: 74 percent said it was justified, and only 7 percent thought the United States should not have taken such action. More significantly, the invasion measurably improved Bush's overall approval ratings, lifting him to 76 percent, a higher level at that point in his term than any president had achieved since John F. Kennedy.[21] The test for a pragmatist is results, and to a politician the ultimate judgment is public opinion and elections. It was therefore not surprising that Bush used polls to respond to a critical question from the press: "Look, you lost some Panamanian lives. . . . Yet 92 percent of the people in Panama strongly supported the action of the United States. Isn't that significant?"[22]

In the end, the invasion liberated George Bush as much as it did Panama. He had been feeling "boxed in," had complained that "our hands are tied."[23] The invasion was his rite of passage, showing him to be a decisive leader prepared to risk force. There were no more charges of weakness. Bush was now free to be the magnanimous patrician. He phoned leaders throughout the hemisphere and listened to their concerns. Later, he explained what he heard:

> I am well aware of how our friends south of our border . . . look at the use of American force anywhere. So I'm concerned about it. I think it's something that's correctable because I think they know that I have tried a lot of consultation, that we have exhausted the remedies in this particular case of multilateral diplomacy. If there is damage, I can repair it.[24]

Bush was not far from the truth. The immediate reaction from Latin America was severe, and in some countries with a long history of U.S. intervention, such as Cuba, Nicaragua, and Mexico, the reaction was outrage. But in much of the rest of Latin America, Bush's consultations, Noriega's depravity, the passage of time, and the importance of the remaining agenda diluted the negative feelings.

Venezuelan President Carlos Andrés Pérez evaluated the event in an important address to the OAS on April 27, 1990: "The crisis ended with the most unacceptable of results, the armed unilateral action of the United States." But he also insisted that Latin America should share some of the responsibility for not using the OAS to take tougher actions against Noriega. He argued that the principle of "non-intervention became a passive intervention against democracy," and he urged his colleagues to work to redefine the principles of the OAS to permit it to take stronger action against dictators.[25]

Reactions to the invasion resonated through other issues. Bush had accepted an invitation in October from the presidents of Peru, Bolivia, and

Colombia for a summit meeting to deal with the drug issue. Because of Panama, the meeting was delayed and abbreviated, but it was held in Cartagena for six hours on February 15, 1990, and the leaders issued a lengthy communiqué announcing the "first antidrug cartel." Bush promised a five-year, $2.2 billion (half economic, half military) regional aid program to assist the fight against drugs.[26] The Andean presidents convinced Bush of the need to provide alternatives through crop substitution and trade policy, and in July the American president opened the U.S. market to sixty-seven Andean products that they had requested.[27]

Bush had a second chance to act magnanimously and erase the effect of the Panamanian invasion when Violeta de Chamorro won the presidency in Nicaragua on February 25, 1990. Bush sent a message to Ortega as well as to Chamorro and promised to help Nicaragua during the transition and afterwards. Administration officials encouraged the contras to disarm, but they had missed their moment of maximum influence. As the contras prolonged their negotiations, the Sandinistas grew worried and insisted that General Humberto Ortega remain head of the army until the negotiations with the contras were completed. The Bush administration opposed this demand, but Chamorro, opting for a strategy of national reconciliation, decided to retain General Ortega.

The old agenda of Nicaragua and Panama had been smoothed, if not removed, but Bush and Baker wanted to prove that this would not lead them to neglect those countries or the rest of Latin America. The administration lifted the trade embargoes against both countries and requested $500 million for each. The amounts were too small to solve the economic problems there, but larger than Congress was initially willing to consider.

Salinas and the Regionalist Option

When Carlos Salinas proposed a free trade agreement with the United States in the spring of 1990, it was a propitious moment. Europe and Japan were concentrating on their own regions. Mexico and most Latin American governments had implemented fundamental economic reforms, privatizing state corporations, deregulating their internal markets, and reducing their trade barriers. They hoped that the General Agreement on Tariffs and Trade (GATT) would open new markets, but as the Uruguay Round of trade negotiations stagnated, they looked to each other to establish subregional trading pacts, and they looked north.

Bush had previously asked Congress to extend the Caribbean Basin Initiative (CBI), and Congress approved the bill after restricting the number of products eligible for the program. Bush's cautious response to Salinas's proposal when they met in June might be explained by Congress's reaction to the CBI and the fact that his trade negotiators were focused on completing the Uruguay Round. But he was soon convinced by Texas friends, and he responded positively to Salinas.[28]

Whether intentionally or not, Salinas had opened the hemispheric floodgates; no one wanted to be left out of the North American market. To respond to this interest, Bush launched his "Enterprise for the Americas" initiative on June 27, 1990. This was a grab-bag of proposals that were partly a follow-up of the Andean Summit and partly a response to the trade issue. It included tariff reductions in the Uruguay Round on products of special interest to the region, a pledge to reduce U.S. government-owned official debt, a $1.5 billion investment fund for privatizations managed by the Inter-American Development Bank, debt-for-nature swaps, and free trade with Latin America. The last point was potentially the most important, and Bush described his objective as "a hemispheric free trade zone from Alaska to Argentina."[29]

Latin American leaders responded promptly and positively. Argentine President Carlos Menem hailed the initiative: "We are passing through the most brilliant moment in our relations with the United States." Uruguayan President Luis Lacalle called Bush to compliment him, and President Pérez of Venezuela called the initiative "the most advanced proposal the United States has ever made for Latin America. It's revolutionary, historical."[30]

After a bruising debate in late May 1991, Congress approved authority for the administration to conduct "fast-track" trade negotiations, and in June trade representatives from the United States, Mexico, and Canada began negotiations on a North American Free Trade Area. By the end of 1991, the U.S. government had negotiated reductions of more than 90 percent in the bilateral official debt for Guyana, Honduras, and Nicaragua; around 70 percent for Haiti and Bolivia; 25 percent for Jamaica; and 4 percent for Chile. By then, the United States had signed fifteen trade "framework agreements" with thirty Latin American and Caribbean nations. These agreements included a declaration of trade and investment principles, a routine consultation mechanism, and an agenda for negotiating reductions in trade barriers.[31]

"To fulfill the New World's destiny," Bush said as he left for a trip to South America in December 1990, "all of the Americas and the Caribbean must embark on a venture for the coming century: to create the first fully democratic hemisphere in the history of mankind."[32] The administration supported free elections in Haiti on December 16, 1990, and pledged aid for the new president, Jean-Bertrand Aristide. It also encouraged free elections in Guyana and a democratic transition in Suriname. In both cases, the administration relied on the OAS and the Council of Freely-Elected Heads of Government to monitor the elections.

In June 1991 the OAS General Assembly met in Santiago, Chile, and passed a resolution committing the organization to democracy and promising to meet in the event that a democratic government was overthrown. Within three months, the Haitian military provided the OAS with its first test. Days after Aristide went into exile, the OAS met and condemned the coup, demanding the reinstatement of Aristide and his constitutional government. When the military ignored this demand, OAS foreign ministers met again on October 8, 1991. Secretary Baker said that the coup would not stand, and all agreed to a diplomatic and economic embargo against the military junta. A team was sent to Haiti to try to negotiate Aristide's return, but they failed.

The administration was divided on whether Aristide's return was desirable. The State Department tried to negotiate an agreement to restore Aristide, but the Pentagon was opposed to using force, and without a credible threat, the negotiations proved ineffectual. The administration's principal concern was stopping the flow of Haitian refugees, and in the spring of 1992, Bush ordered the U.S. Coast Guard to return to the island any Haitians who tried to flee. Candidate Bill Clinton criticized Bush's "cruel policy of returning Haitian refugees to a brutal dictatorship without an asylum hearing," but Bush maintained the policy.

Despite the end of the Cold War, Castro remained. Believing that Castro's tenure could be "measured in months, not years,"[33] the Cuban-American community, led by the Cuban American National Foundation (CANF), urged Congress to bring down the regime by forcing other governments to stop trading with Cuba. This idea was introduced by Representative Robert Torricelli in a bill that tightened the embargo by preventing U.S. subsidiaries in other countries from trading with Cuba. President Bush opposed the bill because its extraterritorial provisions were opposed by our allies, but when Clinton endorsed it after a fund-raiser in Miami during the Florida primary in the spring of 1992, Bush reversed course and signed it and established TV Marti, an expensive and useless television program that Cuba jammed. Torricelli said the law would cause Castro to fall "within weeks."[34]

Soon after the failed coup in Moscow by Soviet hard-liners in August 1991, Gorbachev announced that the Soviet Union would withdraw its military personnel from Cuba and that all future economic activity with Cuba would be based on free trade rather than price subsidies. Castro was irate at both the message and the way it was delivered. The Cuban-American community in Miami was elated.

The Bush administration also joined the Russians and Mexicans in support of UN mediation of the conflict in El Salvador. On New Year's Day 1992, an agreement was reached between the Alfredo Cristiani government and the FMLN to end the twelve-year war that had taken as many as 75,000 lives. The agreement included an important role for the United Nations to monitor both the disarmament of the guerrillas and the investigations of human rights violations by soldiers. A new national civic police force was created, and land reform was guaranteed. Both the government and the guerrillas had realized that neither could prevail on the battlefield and that their nation suffered while they fought. The end of the Cold War caused the guerrillas to reconsider their strategy, and Nicaragua's relative success at reconciliation also helped both sides to realize they could live together.

Politics and Policy: An Evaluation

Because the principal motive for U.S. engagement in Latin America had been a fear of Soviet encroachment, many observers predicted that the end of the Cold War would lead to U.S. neglect. A second expectation was that Bush's predilection for sidestepping rather than resolving difficult issues would soon lead him to concentrate on other matters. Both judgments proved incorrect. Instead of a lack of interest, Bush and his administration displayed almost frenetic attention, with more high-level "telephone summits" and meetings, including six with the Mexican president in two years and a major trip to South America in December 1990 in the middle of the Persian Gulf crisis.

The old agenda of Nicaragua and Panama that had plagued the Reagan administration was removed with an election and an invasion. The

Nicaraguan situation was resolved largely because the Bush administration discarded the belligerence of its predecessor and allowed others to mediate a free election. In Panama, Noriega's annulment of the election in May 1989 was his undoing. Venezuela pursued him in the OAS, giving Bush an exit from the unproductive bilateral confrontation that Reagan had bequeathed him. In the end, this multilateral path did not succeed, but it did provide Bush with a patina of international legitimacy that permitted him to take military action without irrevocably fracturing U.S. relations with his democratic friends in the region. The human, economic, and political costs of intervention were high, but most Panamanians and Americans judged them worth it at the time.

That price rose as Panamanians came to grips with the difficult and slow process of rebuilding their nation's shattered economy, weak political structures, and injured sense of nationhood. The problems of economic recovery and democratic consolidation in Nicaragua and Panama—and in many other new democracies in the hemisphere—proved to be taxing and difficult. Aid from the United States was helpful, but clearly inadequate.

It was not long before Americans lost their enthusiasm for the Panamanian invasion and for Bush's overall policy toward the region. By the fall of 1991, a public opinion survey showed that Americans gave the Bush administration a 5:4 positive rating for its handling of the intervention, and public opinion leaders actually gave Bush a 4:3 negative rating on Panama. Similarly, the American people gave a very low rating to his Latin American policy—3:1 negative in public opinion, 4:1 negative in leadership opinion. In Panama, support for the invasion also declined from 90 percent at the time to 40 percent one year later.[35]

On the Latin American issue that concerned Americans the most, drugs, the Bush administration significantly increased its expenditures, from $6.4 billion in 1988 to more than $11 billion in fiscal year 1992. But the proportion spent on the demand side of the problem (health treatment, education) remained about 30 percent. The United States also increased its military involvement in the Andes, but the president did not achieve the goals that he had set for himself in September 1989. He wanted to reduce the supply of cocaine by 15 percent from 1989 to 1991, but the Drug Enforcement Agency estimated that cocaine production in South America increased in 1990 by 28 percent and in 1991 by at least 10 percent.[36] At a meeting with five Latin American presidents in February 1992 in San Antonio, Bush declared that, together, they were "making significant progress," particularly by increased seizures of cocaine. Mexico and Colombia alone captured the equivalent of $13 billion of cocaine in 1991. But the State Department's own report, issued several days later, admitted that the volume of coca and poppy production rose in 1991, and the price of cocaine on the street of Miami had declined.[37] Stalemate, not victory, is a more accurate way to describe the war between Washington and the drug traffickers, but the American people judged that the war on drugs was being lost. In one poll, only 38 percent of the American people felt that Bush had made progress on the drug problem. A survey by the Chicago Council on Foreign Relations found that people gave Bush a 3:1 negative rating on the drug problem and leaders gave him a 4:1 negative assessment.[38]

On the economic front, the Brady Plan and the Enterprise for the Americas Initiative were welcome acknowledgments of the importance of debt relief, but their impact on most of Latin America was limited. Although debt service as a percentage of Latin American exports declined in 1991 to 22 percent, that was "still very high," according to the United Nations, "and reflects the serious debt problems that persist in most of the countries in the region."[39] On the trade front, Bush pressed his negotiators to complete NAFTA before the Republican Convention in order to place his rival, who depended on labor unions for support, in an awkward position. This was a short-sighted approach to a long-term initiative. In the end, Clinton endorsed NAFTA but promised to improve on it in the area of labor and environmental rights if he were elected.

The foreign policy process during the Bush administration encountered some problems. So proud of its successful invasion of Panama, the Pentagon overreached by announcing the deployment of an aircraft carrier to Colombia. Similarly, the Drug Enforcement Agency acted repeatedly like a rogue elephant, particularly in Mexico, where it was involved in the kidnapping of a Mexican citizen charged with complicity in the 1985 murder of a DEA agent. In the first instance, Bush pulled the Pentagon back; in the second, he failed to discipline the DEA, despite the cost of its behavior to U.S. interests in Mexico. Nonetheless, overall, the foreign policy process probably worked better under Bush than under most of his predecessors.

Bush tested the promise and the limits of a pragmatic style on both Congress and Latin America. The pragmatic style has both a positive and a negative side. On the positive side, his responsiveness to critics and to the region's complaints was welcomed by the region's leaders. What is interpreted as responsive by one side, of course, may appear as caving in to pressure by the other side. For example, his decision to invade Panama could be interpreted as a response to critics, who called him weak. On the other hand, it is hard to see his posturing against Fidel Castro as anything more than pandering to the Cuban-American community, a phenomenon that was hardly unique to him.

Responsiveness, by definition, means that an administration reacts rather than anticipates or plans. And most observers agree that the central weakness of the Bush administration was its lack of a guiding idea, a grand design. The predilection to deal with problems on a piecemeal basis means that sometimes policies do not fit together. For example, less than two years after he was condemned for the first unilateral U.S. intervention in the hemisphere since the 1920s, Bush responded to criticisms of his more cautious response to the coup in Haiti by saying: "I am disinclined to use American force. We've got a big history of American force in this hemisphere, and so we've got to be very careful about that."[40] Still, by taking one issue at a time, and with the stimulus of Salinas, the pragmatic Bush administration stepped toward a new regionalist option.[41]

With George Bush listening, Latin America's new leaders took genuine risks that will benefit their countries in the long term. These risks include reducing state control of the economy, widening the base of civil society, slicing military budgets, and trying to develop deeper economic relations with the United States and the rest of the world. George Bush did not take comparable risks in his hemispheric policy. He preached the free market as if that would solve the problem of endemic poverty, build schools, or construct water systems. He looked to the Soviet Union to solve the problem of Cuba rather than to U.S. policy. But Bush's pragmatism and responsiveness moved the hemisphere forward and built close personal and governmental relations with Latin American democracies on the full gamut of issues.

The Salinas proposal and the Enterprise for the Americas Initiative represented the outline of a new hemispheric economy, just as the "Santiago Commitment" that was approved by the OAS in June 1991 offered the possibility of a democratic community. The pragmatist, however, should be judged by results. In the end, Bush urged the OAS to do more to restore constitutional government in Haiti, and he negotiated NAFTA. But both initiatives would have to await completion under his successor.

Notes

1. "Transcript of Bush-Gorbachev News Conference on Malta Meeting," *The New York Times,* December 4, 1989, pp. 10–11.

2. Statistics are from the UN Economic Commission for Latin America and the Caribbean, *Preliminary Overview of the Economy of Latin America and the Caribbean, 1988 and 1989* (Santiago, 1989); see pp. 19–20 for 1989.

3. Statement of Secretary of State-designate James A. Baker III at confirmation hearings before the Senate Foreign Relations Committee, January 17, 1989. U.S. Department of State Current Policy no. 1146, Washington, D.C., p. 2.

4. Jim Wright, *Balance of Power: Presidents and Congress from the Era of McCarthy to the Age of Gingrich* (Atlanta: Turner Publishing, Inc., 1996), pp. 479–480.

5. See Michael Kramer, "Anger, Bluff—and Cooperation: Behind the Sandinistas' Stunning Election Loss in Nicaragua Is the Secret Story of U.S.-Soviet Partnership in Central America," *Time,* June 4, 1990, pp. 38–45.

6. Andrew Rosenthal, "Bush Hoping to Use Malta Talks to Speed Strategic Arms Pact," *The New York Times,* November 30, 1989, pp. 1, 11.

7. Robert Pear, "Quayle Calls Managua Vote Plan a Sham," *The New York Times,* June 13, 1989, p. A3.

8. Address by Hon. James A. Baker III to the Carter Center of Emory University's Consultation on a New Hemispheric Agenda, Atlanta, Georgia, March 30, 1989, U.S. Department of State Press Release no. 56.

9. Carter Center of Emory University, *The May 7, 1989 Panamanian Elections: Pre-Election Report Based on the Findings of an International Delegation,* March 1989; National Democratic and Republican Institutes for International Affairs, *The May 7, 1989 Panamanian Elections: International Delegation Report,* 1989; and Manuel Noriega and Peter Eisner, *The Memoirs of Manuel Noriega: America's Prisoner* (New York: Random House, 1997), p. 145.

10. See, for example, "Panama Crisis: Disarray Hindered White House," *The New York Times,* October 8, 1989, pp. 1, 6; "Amateur Hour," *Newsweek,* October 16, 1989, pp. 26–31.

11. President's interview with Latin American press, October 25, 1989, Washington, D.C., p. 10.

12. The number declined to 54 percent by the end of the month. R. W. Apple Jr., "Poll Finds Broad Support for Bush But Skepticism about Drugs and Taxes," *The New York Times,* September 26, 1989, p. 12.

13. See Bruce Bagley, "U.S. Foreign Policy and the War on Drugs: Analysis of a Policy Failure," *Journal of InterAmerican Studies and World Affairs* 31 (Summer/Fall 1989).

14. Paul Lewis, "OAS Deems Rule by Noriega Illegal: Group Deplores Panamanian and Accuses His Regime of Rights Violations," *The New York Times,* November 14, 1989.

15. Michael Wines, "U.S. Plans New Effort to Oust Noriega," *The New York Times,* November 17, 1989, p. A3.

16. Michael R. Gordon, "U.S. Drafted Invasion Plan Weeks Ago," *The New York Times,* December 24, 1989, pp. 1, 5.

17. Interview with Bogotá Radio, reprinted in *Foreign Broadcast Information Service* (hereafter *FBIS*), January 3, 1990, p. 35.

18. James Brooke, "U.S. Denounced by Nations Touchy about Intervention," *The New York Times,* December 21, 1989, p. 14; "OAS Resolution Expresses Regret on U.S. Action," reprinted in *FBIS,* December 27, 1989, p. 1.

19. Maureen Dowd, "Doing the Inevitable: Bush Reportedly Felt That Noriega 'Was Thumbing His Nose at Him,'" *The New York Times,* December 24, 1989, p. 5; and R. W. Apple Jr., "Bush's Obsession: President Says Noriega's Hold on Power Has Left Him 'Extraordinarily Frustrated,'" *The New York Times,* December 26, 1989, p. 5.

20. Michael R. Kagay, "Panamanians Strongly Back U.S. Move," *The New York Times,* January 6, 1990, p. 7.

21. Michael Oreskes, "Approval of Bush, Aided by Panama, Hits 76% in Poll: A Rarely Achieved Level," *The New York Times,* January 19, 1990, pp. 1, 11.

22. Transcript of Bush's press conference, *The New York Times,* January 25, 1990, p. A15.

23. Interview with President Bush, *The New York Times,* October 25, 1989, p. 9.

24. Transcript of Bush news conference on Noriega and Panama, *The New York Times,* January 6, 1990, p. 8.

25. Address to the OAS, April 27, 1990.

26. Andrew Rosenthal, "Three Andean Leaders and Bush Pledge Drug Cooperation," *The New York Times,* February 16, 1990, p. 1.

27. Clyde H. Farnsworth, "Bush Planning Aid to Andean Lands," *The New York Times,* July 24, 1990.

28. Peter Truell, "Texans Use Their Influence with Bush to Open U.S.-Mexico Free-Trade Talks," *Wall Street Journal,* August 31, 1990, p. A12; Clyde H. Farnsworth, "Mexican Free Trade Pact Pushed: President Planning to Ask Congress to Authorize Talks," *The New York Times,* September 14, 1990, p. C1.

29. President Bush's remarks on submitting legislation to Congress to implement the initiative, September 14, 1990, Office of the White House Press Secretary.

30. See Shirley Christian, "Bush's Offer of Free Trade Gets Warm Latin Reception," *The New York Times*, August 26, 1990, p. 15; and Clifford Krauss, "Bush to Take Off for South America," *The New York Times*, December 2, 1990, p. 11.

31. UN Economic Commission for Latin America, *Preliminary Overview of the Economy of Latin America and the Caribbean, 1991,* p. 19; "Press Briefing by U.S. Trade Representative Carla Hills," White House, December 13, 1991.

32. Cited in James Brooke, "Debt and Democracy: Officials Say Bush Is Either Reflecting New Reality or Missing Opportunity," *The New York Times,* December 5, 1990, p. A6.

33. José S. Sorzano, "Debating U.S. Cuba Policy: Why Alter a Course That Has Helped to Create the Dead-End Situation That Castro Now Faces?" *Miami Herald,* October 7, 1990, pp. 1, 6.

34. Cited in Wayne S. Smith, "Shackled to the Past: The United States and Cuba," *Current History* (February 1996): 51.

35. John E. Rielly, ed., *American Public Opinion and U.S. Foreign Policy, 1991* (Chicago: Chicago Council on Foreign Relations, 1991), p. 17. The same questions were asked of a national sample of 1,662 people and a selected sample of 377 leaders in senior positions with knowledge of international affairs. The Panama poll in *La Prensa* was cited in Center for International Policy, *These Noble Goals* (Washington, D.C., June 1991), p. 6.

36. Washington Office on Latin America, *Clear and Present Danger: The U.S. Military and the War on Drugs in the Andes* (Washington, D.C., October 1991), pp. 7, 93–95.

37. U.S. Department of State, *International Narcotics Control Strategy Report* (Washington, D.C., March 1992); Joseph Treaster, "Bush Sees Progress, but U.S. Report Sees Surge in Drug Production," *The New York Times,* March 1, 1992, p. 8.

38. Robin Toner, "Poll Finds Postwar Glow Dimmed by Economy," *New York Times,* March 8, 1991, p. A11; Rielly, ed., *American Public Opinion,* p. 17.

39. UN Economic Commission for Latin America, *Preliminary Overview, 1991,* p. 19.

40. Quoted in Thomas L. Friedman, "A Regional Group Moves to Isolate Haiti's New Junta," *The New York Times,* October 3, 1991, pp. A1, 6.

41. See Abraham F. Lowenthal, "Rediscovering Latin America," *Foreign Affairs* 69 (Fall 1990): 41.

6

THE CLINTON ADMINISTRATION: A TEST OF (POSTWAR) POLITICS

A November 30 [1993] remark [by President Bill Clinton] to the press—that the NAFTA expansion was "something I have long supported"—suggested that by repeating the concept so frequently, the president had come to deeply feel it.[1]

—RICHARD E. FEINBERG, NATIONAL SECURITY ADVISOR FOR LATIN AMERICA TO PRESIDENT CLINTON

In December 1991, the Soviet Union disappeared, depriving U.S. policymakers of the lodestar they had used for forty-five years to map their way across the international political landscape. The public adjusted to this transformation faster than most leaders, and in the first post–Cold War election, they altered one criterion they had used to judge the candidates. Suddenly, the foreign policy experience of George Bush, still aglow from his victory in the Persian Gulf, had become a liability, and the lack of diplomatic expertise of Bill Clinton became an asset. No longer concerned about the Soviet threat, the American public turned their attention to domestic problems, as they had after every war. The public suspected that George Bush was more concerned about the world's problems than their own. Bill Clinton read the shift in the national mood better and concentrated his campaign on the economy.

Bill Clinton, who had spent almost his entire adult life running for office, was an exceptionally skillful politician in the best and the worst sense of the term. He understood what the American people wanted, and he articulated their aspirations and concerns as effectively as anyone; yet by trimming his sails to public opinion, he also emitted a scent of opportunism. This did not mean, as some critics contended, that he was a slave of public opinion polls. He occasionally took positions or made decisions that he knew were correct but unpopular, notably on Bosnia and Haiti, but he shaped his argument and he tacked masterfully to keep the political wind at his back. This permitted him to reverse course in a moment, if he needed to do so, as he did on the Helms-Burton law on Cuba after Fidel Castro's air force shot down two civilian aircraft. But it also meant that he would scour the domestic agenda to find a new post–Cold War rationale for remaining engaged in the world. He tried, for example, to equate job creation with access to new markets, but that did not take as well as making war on illicit drugs.

The irony of Clinton's election in 1992 was that he won because of the economy and his domestic agenda, but no matter how hard he tried, he could not avoid tackling Bush's unfinished foreign policy agenda to Latin America, specifically, Haiti, NAFTA, and the Enterprise of the Americas Initiative. He stumbled before addressing each of these issues, but in the end he secured the approval of NAFTA by Congress; restored constitutional government to Haiti; and convened an unprecedented Summit of the Americas to pledge a Free Trade Area of the Americas (FTAA) by 2005.

Having achieved these three goals in two years, Clinton's administration paused and never quite got its engine started again, at least in Latin America. The capture of the Congress by a resurgent Republican Party and the failure to anticipate the Mexican peso crisis diverted Clinton's attention and undermined his ability to realize the Summit's goals. He did not take advantage of the opportunity presented by each challenge to construct an enduring and effective approach to the region. There did not seem to be any political incentive in doing that, and politics, after all, was the criterion on which his administration often made its choices and judged its results.

Completing the Bush Agenda

President Bush signed the North American Free Trade Agreement (NAFTA) in December 1992 and left the heavy lifting of gaining congressional approval to Clinton. Despite Secretary of State James A. Baker's promise in 1991 that the coup in Haiti would not stand, the generals were still there when Bush left office. Finally, despite promises to

Chile and the rest of Latin America about free trade agreements, Bush couldn't even persuade Congress to give him authority to negotiate such agreements. Clinton also had made his share of promises in the campaign, but most of those were in the area of domestic policy. If he had had a choice, Clinton would probably have preferred to postpone action on these issues indefinitely, or at least until he had completed his own agenda—closing the deficit and securing a health program—but he didn't have that luxury.

The challenge of Haiti was twofold: What should be done to prevent another wave of Haitian refugees, and how much effort should be invested to restore Jean-Bertrand Aristide to the office of the presidency? During the transition, Bush administration officials convinced Clinton that a new wave of refugees would sail to the United States unless he continued Bush's policies to prevent them. Although he had been very critical of Bush for sending back the refugees, Clinton announced in early January that he would continue the same policy. This was a signal of the importance that the refugee problem would play in the new administration's foreign policy calculations. At the same time, to placate the Black Caucus, who supported Aristide and were a vital constituency of the Democratic Party, he personally promised Aristide that he would return to Haiti. Clinton's promise was a recognition that he could not sustain a policy of returning Haitians without a definitive political solution to the Haitian crisis.

The promise to restore Aristide in Haiti proved easier said than done. The president supported UN sanctions and the efforts by UN envoy Dante Caputo to negotiate an agreement on Governor's Island on July 3, 1993. The agreement involved the lifting of sanctions; appointment of a new prime minister; amnesty for the military; the arrival of 1,300 U.S. and UN peacekeeping officers; and finally, the return of Aristide. On October 11, Haitian paramilitary thugs blocked the landing of U.S. troops aboard the *Harlan County;* fearing a repetition of the recent slaughter of American peacekeepers in Somalia, Clinton withdrew the ship. It took another year before the administration was prepared to back diplomatic efforts with a credible threat.

The cost of accomplishing that goal was perceived as so high that the president was tempted to put the issue aside. However, the congressional Black Caucus wouldn't let him. When Randall Robinson, the director of TransAfrica, began a hunger strike, the publicity finally forced the president to act. In July 1994, pressed by Washington, the UN Security Council passed a resolution calling on member states to use force to compel the Haitian military to accept Aristide's return. This was a watershed event in international relations: the first time that the UN Security Council had authorized the use of force for the purpose of restoring democracy to a member state. In August, preparations for an invasion began.

On September 15, in a national address, President Clinton declared that all diplomatic efforts had been exhausted, and he publicly warned the Haitian military leaders to leave power immediately. In fact, the U.S. government had stopped talking to the Haitian military six months before. Nonetheless, General Raoul Cedras, the commander of the Haitian military, had opened a dialogue during the previous week with former President Jimmy Carter, whom he had met during the 1990 elections. Carter informed President Clinton of the talks, and the president decided on Friday, September 16, to send Carter together with Senator Sam Nunn and General Colin Powell to try one last time to negotiate the departure of Haiti's military leaders by noon on Sunday.[2]

Within one hour of their first meeting with the Haitian military high command, the three statesmen had convinced the generals that an invasion would occur if the talks failed. The Haitian military wanted to preserve their institution and prevent Aristide from unleashing the masses against them. By 1:00 P.M. on Sunday, September 18, they agreed to allow the peaceful entry of U.S. forces into Haiti and the restoration of President Aristide. Details remained to be negotiated when Haitian General Philippe Biamby burst into the room with the news that the 82nd Airborne was being readied for attack, a fact not known to all the members of the Carter team. Biamby accused the Americans of deception and informed them he was taking Cedras to a secure area where they would prepare for the invasion.

It is hard to find a better example of the difference between a credible threat, which was essential to reach an agreement, and the actual movement of troops, which in this case and at this moment was counterproductive. Because the Carter team had conveyed a threat with credibility but without brandishing it, Cedras was ready to sign the agreement. After learning the attack was underway, he refused to sign or even to negotiate further.

To keep alive the chance for an agreement, Carter changed the venue of the talks from the Military Headquarters to the Presidential Palace, and he asked Cedras to accompany him. There, the de facto President

Emile Jonaissant agreed to sign the agreement. This then created problems for President Aristide, who was in Washington, and was reluctant to accept an agreement with people he viewed as illegitimate usurpers. With the U.S. Air Force halfway to Haiti, President Clinton finally ordered them recalled, and authorized Carter to sign the agreement on his behalf.

The president asked Carter, Nunn, and Powell to return to the White House immediately, and they asked me, their principal adviser, to remain to brief the U.S. ambassador and Pentagon officials, who had not participated in the negotiations, and to arrange meetings between Haitian and U.S. military officers. This proved to be extremely difficult because the Haitian generals went into hiding, and U.S. government officials in Port-au-Prince distrusted the Haitian generals and expected a double-cross like that which occurred when the *Harlan County* tried to land.

With less than two hours before touchdown by the U.S. military, I finally reached Cedras and arranged the crucial meetings that permitted U.S. forces to arrive without having to fire one shot. Twenty thousand U.S. troops disembarked without a single casualty or even one civilian hurt. There was no question that U.S. forces would have prevailed in an invasion, but because of the *Harlan County* incident, the Somalia experience, and the need to minimize U.S. casualties, the U.S. military had planned a ferocious assault that would have meant hundreds, perhaps thousands, of Haitian casualties, and inevitably, some American deaths. General Hugh Shelton, the commanding officer and later chairman of the Joint Chiefs, said that such an invasion would have engendered long-term bitterness among some Haitians, making it more difficult to secure order and build a democracy. General Cedras stepped down from power on October 12, and three days later, Aristide returned.

Before his inauguration, Clinton also met with Mexican President Carlos Salinas. The president-elect affirmed his commitment to NAFTA and promised he would expedite the completion of side agreements on labor and the environment.[3] But upon taking office, he decided to give highest priority to reducing the budget deficit, and when Congress approved that, his political advisers suggested a further postponement until after his health plan was approved.[4] The problem was that NAFTA mandated that it would take effect on January 1, 1994, so the administration could not delay any longer. Negotiations were completed on the side agreements quickly, and NAFTA was signed at the White House with the support of all the former presidents on September 14, 1993. Clinton then launched a full-court press to gain congressional approval.

The debate within the Democratic Party was more divisive than between the Democrats and the Republicans. The side agreements bought some support from moderate environmental groups, but none from the unions. The toughest battle was in the House of Representatives, but on November 17, the president won, 234–200. One hundred and thirty-two Republicans voted with the Democratic President, and only 102 Democrats. Three days later, the Senate approved NAFTA by a vote of 61 to 38. The president had his second victory (after the budget), and his first foreign/domestic policy accomplishment.

Like NAFTA, Haiti was transformed from an unwelcome problem into a success story, at least for the moment, but the process by which the administration made that journey was so messy and, at times, so accommodating to demands of pressure groups, that the president was denied the credit that he deserved.

The Summit and Other Pieces of the Hemispheric Agenda

NAFTA and Haiti were the main issues in inter-American relations, but hardly the only ones. Latin America hoped NAFTA would be the first U.S. free trade agreement in the area—not the last. Haiti's was the first democratic government in the Americas overthrown in the 1990s, but it was not the only one threatened. Peru's President Alberto Fujimori closed his Congress in 1992. A group of Venezuelan military officers attempted two coups. In Central America, every government except Costa Rica faced an embittered but strong military, and in the Andes, drug traffickers corrupted and terrorized weak democracies.

The administration was slow in making appointments and erratic in coordinating policy, and one result was that the rest of the U.S.–Latin American agenda was addressed at the middle levels of the bureaucracy in a highly compartmentalized way. This evoked complaints from some Latin leaders that the administration was ignoring the region,[5] and it led Senator Christopher Dodd, the chairman of the Subcommittee on Western Hemisphere Affairs, to call the administration's performance "amateur hour."[6]

In December 1993, still uncertain about what it would do about Haiti, the administration decided to build on its success with NAFTA. On a visit to Mexico, Vice President Al Gore proposed a Summit of all "democratically elected heads of state" of the Americas. It was a bold idea, but the administration was slow to follow up. It took a four-month-long lobbying campaign by Florida's politicians before the administration even decided to hold the Summit in Miami. Then, it waited until almost the eve of the Summit in December 1994 before deciding on its goals. That did not permit enough time to package the ideas into a coherent program or to build the relationships needed to give it momentum.[7]

The main domestic issue driving American foreign policy toward the region remained drugs. It sat at the intersection between domestic fears and foreign threats. Democrats and Republicans accused each other of not doing enough to keep drugs from America's children. The result was that while the overall government budget contracted, expenditures to fight drugs soared, and from Latin America's perspective, America's preoccupation with the drug war replaced its previous obsession with the Cold War.[8]

The Clinton administration's strategy contained all of the elements of its predecessors': eradication, crop substitution, cartel busting, and interdiction and, in the United States, education, treatment, and enforcement to reduce demand. Over time, it placed more stress on the demand side of the equation, but two-thirds of the expanded funding continued to be devoted to interdiction and enforcement.[9] The drug program appropriated an increasing share of a much reduced aid program to Latin America, and the drug program in Peru, Colombia, and Bolivia easily surpassed the aid program to all of Latin America.

By the 1990s, most Latin American governments had come to realize that drug trafficking was a more serious menace to their political and territorial integrity than it was to the United States. However, instead of the shared threat being a stimulus to a cooperative approach to the problem, Congress used the aid to mandate a new paternalism. The State Department was required by law to either certify that individual governments were cooperating or suspend aid. This created a demeaning process. Instead of building more mature relationships, the United States was compelled to grade Latin American governments each year, and they naturally resented it.

The Clinton administration's policy toward Central America was also shaped to a great degree by Congress, but unlike the widespread concern about drugs, a few members of Congress—mainly those who were still fighting the Cold War—influenced the policy. This approach was particularly tragic because the governments in the region were desperate to escape the Cold War demons that had ravaged their countries in the 1980s.

In Nicaragua, instead of encouraging national reconciliation, the State Department, under pressure from Congress, withheld aid in a manner that exacerbated divisions within the country and made resolution of problems, like those over property, more difficult. In response to newspaper reports of atrocities in El Salvador that had occurred at the beginning of the Reagan administration, Secretary of State Warren Christopher appointed a review panel, whose report was criticized by the *Miami Herald* as "disturbingly evasive."[10] Administration officials repeatedly denied information to Jennifer Harbury, an American lawyer, about her husband, a Guatemalan guerrilla, who had been captured by the Guatemalan military. In 1995, a Democratic congressman disclosed what the administration had withheld: A Guatemalan colonel was a paid agent of the Central Intelligence Agency when he was alleged to have been involved in the torture and death of Harbury's husband and in the obstruction of an investigation into the murder of an American citizen in Guatemala in 1990. When Guatemalan President Jorge Diaz Serrano shut down Congress in May 1993, the Clinton administration suspended aid, causing the military to abandon Serrano and facilitate a transition to another civilian president. The administration also supported the UN-sponsored peacemaking efforts with the guerrillas.

The administration delayed in making a decision on its goals for the Summit because it wanted first to secure congressional approval of three trade-related goals: fast-track negotiating authority to extend NAFTA, an interim trade program that would permit quasi-parity to NAFTA for the small Caribbean Basin countries, and the GATT agreement. By October 1994, the administration had given up on its first two goals, and the vote on GATT was postponed until after the November congressional election. That election brought the Republicans to power and demoralized the Clinton administration, which failed to recognize—until the last moment—the historic moment presented by the Summit. It occurred at a time of convergence in the hemisphere of two phenomena, democracy and freer trade.[11] A shared perspective among the thirty-four heads of state, all of whom were civilians and had won competitive elections, was possible.

Of course, NAFTA and the Summit were born in original sin in the sense that a founding member of the democratic community—Mexico—was not democratic. By the August 1994 presidential elections, Salinas had dispensed with the crude methods for rigging the election, but numerous problems remained, most due to the PRI's use of state resources for its candidates and the lack of autonomy of the Federal Election Institute (IFE). The United States downplayed these electoral problems and mistakenly left the impression that it endorsed the PRI candidate.[12] The U.S. ambassador described the election as "a major advance for democracy in Mexico." A *New York Times* editorial described it, more accurately, as "the least tainted election in decades."[13]

South America made more progress. In the southern cone, Brazil and Argentina had been rivals almost since their independence, but the civilian presidents realized that only the military would benefit if they failed to cooperate. These two South American giants ended their nuclear weapons programs, reduced their defense expenditures, and, in 1991, joined with Uruguay and Paraguay to establish a Common Market, Mercosur. Four years later, Mercosur made 90 percent of their trade duty-free. On the same date, the Andean Pact countries established common external tariffs, ranging from 5 to 20 percent, and the Group of Three—Mexico, Venezuela, and Colombia—pledged to eliminate all tariffs and quotas within a decade. From 1991 to the Summit, the region reduced its trade barriers by 80 percent.[14] Regional integration was proceeding at a fast pace. Each country had learned the benefits of freer trade and was prepared to accelerate the process and widen it.

At the Summit in Miami, the presidents agreed to a "Declaration of Principles" and "A Plan of Action"—fulsome statements of solidarity on behalf of democracy, prosperity by economic integration and free trade, and sustainable development through environmental protection. Apart from the rhetoric and the many committees established to discuss a wide agenda, one goal stood out: The presidents agreed to conclude negotiations on a Free Trade Area of the Americas no later than 2005. That single goal made the Summit a success.

The Rise of the Republicans and the Fall of the Peso

For the Clinton administration and much of Latin America, the Miami Summit was a moment of sunshine between two ominous clouds—the Republican takeover of Congress, which jeopardized Clinton's domestic and international programs, and the collapse of the Mexican peso, which called into question the premise of the Summit, that Latin America was on a high-speed trajectory to the first world.

The Republicans won control of Congress with a clear, but exclusively domestic, agenda: the "Contract with America." If the first shoe to fall after the Cold War was the election of a domestic President Clinton, then the second thud was the Republican takeover of Congress in November 1994. The victory was so one-sided that the Republicans immediately assumed that Clinton would be a one-term president, and four Republican senators began running for his office. The country's business was put on hold.

The agenda of the congressional Republicans was to reduce taxes and government. On the international side of the ledger, they favored increased expenditures for defense and less for foreign aid and international organizations. They were deeply suspicious of treaties and any international obligations that constrained America's freedom of action. The vast majority of Republicans were in favor of free trade without any conditions, but there was an influential group, led by Senator Jesse Helms, the new chairman of the Senate Foreign Relations Committee, who opposed free trade and any financial support for Mexico. Helms viewed the Cold War as a continuing struggle, and although he opposed foreign aid, he approved some aid so that he could withhold it if a government was unresponsive to his concerns.

Most Republicans opposed President Clinton's strategy to restore President Aristide to Haiti, largely because they viewed Aristide as an unstable, anti-American leftist. After Aristide's return, the Republicans were averse to supporting him. This became moot since subsequent elections in Haiti for the Parliament and president in 1995 were flawed, and the new Parliament would not approve the government's budget or other agreements that would have permitted the delivery of more than $500 million in promised development aid. In the meantime, UN and subsequently Canadian forces kept law and order and an artificial lid on Haiti's inequitable social cauldron. Both Haiti and U.S. policy were stalemated.

The other Caribbean country whose destiny was shaped by a partisan struggle in the United States was Cuba. The Clinton administration was acutely sensitive to the concerns of the Cuban-American community, but one preoccupation trumped that: the fear of another Mariel boatlift. Clinton attributed his loss for reelection as governor of Arkansas in 1980 to the relocation of Mariel refugees to Fort Chafee.

Faced with signs of unrest in August 1994, the Castro government allowed more than thirty thousand people to flee the country on rafts. The White House proposed a migration agreement with Cuba that included increased legal Cuban emigration to the United States and a halt by the U.S. Coast Guard of Cuban rafters, who would be sent to another country or to the U.S. base at Guantanamo, Cuba. To assuage the Cuban-

American community, which was upset that the United States would send Cubans home, the president tightened sanctions, restricted travel, and reduced remittances.

The September 1994 migration agreement proved unsustainable. Only one country—Panama—came forward to accept Cuban refugees, and six months later, after the Cubans rioted and the United States failed to demonstrate its gratitude, the Panamanians decided to return the fifteen thousand refugees to Guantanamo. The U.S. military in Guantanamo feared riots if there were no permanent solution. The problem was that if the Cubans in Guantanamo were sent to the United States, that would violate the September accord with Cuba and stimulate a new flow of refugees. Therefore, the United States proposed to Cuba that the Guantanamo-based refugees be sent to the United States, but to prevent a new exodus, the U.S. would intercept at sea and return to Cuba any future migrants. In other words, Cubans fleeing the island were no longer automatically considered refugees; they would be returned to Cuba if they were stopped at sea and failed to prove they had a well-founded fear of persecution. This secret agreement was announced on May 6, 1995, and it enraged the Cuban-American community. The Clinton administration was saved by a public opinion survey from the *Miami Herald* on May 15 that showed the majority of Florida residents supportive of the president's decision restricting immigration. The Clinton administration had stumbled upon a Democratic answer to California's anti-immigrant Proposition 187, which passed in November 1994 by a 3–2 margin.[15]

The Cuban-American National Foundation retaliated by persuading Senator Jesse Helms to introduce a bill with Congressman Dan Burton of Indiana to try to topple Fidel Castro by tightening the embargo, discouraging foreign investment, and precluding meaningful negotiations until Fidel Castro was removed from power. The bill would permit Cubans, who had become U.S. citizens, to sue in U.S. courts anyone who was using their property. Helms had already applied this standard to Nicaragua, even though it was judged contrary to international law. The administration strenuously opposed the bill until the Cuban Air Force shot down two Cuban-American aircraft for violating Cuban airspace. The president then signed it on March 12, 1996, the day of the Florida presidential primary.

The promise of the Summit of the Americas to negotiate an FTAA was confounded by the collapse of the Mexican peso, just ten days after Mexico's model was praised at the Miami Summit. On December 20, 1994, Mexico devalued the peso by about 13 percent and then let it float. It sank, as capital fled the country. Mexican President Ernesto Zedillo had taken office just three weeks before, and his team fumbled trying to put together an economic plan to reattract confidence and capital.

It was the end of the best and the worst of years for Mexico. The year began with NAFTA and the attack by a guerrilla group—the Zapatistas—in the poor southern province of Chiapas. It was also an election year in which the presidential candidate of the PRI was assassinated together with the secretary general of the party. Trade expanded by more than 20 percent, but capital fled. To retrieve it, the Mexican government offered "teso-bonos": bonds denominated in dollars at very high interest rates. Ernesto Zedillo, Salinas's second choice, won the presidential election and went to Washington on November 23, 1994, to seek Clinton's help. He found the president disoriented by the results of the congressional elections. Zedillo needed help and a coordinated approach to the weak peso, but instead Clinton publicly "expressed confidence in Mexico's economic prospects."[16]

Within a month, the peso collapsed together with the Mexican government's credibility. There were many warning signs. Subsequent investigations by Congress showed that the administration was aware of the problem but did not approach Mexico with ideas on how to address it.[17] The first reaction by the director of the Clinton administration's National Economic Council, Robert Rubin, who had just been named secretary of the treasury, was "to let the market sort it out."[18] Mexico assembled an economic plan, and on January 12, the Clinton administration announced its support with an endorsement by the new Speaker Newt Gingrich and the new Majority Leader Bob Dole. Their party followers rebelled, and the two of them deserted the president. On January 31, President Clinton announced a larger, $53 billion package that included $20 billion from the U.S. Exchange Stabilization Fund. The Republican leaders were content for the president to use that fund by Executive Order rather than bring it to a vote. Unfortunately, another month would pass before the agreement was signed, and by that time, Mexican reserves had declined so much that the government had to accept an unusually austere economic program. The result was massive unemployment, a catastrophic number of bankruptcies, a 7 percent decline in Mexico's gross domestic product for 1995 (the worst drop since 1932), a maimed presidency, and a discredited NAFTA.[19]

NAFTA had not failed. The problem was that NAFTA was only a trade agreement; it was inadequate to the challenge of integrating three such divergent economies. Because of NAFTA, Mexico attracted large movements of short-term capital, but there was no coordinating mechanism to monitor or cope with the fast exit of such capital.

The Mexican crisis rippled through Latin America as foreign capital fled the region. Decisive actions by Argentina's finance minister prevented a major devaluation, but the economy declined 3 percent. Fernando Henrique Cardoso, Brazil's brilliant new president, kept inflation under control and continued to restructure the economy, but the peso crisis was a signal that Latin America had not escaped the volatility of the past, and that the United States had no greater power of foreseeing such crises than the other nations.

Second Term Stalemate

Bill Clinton won reelection in November 1996, easily beating Bob Dole, even in Florida, where his decision to sign the Helms-Burton law on Cuba apparently earned him enough Cuban-American votes to secure the state. In his second inaugural address, Clinton spoke of building bridges to the twenty-first century, but he spent most of his second term protecting his back, fighting personal battles at home and ancient struggles abroad. An angry Republican majority in Congress transformed Clinton's humiliating personal scandal into the nation's first impeachment trial since Andrew Johnson's. In addition to fighting for his political survival, he was compelled to cope with the crises in former Yugoslavia, Russia, and China, three countries trying to locate the exit from the Cold War. Latin America was largely shunted aside, and the promise of the Free Trade Area of the Americas went unfilled.

This is not to say that the region went out of business in the last years of the twentieth century, only that the United States did not play the leadership role that it could have on the positive agenda of democracy and free trade. Instead, the United States pursued a transnational police agenda against drugs, money laundering, corruption, and illegal migration, while Latin America grappled with difficult economic and democratic reforms.

The economic reforms that had begun in the aftermath of the debt crises of the early 1980s continued, albeit at a slower pace, as old industries had trouble adjusting to new international competition. This was one reason why there was no progress on trade negotiations after the Miami Summit. A second reason was that Brazil, with about half of South

America's population and gross product, wanted time to consolidate Mercosur and extend it to the other countries of South America. It hoped to establish a South American Free Trade Agreement (SAFTA) that would be able to negotiate with NAFTA on the basis of greater equality. A third reason was that Mexico and Canada were not eager to share their exclusive access to the world's largest market. But the fourth reason is pivotal: The U.S. president could not obtain fast-track negotiating authority from Congress, and without that, no government wanted to make a commitment. So the question is, why, at the peak of its power, would the United States not be able to lead, particularly as the objective was to persuade Latin America to open its market as wide as that of the United States?

There are several answers to the question. Starting at the tactical level, Clinton waited too long, until September 1997, before introducing the bill. He did not prepare as he had done for NAFTA, and the business community did not throw its weight behind the proposal. Second, the two political parties had polarized on trade issues since the 1994 elections. The Republicans had accepted side agreements on labor and the environment in 1993, but they had shifted to the right in 1994, and by 1997, they insisted on a more laissez-faire trade negotiation. At the same time, the Democrats had become more dependent on the labor unions, and therefore more resistant to freer trade. Clinton could have brokered an agreement with the Democrats and tried to secure enough Republicans to pass a bill with provisions for labor and the environment, but he chose a "Republican strategy" instead: to seek a clean bill. After two months of jockeying, he had alienated the Democrats, and the Republicans deserted him. At a third level, the American people were still digesting two large trade agreements—NAFTA and the WTO—and were not ready for another. Even U.S. multinational corporations, which had always been the gladiators for free trade, did not step into the arena. As a result, for the first time in a century, a president failed to obtain authority to negotiate trade agreements, and without a U.S. commitment, Latin America did not want to bargain.

The thirty-four democratic presidents convened in April 1998 for the second Summit of the Americas. As both Presidents Bush and Clinton had promised Chile that it would be the first country in line for a free trade agreement, it was particularly embarrassing that the site was Chile's capital, Santiago. All the leaders understood that serious negotiations on trade were not possible until the United States had fast-track authority, but they decided to launch the FTAA anyway and established eleven groups to begin work on different elements of the agreement. In part to deflect attention from trade, the leaders placed "education" as the premier issue on an agenda that read like a laundry list of every imaginable subject. Although education was of undoubted importance, most governments, including the United States, addressed it as a local or state responsibility, with less involvement at the national level and none at the hemispheric level.

Between NAFTA and the subregional integration agreements in South America were a string of twenty-three vulnerable and smaller economies in the Caribbean and Central America. Although the region as a whole was a larger market for U.S. exports than Brazil or France, it could no longer compete with Mexico because of its preferential access to the U.S. market. The region asked for "NAFTA Parity," and Clinton agreed, but it took five years of lobbying Congress before he could sign the U.S.-Caribbean Trade Partnership Act on May 18, 2000. The law fell short of "parity," but it relaxed import restrictions on selected products, such as textiles and apparel.[20] This was an important step for these countries, but securing congressional support proved so difficult that the administration could not fit this piece of the trade puzzle into a broader geo-economic strategy, even if it had conceived one.

In the final years of the twentieth century, democracy did not retreat in the Americas, but it did not advance, and it was under siege in some countries. The idea of "no reelection" had been Mexico's contribution to political stability in the Americas, and it was based on a simple premise: The best way to ensure a free and fair election is to prevent an incumbent from running. Therefore, when incumbent presidents in Argentina, Brazil, and Peru tried to revise their countries' constitutions to permit reelection, this caused considerable anxiety. In the end, all three succeeded in winning reelection without serious dispute. Democracy was stronger in Argentina and Brazil, but Alberto Fujimori of Peru trespassed across the boundaries of accountability when he fired the Supreme Court justices who said the new reform could not tolerate a third term.

The pleasant surprise of the 1990s was the progress of democracy in Central America, which had preoccupied the United States during the previous decade. In the October 1996 presidential election in Nicaragua, the Sandinistas were beaten by the conservative mayor of Managua, Arnoldo Aleman, and yet both sides reconciled. In Guatemala, on December 29, 1996, the government signed an agreement with the guerrillas, ending the longest civil war in Central America—a war that had claimed 100,000 lives. The revolutionaries were to be incorporated into the political system much as they had been in El Salvador, where former guerrilla leaders won key municipalities and second place in the national elections behind their formal enemies, ARENA. In November 1998, when Hurricane Mitch wreaked havoc throughout Central America, the United States provided $600 million in aid, and the democratic governments not only survived, they used the foreign aid effectively.

The only country that made more progress toward democracy was Mexico. During the 1990s, the opposition pressed for, and the government grudgingly conceded, the need to have an independent and professional Federal Election Institute (IFE). By the 2000 presidential election, the candidates of the three major parties expressed their confidence in IFE and declared that they would accept the results if the voting was secret and the count was fair. On July 2, Vicente Fox, the presidential candidate of the Alliance for Change and the National Action Party (PAN), defeated Francisco Labastida, the candidate of the PRI, by a margin of 42.5 to 36.1 percent. President Ernesto Zedillo orchestrated the announcement of the results by the director of the IFE and the concession speech by the PRI candidate. An historic transition occurred.

In the late 1990s, the Central American disease of political instability seemed to migrate south to the Andean countries. Ecuador was the most unstable. The legislature first dismissed one elected president, Abdala Bucaram, in February 1997, and nearly three years later they pasted a patina of respectability on a military coup against President Jamil Mahuad by elevating the vice president. Nearby in Venezuela, on December 6, 1998, the people elected Colonel Hugo Chavez, the leader of the military coup in 1992, as president. His principal priorities were to change the constitution, shut down the old political parties and institutions, and involve the military in political life. A high oil price in 1999 and 2000 made it possible for him to achieve these goals. In Bolivia, Hugo Banzer, a military dictator of the 1970s, became a moderate politician two decades later and won election as president in August 1997.

The Andean country with the most serious problems in the 1990s was Colombia, which also had the longest history of democracy. The government faced a three-sided war against narco-traffickers, who supplied about 80 percent of the cocaine used in the United States; two long-standing guerrilla groups, the FARC and ELN; and a plague of corruption and violence, exacerbated by brutal paramilitary forces. The election of Ernesto Samper in 1994 amid reports that he had received campaign contributions from drug lords caused the United States to freeze relations, and the result was that all three wars grew worse. In 1998, Andres Pastrana was elected president, and the United States was almost as desperate to come to his support as he was to seek help. Pastrana developed a $7.3 billion "Plan Colombia," and the United States pledged its support, mostly in military aid and equipment. This occasioned a heated debate in Congress as to whether the United States was about to embark on a "new Vietnam," a wholly implausible analogy, but one that still could raise the temperature of a debate. In the end, Congress approved $1.3 billion in aid for a two-year period with stringent human rights conditions, and the president signed the law on July 13, 2000.

The only country in the hemisphere that made less democratic progress than Haiti was its communist neighbor, Cuba. Castro fully exploited the Helms-Burton bill to win overwhelming majorities in the United Nations each year, condemning the law. He permitted some economic reforms that allowed food to reach the market, and he encouraged an enclave tourist industry. After the death of Jorge Mas Canosa, the leader of the Cuban American National Foundation, in late 1997, the community's power fragmented and waned, and Clinton used the opportunity of Pope John Paul II's visit in January 1998 to relax some travel restrictions and permit more remittances, which soon exceeded U.S. aid to all of Latin America. Castro responded as he had in the past—by arresting anyone who questioned his authority. United States policy remained as stalemated as Cuba.

The problem was that Clinton's strategy was fundamentally flawed. In a revealing comment, Clinton acknowledged that "the hardest-line people in Miami are basically responsible for the policy." Clinton believed that "the ball is in Cuba's court. . . . The United States will attempt to work out an accommodation with Cuba in which as they become more open, we will take more forward-looking steps to reach out to them. If they close up, we will close up."[21] Castro understood, as Clinton did not, that an open relationship was dangerous to an authoritarian government, and so when the United States opened, he closed.

The democratization of the region permitted some tentative steps toward resolving long-standing territorial disputes. The boundary dispute between Ecuador and Peru had erupted into war in January 1995, but its neighbors and the United States mediated and helped the two sides reach agreement on October 26, 1998. Chile and Argentina resolved all twenty-four territorial disputes between them.[22] A skirmish between Nicaragua and Honduras over some islands also led to an effort to resolve this long-standing dispute. These are actually just a few of the many disputes that remain from colonial days. Democracy has made their resolution possible but not automatic.

Democracy has also encouraged reductions in the size of some Latin American governments' armed forces and defense expenditures, but again, the absence of an agreement to restrain arms purchases may mean this trend could change. On leaving power in 1989, General Augusto Pinochet of Chile compelled the civilian government to accept measures that would assure increased resources for Chile's military. The air force sought bids for supersonic aircraft from France, Sweden, or the United States, and U.S. defense contractors did not want to lose that opportunity. They persuaded the U.S. government in August 1997 to revise a twenty-year policy of not selling advanced supersonic aircraft to the region. The civilian presidents in Argentina and Brazil feared that expensive arms purchases by Chile would lead their armed forces to put pressure on them to follow suit. The arms race was postponed by an unlikely set of dynamics beginning with the Asian financial crisis, which reduced the price of commodities, including copper, on which Chile's defense purchases relied. The final ironic twist on this episode was the arrest of Pinochet in England in October 1998 for the crimes he had committed after seizing power in 1973. His seventeen-month incarceration, and the election of Socialist Ricardo Lagos as president further weakened the military position.

The agenda that preoccupied the United States most in the second term of the Clinton administration was a transnational police agenda that centered on drug trafficking but included problems of money laundering, corruption, illegal arms trafficking, and undocumented migration. In some ways, this agenda could be considered the dark side of integration. As barriers to the legitimate movement of goods, capital, and people declined, the possibilities for illegitimate traffic naturally increased. The U.S. government was predisposed to address these problems in the hemisphere unilaterally, and this offended many neighbors. In 1990, in Mexico, U.S. agents kidnapped a Mexican who was accused of being involved in the torture of a DEA agent. That person, Humberto Alvarez Machain, was exonerated by a U.S. judge in 1993 for lack of evidence. After promising not to repeat such an intervention, American customs agents lured scores of mid-level Mexican bankers into the

United States through a "sting" operation, named Casablanca, in May 1998, and arrested them on money laundering charges. The Mexican government was irate. In the Caribbean, the United States pressured the governments to accept "ship-rider agreements" that permitted U.S. ships to enter the territorial waters of these countries without bothering to seek permission in order to pursue alleged drug traffickers.[23]

Perhaps the most difficult policy for Latin American governments to accept was the annual certification by the State Department of countries based on whether they cooperate with the U.S. on stopping drug trafficking. On the one hand, the U.S. government claimed it wanted a partnership, and on the other, it acted unilaterally. As Latin resentment increased, the United States agreed to establish a mechanism in the OAS to review the war on drugs on a multilateral basis, but the annual certification process remained.

Since 1990, funding for drug programs has increased dramatically, but there has been no reduction in the number of hard-core drug users in the United States.[24] The war was successful in reducing coca crops in Bolivia and Peru, but there was a corresponding increase in Colombia. This pattern is an old one: Individual producer or transit countries can be effective in reducing drug flows, but as long as the demand in the United States for illegal drugs does not change, other producers will replace the ones who are eliminated. President Clinton's appointment of General Barry McCaffrey as director of the White House Office of National Drug Control Policy was a deft political move, and McCaffrey is a very effective leader, but the overall policy message was ironic. The two most visible and important Latin American policymakers in the Clinton administration were McCaffrey and General Charles Wilhelm, the head of Southern Command—both military leaders, whose focus was drugs. The drug issue was the administration's highest priority in the region, but it not only failed to reduce drug trafficking; it pursued that goal in a way that made it more, not less, difficult to achieve a true partnership.

The Postwar Political Template and the Clinton Paradox

Bill Clinton was the first U.S. president to take office after the Cold War, and he moved to the rhythm of a postwar era. The anticommunist landmarks that had guided his predecessors across a treacherous international political landscape were no longer of use. The compass bequeathed to him by the American electorate compelled him to look toward domestic concerns, including the fiscal deficit, crime, drugs, and health care. Secretary of State Warren Christopher's role was to counsel the president on how to avoid mistakes or foreign commitments. Latin America was among Christopher's lowest priorities. He only visited South America in February 1996 after being criticized for visiting Syria seventeen times and the region not once.[25]

Christopher's successor, Madeleine Albright, along with National Security Advisor Sandy Berger and Secretary of Defense William Cohen, represented the most politically attuned security team ever assembled by a president, and together with the most political of presidents, they explored ways to make America's international interests resonate for a largely uninterested public. Clinton talked of the connection between trade and jobs, between weapons of mass destruction in Iraq and security in Oklahoma, between drug addiction in our inner cities and the crisis in Colombia. But despite his eloquence, he never found the right notes, nor could he play them in a way that moved the country.

In the hemisphere, the Clinton administration inherited two problems, Haiti and NAFTA. At the end of agonizing journeys, the president made the tough decisions to use force to restore Aristide in Haiti and to launch a full-court political press to secure the approval of NAFTA. He followed up both initiatives with a Summit of the Americas, which set a hemispheric goal of free trade by the year 2005. These, together with his rescue package for Mexico, were significant achievements on issues that were not popular. In a sense, these accomplishments represented the completion of both his predecessor's agenda and his own. After that, the administration seemed to tread water—failing to get the authority to negotiate the FTAA, failing to organize a forward-looking coalition of countries to preempt the democratic challenges in the Andes, and failing to shore up weak reeds like Haiti or advance democracy's promise in Cuba.

As a result, the administration's overall policy toward the Americas seemed less, not more, than the sum of these parts. The President made wise and sometimes politically courageous decisions, but he received little credit for them. Indeed, he was frequently criticized for being excessively responsive to interest groups and captive to public opinion surveys. What accounts for this paradox?

The answer lies not in the president's achievements but in the journey—the process—before and after the decisions. The administration initially treated NAFTA and Haiti as distinct problems rather than as opportunities to grasp a "regionalist option" or construct a democratic community or merge them into a broader strategic framework. Richard Feinberg, Clinton's first national security advisor for Latin America, wrote that even the trade decisions were each made in an ad hoc manner: "The decisions on Chilean accession and NAFTA-parity had occurred in isolation from any broader strategic framework. Rather, they were made incrementally and in response to particular political pressures and situational meetings with foreign officials."[26] Similarly, mid-level groups in the administration addressed the rest of the hemispheric agenda—drugs, immigration, Central America, and Cuba—without relating each issue to the others or to a hemispheric strategy.

Ironically, the mistake-avoidance strategy that typified the State Department's approach may have sapped more of the president's time and capital than would have been the case had he either moved decisively at the beginning or fashioned a longer-term strategy, as Franklin D. Roosevelt had done. Within one year of America's entry into World War II, Franklin Roosevelt began to prepare for the shift in the public mood that he expected when the war would end. He designed international institutions and forged a bipartisan consensus to keep America engaged globally despite the desire to avoid entangling alliances. Instead of formulating a similar foreign policy to counter the swing in mood in the post-Cold War era, Clinton administration officials argued that "containment" was not discovered in a day; it was a product of trial and error. There is some truth to that, but FDR's strategy locked the United States into an internationalist world before the Cold War.

On the issues of Central America and Cuba, U.S. policy seemed driven by the most determined interest group—whether in Congress or in Miami—using a political template. If a crisis did not engage the public or attract the media or an interest group, the administration did not pay much attention to it. It could not afford, however, to ignore intense objections from a core constituency group, such as the congressional Black Caucus on Haiti or labor unions on trade. It was wary of antagonizing a Florida ethnic group, like the Cuban-Americans, unless a broader national domestic interest, for example, on stopping refugees, compelled a recalculation.

What was missing in these political judgments was some picture of what the world should look like and how U.S. policy should try to influence its shape. In the Americas, the United States did not face a problem, but rather an unprecedented opportunity: to create a community of democratic, market-oriented neighbors. A strategic approach would have mobilized prestigious U.S. statesmen to try to persuade Latin leaders, who wanted NAFTA extended but did not much care for Haiti, of the need to address the two sides of the Americas' challenge. Such an approach could have been mutually reinforcing: If Congress saw Latin America as cooperative on Haiti, it might have been more sympathetic to extending NAFTA. Assembling such a package would not have been easy and could not emerge by sending cautious mid-level officials to the region. It would have required detailed plans on economic integration and democratic reinforcement.

The State Department was on the margins of both negotiations. If one were to believe the rhetoric about the centrality of NAFTA to its policy, then the Department of State should have redesigned itself not to preempt Jesse Helms but to ensure that each interest would be woven into a thick fabric representing the entire nation. The administration did not pursue a strategic approach because the motives driving its policy were domestic and compartmentalized: interests and interest groups; the fear of refugees, drugs, and terrorism; and the desire to please groups of "hyphenated" Americans.

The geo-politics were never more propitious. The democratic transformation of Argentina and Brazil permitted the two rivals to become partners, and both sought a cooperative relationship with the United States. Argentina undertook UN peacekeeping missions—an opportunity to employ their military constructively and build new bonds with the United States. But instead of building on this opportunity, Congress and the president could not find a compromise to advance free trade, and the middle levels of the U.S. government gave disproportionate attention to peripheral issues such as intellectual property rights in Argentina and the drug issue in Brazil, both of which drove leaders away from a unifying strategy, not toward one.

The Summit provided the vehicle to pursue an Americas strategy that was broader than these two relationships and as full as the inter-American agenda. Unfortunately, the administration wasted the better part of a year before it began to consult with Latin America. By the time that the Summit was held in December 1994, the attention of the American people had shifted, the Republicans had captured Congress, and the regional spillover of the peso crisis was about to spoil the party. The decision to hold the Summit in Miami made political sense given the intensity of the community's interest and commerce in the region, but it invited a public focus on the one head of state who was not there, Fidel Castro, rather than on the thirty-four who were. Moreover, the press did not fathom the significance of the event. This was even truer of the Second Summit in Santiago in 1998.

President Clinton recognized the importance of the summits, and in the course of discovering that his domestic agenda was shared by his colleagues, he began to articulate the overarching concept of an Americas policy. But after 1994, he could not deliver, and he almost seemed to lose interest. The opportunity to fill in the outline of a democratic community drawn so graphically by the president passed.

The Clinton administration's second term was full of missed opportunities. The promise of the FTAA was unfilled because the president mishandled the request for fast-track negotiating authority. The administration's drug control policy was its highest priority; because it was managed by two generals, it sent a signal that no interest—not even democracy—was more important, and that the negative, transnational crime agenda trumped the positive agenda of trade and democracy.

The United States and Latin America defended democracy in several instances but failed to forge a consensus on a proactive strategy. The consequences were evident at the OAS General Assembly in Windsor, Canada, in June 2000. The foreign ministers were divided on what to do about the election fraud in Peru. Instead of demanding a new election, the OAS sent a high-level mission to promote negotiations with the opposition. They failed to make progress until a secret videotape was released of Vladimiro Montesinos, the head of intelligence, bribing an opposition legislator to support Fujimori. This led to a firestorm of protest, and on September 16, 2000, Fujimori announced new elections for president and said that he would not run.

The U.S. government failed to negotiate an agreement to limit arms purchases in the region, and although it took a few tentative steps toward a multilateral approach on drugs, it did not seek to repeal the annual certification process. The symbol of the administration's diminished interest was the reluctance on the part of the president or the secretary of state to attend the concluding ceremonies transferring authority over the Canal to Panama on the last day of the century. The Mexican president, the king of Spain, and former president Jimmy Carter attended, but U.S. government leaders chose not to be party to an event that symbolized the new partnership between North and South America.

Still, President Clinton's choices on NAFTA, Haiti, the Miami Summit, and the peso crisis were the defining ones of his policy toward the Americas. NAFTA is a revolutionary event that will reshape North America, and if the model is extended and deepened, it will redefine the hemisphere. United States leadership in securing UN and OAS decisions to restore Aristide to power was also pivotal, although more as a collective statement on democracy by the Americas than what it did for Haiti.

In some ways, Clinton's greatest challenge in international affairs was to find the language that would keep America engaged after the threat diminished; Americans wanted a government that would concentrate on domestic affairs. This was the supreme test of a politician who was also commander-in-chief. In the end, one of the most articulate presidents did not find the words to persuade the American people that their destiny depended on internationalism. Nor did he find the formula that could bring the Democratic Party and its most important constituent group, labor unions, to accept a new trade policy. Clinton made positive decisions at the beginning of his term on U.S. policy toward Latin America, and he made few very serious mistakes. In failing to grasp the opportunities that were available to build a hemispheric democratic community, Clinton may have passed the test of politics, but he failed the test of a statesman.

Notes

1. Richard E. Feinberg, *Summitry in the Americas: A Progress Report* (Washington, D.C.: Institute for International Economics, 1997), p. 66.

2. I was an adviser to the Carter team and have described parts of the negotiations in "A Short History of Haiti," *Foreign Service Journal* (November 1995): 20–25; and "More and Less Than It Seemed: The Carter-Nunn-Powell Mediation in Haiti, 1994," in Chester A. Crocker, Fen O. Hampson, and Pamela Aall, eds., *Herding Cats: Multiparty Mediation in a Complex World* (Washington, D.C.: U.S. Institute of Peace Press, 1999), pp. 507–525.

3. Thomas L. Friedman, "Clinton Says U.S. Will Act Fast on Trade Pact If . . . ," *The New York Times*, January 9, 1993, p. 8.

4. Bob Woodward, *The Agenda: Inside the Clinton White House* (New York: Simon & Schuster, 1994), pp. 55, 314–319.

5. The Venezuelan president said: "What troubles me is that there doesn't seem to be a Clinton administration policy toward Latin America. We obviously maintain a friendly, favorable expectation that President Clinton will maintain

the tradition [of support for Latin America] of other Democratic presidents such as Kennedy and Carter. But we're not seeing an interest in Latin America." Cited in Andres Oppenheimer, "Latins Fear Region Will Be Ignored," *Miami Herald*, April 26, 1993, p. 10.

6. Dodd was upset at the slow pace of appointments and the "mixed messages" on NAFTA, with the budget director calling it "dead" and the treasury secretary saying it remained a high priority. See Christopher Marquis, "Latin Policy: 'Less of the Same,'" *Miami Herald*, May 10, 1993, pp. 1, 7.

7. For the best analysis of the weakness, delay, and strengths of the Summit process and outcome, see Richard E. Feinberg, *Summitry in the Americas: A Progress Report* (Washington, D.C.: Institute for International Economics, 1997); and Peter Hakim and Michael Shifter, "U.S.-Latin American Relations: To the Summit and Beyond," *Current History* 94, no. 589 (February 1995): 49–53.

8. Bernardo Vega, *The Second Cold War: U.S. and Caribbean Law and Order* (Washington, D.C.: Center for Strategic and International Studies, Policy Papers on the Americas, Vol. IX, Study 7, September 9, 1998). Vega was the Dominican Republic's ambassador to Washington.

9. Abraham F. Lowenthal, "United States-Latin American Relations at the Century's Turn: Managing the 'Intermestic' Agenda," in Albert Fishlow and James Jones, eds., *The United States and the Americas* (New York: W. W. Norton, 1999), p. 120.

10. *Report of the Secretary of State's Panel on El Salvador*, July 1983, pp. 3, 10. "Half Truths of Whole Cloth: U.S.'s Salvador Report," *Miami Herald*, July 17, 1993.

11. For the development of the idea of a convergence of democratic and market values in the context of a "hemispheric democratic community," see Robert A. Pastor, *Whirlpool: U.S. Foreign Policy Toward Latin America and the Caribbean* (Princeton: Princeton University Press, 1992), especially chap. 15, "Crossing the Sovereign Divide: The Path Toward a Hemispheric Community;" and *Convergence and Community: The Americas in 1993*, A Report of the Inter-American Dialogue (Washington. D.C.: Aspen Institute, 1992).

12. This was due to an ill-advised congratulatory statement by the White House spokesperson on the nomination of the PRI candidate. It was strongly criticized by leaders from the main opposition parties. See "PAN, PRD Protest U.S. Spokesperson Remarks," *FBIS*, 3 December 1993, p. 15.

13. The ambassador's comment was in *The New York Times*, August 25, 1994; the editorial was "Mexico's Political Crisis," *The New York Times*, October 11, 1995. For a detailed analysis of the election, see Council of Freely Elected Heads of Government, Carter Center of Emory University, *The August 21, 1994 Mexican National Elections: Fourth Report* (January 1995).

14. James Brooke, "On Eve of Miami Summit Talks, U.S. Comes Under Fire," *The New York Times*, December 9, 1995, p. A4.

15. John Lantigua and Stephen Doig, "Limit Cuban Immigration: Yes, Most in Survey Agree," *Miami Herald*, May 15, 1995, pp. 1, 16. For a good analysis of why Clinton risked a little by alienating the Republican Cuban-American vote, but gained a lot by "sending a big message on immigration to other important states such as California," see William Schneider, "Immigration Politics Strikes Again," *National Journal*, May 13, 1995, p. 1206.

16. Cited in "White House Statement," *Foreign Policy Bulletin* (January/April 1995): 26. Interviews with senior Mexican officials, January 1995.

17. The Senate Banking Committee compiled numerous documents from the Treasury Department and prepared a detailed and authoritative chronology based on those documents. See "Report on the Mexican Economic Crisis," presented by Senator Alfonse D'Amato, 104th Cong., 1st sess., June 28, 1995, especially App. E.

18. Cited in David Sanger, "The Education of Robert Rubin," *The New York Times*, February 5, 1995, pp. III, 1,3.

19. "Poll Records Mixed Results for Zedillo," *Reforma*, republished in *FBIS*, 21 November 1995, pp. 10–12.

20. Office of the White House Press Secretary, Remarks by the President on the Signing of the Trade and Development Act of 2000, May 18, 2000.

21. Cited in Christopher Marquis, "'The Ball Is in Cuba's Court,' Clinton Says," *Miami Herald*, October 17, 1997, p. 22A.

22. See David R. Mares, "Securing Peace in the Americas in the Next Decade," in Jorge I. Dominguez, ed., *The Future of Inter-American Relations* (New York: Routledge, 2000), pp. 35–48.

23. See Tom Farer, ed., *Transnational Crime in the Americas* (New York: Routledge, 1999).

24. See Office of National Drug Control Policy, *National Drug Control Strategy, 1999* (Washington, D.C., 1999); Mathea Falco, "U.S. Drug Policy: Addicted to Failure," *Foreign Policy* 102 (Spring 1996): 124; Coletta Youngers, "Fueling Failure: U.S. Drug Control Efforts in the Andes," *Issues in International Drug Policy* (Washington, D.C.: Washington Office on Latin America, April 1995).

25. Thomas L. Friedman, "Three Little Words," *The New York Times*, February 11, 1996, p. E15.

26. Feinberg, *Summitry in the Americas*, p. 70.

7

INTERBRANCH POLITICS AND THE AMERICAN DIALECTIC

We can tell the Latin Americans just so many times that the Executive does not agree with an action taken by Congress. But inevitably, after a while, Congressional actions become viewed here [Brazil] *as part of the landscape of American foreign policy.*[1]

—SECRETARY OF STATE HENRY A. KISSINGER, 1976

From the Monroe Doctrine to the Reagan Doctrine, from McKinley's Spanish-American War to Bush's invasion of Panama, from the building of the Panama Canal by Theodore Roosevelt to its return by Jimmy Carter, from FDR's Good Neighbor Policy to JFK's Alliance for Progress, from William Howard Taft's "dollar diplomacy" to Bill Clinton's Summit of the Americas—U.S. policy toward Latin America has been identified with presidents and sculpted by their initiatives and interventions.

It comes as no surprise, then, that the dominant metaphor used to describe the foreign policymaking process is that of the president driving the car-of-state, with Congress and the American public in the back seat.[2] But this view of the foreign policymaking process fails to account for the policies that have been imposed on reluctant or resistant presidents, and it cannot explain the many presidential initiatives that have been rejected by Congress. In the last three decades, an analysis that focused solely on the president could not explain the end of U.S. involvement in Vietnam, the imposition of sanctions on South Africa, or the evolution of U.S. policy toward Cuba.

Even our survey of foreign policy toward Latin America during the last four administrations suggests that an understanding of U.S. policy must incorporate the influence of society's changing moods and the role of Congress in articulating those swings. Congress's voice in many of the policies is evident, and in some cases it is dominant. Instead of viewing Congress as an interest group trying to influence the executive, a more accurate approach would view the two institutions as separate and nearly equal. Each shapes policy and is the most important actor in the other's arena. This is because the Constitution gives substantial powers in the area of foreign policy to both branches. Although the president is commander-in-chief, Congress has the power to declare wars. The president nominates ambassadors and proposes a budget, but the Senate confirms or rejects his appointments, and Congress re-does the budget. Congress has powers over trade, immigration, and all the domestic issues that moved to the center of the foreign policy agenda at the end of the Cold War and after decades of growing economic interdependence. In brief, the Constitution is not a system based on the "separation of powers," but rather, as Richard Neustadt observed in *Presidential Power*, a system of "separate institutions sharing powers."[3]

"U.S. foreign policy" ought to be defined not as a president's declaration but as the product of an interactive process by which Congress and the president reconcile their different conceptions of the national interest with their varying perceptions of international realities. An effective policy requires that each branch be responsive to the other. If either branch refuses to compromise, the policy and the nation will suffer. To attempt to identify the more powerful of the two branches is a futile and sometimes misleading exercise. Congress's power might actually be greater when it is least apparent, that is, during moments of quiet cooperation rather than public confrontation. Responding to the law of anticipated reactions, the president might choose not to contest an issue or to yield to congressional preferences before drafting a bill. A more useful question is what effect Congress and the interaction between the two branches have on foreign policy.

The principal debates on U.S. policy toward Latin America have seldom occurred within the executive branch. The president appoints advisers whose view of the world resembles his own, to varying degrees, and the more these officials work together, the more their views meld into an administration position. The most important debates are between the two branches, not within the multiple bureaucracies.

It is tempting to trace the role of Congress in the formulation of U.S.

policy toward Latin America. One could start with the Monroe Doctrine, in which the views of the Speaker of the House had great weight, but such a comprehensive survey would require another book. Instead, I briefly develop five case studies that span the last forty years of the twentieth century. Each represents a pivotal moment in U.S. policy toward Latin America, and each illustrates the use of a different policy instrument:

1. U.S. policy on expropriations and investment disputes (1961–1969) is an example of the way Congress uses the aid bill to make policy.
2. U.S. policy on human rights (1975–1985) is routine executive diplomacy.
3. The negotiation and ratification of the new Panama Canal Treaties required a two-thirds vote of the Senate.
4. U.S. policy toward Nicaragua (1978–1989) included diplomacy, aid, and covert actions.
5. The U.S. invasions of Grenada in 1983 and Panama in 1989 were acts of war.

If all five cases were treaties, we would be able to test the nature of interbranch relations only for treaties. But because the cases reflect a wide range of foreign and defense policies, we are better positioned to understand the role of Congress and interbranch politics in the making of U.S. foreign policy toward Latin America.

The Cases

Aid and Expropriations

On March 13, 1961, while Cuban exiles were making final preparations for an invasion in the Bay of Pigs, President John F. Kennedy unveiled his ten-year, $10 billion aid plan for an Alliance for Progress. He requested $3 billion for the first three years to permit the region's leaders to make long-term development plans. Congress applauded the program and then reduced it by $600 million and insisted that Kennedy request aid annually. This was not the first time—nor would it be the last—that the president would ask for multiyear appropriations and Congress would reject the request and reduce the amount. Congress also differed on the priorities that should be given to certain interests. The first important difference was on how the United States should respond to Latin American expropriations of U.S. investments.

In 1962 a governor of a state in Brazil expropriated a subsidiary of ITT. Fearful that such activities could spread throughout Latin America, Senator Bourke Hickenlooper of Iowa introduced an amendment to deny aid to a government that expropriated American property without "adequate, effective, and prompt compensation." The Kennedy administration took the same negative stance toward this amendment that its predecessor had taken toward a similar one three years before. In a press conference President Kennedy called the amendment "unwise," and Secretary of State Dean Rusk told the Senate Foreign Relations Committee: "There can be no difference between us . . . on the objective of doing everything that we can to create the right kind of environment for private investment. But I do think that such a [mandatory] provision would create very severe complications in our relations with other governments."[4]

The traditional roles were reversed, with Congress trying to make policy and the State Department attempting to obstruct, claiming that new legislation was neither necessary nor desirable. In the end, Hickenlooper's amendment passed, but only after the State Department diluted it to allow a one-year delay before the executive would have to suspend aid. Expropriations continued, and many members of Congress questioned the administration's commitment to using the new instrument. In 1963 Hickenlooper and Senator Wayne Morse introduced a more stringent amendment that applied to a much wider class of investment disputes.

Rusk adopted a different strategy to defeat the new amendment. Although he had called the original Hickenlooper amendment ill conceived, in 1963 he testified that it "has been a good thing," and the administration suspended aid to Ceylon for failing to compensate an American oil company. The amendment had enjoyed widespread support in Congress because of the feeling that the administration was unconcerned about U.S. investments. The action against Ceylon served to undercut support for the amendment. The administration regained its prerogative at the price of accepting Congress's policy.

Human Rights Policy

Although Jimmy Carter is credited with instilling a concern for human rights in U.S. foreign policy, the policy originated in Congress in the early 1970s and was defined by Congress's battle with a recalcitrant executive before Carter was elected. Representative Donald Fraser, chairman of a House foreign affairs subcommittee, provided the intellectual leadership to translate America's moral impulse into a coherent policy for reducing aid to countries that abused the rights of their citizens. Hearings in his subcommittee resulted in a report in March 1974, *Human Rights in the World Community: A Call for U.S. Leadership,* that offered twenty-nine specific recommendations on ways to incorporate human rights into U.S. foreign policy.[5]

The violent overthrow of Chilean President Salvador Allende provided Congress with a concrete case to which Fraser's recommendations could be applied. Despite reports of widespread torture and "disappearances," the Nixon administration increased aid to the military government nearly twenty-fold. Led by Representative Dante Fascell and Senator Edward Kennedy, Congress amended the aid law with a nonbinding sense of Congress's resolution that "the President should deny any economic or military assistance to the government of any foreign country which practices the internment or imprisonment of that country's citizens for political purposes." The administration ignored this resolution and instead asked for more aid. The next year, in December 1974, Congress set a ceiling on economic aid and prohibited military aid to Chile.

Again the president disregarded Congress's intent and boosted aid to Chile by shifting funds from other projects. In 1975 Congress took a further step: It prohibited aid not just to Chile but to any government that engages in gross violations of human rights, "unless such assistance will directly benefit the needy people in such country." The pattern of interaction was repeated until Congress denied the executive any discretion.

The branches differed on policy and prerogative. The administration wanted to support a government "that can pull Chile together in the long-term" and help it to recover after the anti-American leftist rule of Allende. It did not want to say that it opposed human rights, however, so it disguised its intent by wrapping it in a blanket of other interests. The human rights issue in Chile was "a part of a large relationship," according to Deputy Assistant Secretary of State Harry Shlaudeman, "a part which has to be weighed against other parts."[6] Secretary of State Henry Kissinger rejected Congress's signal to reduce aid to Chile on grounds of effectiveness, but he was really arguing prerogative: "We have generally opposed attempts to deal with sensitive international human rights issues through legislation—not because of the moral view expressed, which we share, but because legislation is almost always too inflexible, too public, and too heavy-handed a means to accomplish what it seeks."[7]

When Kissinger requested more aid for Chile, Congress concluded that he was pursuing silent, not quiet, diplomacy on human rights. "Suppose you are in the Pinochet government," Representative Donald Fraser asked an administration witness with tongue in cheek, and despite gross human rights violations "our Ambassador and AID mission was continuing to negotiate new loans and new assistance. What would be the message you would get?"[8] That message was different from the one Congress wanted the administration to send, and so it tied the president's hands. Fraser expressed a "growing congressional frustration at the increasing tendency of the executive branch to ignore the statutes enacted by Congress."[9]

After Carter took office and elevated human rights to be the "soul" of his foreign policy, some members of Congress tried to pass bills that would apply the policy to the Export-Import Bank, the International Monetary Fund, and the General Agreement on Tariffs and Trade. Carter opposed these efforts for the same reasons of prerogative that Nixon and Ford had cited. Carter explained at a press conference his opposition to an amendment sponsored by Representative Tom Harkin to require the United States to vote against loans by the international development banks to countries that violate human rights: "To have a frozen mandatory prohibition against our nation voting for any loan simply removes my ability to bargain with a foreign leader whom we think might be willing to [improve] human rights. . . . We need to have the flexibility."[10] Congress as a whole judged that Carter, unlike Nixon or Ford, would use the flexibility to pursue these goals, and it rejected the human rights amendments.

Congress began to pass restrictive human rights amendments again after the inauguration of Ronald Reagan, who was more committed to stopping leftist subversion than to curbing human rights violations by "friendly" regimes. The Reagan administration requested unconditional aid for the Salvadoran government, but Congress responded by attaching human rights conditions. The administration dodged the conditions, and the human rights situation worsened. In 1983 Congress decided to legislate with precision. It would withhold 30 percent of authorized military aid until a verdict was given in the trial of those soldiers accused of murdering four American churchwomen in November 1980. The strategy worked. In May 1984 four National Guardsmen were found guilty, the first time members of El Salvador's security forces were convicted of murder.

Panama Canal Treaties

From the beginning of negotiations for new Panama Canal treaties in 1965 through their ratification in 1978, Congress defined the timing of the talks and the parameters of the treaties. President Lyndon Johnson was wary of congressional opposition to the treaties and decided not to test it. Soon after Secretary of State Henry Kissinger negotiated a joint statement of principles with his Panamanian counterpart in February 1974, Senator Strom Thurmond introduced a resolution with thirty-four co-sponsors (enough to prevent ratification of a treaty), and Representative Dan Flood and 120 representatives introduced similar resolutions, urging the president to stop negotiations and "retain continued undiluted sovereignty over the Canal Zone." Thurmond and Flood effectively precluded any further negotiations until Carter's inauguration.

Carter instructed his negotiators to consult more regularly and fully with the Senate during the course of their talks, and Senator Howard Baker, then minority leader, acknowledged that they had consulted more than ever before when hearings on the treaties commenced.[11] As a result of those consultations, the Senate leadership defined the conceptual boundaries of the treaties, requiring that the United States retain rights to defend the Canal permanently and not pay Panama for giving up the Canal. Then, in its second-longest treaty debate, the Senate tightened two provisions of the treaty to eliminate any ambiguity on the unilateral right of the United States to defend the Canal and to grant to the U.S. Navy the right to transit the Canal on a priority basis during an emergency.

U.S. Policy toward Nicaragua

In 1978–1979, as the Carter administration tried to mediate a transition from Anastasio Somoza, congressional pressures were felt on both sides of the issue. Liberals in Congress argued that Carter should push harder to get Somoza to resign, and Somoza's conservative friends insisted that the United States support him or leave him alone. Because the administration's efforts were primarily diplomatic and did not require congressional consent, Congress was never compelled to take a unified position, and the two-sided pressures left the Carter administration free to pursue its preferred policies.

After the Sandinistas took power in 1979, Carter sought $75 million in aid for the new government to try to put relations on a good footing. Between Carter's request in November 1979 and the approval in the summer of 1980, Congress wrestled with the policy and all its implications. The final law carried a laundry list of conditions and limitations on the use of the aid, all of which the Carter administration opposed but was obliged to accept. The key condition was that before he disbursed aid, Carter would have to certify to Congress that Nicaragua was not supporting insurgencies. The inclusion of this condition was a sign—another appeared during the negotiations over the Canal treaties—that Congress viewed the administration as insufficiently committed to U.S. security interests in the region. But the limitation helped to contain the Sandinistas until late November 1980, when the situation in the region and in Washington changed so much as to undermine the effectiveness of the threat of an aid cutoff.

After Ronald Reagan was inaugurated, and U.S. priorities in the region changed, Congress pivoted around the president and applied its pressure on different points. Instead of insisting that the administration take tougher positions on security issues, as it had done with Carter, Congress pressed Reagan to give greater weight to human rights and negotiations in El Salvador and Nicaragua. At first, Congress accepted U.S. support for the contras, provided it was aimed at interdicting arms from the Sandinistas to the Salvadoran rebels. As it became clear, however, that the contras' goal was to overthrow the Nicaraguan government, Congress retreated and encouraged President Reagan, with increasing persistence, but also some equivocation, to stop supporting the contras.

Congressional reasons for opposing the contra program were almost as numerous as the members who voted against it, but the connecting threads were that the policy was wrong and that the contras could not succeed—a combination of the moral and the practical. Despite Reagan's very potent national security arguments, these congressional concerns guaranteed a close debate. When Sandinista acts appeared to confirm Reagan's view of them—for example, when Ortega flew to Moscow—the president obtained the aid. On the other hand, when the Central Americans signed the Arias Plan in Guatemala in August 1987 and asked Congress to stop providing military aid to the contras, Congress felt it had the ballast to reject Reagan's arguments and give the negotiations a chance. Congress's decision proved to be crucial in winding down the war and paving the way toward a free election in Nicaragua in February 1990.

The Grenada and Panama Invasions

The invasions of Grenada in October 1983 and of Panama in December 1989 were presidential decisions taken with minimum consultation with Congress. The country's immediate reaction to these decisions was to "rally around the flag" and wait to see whether the action would succeed or become another quagmire. In each case the invasion was quick and effective, and public opinion in the targeted country as well as in the United States was overwhelmingly favorable.

The Democrats' initial skepticism about the Grenadian invasion was overcome after a high-level visit established that the islanders regarded the invasion positively. Congressional reaction to intervention in Panama was more complicated. In some ways, Congress invited the invasion. After the unsuccessful coup against Noriega on October 3, 1989, congressional Republicans and many Democrats charged Bush with timidity, suggesting that a quicker reaction would have displaced Noriega. Bush felt the pressure, though he tried to deny it. When American soldiers were harmed in mid-December, the president decided to use that as the justification for a quick takeover of the country. He succeeded, and criticisms of his leadership diminished sharply.

The Impact of Interbranch Politics

The dominant model of a presidentially driven foreign policy is of limited use. Although Congress's hand is not always noticeable, its signature can be identified on virtually every policy. By and large, Congress finds neglected interests and presses a reluctant president to integrate these into his foreign policy.

The five case studies of U.S. foreign policy toward Latin America during the last four decades show that the eventual policy diverged sharply from initial presidential preferences. Had it not been for Congress and interbranch politics, the Alliance for Progress would have had far more funds, for more years, and without conditions on the treatment of U.S. investment. Without Congress, the human rights policy would have been little more than rhetoric; U.S. rights to defend the Panama Canal would have been ambiguous, although the treaty would have been completed sooner; the contras would have been flush with money; and Bush might never have invaded Panama.

With the end of the Cold War and the decline of the security threat, Congress pressed its concerns on a broad range of domestic issues, including drugs, immigration, and trade, and ethnic and interest groups played a larger role. There can be no doubt that the president pursued these concerns much more vigorously because of Congress than if there had been no pressure from the second branch.

When is the perspective from interbranch politics most useful? It depends largely on the vehicle that carries a particular policy. By "vehicle," I mean a treaty, a diplomatic demarche, a law, a speech, an act of war. If the policy is a treaty like the ones governing the Panama Canal or an aid bill like the Alliance, then Congress's role is central, and a national debate is unavoidable. If the policy is diplomacy, as was the case in the Nicaraguan mediation of 1978–1979, or an invasion, then the executive branch can determine its own timing and approach. The power of Congress is less visible in executive-dominant policies, but it is always present because important presidential actions almost always involve a promise of aid or a threat of sanctions, and the absence of congressional support risks empty promises and ineffectual threats. Moreover, the president understands that if he ignores Congress on an issue important to its members, he risks losing their support on issues more important to him.

Congressionally driven "policies" through resolutions and hearings sometimes have an important effect on foreign countries. For example, Senator Jesse Helms chaired a Senate Foreign Relations subcommittee hearing in 1985 on fraud and corruption in Mexico and drove the Mexican government to distraction. Resolutions on trade issues also have an impact in Europe and Japan even if they never become law. The main purpose of these congressional-dominant policies is to send signals to three groups: (1) constituents, to recognize that their elected representatives have heard their complaints and therefore deserve to be reelected; (2) the administration, to pursue a particular interest more vigorously; and (3) a foreign government, to correct a particular problem, whether that requires opening a market or a political system. If the administration and the foreign government respond to the signal, then Congress is unlikely to bind its concern into law.

On Central America, Congress helped balance U.S. policy and ensure that a wider range of U.S. interests was pursued. Congress repeatedly compensated for presidential preferences, for example, by compelling Carter to certify that the Sandinistas were not providing arms to the FMLN and by requiring Reagan and Bush to prove that the Salvadoran government was investigating political murders.

Congress initiated and pressed a reluctant administration to give priority to defending human rights, protecting U.S. investments, and stopping drug trafficking. Although concerned about the same problems, the administration would typically not give these domestically driven interests as high a priority if Congress did not insist on it. "Bureaucracies, unmolested," Kenneth Waltz wrote, "are not famed for their creativity."[12] When Congress's signal is received and affects the administration's policy, the president can speak effectively for the entire government. Indeed, Congress provides additional and credible leverage to the president's negotiators because the foreign government will know that Congress will take action if there is no response.

The degree of trust and responsiveness between the two branches is a pivotal determinant of effective policy. In the spring of 1991 Congress felt considerable pressure from unions and environmental groups to reject the president's request for authority to negotiate a free trade agreement with Mexico on a fast track. Representative Richard Gephardt, Democratic majority leader of the House, sent President Bush a letter outlining the concerns that he and some other members of Congress had about a possible agreement. If Bush had stonewalled the letter, he probably would have failed to gain congressional approval. Instead, the president responded with a serious and detailed program, which permitted Gephardt to inform his constituents: "On many of the issues, they [the Bush administration] have moved a good distance responding to Congressional pressures."[13] When the president is responsive, Congress will delegate more power and grant more discretion to use that power, and the beneficiary will be U.S. interests.

Conversely, when the executive is unresponsive, Congress will eventually tie its hands, to the detriment of U.S. interests. During a visit by Secretary of State Henry Kissinger to Brazil in 1976, *The New York Times* reported that "both supporters and opponents of the Brazilian government view Washington's concern with human rights as more a product of Congressional pressure than initiative from the Executive Branch."[14] In this case, the secretary's failure to convey a national concern had two effects. First, Brazil did not take U.S. concerns about human rights seriously, and second, Congress decided to restrict the president's flexibility to negotiate by imposing mandatory sanctions. On another matter, Senator Edmund Muskie reprimanded an administration witness who had apparently altered the intent of a law: "To have you twist [the law] as you have is a temptation to this Senator to really handcuff you the next time."[15]

The U.S. political system is so open that there is always someone to articulate an idea, interest, or ideal—or, more likely, combine the three into a policy recommendation. If the recommendation is compelling and suits the needs and perspective of the president, then it becomes U.S. policy. If the executive branch proves uninterested or unresponsive, the proposal passes to the second great container, Congress. Given the diversity of the membership and their need for public recognition, a member can always be found to propose a new idea. Whether the proposal gathers a critical mass and becomes law, however, depends on public opinion, congressional politics, and the merits of the idea. These three factors are intimately related: If public opinion supports a proposal, Congress will accept it, and it will fill a policy niche. That is how legislative initiatives emerge and pass. The search by an ambitious member of Congress for a policy niche—a neglected interest or ideal —is often the engine in the foreign policy process, balancing an administration's policy or compensating for its inadequacy.

The executive branch can try to co-opt, preempt, or resist the initiative. To co-opt or preempt means to absorb the idea into its own policy. To resist means to risk a collision and a self-defeating policy. The existence of the two branches ensures that the policy that evolves from the American dialectic reflects the breadth of U.S. national interests and ideals. The exact permutation depends on the responsiveness of both branches and the peculiar way in which the two institutions reflect domestic demands and perceive the international landscape.

The executive-dominant model assumes that the optimum foreign policy is the product of a rational choice by the president and his advisers. But such rational choices led to Vietnam, the Bay of Pigs, the Chilean intervention, and Iran-Contra. Congress had little or no voice in these debacles, but it did have a compelling voice in the human rights policies, the Panama Canal Treaties, and the bipartisan accord on Central America—all of which served U.S. interests effectively.

Congress is certainly not the sole repository of wisdom on foreign policy. It has made many mistakes. But as Francis O. Wilcox, who served at different times as a staff director of the Senate Foreign Relations

Committee and as an assistant secretary of state, recognized: "If Congress has frequently seemed to be going in one direction and then in another, that is partly because it is a collection of poorly coordinated, strong-minded individuals. But more importantly, it is because that is the way the White House and the Kremlin have moved as well."[16]

The point is not that one branch makes better or worse policy but that the debate between the branches offers the most thorough and systematic mechanism for locating the national interest. Each branch brings its unique perspective and capabilities to the search for the best match between U.S. interests and geopolitical realities. Each institution has its own biases or, as Thomas E. Mann calls them, "distinctive competencies."[17] In contrast to the congressional need for public initiatives, the executive responds to routine, prefers privacy, and guards bureaucratic turf with ferocity.[18] The executive prefers as few laws and as much discretion as possible because when the policy moves to the congressional arena, the executive risks having its prerogative circumscribed. Compared with the executive's zealous protection of its privileges, Congress is much more ambivalent about protecting its turf and will do so only if there is an obvious electoral advantage. Sometimes, as in the case of trade policy, Congress delegates responsibility to the executive to protect itself from interest groups. But even in those cases, it keeps the executive on a short and tight leash, requiring the president to return at regular intervals for a new grant of authority.[19]

Each branch is capable of initiating foreign policy, defining objectives and priorities, and obstructing them. Although Congress often sounds as if it speaks with 535 separate voices, the institution *qua* institution speaks when members vote; and although there might be 535 motives, it is still possible to divine an intent by reading the product—the law—and deducing the president's original request.

The dominant model of executive-driven foreign policy is clearly inadequate, but it should not be replaced by a congressional model. What is needed is an interbranch perspective that investigates both the successes and the collisions in U.S. foreign policy by probing the relationship between the two branches. Such an approach can offer new insights for enhancing the ability of the United States to make effective foreign policy by using each branch's comparative advantage.[20]

United States policy toward Latin America is different from the president's signature at the bottom of a decree. The policy is the result of a debate in which Congress articulates neglected national interests or changing domestic priorities. What is most fascinating is that the congressional dialectic is not ideological. Whether led by Democrats or Republicans, Congress has acted as a balance: It encouraged conservative presidents like Nixon, Ford, and Reagan to respect human rights, and it persuaded liberal presidents like Kennedy and Carter to pay more attention to security issues and protect U.S. businesses abroad. In the cases of George Bush and Bill Clinton, the ultimate pragmatists, Congress helped them find the mid-point between liberals and conservatives. Overall, Congress has tended to serve as the great compensator.

Interbranch competition is permanent, sewn into the Constitution that established two separate institutions—Congress and president—but insisted that they share the powers to declare and make war, to appropriate and spend money, and to make and collect taxes and tariffs. To argue that congressional assertiveness—whether new or old—is the cause of conflict is equivalent to arguing that today's high divorce rate is due to the "new assertiveness" of women. Sometimes Congress and women are culpable; sometimes the president and men are to blame. When one branch trespasses over the constitutional boundary, breaks the rules, or deceives the other, as the Reagan administration did on the contra affair, then the interaction becomes unproductive and foreign policy suffers. Like the possibility of divorce in marriage or war in the international system, interbranch conflict in U.S. politics can never be ruled out. But the wise statesman will find a way to advance U.S. interests without having to pay the high price of war.

Notes

1. Quoted in Jonathan Kandell, "The Latins and the U.S.: Kissinger's Tour Just Made More Clear That Congress Complicated Relations," *The New York Times,* February 27, 1976, p. 2.

2. See Robert A. Dahl, *Pluralist Democracy in the United States: Conflict and Consent* (Chicago: Rand McNally, 1967), p. 136; Louis Henkin, *Foreign Affairs and the Constitution* (New York: W. W. Norton, 1976), p. 123. Both use the car-driving metaphor.

3. Richard Neustadt, *Presidential Power* (New York: Wiley, 1960).

4. U.S. Senate, Committee on Foreign Relations, *Hearings on Foreign Assistance Act, 1962,* 87th Cong., 2d sess., p. 31.

5. For the emergence and evolution of the human rights policy, see Robert A. Pastor, *Congress and the Politics of U.S. Foreign Economic Policy* (Berkeley: University of California Press, 1980), pp. 301–321.

6. U.S. House of Representatives, Committee on International Relations, *Hearings: Human Rights in Chile,* 93d Cong., 2d sess., June 12, 1974, pp. 132–133.

7. "U.S. Policy on Rights Backed by Kissinger," *The New York Times,* October 20, 1976, p. 3.

8. U.S. House of Representatives, Subcommittee on International Organizations of the Committee on International Relations, *Hearings: Chile, the Status of Human Rights and Its Relationship to U.S. Economic Assistance Programs,* 94th Cong., 2d sess., April-May 1976, p. 36.

9. Ibid., p. 117.

10. *Public Papers of the Presidents of the United States, Jimmy Carter, 1977* (Washington, D.C.: Government Printing Office, 1978), vol. 1, April 15, 1977, p. 636.

11. Baker said that the U.S. negotiators "did much more [in consulting with the Senate] than anybody I have ever known has done." U.S. Senate Committee on Foreign Relations, *Hearings: Panama Canal Treaties, Part I,* 95th Cong., 1st sess., September–October 1977, pp. 87–88.

12. Kenneth Waltz, *Foreign Policy and Democratic Politics* (Boston: Little, Brown, 1967), p. 104.

13. Statement on Fast-Track Authority by Congressman Richard A. Gephardt, 102d Cong., 1st sess., May 9, 1991, Washington, D.C.

14. Kandell, "The Latins and the U.S.," p. 2.

15. Cited in Louis Fisher, "Micromanagement by Congress: Reality and Mythology," in L. Gordon Crovitz and Jeremy A. Rabkin, eds., *The Fettered Presidency: Legal Constraints of the Executive Branch* (Washington, D.C.: American Enterprise Institute, 1989), p. 152.

16. Francis O. Wilcox, *Congress, the Executive, and Foreign Policy* (New York: Harper & Row, 1971), p. 133.

17. Thomas E. Mann, "Making Foreign Policy: President and Congress," in Mann, ed., *A Question of Balance* (Washington, D.C.: Brookings Institution, 1989), p. 2.

18. The master scholar and practitioner of bureaucracies is Henry A. Kissinger. See his "Domestic Structure and Foreign Policy," *Daedalus* 95 (Spring 1966).

19. I. M. Destler, *American Trade Politics: System under Stress* (Washington, D.C.: Institute for International Economics, 1986).

20. For an essay on why Congress provides a strategic advantage to the United States in the field of foreign policy and how that asset can be enhanced, see Robert Pastor, "Congress and U.S. Foreign Policy: Comparative Advantage or Disadvantage?" *Washington Quarterly* 14 (Autumn 1991).

Part 2

RECURRING PROBLEMS

ESTRAGON: *I can't go on like this.*

VLADIMIR: *That's what you think.*

—**SAMUEL BECKETT, *WAITING FOR GODOT***

One thread that connects Carter, Reagan, Bush, and Clinton to each other and to many of their predecessors is that their policies respond to similar questions. More broadly, one could view U.S. foreign policy toward Latin America and the Caribbean as the sum of the answers to a set of recurring questions that range from the quantity to the quality of attention that the United States should give to the region. The pivotal question, however, has always been the strategic one: How should the United States deal with instability that could present an opportunity for a rival power to gain a foothold in the hemisphere? The Monroe Doctrine of 1823 that declared the hemisphere off-limits to European recolonization was the first answer by the U.S. government to that question, and its message—that foreign rivals are unwelcome—has been repeated often.

The instability question has sometimes been posed in terms of whether the United States could accept Latin American revolutions. A definitive answer to this question proved elusive, partly because it blurred two distinct challenges: first, succession crises where dictators face a broad-based challenge that is led by anti-American guerrillas; and second, anti-American revolutionary governments in the region. The first challenge was serious precisely because the second problem of revolutionary regimes proved so troubling for the United States. Policymakers have therefore believed that U.S. influence is greater, and the risks to world peace fewer, if the United States acts to avert a hostile group from taking power than if it tries to prevent an anti-American regime from asking help from its rival.

Chapter 8 examines the U.S. approach to seven succession crises and seeks to determine which policy was most effective in preventing anti-American revolution and promoting democracy. Chapter 9 tries to explain why the United States and the revolutionary governments of Cuba, Nicaragua, and Grenada always clashed and whether an alternative approach might have advanced U.S. interests more.

After a revolution occurs, policymakers are inevitably asked to explain why they failed to anticipate the revolution. The U.S. style is to react to crises and then react to criticism by forging longer-term economic and political policies aimed at precluding future revolutions. Chapters 10 and 11 explore the paths that the United States has taken to try to promote long-term economic development and peaceful political change.

These questions on development and democracy are being asked today. The first two questions, on dictators and revolutionaries, compelled presidents to take notice of Latin America throughout the twentieth century. They seem less pressing with the end of the Cold War just as they did after the First and Second World Wars. Nonetheless, it would be a mistake to conclude that a variant of these two questions will never recur or that an analysis of the history of how the United States has dealt with them in the past is of little use in the future. If the inter-American community fails to promote development and assure democracy, then the first two challenges will become pertinent again.

President Ronald Reagan urged Americans to remember "our history in Central America so we can learn from the mistakes of the past." Then, he repeated one of the recurrent mistakes of history, underestimating the potency of Latin American nationalism when confronted by U.S. hostility.

Some issues and interests are changing, but the central U.S. concerns that stem from Latin American proximity and instability remain. In the past, the United States was most concerned that instability could lead to anti-American regimes. Today, it is preoccupied that instability could lead to massive flows of refugees, or that drug traffickers can exploit weak regimes to do their illicit business.

8

SUCCESSION CRISES: THE BOUNDARIES OF INFLUENCE

Experience teaches us that, generally speaking, the most perilous moment for a bad government is one when it seeks to mend its ways.

—ALEXIS DE TOCQUEVILLE

After World War II, one of the most frustrating and dangerous predicaments that the United States faced was coping with the revolutionary regimes in Cuba, Iran, and Nicaragua. In Cuba in 1962, the United States and the Soviet Union came closer to nuclear holocaust than at any other place or moment. In Iran, America was humiliated by a religious leader, who violated the first rule of international diplomacy by kidnapping U.S. diplomats. And in Nicaragua, President Reagan fought a war that divided and maimed a small country and nearly destroyed his presidency.

The shock of dealing with these three revolutionary regimes was all the more difficult because they replaced dictatorships that were friendly to the United States. Some Americans concluded that the problem was the dictator, but protracted dictatorships have not always given way to hostile revolutionary regimes: The assassination of Dominican dictator Rafael Trujillo in 1961 led to a period of instability but eventually to democracy, and Chilean dictator Augusto Pinochet transferred power soon after losing a plebiscite in 1988. Why were some dictators replaced by revolutionary regimes while others were not? Did U.S. foreign policy make the difference?

Succession crises occur when a declining dictator, who has been friendly to the United States but repressive to his own people, faces an imminent or potential national movement to unseat him. The element that transforms this issue into a national security problem for the United States is the possibility that an anti-American group will assume control of the national movement. The essence of the challenge for the United States, however, is not how to deal with the revolutionaries (the subject of the next chapter) but rather how to persuade or coerce the declining dictator to yield power in such a way that the successor is least likely to be anti-American and most likely to be democratic. In this chapter I begin by defining succession crises, then analyze seven cases with different outcomes, and, finally, seek to explain why revolutions occur or are preempted, why U.S. policies have been similar in apparently different circumstances, and what lessons can be drawn for dealing with future succession crises.

A surprising aspect of these seven succession crises is the similarity of U.S. policies over a span of thirty years. An effective formula eluded all the presidents. George Shultz, Reagan's secretary of state, mused: "How do you go about the move from an authoritarian governmental structure to one that is more open and democratic? The more you study that, the more you see that it is hard."[1]

Defining the Problem

When a dictator who has been in control for a long time does not allow for peaceful change by free elections, the opposition has the options of acquiescence, nonviolent resistance, or violent change. In most of the developing world, the first two options are soon abandoned, and the only question is whether the opposition takes power quickly, through a coup d'etat, or through a protracted succession crisis. To identify the explanatory variables, this chapter examines a sample of seven succession crises that involved a substantial American role and had different outcomes: Cuba (1958–1959), the Dominican Republic (1960–1961), Haiti (1961–1963 and 1985–1986), Iran (1978–1979), Nicaragua (1978–1979), the Philippines (1983–1986), and Chile (1988–1989).

Each crisis began with a key event that shook the dictator, and it ended with his death, exile, or transfer of power. The United States played a large role in the internal affairs of all of these countries. Only Chile had not been occupied by U.S. troops. The Philippines was a U.S. colony, and at one time the constitutions of Cuba, Nicaragua, the Dominican Republic, and Haiti included clauses that granted rights to the

United States to intervene. Even after the United States repealed these rights and withdrew its troops, the psychological residue of this period of U.S. control continued to contort local politics.

When dictators took power in each of these countries, they supported U.S. foreign policies and tried to make it appear as if the United States supported them. Their purpose was to try to neutralize their opposition. The United States sometimes rejected this identification; at times, it acquiesced; and sometimes it embraced the dictator. Unfortunately, most of the people in these countries exaggerated the last relationship, identification, with the effect that the dictator's enemies viewed the United States as their enemy as well. Thus, the United States was drawn into succession crises that were violent struggles between indefensible dictators and anti-American revolutionaries.

The objectives of the United States in these crises exhibited a similar pattern and were defined with astute precision by President Kennedy as he surveyed the Dominican Republic after the assassination of Rafael Trujillo in 1961: "There are three possibilities in descending order of preference: a decent democratic regime, a continuation of the Trujillo regime, or a 'Castro' regime. We ought to aim at the first, but we really can't renounce the second until we are sure that we can avoid the third."[2] The worst outcomes for Washington occurred in Cuba, Iran, and Nicaragua, where anti-American, undemocratic regimes took power. The best outcomes occurred with the democratic transitions in the Philippines and Chile. The Dominican Republic and Haiti represent ambiguous outcomes because a (flawed) democracy eventually took hold, but only after years of instability and major U.S. interventions.

The succession crises passed through four stages that serve as signposts for narrating the cases and for showing how the changing relations among the various actors led to different outcomes. The first stage is the *identification* of the dictator with the United States in the country's collective mind. (Sometimes that is an accurate reflection of U.S. policy, and sometimes it is a misperception based on the historical rather than the contemporary relationship.) As middle-class disenchantment and rebel violence against the dictator increase, or as traumatic events cause local and international actors to fear a revolutionary outcome, U.S. policy moves to the second stage, *distance and dissociation.* The third stage occurs as the dictator weakens and the insurgency strengthens. At this time, moderate groups seeking change either *ally with and legitimize the rebels* or remain independent. If an alliance is forged, then the United States moves toward the fourth stage, persuading *the military to reject the dictator and support a "third force,"* a moderate alternative to the insurgents and the dictator. The emergence of a third force or the defection of important military figures can preempt the revolution. If this fails, then the U.S. must decide whether to intervene or to allow the insurgents to take power.

Moderate leaders and groups existed in all of the countries and could be defined as those who were interested in peaceful, nonviolent democratic change. In Chile, the moderates were the strongest force; in Haiti, the weakest. Other variables that help to explain why some revolutions succeeded and most failed were (1) the existence of a guerrilla insurgency, (2) the nature of the military response, and (3) the promise of genuinely free elections (see Table 8.1). The pattern of outcomes suggests that

1. If the guerrillas stay independent of moderates, they are less likely to succeed.
2. If the guerrillas ally with moderates and friendly regional governments, and if the military remains united until the dictator flees, then the prospects for an anti-U.S. revolutionary regime are the highest.
3. If the military divides and some or all of its leaders defect from the dictator, and if there are no elections, then a military takeover is most likely.
4. If the middle sector supports elections, and if the military divides but does not collapse, then the prospects are best for democracy.

The Cases

Cuba, 1958–1959

Between August 1933 and New Year's Day 1959, with the exception of an eight-year period beginning in 1944, Fulgencio Batista ruled Cuba. When polls showed he might lose the election in 1952, he seized power. This led to widespread protests, some violent, including an attack against one of his barracks led by young Fidel Castro on July 26, 1953. But Batista prevailed, and in this period of identification, U.S. Ambassador Arthur Gardner (1953–1957) praised him.

TABLE 8.1 Succession Crises and U.S. Foreign Policy

Countries and Revolutions	*Dictatorship*	*Outcome*	*Does U.S. Policy Follow Pattern?*[1]	*Was There a Guerrilla Movement?*	*Role of Middle Sector and Regional Actors*	*Military Defection from Dictator/ Collapse?*	*Characteristics of Elections*
1. Cuba (1958–59)	Fulgencio Batista, 18 years (1933–44); (1952–59)	Anti-U.S. revolution	Yes	Yes	Allied with guerillas	No/Yes	Fraud/Abstention (1958)
2. Nicaraugua (1978–79)	Somoza family, 43 years (1936–79)	Anti-U.S. revolution	Yes	Yes	Allied with guerillas	No/Yes	Fraud/Abstention (1972); none in 1979
3. Iran (1978–79)	Shah, 37 years (1941–79)	Anti-U.S. revolution	Ambiguous	Yes	Alienation	No/Yes	None
4. Dominican Republic (1960–61)	Rafael Trujillo, 31 years(1930–61)	Military takeover	Yes	No	Disassociation from dictator	Yes/No	None
5. Haiti a. (1961–63) b. (1985–86)	Duvalier family, 29 years (1930–61)	No change (1963); military takeover (1986)	a. Yes b. Yes	a. No b. No	Disassociation from dictator	a. No/No b. Yes/No	None
6. Philippines (1983–86)	Ferdinand Marcos, 21 years (1965–86)	Democracy	Yes	Yes	Autonomous opposition	Yes/No	Free, but attempted theft
7. Chile (1988–89)	Augusto Pinochet, 17 years (1973–90)	Democracy	Yes	Yes, but weak	Support for election	Yes/No	Free

[1]"Yes" indicates that in this case, U.S. policy followed the pattern of (1) identification, followed by (2) distance/dissociation, and then, in reaction to the moderates' alliance with the left, by (3) encouraging the military to reject the dictator, and (4) seeking a moderate "third force."

By 1957, however, the protests against Batista had become increasingly violent, and the moderate sectors began to lend their support to the young rebels. Castro, who had been exiled, returned to Cuba with a small band in December 1956. He tried to place his guerrilla movement at the center of the opposition by issuing moderate manifestos calling for free elections, a constitutional government, and agrarian reform. On March 1, 1958, Cuban bishops called for an investigation of the regime's brutality and asked Batista to step down in favor of a government of national unity. Earl Smith, the new U.S. ambassador, also criticized the repression, but the clearest sign of a new policy of distancing and dissociation from the regime was the U.S. arms embargo against Batista announced by Secretary of State John Foster Dulles on April 8, 1958. The next day, Castro called a general strike.

On July 20, 1958, representatives of all the opposition groups met in Caracas to sign a pact that named an opposition government led by a moderate judge as president and Castro as commander-in-chief. This legitimization of the leftist guerrillas represented the third stage of the succession crisis. The Venezuelan site was symbolic of the support Castro began to receive from Latin American democratic forces. Costa Rican President José Figueres had already given him a planeload of arms on March 30, 1958, and Carlos Andrés Pérez, a leader of the Venezuelan Social Democratic party, also sent arms to Castro. Figueres later explained: "[I] helped Fidel Castro as much as I could because . . . we were completely willing to help overthrow all military dictatorships. We didn't know . . . what were Fidel Castro's ideas regarding Communism at the time."[3]

The fourth stage—the search for a third force—occurred after the opposition decided not to participate in what turned out to be a fraudulent election in November 1958. Senior officials in the Eisenhower administration asked William Pawley, an American businessman who had founded Cubana Airways, to undertake a secret mission. Pawley later described his goal as to "get Batista to capitulate to a caretaker government, unfriendly to him but satisfactory to us, whom we would immediately recognize and give military assistance to in order that Fidel Castro should not come to power."[4] Pawley proposed that Batista transfer power to Colonel Ramón Barquín, who had tried but failed to overthrow Batista in 1956. Batista refused.[5]

In December the Eisenhower administration desperately sought to locate and support a third force. The CIA tried to get Barquín released from prison and have him join Justo Carrillo and other moderates. Castro was wary of these plots, concerned that if Batista were replaced by someone credible and independent like Barquín, the revolution could come to a halt. But Batista unwittingly saved Castro when he transferred power to one of his staff, General Eulogio Cantillo, and then flew to Miami.

Cantillo, however, decided it was futile to try to hold the army together, and he handed power to Barquín, who was released from prison. Barquín then surprised everyone by telephoning Castro and surrendering the army, giving up, according to historian Hugh Thomas, "what chance there was of a government of the center."[6] The Cuban military disintegrated quickly, and Castro's soldiers took control of the remaining army units while he gathered political support on his journey to Havana.

Dominican Republic, 1960–1961

Both the Eisenhower and the Kennedy administrations concluded that "Castro's road to power was paved by the excesses of Batista" and that similar conditions existed in the Dominican Republic under a brutal dictator, General Rafael Trujillo, who had ruled since 1930.[7] Even before Castro took power, the United States had begun to distance itself from Trujillo because of his notorious repression. Ambassador Joseph Farland adopted a cool approach to the dictator and opened the U.S. embassy to Dominican dissidents.[8]

Such efforts accelerated after Castro's victory. In April 1960 President Eisenhower approved a contingency plan: If the situation deteriorated, "the United States would immediately take political action to remove Trujillo from the Dominican Republic as soon as [a] suitable successor regime can be induced to take over with the assurance of U.S. political, economic, and—if necessary—military support."[9] He then sent Pawley to talk to Trujillo, who said prophetically, "I'll never go out of here unless I go on a stretcher."[10]

The April 1960 plan to remove Trujillo was not implemented, but Kennedy continued Eisenhower's policy of encouraging dissidents to overthrow the general. The failure of the Bay of Pigs invasion on April 17, 1961, made Kennedy more cautious, however, lest a coup create a power vacuum that could be exploited by Castroite radicals. Kennedy instructed the CIA to "turn off" the coup. The rebels replied that the coup was their affair.[11]

At a National Security Council meeting on May 5, 1961, Kennedy decided "that the United States should not initiate the overthrow of Trujillo before we knew what government would succeed him, and that any action against Trujillo should be multilateral."[12] Henry Dearborn, the U.S. embassy contact with the dissidents, reminded the State Department that the embassy had been supporting efforts to overthrow Trujillo for a year. Dearborn cabled that it was simply "too late to consider whether United States will initiate overthrow of Trujillo."[13]

As the rebels were about to strike, Kennedy was torn between his fear of being held responsible if the coup failed or led to instability and his hope that it would succeed.[14] The White House therefore sent a cable to Dearborn on May 29, 1961, affirming that U.S. policy was "not [to] run [the] risk of U.S. association with political assassination, since [the] U.S. as [a] matter of general policy cannot condone assassination." At the same time, the cable implied approval if the dissidents succeeded. In short, U.S. objectives were deliberately contradictory: to encourage the rebels to think they had U.S. support if they succeeded, but to dissociate from them if they failed. The next day, May 30, 1961, Trujillo was shot and killed.[15]

The new problem was how to maintain order, facilitate a transition to constitutional democracy, and keep Trujillo's sons from power. Kennedy sent a flotilla of nearly forty ships to the Dominican coast as a warning to the Trujillo family, but he was also bothered by the factionalism of the Dominican opposition. "The key in all these countries," said Kennedy, "is the emergence of a leader. . . . The great danger . . . is a take-over by the army, which could lead straight to [another] Castro."[16]

In December 1962 Juan Bosch, a Social Democrat, was elected president, but the military overthrew him within a year. When some of the military tried to restore Bosch to power in 1965, the country fell into civil war, and President Johnson dispatched twenty-two thousand American soldiers to restore order and prevent radicals from taking power. Presidential elections were held within a year and were repeated at four-year intervals after that. The year 1978 witnessed the first peaceful transfer of power from one political party to another; the second occurred in 1986.

Haiti: Two Phases

The same concern that led the United States to take preventive action in the Dominican Republic guided it to Haiti, where another brutal dictator, François "Papa Doc" Duvalier, had ruled since 1957. Initially, the State Department considered a plan proposed by Undersecretary of State Chester Bowles to assemble a donors' consortium and offer Duvalier substantial aid if he accepted democratic and financial reforms. If Duvalier rejected the plan, the United States would impose an embargo against Haiti. The plan was not approved because of the administration's "reluctance to offer so much as Bowles proposed to such a government and the conviction of Haitian experts that Duvalier would accept neither proposal."[17]

After the Cuban missile crisis, President Kennedy personally initiated a review of policy toward Haiti. At the end of that review, in January 1963, Kennedy decided that the "replacement of Duvalier was a prerequisite to the achievement of U.S. interests in Haiti," but he insisted on three conditions before he would approve a plan to implement that objective: (1) the plan would have to have a high probability of success; (2) assurances were necessary that the new regime would be better than the existing one; and (3) the plan would have to be implemented by Haitians or by a third country. These preconditions, of course, rendered the proposal impracticable.[18] The administration's sense of urgency was based on a fear that the longer Duvalier stayed in power, the more likely he would be replaced by a Castroite revolution. The premise proved to be flawed: Papa Doc and his son, Jean-Claude "Baby Doc" Duvalier, who became president after his father's death in 1971, continued to rule for twenty-three years after Kennedy's death.

During the younger Duvalier's tenure, U.S. policy remained relatively consistent in a broad sense. The United States either ignored Haiti or used a carrot-and-stick approach—promises of aid and threats of withdrawal—to encourage Duvalier to respect human rights, open the political system, end corruption, and cooperate on controlling illegal emigration to the United States. Within these broad parameters, Carter tended to make more human rights demands on the Haitian government and give less aid, whereas Reagan made fewer demands and delivered more aid, increasing it from about $30 million in 1981 to about $56 million in 1985. Nonetheless, Congress added stiff human rights conditions to Reagan's aid. In July 1985, Baby Doc held a referendum, and more than 99 percent of the voters confirmed him as president-for-life. Soon after that, violence erupted in numerous towns, culminating in November with riots in Gonaives, which many observers regard as the beginning of the end of the regime.[19] On January 29, 1986, riots spread over the island.

Duvalier proclaimed martial law, and the middle class distanced itself from Duvalier, as did Secretary of State George Shultz in announcing that new aid commitments to Haiti would be delayed. The pressure on Duvalier to resign increased from all sectors, including the military and Haiti's neighbors, notably Jamaica. On February 6, 1986, Duvalier asked the U.S. embassy to provide a plane for his departure.

When asked about the role of the United States in the last week of the regime and whether the U.S. ambassador gave Duvalier "any strong advice to leave," President Reagan responded that the United States had never given any such advice and that Duvalier had "never asked us for any." The only role played by the United States, according to Reagan, was "providing an airplane to fly him to France."[20]

Military juntas promised free elections, but none delivered until Supreme Court Justice Ertha Pascal-Trouillot was appointed provisional president in March 1990. She invited international observers for the election on December 16, 1990. Jean-Bertrand Aristide won two-thirds of the vote, but he was deposed nine months later. The military ruled Haiti until U.S. soldiers restored Aristide in October 1994.

Nicaragua, 1978–1979

The Cuban example haunted all the key actors in the Nicaraguan succession crisis, but that did not preclude them from repeating virtually the same actions as had occurred in Cuba.[21] In 1936, three years after his uncle, President Juan Sacasa, appointed Anastasio Somoza García as commander of the National Guard, Somoza overthrew him. He and his two sons ruled Nicaragua as a family fiefdom until the Sandinistas overthrew the youngest son, Anastasio Somoza Debayle, on July 17, 1979. The Somozas cultivated a public image of partnership with the U.S. government, although the latter tried to persuade each of them to step down or refrain from seeking reelection on four different occasions (1945, 1947–1949, 1963, 1978–1979). Nonetheless, the perception of identification, partly the result of two obsequious U.S. ambassadors, remained more influential than the reality of a complicated relationship.

In 1975 the Ford administration distanced itself from Somoza because of increasing concern about his corruption and repression, and it opened contacts with the opposition. This trend was accelerated when Carter took office in 1977. The decisive event that triggered the Nicaraguan insurrection was the assassination in January 1978 of Pedro

Joaquín Chamorro, the editor of *La Prensa* and leader of the moderate opposition. The moderate sectors were transformed from passive opponents into new militants who would consider alliances with the left to depose Somoza.

The Sandinista National Liberation Front (FSLN), which had been founded in 1961 as a Marxist, Castro-oriented guerrilla group, had decided in the mid-1970s to broaden its membership, expand its relationships internationally, and tone down its Marxist rhetoric. Frightened by the power of a September insurrection, the U.S. government arranged multilateral mediation under the auspices of the OAS to facilitate a democratic transition. The effort failed, and the Carter administration imposed sanctions on Somoza in February 1979. Between then and June, the moderate opposition and democratic Latin American governments gradually moved toward an alliance with the Sandinistas. Costa Rica, Panama, Venezuela, and Cuba provided political support and covert military aid to the Sandinistas. Until the Sandinistas launched their "final offensive" in mid-June 1979, the U.S. government remained unaware of the nature and depth of their strength.

The United States desperately sought to fashion an "executive committee"—a non-Somocista third force—to negotiate with the Sandinista-led junta. Unfortunately, most members of the moderate leadership had already allied with the Sandinistas. The U.S. government also tried to locate post-Somoza leadership for the National Guard, but these efforts failed because Somoza blocked the appointment of General Julio Gutiérrez (favored by the United States) as commander, just as Batista had blocked Colonel Barquín, and he shielded the Guard from any contacts with the United States. Carter promised aid to new Guard leaders only if they attracted some support from Latin American leaders, but this proved impossible. In the end, a transitional agreement involving Somoza's successor (Francisco Urcuyo), the Guard, and the Sandinistas was disregarded by both the Sandinistas and Somoza after Somoza's flight on July 17, 1989.[22] Two days later, the Sandinistas marched into Managua.

Iran, 1978–1979

The period of Nicaragua's succession crisis overlapped with that of Iran's, but Carter and his senior advisers were much more directly engaged in the latter crisis because of the impact that events in Iran could have on

U.S. interests in the Persian Gulf and on U.S.-Soviet strategic relations. Carter judged that "our nation would not be threatened by the Sandinistas as it would be by the fall of the Shah."[23] In his memoirs, Zbigniew Brzezinski mentions Nicaragua in a sentence but devotes more than a chapter to the Shah's fall, calling it the "administration's greatest setback" and "disastrous strategically."[24]

The Shah of Iran had been on the Peacock Throne since 1941. Because of his anticommunism and his nation's long border with the Soviet Union, he had forged a close relationship with the United States. In 1953 the CIA helped him secure the resignation of Mohammed Mossadegh, who was then prime minister, creating the myth of the Shah as "a pliant creature of the United States." That perception remained "a vivid political reality" in Iran, although twenty years later an arms agreement with President Nixon signified a reversal of roles, with the Shah dictating the terms of the relationship.[25] Carter tried to persuade the Shah to reduce his military purchases and curb his secret police, but the Shah did it his own way. On January 9, 1978, the Shah's police opened fire on a religious demonstration, and the Iranian revolution began.[26] Whereas Carter urged Somoza to accept a vote on his tenure, his message to the Shah was different:

> Whatever action he took, including setting up a military government, I would support him. We did not want him to abdicate. [The Shah was] a staunch and dependable ally . . . [who] remained the leader around whom we hoped to see a stable and reformed government. . . . We knew little about the forces contending against him, but their anti-American slogans and statements were enough in themselves to strengthen our resolve to support the Shah.[27]

Despite Carter's position, the U.S. ambassador in Teheran decided by November 1978 that the Shah should abdicate and that the United States should work with the Ayatollah Khomeini to try to moderate his anti-Americanism. At the end of December 1978 the Shah tried to regain control by appointing Shahpour Bakhtiar as his prime minister. Bakhtiar, however, called for the Shah to leave and for the secret police to be disbanded. Carter reluctantly recognized that "the Shah would have to leave the country before order could be restored."[28]

Soon after the Shah's departure on January 16, 1979, Bakhtiar was overwhelmed by the followers of the Ayatollah Khomeini. On February 1 the Ayatollah flew into Teheran, and by February 11 he controlled the government and the military.

The Philippines, 1983–1986

As a former colony of both Spain and the United States, the Philippines shares a number of characteristics with the nations of the Caribbean Basin. Unlike the Caribbean nations, however, the Philippines had a history of contested elections from independence in 1946 until Ferdinand Marcos declared martial law in 1972. Marcos, once a popular leader, had won election as president in 1965 and 1969, but during the 1970s he grew increasingly corrupt and repressive.

The Catholic Church, led by Jaime Cardinal Sin, played an important role in supporting and legitimizing the protest against the dictator. The assassination in August 1983 of Benigno Aquino Jr., the principal opposition leader, polarized the country, and the guerrillas profited. The Communist New People's Army, which numbered in the hundreds when Marcos declared martial law in 1972, increased to more than twenty thousand armed men by the time Marcos quit power in 1986.[29]

Reagan initially criticized Carter's human rights policy and identified with Marcos. When Vice President George Bush visited the Philippines in July 1981, he complimented Marcos: "We love your adherence to democratic principles and democratic processes."[30] The next year Reagan warmly welcomed Marcos on a state visit to Washington.

The killing of Benigno Aquino and the growing power of the insurgents finally impelled the Reagan administration to distance itself from Marcos and press for reforms. President Reagan's planned state visit to the Philippines in November 1983 was canceled. A State Department policy paper written in November 1984, and leaked to the press five months later, warned: "An overriding consideration should be to avoid getting ourselves caught between the slow erosion of Marcos's authoritarian control and the still fragile revitalization of democratic institutions." The State Department recommended pressuring Marcos to accept a democratic political succession.[31] Marcos acquiesced to some of the minor demands but blasted the United States for interfering in Philippine politics.[32] American conservatives grew uneasy about the insurgency, while liberals demanded that Reagan "repudiate any notion of propping up Ferdinand Marcos."[33]

The Reagan administration was divided. The president viewed Marcos as a friend; having criticized Carter for abandoning America's friends, he was loath to do the same. The Defense Department was "impressed with Marcos's grit" and anxious about U.S. military bases. The CIA and the State Department were convinced that Marcos's continuance in power would lead to another Nicaragua.[34] The administration resolved its bureaucratic conflict by encouraging Marcos to hold a free election before 1987. Apparently believing he would win, either freely or by manipulation, Marcos announced on U.S. television that he would schedule a new election. The Philippine opposition, unlike that in Nicaragua, never seriously considered supporting the guerrillas against Marcos. Although initially divided, it eventually united behind the candidacy of Corazon Aquino, the widow of the slain leader. The National Citizens Movement for Free Elections (NAMFREL), an independent poll-watching organization, had experience observing elections.

Marcos manipulated the results of the elections held on February 7, 1986, but he was caught and denounced by NAMFREL, the international press, and a U.S. delegation led by Senator Richard Lugar. Supported by the Church, many businesses, and the united opposition, Corazon Aquino launched a nonviolent protest. Reagan equivocated, blaming "both sides" for electoral fraud, to the embarrassment of the U.S. ambassador and Aquino.[35] In his memoirs, Reagan admits he did not think Marcos committed fraud until Lugar briefed him in Washington. On February 22, Defense Minister Juan Ponce Enrile and Vice Chief of Staff General Fidel Ramos announced their support of Aquino and asked Marcos to resign. Two days later army rebels, surrounded by the civilian opposition and a group of nuns, approached the presidential palace. Marcos faced the choice of resigning or ordering the soldiers loyal to him to fire at the crowd. Only then did Reagan decide to withdraw his support from Marcos.[36]

The White House issued a statement urging Marcos to permit a peaceful transition to a new government. Marcos then phoned Senator Paul Laxalt, who was close to Reagan, to ask whether that statement "was genuinely from President Reagan" or reflected only the views of the State Department, which he did not trust. Laxalt affirmed that it came from Reagan. Then Marcos asked Laxalt if Reagan wanted him to resign. Laxalt called Reagan, who told the senator that Marcos "would be welcome to come to the United States."[37] As happened between Carter and Somoza, Reagan would not ask Marcos to resign, nor would he defend him. Laxalt then told Marcos that he could not answer the question directly, but when asked his own views, Laxalt said: "Cut and cut cleanly. The time has come."[38] Marcos decided to leave.

Chile, 1988–1989

As it had with the Philippines, the Reagan administration at first repudiated Carter's human rights policy and sought warm relations with Chile's dictator, General Augusto Pinochet, who had held power since 1973. But in 1984, the administration returned to a policy similar to Carter's for three reasons: violence by a small, determined leftist group; intensified demands for a return to democracy by the moderate opposition; and the desire to show that its commitment to democracy was not just a ploy for obtaining aid for the contras in Nicaragua. The administration decided to show it was serious about democracy in Nicaragua by supporting it in Chile.

As *The New York Times* reported on December 2, 1984: "Mediation in Chile Termed Essential by U.S. Officials: Review Produces a Consensus for a Major Effort to Avoid 'Another Nicaragua.'" The administration abstained or voted against loans to Chile in the international development banks; it urged a democratic transition, but it was unwilling to overthrow Pinochet.[39] Indeed, the consensus in the policy review was that the United States should not even "take sides"; rather, it should be an impartial mediator between Pinochet and the opposition.

Chile's succession crisis was the most gradual and controlled of all the cases examined here, probably because the country had a long democratic and constitutional tradition before Pinochet's 1973 coup. The polarization during the Allende government (1970–1973) and the resulting coup were traumas that the majority of the Chilean public did not want to repeat. With U.S. encouragement, the opposition succeeded in negotiating the terms for a free plebiscite on Pinochet's tenure. Pinochet thought he could win a free election and wanted to ensure that it would not appear tainted. International observers raised the price of rigging the vote count or disregarding the outcome.

On October 5, 1988, nearly 4 million Chileans went to the polls, representing 97 percent of the registered voters. They rejected Pinochet by 54 to 43 percent. Although there was some reluctance on Pinochet's part to accept the results, the other military members of the junta quickly issued a statement that the opposition had won. This cleared the way for a presidential election on December 14, 1989, and the Christian Democratic victor took office on March 11, 1990.

Outcomes and Explanations

Three of the crises discussed here culminated in nondemocratic, anti-American revolutionary regimes—the worst outcome from the perspective of the United States and local democrats. Two of the cases ended with democracies, the best outcome; and two led to military takeovers. How to explain the differences?

The middle sector played the pivotal role in every case. Indeed, each crisis could be said to have begun, at least from the U.S. perspective, when middle-class opposition to the dictator became militant. In three cases the decision by centrist groups and democratic governments to support a violent overthrow of the regime provided legitimacy to the revolutionaries and neutralized a U.S. role. In Cuba and Nicaragua, the center, supported by democratic governments in the region, aligned with the guerrillas. In Iran the moderate National Front aligned with Khomeini and expelled Bakhtiar when he entered the Shah's government. The middle sectors chose the risky option of supporting the revolutionaries out of frustration with the dictator's intransigence and in the hope that they could moderate the revolutionaries if they helped them. Squeezed between a repressive dictator and anti-American revolutionaries, the United States would not support the dictator, but it could not intervene against the revolutionaries because the latter had the support of the middle groups.

In the two successful cases—the Philippines and Chile—the middle sectors did not ally with the guerrilla insurgency, and the guerrillas did not enjoy any support from democratic governments. In the Dominican Republic and Haiti the middle sectors were relatively weak, and there was no insurgency. This eliminated the prospect of a worst-case scenario from the U.S. perspective, but it meant that the military filled the power vacuum after the dictators departed.

The role of the military also had important effects on each outcome. The military remained loyal to the dictator in the cases of Cuba, Nicaragua, and Iran, and all three militaries collapsed when the dictators left. Some observers thought that the disintegration of the Nicaraguan National Guard was due to the lack of U.S. assurances, but these were given in Cuba and Iran with no effect. Military defection from dictators in the Dominican Republic, Haiti, the Philippines, and (to a limited extent) Chile permitted nonrevolutionary successor regimes to emerge.

Elections were important to the success of democracy in the Philippines and Chile, where the opposition negotiated conditions that permitted detection of fraud. In these two cases, last-minute efforts to manipulate the vote or the count failed. Whether or not the dictator was prepared to accept his loss initially, the election denied him legitimacy more effectively than all the earlier demonstrations and strikes. Thus, elections served as the best avenue for peaceful change, even for countries emerging from long periods of tyranny.

The United States was important in encouraging elections in these cases, but it had encouraged free elections unsuccessfully in Cuba, Nicaragua, and Haiti. The reason for the policy's success or failure had less to do with the United States than with the history of the other country. Nicaragua and Haiti had never held a free election, and Cuba's experience with democracy was negligible. In these countries the opposition was divided into small factions, many of which preferred to withdraw under protest rather than participate in the elections. In contrast, both the Philippines and Chile had enjoyed free elections, and the opposition was willing to risk participation. In both cases, the dictator convinced himself that he could win, either honestly or with minimal fraud.

Negotiating the terms for free elections proved more effective than negotiating transitions. In Nicaragua, a negotiated transitional arrangement fell apart the day after Somoza's departure. The negotiated exit of the Shah also failed within days of the arrival of the Ayatollah. Only when elections legitimized a successor regime did prearranged transitions work.

A final factor that explains the different outcomes is the influence of recent similar experiences on the decisionmakers. The trauma of Castro's victory impelled both local and international actors to try to precipitate changes in the Dominican Republic and Haiti to preempt revolution. Similarly, two decades later, the Nicaraguan trauma had a profound influence on the crises in Chile and the Philippines. The moderate sectors appear to have learned the principal lesson of the Nicaraguan revolution: unite, participate in elections, and resist the siren calls of the insurgents. From the outside, efforts to encourage and monitor elections seem to offer the most promise for a graceful and successful exit from succession crises, although local actors and experiences remain the principal cause of the success or failure of elections.

The Realm of Choices for U.S. Decisionmakers

To say that U.S. policy alone cannot explain the different outcomes in these seven cases does not mean that U.S. policy was irrelevant, only that the decisive factors were indigenous. To understand how the United States can improve its ability to facilitate democratic transitions from succession crises, it is essential to analyze the range of options available to U.S. policymakers.

As the crisis unfolds, the United States has three options: (1) let events take their course, (2) bolster the dictator, or (3) oppose the dictator. In each of the cases discussed, with the partial exception of Iran, the U.S. government chose to oppose the dictator by promoting a democratic transition. Even a conservative administration could not continue supporting a dictator if the middle groups in that country reject him. This explains Eisenhower's distancing from Batista and Reagan's from Marcos and Duvalier. Carter continued to support the Shah simply because he was viewed by Washington as more liberal than the alternative.

Several administrations considered very seriously the option of trying to overthrow the dictator. In the case of the Dominican Republic, both Eisenhower and Kennedy encouraged a conspiracy to unseat Trujillo. As the day of decision approached, Kennedy tried to stop the conspiracy and, when that failed, to dissociate from it. For a similar reason, U.S. presidents also did not ask dictators to resign (except at the very last moments in Cuba and Nicaragua), nor did they apply sufficient pressure to compel them to resign in either the successful or the unsuccessful cases.

There is only one known case, Vietnam, where a U.S. president encouraged a coup against a "friendly" dictator. In 1963 the United States concluded that the war in South Vietnam could not be won so long as Ngo Dinh Diem was president, and Kennedy approved a military coup to overthrow him. The president weighed this decision carefully from August until the assassination of Diem on November 1, 1963.[40] Four years later, in its report on the war, the Pentagon described the coup as a lamentable watershed: "Our complicity in his overthrow heightened our responsibilities and our commitment in Vietnam."[41] None of Kennedy's successors would repeat his mistake.

There are other reasons why this option was rejected. Friendly dictators represent an indirect rather than a direct threat to U.S. interests. The main threat posed by Batista and the other dictators was that their continuing presence in power increased the chances of a revolutionary military victory. If the United States forced out the dictators, the consequences might have been instability, as occurred in the Dominican Republic and Vietnam, or a clearer path to power for the revolutionaries. This partly explains why Kennedy backed away from a coup against Trujillo and virtually precluded a Haitian coup by setting stringent preconditions.

It is not surprising that the United States has proposed elections as the best middle path between the dictator and the revolutionaries. Presidents as different as Calvin Coolidge and Jimmy Carter have regarded elections as the way to resolve succession crises. The idea is born of America's national experience, not the other country's. Public opinion polls in the United States show a marked preference for removing dictators by elections rather than by force, even if the results favor Communists.[42]

In summary, as the United States traversed the four stages in each of the seven succession crises, it was guided by its national experience through a polarized terrain of unattractive options. In some cases, although not all, the search for a middle option was fruitful. From the beginning to the end of the crises, the moderate groups stimulated, guided, and defined the parameters of U.S. policy, although they were often unaware of their influence. Whereas Americans proposed elections as the solution, few if any moderates in these nations thought in those terms. They wanted the dictator out and believed that only the United States could accomplish that. When the United States failed to remove the dictator, the moderates allied with the revolutionaries, thinking that, in the end, the United States would never let the revolutionaries take power. One Nicaraguan businessman recalled that "many people told us [during the revolution] that this was going to be another Cuba, but we did not think it could happen. . . . Surely, the U.S. was not going to let this become another Cuba."[43] But when the moderates joined the Sandinistas, they removed the middle option on which the United States relied. The worst outcomes occurred when signals were misunderstood between the moderates, who thought they were following the United States but were actually leading it, and the United States, which was a step behind them.

In considering future U.S. policies, then, the only real choices are within the parameters of promoting liberalization. Because military intervention is ruled out, the United States cannot control or even manage a succession crisis. The issue for U.S. policymakers is how to influence the crisis from the periphery of events. The outcome will depend, first and last, on the decisions of local actors—on the dictator, the military, the moderate opposition, and the radicals—but U.S. influence and timing can exert an important influence.

The best outcomes occurred when a dictator agreed to elections, a united opposition chose to participate and could negotiate the terms for free elections, and the dictator was forced to accept the election results. Outside mediators can play a crucial role in this process, as they did in Nicaragua in 1989–1990 (see Chapter 13). The United States needs better information on the actors than it has had in past succession crises. A dictator's personal needs and weaknesses should be the object of intense and continuing study. The United States should pursue contacts with the military at all levels.

The most delicate and important relationships are with the moderate opposition and the insurgents. When moderates divided and allied with the insurgents, they forfeited their future. As a succession crisis approaches, the United States should develop a comprehensive strategy aimed at all four stages of the crisis: (1) isolate the dictatorship through a clear, multilateral human rights policy; (2) facilitate the dictator's exit through negotiations that reflect a full understanding of his weaknesses and needs; (3) assist in the transition toward free elections through international mediators and observers; and (4) aid the consolidation of democracy.

By the time a dictator begins to fall, the boundaries of U.S. influence have already narrowed. Long before that happens, the United States should work with other democracies in the hemisphere and use the reservoir of American resources to aid democratic institutions.

Notes

1. Quoted in Elaine Sciolino, "Panama's Chief Defies U.S. Powers of Persuasion," *The New York Times,* January 17, 1988, p. E3.

2. Quoted in Arthur M. Schlesinger Jr., *A Thousand Days: John F. Kennedy in the White House* (Boston: Houghton Mifflin, 1965), p. 769.

3. Figueres's involvement is documented in a hearing of the U.S. Senate, Committee on the Judiciary, *Communist Threat to the United States through the Caribbean: Hearings before the Subcommittee to Investigate the Administration of the Internal Security Act and Other Internal Security Laws, Part 8,* 86th Cong., 2d sess., January 22–23, 1960, pp. 447–54. Pérez acknowledged his help in an interview with WGBH-Public Television (Boston) in New York, May 2, 1984.

4. Quoted in Hugh Thomas, *Cuba: The Pursuit of Freedom* (New York: Harper & Row, 1971), pp. 1015–1016.

5. Ibid., p. 1018.

6. Ibid., p. 1028.

7. The quotation and conclusion are from Secretary of State Dean Rusk, testimony before the U.S. Senate, *Alleged Assassination Plots Involving Foreign Leaders,* an interim report of the Select Committee to Study Governmental Operations with Respect to Intelligence Activities, 94th Cong., 1st sess., November 20, 1975, pp. 191–192 (hereafter cited as Senate Report on Assassinations, 1975).

8. Bernard Diederich, *Trujillo: The Death of the Goat* (Boston: Little, Brown, 1978), p. 41.

9. The quotation is from a memorandum from Secretary of State Christian Herter to the president, April 14, 1960. Presidential approval was indicated in a letter from Herter to the secretary of defense, April 21, 1960. Senate Report on Assassinations, 1975, p. 192.

10. Quoted in Stephen G. Rabe, *Eisenhower and Latin America: The Foreign Policy of Anticommunism* (Chapel Hill: University of North Carolina Press, 1988), p. 156.

11. Senate Report on Assassinations, 1975, pp. 197–205, 257.

12. Ibid., p. 209. Record of actions by National Security Council, May 5, 1961; approved by the president, May 16, 1961.

13. Senate Report on Assassinations, 1975, p. 212.

14. Kennedy escaped blame for the instability that resulted because his role was not disclosed for ten years.

15. In its analysis of this final cable, the Senate committee addressed the question of whether it was "designed to avoid a charge that the United States shared responsibility for the assassination." The committee concluded that the cable's "ambiguity illustrates the difficulty of seeking objectives which can only be accomplished by force—indeed, perhaps only by the assassination of a leader—and yet not wishing to take specific actions which seem abhorrent." Senate Report on Assassinations, 1975, pp. 212–213, 263.

16. Quoted in Schlesinger, *A Thousand Days,* pp. 770–771.

17. Edwin Martin, "Haiti: A Case Study in Futility," *SAIS Review* 1 (Summer 1981): 66. Martin was assistant secretary of state for inter-American affairs from 1962 to 1963.

18. Ibid., p. 63.

19. Georges Fauriol, "The Duvaliers and Haiti," *Orbis* 32 (Fall 1988): 601.

20. President Reagan's press conference of February 11, 1986, reprinted the next day in *The New York Times,* p. 10. Others, including Georges Fauriol, "The

Duvaliers and Haiti," and Elizabeth Abbott, *Haiti: The Duvaliers and Their Legacy* (New York: McGraw-Hill, 1988), have written that the U.S. embassy played a much larger role in Duvalier's departure; if true, this would mean that President Reagan either deliberately misled the American people or did not know what his administration had done in Haiti.

21. See Robert A. Pastor, *Condemned to Repetition: The United States and Nicaragua* (Princeton: Princeton University Press, 1987).

22. On the tenth anniversary of the revolution, the Sandinistas published the transcripts of the exchange in which Humberto Ortega, then head of the Sandinista army, demanded the surrender of Federico Mejía, the Guard commander, making clear his intention to capture Managua, thus violating the previous agreement. "Las Ultimas Horas de la Guardia Somocista: El Frente Jamas Detuvo Avance Hacia Managua," *Barricada* (Managua), July 19, 1989, pp. 6–7.

23. Interview with former President Jimmy Carter, November 12, 1987, Atlanta, Georgia.

24. Zbigniew Brzezinski, *Power and Principle: Memoirs of the National Security Adviser, 1977–1981* (New York: Farrar, Straus & Giroux, 1983), p. 354.

25. For Iranian perceptions and the Nixon agreement, see Gary Sick, *All Fall Down: America's Tragic Encounter with Iran* (New York: Random House, 1985), pp. 7, 20.

26. Ibid., p. 34.

27. Jimmy Carter, *Keeping Faith: Memoirs of a President* (New York: Bantam, 1982), p. 440.

28. Ibid., pp. 442–443.

29. Theodore Friend, "Marcos and the Philippines," *Orbis* 32 (Fall 1988): 572.

30. "In Toast to Marcos, Bush Lauds Manila Democracy," *Washington Post*, July 1, 1981, p. A20.

31. Don Oberdorfer, "U.S. Pressing for Democratic Succession in Philippines," *Washington Post*, March 12, 1985, p. A11.

32. "Marcos Faults U.S. Role in Philippine Politics," *The New York Times*, March 19, 1984, p. A7.

33. Stephen J. Solarz, "Last Chance for the Philippines," *New Republic*, April 8, 1985, pp. 12–17.

34. See Fred Barnes, "White House Watch: Civil War," *New Republic*, March 10, 1986, pp. 8–9.

35. Sandra Burton, *Impossible Dream: The Marcoses, the Aquinos, the Unfinished Revolution* (New York: Warner Books, 1989), pp. 361–363, 371.

36. Ronald Reagan, *An American Life* (New York: Simon & Schuster, 1990), pp. 362–367.

37. Paul Laxalt, "My Conversations with Ferdinand Marcos: A Lesson in Personal Diplomacy," *Policy Review* 37 (Summer 1986): 2–5.

38. For Laxalt's comments, see Charles Mohr, "Laxalt Says Marcos Vote Was Suggested by CIA," *The New York Times,* July 18, 1986, p. 5; for the White House statement and background comments, see Seth Mydans, "Marcos Ignores Plea by U.S. and Vows to Stay in Office; Rebels to Swear in Aquino," *The New York Times,* February 25, 1986, pp. 1, 5; Bernard Gwertzman, "Reagan Sent Marcos Secret Message 12 Hours Before White House's Plea," *The New York Times,* February 28, 1986, p. 6.

39. Bernard Gwertzman, "Mediation in Chile Termed Essential," *The New York Times,* December 2, 1984, pp. 1, 4; Joel Brinkley, "U.S. to Abstain on Loan to Chile to Protest Human Rights Abuses," *The New York Times,* February 6, 1985, p. 4.

40. A White House cable to Ambassador Henry Cabot Lodge on October 5 insisted that "this effort be totally secure and fully deniable." National Security Adviser McGeorge Bundy cabled Lodge on October 25 to convey President Kennedy's concerns about the hazard of an unsuccessful coup, but he did not try to stop it. See *The Pentagon Papers: As Published by The New York Times* (New York: Bantam Books, 1971), pp. 158–233; quotations from pp. 216, 219. See also Ellen J. Hammer, *A Death in November: America in Vietnam, 1963* (New York: Dutton, 1987).

41. *The Pentagon Papers,* p. 158.

42. In a 1986 poll 40 percent of Americans agreed that the United States should push a reluctant dictator to hold elections, even if the Communists would win; 33 percent disagreed. *National Journal,* May 17, 1986, p. 1224.

43. Ramiro Gurdian, "Nicaragua: A View from the Private Sector," *Caribbean Today* (December 1983): 5–6.

9

REVOLUTIONARY REGIMES: WHO PUSHED FIRST?

> *There are some lessons. . . . High among them is the degree to which fear can lead events irreversibly to destruction. Maurice Bishop's fear, for example, of external intervention was clearly a factor in making that intervention more probable. But he was not only a victim of fear, he was a generator of it. . . . What is the lesson then? Surely that dogmatism of right or left that drives out tolerance and fails to take account of the anxieties its own intolerance generates will ultimately lead to desperate measures; and make harder the triumph of practicality over inclination.*[1]
>
> —SHRIDATH RAMPHAL

At about noon on March 13, 1979, David Aaron, the deputy assistant for national security affairs, phoned me in my office at the National Security Council: "Pastor," he bellowed with an unusual mixture of anger and irony, "did you lose Grenada?"

Eric Gairy, Grenada's prime minister, had been overthrown that morning by a group of leftists known as the New Jewel Movement (NJM). Gairy could be cruel, but he was also bizarre, a devotee of strange hobbies, including unidentified flying objects. Gairy had led Grenada to independence in 1974, but the NJM intercepted him taking it to outer space.

"It wasn't me, sir," I responded to Aaron's question, feigning the expression of a butler being accused of stealing his master's silverware. "Besides," I continued, "as far as I know, Grenada is still about 100 miles north of Venezuela. It's not lost." Aaron wasn't laughing: "The coup isn't funny." It wasn't. And it was. Both assertions were true, and that internal contradiction concealed the essence of the quandary faced by the United States in that small country and, more generally, with all revolutionary regimes.

Grenada is located at the Caribbean crossroads of comedy and tragedy. An island of fewer than 100,000 people, Grenada is twice the size of Washington, D.C., but has one-sixth the population. The coup that brought a group of closet Marxist-Leninists to power was another example of a recurring North American fear of "losing" a country on its border. For those who failed to recognize the significance of the regime change in 1979, President Ronald Reagan brought the issue to American homes in a televised address four years later. Reagan warned that the new airport being built there by Cubans could be used by our rivals or against our friends. Six months later, U.S. troops parachuted onto the new airfield and installed a government friendlier to Washington.

Grenada is much smaller than Nicaragua or Cuba, but the pattern of the U.S. response to the revolutionary regimes in each of these countries was cut from the same cloth: beginning with a suspicious but respectful cordiality, moving to a resentful dissociation, and concluding with confrontation. If the United States was ineffective when responding to succession crises, it has been counterproductive when trying to cope with revolutions in Latin America. In each case, the United States elicited the opposite of what it wanted with regard to the internal and external character of the revolutionary regime. The same could be said of each of the regimes: They sought respect from the United States but pursued policies that provoked U.S. hostility.

In each case, the questions posed were whether (1) the United States clumsily pushed the regimes into the waiting arms of its adversaries; (2) the revolutionary regimes leaped onto the unsuspecting shoulders of the Russian bear because of the ideology of their leadership; or (3) some interactive logic compelled both sides to produce the opposite of what they wanted. Scholars continue to disagree on the answers to these questions as they apply to Cuba and Nicaragua.[2] The Grenada case perhaps offers the best opportunity to answer them because of the available resources, including a huge cache of documents removed by U.S. forces after the invasion and some documents on U.S. policy that have been declassified since then.[3]

The Setting

The international spotlight on Grenada failed to illuminate the simple fact that its politics and problems were those of a very small island dominated by a quasi-religious leader, Eric Gairy, from its first free election in 1951 until the revolution of 1979. Upon returning to Grenada from Trinidad's oil fields in 1949 at the age of twenty-seven, Gairy organized poor estate workers. He attracted a devoted following after successfully confronting the planters and the British bureaucracy. Over time, however, Gairy developed "into a feared and somewhat eccentric Negro shepherd-king."[4] By the 1970s, Gairy was extorting money, terrorizing opponents, and lecturing on UFOs. He was an embarrassment to the newly educated Grenadians, whose path to power was blocked by his continued popularity among the poor. Over a twenty-five-year period, Gairy lost only two of eight elections. On December 7, 1976, the last election before the revolution, a coalition of three parties, which included the NJM, won 48.6 percent of the vote, but Gairy won a majority and nine of fifteen seats in the Legislative Assembly.

One month later, the Carter administration took office, eager to formulate a new policy toward the Caribbean that emphasized development and regional cooperation. Grenada was not on the radar screen of senior administration officials. However, in February 1979, the Treasury Department's Bureau of Alcohol, Tobacco, and Firearms (ATF) arrested two Grenadians in Baltimore and charged them with illegally shipping weapons to Grenada. On March 12, two ATF agents and an embassy officer arrived on the island as Gairy was leaving.[5] The agents worked with Grenada's police, who arrested one NJM leader and interrogated others. NJM leaders learned quickly about the police inquiries, and five leaders—Maurice Bishop, Bernard Coard, and three others—called a secret meeting on March 13. Bishop's father had been killed by Gairy's thugs, and the NJM leaders feared that Gairy had learned of their arms smuggling and had given orders to the police to assassinate them in his absence.[6] The five voted 3–2 to launch a coup.[7] At 4:00 A.M., about forty-five members of the NJM attacked the True Blue police barracks with twenty-one guns and then seized the radio station. Two policemen were killed. The people of Grenada woke up to learn that Radio Grenada had become Radio Free Grenada and that they had been liberated.

First Phase: The Empty Embrace

Upon learning of the coup, British Prime Minister James Callaghan sent a frigate to Grenada and phoned Prime Minister Tom Adams of Barbados for his views. Adams told him that Gairy was indefensible and that Bishop had phoned him and pledged early elections. Adams invited the leaders of five neighboring states to Barbados for meetings on March 14 and 15.[8] All were deeply concerned about the implications of the first violent change of government in the area. Most knew Bishop, Coard, and some of the other NJM leaders either personally or through reputation as men of the "left." The question, they asked themselves, was how far left, and what were their intentions?

In the communiqué issued after their first day of meetings, the five leaders asserted "that the wider interests and unity of the area and of Grenada in particular require a return to constitutionality as soon as possible." Bishop phoned these leaders and others, including U.S. Ambassador Frank Ortiz, and the Caribbean communiqué took note of "the stated declaration of the leaders of the regime in Grenada to hold free and fair elections and . . . the hope that this would be done without delay."[9]

In the United States, a National Security Council subcommittee (mini-SCC) met the same day, March 15. Representatives of all the agencies had the same suspicions about the new leaders in Grenada as the Caribbean leaders had. Despite the many assurances, there were other unsettling signs in Grenada. The broadcasts from Radio Free Grenada sounded more like the propaganda of a communist regime than the newscasts of a democratic nation. More troubling was Bishop's dismissal of the police force and army and their replacement by an NJM People's Revolutionary Army.

The discussion in the mini-SCC reflected predictable bureaucratic differences: The Pentagon viewed the potential threat more anxiously; the State Department took a more relaxed approach. Nonetheless, a consensus soon emerged that a return by Eric Gairy was untenable. As there were no obvious alternatives, the group recommended to the president that the United States support Great Britain and the Eastern Caribbean nations in their efforts to influence the new regime to make good on its promise of early and free elections. After the Eastern Caribbean nations recognized the new regime, the State Department followed suit on March 22.[10]

On the same day, Ortiz, who was stationed in Barbados but also accredited to Grenada, was instructed to travel to Grenada to inform the new leaders of the U.S. aid program and to communicate U.S. interest in cooperative relations. The United States also offered to increase the number of Peace Corps volunteers on the island. When Bishop expressed interest, Ortiz said that a new group could arrive within one or two weeks. In addition, Ortiz described the Special Development Activities Fund (SDA), which could be used for grants of $5,000 for community-related projects. Although the amount was small, these grants were popular in the region because they could be disbursed quickly. Again, Bishop expressed interest. Ortiz emphasized the importance of early elections. Bishop refused to fix a date and said the PRG had not yet decided whether to continue the "alien" Westminster system or create a "real" democracy, like that of ancient Greece.

In his report to Washington, Ortiz recommended "forebearance and patience and avoiding unnecessary confrontation until the new government is more comfortable in its relationship with us."[11] This approach was accepted. The State Department informed its ambassadors in the region that "our main purpose is to keep Grenada from drifting into the Cuban orbit. We continue to feel that this can best be accomplished by working with the new government, showing understanding for its efforts to strengthen democratic institutions and processes, while giving fair warning that attempts to abridge these norms will inevitably have an adverse impact on our relations."[12]

Two days later, on March 25, Bishop held another rally and broke one of his pledges. He suspended the constitution and decreed "ten fundamental People's Laws," which included the continuation of emergency arrest powers for the People's Revolutionary Army. He soon began to receive arms shipments. A Guyanese ship landed in Grenada on March 22 with supplies—and possibly arms. On April 4, 7, and 8, three Cuban planes landed at Pearls airport and unloaded arms, and on April 9, a second Guyanese ship arrived in St. George's with Cuban arms.

At the same time, Bishop's speeches and his government's radio broadcasts began to warn of an imminent invasion from a neighboring island by Gairy's mercenaries. At a press conference on April 9, Bishop said that he would request arms from the United States, United Kingdom, Canada, and Venezuela to prevent a countercoup by Gairy. He added parenthetically: "We have also asked the governments of Cuba and other Caribbean countries for assistance in military training so as to prevent an attack planned by mercenaries against our country." This announcement appeared to be a trial balloon.

Ambassador Ortiz was sent to assure Bishop that Gairy would not invade the island and to inform him that U.S. relations would be affected if Bishop developed close military ties to Cuba. Ortiz arrived on April 9 and was left to wait all day to see Bishop. While waiting, he witnessed the army shooting at but missing a small plane contracted by Holiday Inn to take tourist photographs of the beach and hotel.

Ortiz first saw Coard and emphasized the importance of tourism to Grenada. Then he warned Coard "that incidents such as one I had just witnessed [the shooting at the plane] and the invasion scares would frighten tourists away." In his conversation with Bishop later the same day, Ortiz reiterated his previous offer to send AID officials and Peace Corps volunteers, but Bishop said he was not ready for them. When Bishop asked for military aid, Ortiz explained that the Grenadian government should decide what it wanted and make a formal request. When the ambassador then pressed Bishop on his promise to hold elections soon, Bishop showed "some annoyance."[13]

Ortiz then provided proof that Gairy was in San Diego, not on a neighboring island, as Bishop had claimed, and he assured Bishop that the United States would prevent any invasion attempt. He urged Bishop to try to calm the people by conveying the information about Gairy, but Bishop declined. Ortiz then made his point on Cuba:

> Although my government recognizes your concerns over allegations of a possible counter-coup, it also believes that it would not be in Grenada's best interests to seek assistance from a country such as Cuba to forestall such an attack. We would view with displeasure any tendency on the part of Grenada to develop closer ties with Cuba.[14]

Ortiz asked Bishop whether he had been offered any Cuban aid, and Bishop said no but that he would accept aid from any source if there were a mercenary invasion. The truth was that Bishop had already received weapons from Cuba. In an interview many years later, Coard admitted that Cuba had paid no attention to the New Jewel Movement until the coup. The next day, Castro passed them a message that he would send weapons and provide training to the NJM, and he also agreed to establish party-to-party relations.[15] Although not authorized to leave a copy of the talking points, Ortiz did so because he thought Bishop had not absorbed the points. Later that day Bishop met the British ambassador, who also offered to send an aid team and a group of security advisers. Bishop thanked him and promised to let him know when they should come. He never did.[16]

On April 13, Bishop blasted the United States in his first major speech. With the deftness of an accomplished orator, Bishop used Ortiz's demarche to assert the revolution's nationalist credentials and paint the United States as an insensitive bully trying to push around small Grenada. "The Ambassador," Bishop told the crowd, "went on to advise us that if we continue to speak about what he called 'mercenary invasions by phantom armies' that we would lose our tourists. He also reminded us of the experience which Jamaica had had in this regard a few years ago. As some of you will undoubtedly recall, Jamaica at that time had gone through a period of intense de-stabilization." Striking an aggrieved posture, Bishop told his people that "we have always striven to develop the closest and friendliest relations with the United States." But when Grenada requested aid, the United States offered only $5,000. "Sisters and brothers, our hospitals are without medicines. . . . Is [that] all the wealthiest country in the world can offer?"

Then, after insisting that Gairy was about to launch an invasion, Bishop read from the talking points that Ortiz had left, explaining that the United States would not permit Grenada to ask for help from or have relations with Cuba. "We reject entirely the argument of the American Ambassador. . . . If the government of Cuba is willing to offer us assistance, we would be more than happy to receive it." He concluded his speech with powerful symbolism: "No country has the right to tell us what to do or how to run our country, or who to be friendly with. . . . We are not in anybody's backyard, and we are definitely not for sale. . . . Though small and poor, we are proud and determined."

The next day, as if in reaction to Ortiz's demarche rather than at the end of an eight-day voyage from Havana, the Cuban ship *Matanzas* docked at St. George's. Fifty Cuban technicians and many crates of arms were unloaded. The PRG then announced the establishment of diplomatic relations with Cuba. On the same day, Bishop called the U.S. chargé in Barbados and demanded that he send the AID officials promised by the ambassador right away. The embassy, not having yet fully absorbed his speech, sent an AID officer, but no high Grenadian official would meet him.

The speech, however, and an article by Karen DeYoung of the *Washington Post,* defined the way most of the world, with the exception of the

U.S. government, would perceive the new revolution. DeYoung reported that the "strong U.S. diplomatic response . . . may succeed only in pushing Grenada further to the left." Whereas the Cubans were responsive and helpful to the revolution, the United States only expressed "concern" and "displeasure" and regret over budgetary procedures. Moreover, according to DeYoung, public opinion on the island had turned against the United States, now regarded as "a bully and a stingy one to boot."[17]

Bishop's speech represented a turning point. The sequence of events leading up to the speech—the secret arrival of Cuban arms and advisers, the requests for help from the West without any follow-up—led most analysts in the U.S. government to conclude that Bishop had deliberately staged the confrontation with the United States. Bishop had been waiting for the right opportunity to denounce Washington, establish his nationalist credentials, and justify a relationship with Cuba, and Ortiz's demarche gave him that opportunity.[18]

In October 1982 I described this perception to Bishop and Coard, and both listened with what I perceived as genuine incredulity. Coard answered most candidly: "Look, this was our first revolution. We were very inexperienced." Bishop was more colorful: "We are a lot like Americans. If you kick us in the shins, we will kick you in the balls." Both insisted that Bishop's speech on April 13 was not premeditated; it was an emotional reaction to their perception of Ortiz's "lectures." In January 2000, Coard repeated that Bishop's response was not orchestrated before the conversation with Ortiz, but he did admit that the entire revolutionary elite were "paranoid" at the time: "We were like Joe McCarthy in reverse. He saw Communists under every bed, and we saw the CIA under every bed."[19]

Ortiz's demarche reinforced their image of the United States as bent on destroying their young revolution. And their response, in turn, confirmed the impression in Washington that these young Marxists wanted to provoke the United States to justify their militarization and alliance with Cuba.

Second Phase: Moving Apart

Soon after Bishop's speech on April 13, the U.S. government reevaluated its policy. By mid-April, the People's Revolutionary Army had grown from about fifty men to about two thousand (including the militia), eclipsing all the other armies of the region combined. Even though there was very little criticism of the regime, it imprisoned about eighty political and union leaders. The PRG admitted receiving arms from Cuba and other countries, later estimated at about 3,400 rifles, 200 machine guns, 100 heavy weapons, and ammunition.[20]

At a mini-SCC meeting on April 27, 1979, everyone agreed to keep pressing the regime to hold free elections, but the participants disagreed on the best strategy to accomplish that goal. Some argued that Bishop was still co-optable, and the United States should give more aid to the regime, reassure its neighbors, and encourage the Europeans to do more. Others argued that the April 13 speech signaled a turning toward Cuba and that U.S. policy ought to aim at assisting the rest of the Caribbean with a "regional strategy." The mini-SCC recommended the "regional strategy" to the president, and he approved it.

The co-optation strategy was rejected for four reasons. First, most analysts thought it had been tried and rejected by Bishop, who never followed up any request for aid from the United States, made clear his preference for a closer relationship with Cuba, and used every opportunity to attack Washington. Second, most feared that providing more aid to the one radical regime in the area would undermine the democracies and lend support to radicals on the other islands. Third, the strategy was most congruent with the administration's preference for approaching such problems with regional friends. And fourth, the other nations could probably have a more positive influence on the PRG than the United States could. It appeared that the NJM was comfortable with the United States as its enemy, and therefore the United States should try to avoid giving it a target.

Between April and November 1979, the United States pursued the regional strategy while continuing to explore the possibilities for good relations. For example, in response to Bishop's repeated interest in extraditing Gairy, U.S. Ambassador Sally Shelton, who had replaced Ortiz in the fall of 1979, persuaded the director of the Justice Department's extradition office to visit Grenada to help the government prepare its case. Neither Bishop nor any senior official in his government met him when he arrived.[21]

Grenada reserved its closest relationships for Cuba and the Soviet Union, and its opposition to a UN resolution condemning the Soviet invasion of Afghanistan was one public sign. The documents reveal an even closer relationship, although the PRG was more the pursuer than the pursued, and the Soviet Union gave less aid than Cuba. Within Grenada, the NJM took a hard-line approach, closing independent newspapers, imprisoning political opponents, prohibiting activities by other political parties, and manipulating labor unions. But the government was more flexible with private business and promoted tourism—a curious priority, given the revolutionary rhetoric.

During the remainder of the Carter administration, the United States expanded development programs for Grenada's neighbors. The British improved the region's police forces, and the United States helped to establish a regional coast guard. The nations of the region developed informal arrangements to help each other in times of emergency.

Phase Three: Isolation, Intimidation, and Intervention

The Reagan administration discarded the lower profile of its predecessor and turned up the stridency in its rhetoric toward Grenada. It intensified its efforts to isolate the regime and ended Carter's support for the Caribbean Development Bank (CDB) unless it excluded Grenada. Although most of the Caribbean governments were unsympathetic to the Grenadian regime, they closed ranks behind it to block the U.S. effort.[22] Instead of taking advantage of this misstep to heal relations with Grenada's neighbors, however, Bishop stepped up his verbal attacks on them. The administration ended diplomatic contacts, refusing to accredit a Grenadian ambassador to Washington or to seek accreditation from Grenada for its ambassador in Barbados.

The administration then launched the largest NATO military maneuvers in the Caribbean up to that time. The amphibious operation off Puerto Rico was called "Amber and the Amberdines," an obvious allusion to Grenada and the Grenadines. The PRG received the message; indeed, it publicized the exercises more than the Reagan administration and warned that an invasion would occur before November 1981.

Whereas Carter had avoided singling out Grenada in his statements so as not to exaggerate its importance or lead its neighbors to believe that U.S. interest in them was simply a by-product of its hostility to Grenada, Reagan took a different approach. In an address in February 1982, the president denounced "the tightening grip of the totalitarian left in Grenada and Nicaragua." In his annual report to the Congress on the defense budget, on February 8, 1982, Secretary of Defense Caspar Weinberger bluntly described Grenada as "a Cuban satellite."[23]

The prime ministers of Barbados, Antigua, Dominica, St. Lucia, and St. Vincent signed a "Memorandum of Understanding" on security cooperation on October 29, 1982. While traveling in the region at this time, I was told by several leaders who signed the memorandum that it was due to their increasing fear of the Grenadian regime. Bishop and Coard, however, saw it as part of the Reagan administration's strategy to confront them and seek a pretext for an invasion.[24]

The year 1983 began with a war of words and ended with a real war. On March 10, 1983, President Reagan ridiculed those who claimed that, because Grenada was small and poor, the U.S. should be relaxed. Referring to the airport and Grenada's major export crop, Reagan declared, "It isn't nutmeg that's at stake in the Caribbean and Central America. It is the U.S. national security." On March 23, Reagan used satellite photographs of the airport built by the Cubans in Port Salines to show that "the Soviet-Cuban militarization of Grenada can only be seen as power projection into the region."

Bishop matched Reagan blast for blast. He denounced the U.S. president for his "usual lies and threats." When U.S. marines land, he warned, "every last man, woman and child in our country will fight with full resolve, until the aggressor is removed from our soil."[25] Bishop then declared the Westminster parliamentary system "a dead corpse." After Reagan's speech on March 23, he placed the People's Revolutionary Army on alert to defend against "the warmongering Reagan" and his "fascist clique in Washington" because an invasion was coming soon.[26]

At the invitation of sympathetic groups in Washington, Bishop visited in June 1983. The administration first ignored him, but after critical editorials and press reports, a thirty-minute meeting was hastily arranged with National Security Adviser William Clark and Deputy Secretary of State Kenneth Dam on June 7, 1983. In advance of the meeting, Bishop's advisers suggested he press the United States to exchange ambassadors, extradite Gairy, and cease economic destabilization. According to notes taken by the Grenadians, both sides agreed on the need for dialogue, but Clark said the United States was more interested in Grenada's conduct, and specifically with Soviet influence in the region, which "is not acceptable."[27] Clark also expressed the hope that Grenada would maintain the parliamentary system and not adopt a Soviet model of government.

In an interview with the *Washington Post* before the meeting, Bishop insisted that he had given "concrete assurances ad nauseum" to the United States that the new airport was intended strictly for commercial purposes.[28] In my conversations with Bishop and Coard in October 1982, I probed them about the airport. Bishop told me that it "would not be used as a transit for Soviet or Cuban military aircraft, e.g., to ferry soldiers to or from Africa, or for any other military purpose. Grenada would not even use the airport to receive weapons or armaments from the Soviet Union or Cuba." I passed this message to the State Department with my comment that he could be lying or change his mind but that the United States ought to try to obtain those assurances from him. The State Department never attempted to negotiate this issue with the PRG. Indeed, neither side used the meeting to discuss this point. Negotiations were viewed by Bishop and Reagan as weapons in a propaganda war rather than as tools for accommodating interests.

Some observers have argued that the administration's confrontational strategy divided the NJM and led to the murder of Maurice Bishop and several colleagues by the Coard-Austin faction in October 1983. The documents do not support such a conclusion, nor did my interviews in Grenada. In the crucial debates in the fall of 1983 over the direction of the revolution, no one in the PRG raised the U.S. posture as a reference point for choosing one path or another. Was Reagan's invasion of October 25 the culmination of his strategy?

Here, the evidence shows that the administration did not seriously contemplate an invasion until a few days before it occurred; in fact, the administration was singularly unprepared for it. American forces did not have good maps of the island, and they did not know where American students were located, even though Reagan claimed that their principal mission was to liberate the students. In his memoirs, Reagan recalls that he was awakened at 4:00 A.M. on Saturday, October 22, by National Security Adviser Robert McFarlane and informed that the Organization of Eastern Caribbean States (OECS) had requested U.S. intervention. Reagan justified the invasion as a rescue mission to save U.S. medical students, restore democracy to Grenada, and prevent a Soviet and Cuban takeover. The OECS request made it legal, he said; in fact the treaty required a unanimous decision by the six member nations and only four had made the request. The administration's two other justifications for the invasion were also flawed: The American students were endangered not by the Grenadan military regime established after Bishop's murder but by the invasion, and no evidence was ever found that the Soviets or Cubans were taking over the island. A good reason for the invasion was the need to be responsive to some Caribbean nations that felt threatened and wanted to restore democracy, but that might have been achieved in other ways.[29]

Both the NJM and the Reagan administration seemed to harbor fantasies of destroying the other, and Bernard Coard no doubt aspired to replace Maurice Bishop. But despite these wishes, Coard did not scheme with the Soviet Union or Cuba to murder Bishop or take over the island, as Reagan said, and Reagan did not plan an invasion, as the NJM charged. Coard and Reagan did not guide these events; events led them.[30]

In October 1983, when Bishop returned to Grenada after an extended trip to Eastern Europe and Cuba, the Central Committee demanded that he comply with a previous decision that he share power with Bernard Coard. Bishop rejected the idea and, after heated debate, was placed under "house arrest" across the street from Coard's house. Tensions and mutual suspicions reached a fever pitch. Bishop requested a meeting with Cuban Ambassador Julian Rizo, but Coard decided to meet with Rizo first, on the evening of October 17. Rizo read a message from Castro, condemning the arrest of Bishop and demanding his release. Coard turned the tables and asked him about Angola: "Was it true that Cuba had intervened in the internal politics of the MPLA [the Popular Movement for the Liberation of Angola] to kill Nito Alves and liquidate his group?"

Rizo was enraged by the question, but Coard persisted, and finally, the Cuban ambassador acknowledged that the report was accurate, and that Cuba did it "because we received an official request from President Agostinho Neto." Upon hearing the reason, Coard asked what Cuba would do if it received a similar request from Bishop.

"He wouldn't answer," Coard recalled, "and so we were really worried."[31]

The next day, October 18, both sides redoubled their efforts to resolve the leadership crisis, and Coard, perhaps fearful of Cuban intervention, decided to abandon the plan for "joint leadership." He went to sleep after midnight, thoroughly exhausted, but sensing that the crisis was over. Early the next morning, October 19, while he was briefing members of the Central Committee, Coard saw a mob arrive at Bishop's house and carry him to the market. Coard, the Central Committee, and the army leaders went to Fort Frederick and learned that their radio and telephone connections had been cut. Their fear that Bishop might seek Cuban intervention was heightened when they learned that Bishop sent a fifty-man team to the telephone headquarters to establish a special phone connection between Fort Rupert, which he had just seized, and the Cuban Embassy.

Lieutenant Colonel Ewart Layne, the army's commanding officer and a member of the Central Committee, instructed Lieutenant Calliste Bernard (known as Commander "Abdullah") to take back Fort Rupert from Bishop with three armored personnel carriers (APC), "using lethal force if necessary."[32] Officer Conrad Mayers commanded the first APC because of his experience in the U.S. Army in Europe. As they rounded the turn into Fort Rupert, the APC was hit with a burst of fire from automatic weapons. Mayers and another soldier were killed, and two others were badly injured. Calliste Bernard, in the second APC, recalled the events:

> It was chaos that day. We were very afraid that the Cubans would take sides. When we arrived at Fort Rupert, we didn't expect what we saw. We were trained not to shoot at the people; we were supposed to be different from Eric Gairy. We didn't expect to face arms. We saw our closest friends die right in front of us. We responded with fire, and I then led the team to Bishop. I roughed him up. We felt the need for revenge; he had let us down. We had a big argument, but I take full responsibility. I could have stopped the execution, but I didn't.

Both Layne and Abdullah concluded that "it was either them or us." If Bishop and his leadership group were not executed, they would invite the Cubans to kill them and other members of the Central Committee. In fact, Fidel Castro later acknowledged that "one of Bishop's comrades went to the Embassy to seek our support. A wire was sent to Havana," but by the time Castro learned of the request, Bishop was already dead.[33]

After Bishop's death, the Grenadian military took power under General Hudson Austin and a sixteen-member Revolutionary Military Council. Coard had already resigned from the Central Committee, and the rest of the group confirmed that he was "paralyzed and in disarray" from the day of Bishop's death. He himself admits to being embarrassed by his behavior, accepts responsibility anyway, and says that if he had not been so "dysfunctional," he would have made the same decisions as those made by Layne and Bernard. Four days later, U.S. troops invaded. The Cubans defended themselves, but not the regime.

Causes and Consequences of the Conflict

Who pushed first? Those who argued that the United States pushed Grenada to the left or to Cuba were wrong. Cuban arms and support arrived covertly while the United States was pursuing a cooperative relationship with the PRG and before the Ortiz demarche of April 10. Moreover, we now know that the NJM described itself as a Marxist-Leninist party before it took power in 1979 and that it identified with the Soviet Union and Cuba in its struggle against U.S. imperialism. The first decisions of the NJM were to adopt *secretly* a communist political model and seize control of the military forces[34] while offering *public* assurances of moderate, democratic intentions. There is no evidence that Bishop's pledge to hold free elections was ever viewed by the NJM as anything more than a temporary tactic to neutralize international opposition.

The PRG invited Cuban arms secretly and received them before requesting Western military aid. Moreover, because the PRG did not pursue its initial requests for U.S. and U.K. military aid, Bishop's appeals look disingenuous. The relationship with Cuba grew closer not because of U.S. hostility but because of the ideology of NJM leaders and the deepening personal relationship between Maurice Bishop and Fidel Castro. Relations with the Soviet Union did not deepen because of Soviet reluctance, despite repeated efforts by the PRG.[35]

Did the PRG push first? Did it deliberately provoke the United States to justify its alliance with Cuba and to establish its nationalist credentials? At the time, I believed this. But after interviews with Bishop and Coard and after reading the documents, I am inclined to accept their point that Bishop's hostile speech on April 13 was partly an emotional reaction to the Ortiz demarche. Ortiz's lectures on the vulnerability of tourism and the dangers of relations with Cuba and his style of delivery confirmed their preconceptions of the United States as an unfriendly imperialist. It was a mistake to oppose Grenada's relations with Cuba instead of just the military relationship, and Ortiz's delivery of a nonpaper was an unprofessional error. Bishop, for his part, erred not only in misunderstanding Ortiz's message but also in neglecting to consider an alternative approach or to calculate the costs of his emotional tirade.

Nonetheless, as an explanation for the collision, this meeting shrinks in importance. Regardless of what the United States said or did, its relations with the PRG were destined to be cool and distant at best, for two reasons: (1) the NJM's preconception of U.S. imperialism as the devil incarnate and its orientation toward the Soviet Union and Cuba and (2) the U.S. judgment that its interests would be adversely affected by the expansion of Soviet-Cuban influence in the Caribbean. Yet, just because relations could not be good does not mean that confrontation was inevitable or that the relationship could not have evolved over time in a more benign way. Perceptions of each other's behavior were crucial in bringing the two governments to confrontation. Each suspected the other of the worst motives and interpreted information in a way that reinforced those suspicions.

The issue for Grenada was not whether the United States was a threat—that was assumed from the beginning—but, rather, what was the best response. Grenada pursued several strategies, but the major instrument was propaganda. As Bishop told me, "our only means of defense [against the United States] is to warn our friends and our people of the threat." Of course, repeated condemnations of Washington served only to confirm the U.S. government's suspicions about the NJM, first creating and then exacerbating a threat that did not initially exist.

Bishop's rhetoric had another important effect: It discouraged tourism to Grenada and thereby hurt the economy.[36] The PRG believed that the U.S. government orchestrated adverse publicity against the revolution, but that was a self-inflicted wound. The U.S. government cannot manipulate the press on a story like Grenada, and indeed, two recurring themes in the U.S. press were that the U.S. government was pushing Grenada leftward and that both Carter and Reagan behaved foolishly. No administration would choose to look bad in the U.S. press just to hurt tourism in Grenada.

The U.S. and the Grenadian governments were sincere in wanting good relations, but each wished to impose terms that were unacceptable to the other. The United States was more honest in stating its conditions, but it was also more intrusive in demanding changes in the PRG's internal and external policies. The PRG pretended that its problem with the United States was that the superpower did not respect its independence and nonalignment, but in fact it understood that the problem was that the United States would not accept its *alignment* with the Soviet Union and Cuba. That is why the NJM concealed the fact that it was a Marxist-Leninist party.

Arguments that the United States opposes revolution because it defends U.S. business interests or fears the contagion of social revolution are not supported by the Grenadian case, where no U.S. business interests were involved and the revolution was neither social nor economic. The replacement of Gairy by wealthier, better-educated, and generally lighter-skinned leaders hardly constituted a social revolution. Ironically, as the revolution evolved, the PRG gradually discarded its dream of transforming the economy and decided to concentrate on tourism—the sector most dependent on the United States.[37] In brief, U.S. concern with the PRG was based not on its economic model or "nonalignment" but on its external relationships with the Soviet Union and Cuba.

What were the options available to the United States? A friendly posture could not be sustained in the absence of reciprocal gestures by the PRG, and unlike Nicaragua, Grenada was simply not worth the political price. The Carter administration did not view the PRG as a security threat that might justify more drastic options, such as subversion, destabilization, or military intervention. The Reagan administration perceived a serious threat but apparently did not pursue these options. Military intervention was judged too costly in the absence of regional support or a justifiable reason, neither of which was available until October 1983. The U.S. couldn't support the regime's opponents because most of them were in jail, and Gairy was viewed as indefensible.

Destabilization, a strategy that the PRG believed the United States had adopted as early as May 8, 1979, would have been easy to implement because two-thirds of Grenada's foreign exchange relied on tourism and the medical school. The United States could have discouraged tourism with a travel advisory and persuaded the medical school to move. But it chose not to do so, perhaps because a strategy of destabilization is a recipe for disaster unless there is a viable opposition that can take advantage. If there was evidence that the PRG was supplying arms to radicals or preparing its airfield for Soviet bombers, the United States probably would have chosen one of these options, but this was not the case.

That left the option of distancing and isolation. This option is not chosen; it is what remains when an administration realizes that it has no other options.

Both the Carter and the Reagan administrations "distanced," although their different approaches illustrate the breadth of this option. Carter initially tried co-optation and then retreated to an approach that stressed development and security assistance to Grenada's neighbors and a low profile, believing that a strident approach would only make the PRG look heroic and the United States foolish. Whereas Carter viewed Grenada as a small, radical problem in the Eastern Caribbean, Reagan approached Grenada as an object in the East-West struggle. His administration viewed negotiations with the regime as a wasted effort. In addition, the administration tried to isolate the PRG.

The two strategies had different effects on the region. Most leaders were more comfortable with Carter's multilateral, development-oriented approach, although a few preferred Reagan's security approach. But the increased attention and aid by both administrations undoubtedly assisted development, contributed to security, and reinforced the region's democracies.

As to their effect on the PRG, there is no evidence that either U.S. strategy made a difference, except perhaps that Reagan induced the Bishop regime to greater heights of paranoia. American policy did not seem to affect either Grenada's political direction or its relations with Cuba and the Soviet Union, the two key U.S. interests. In an interview in September 1983, Bishop seemed to suggest that the continuity in U.S. policy was more evident to him than the difference: "All United States administrations, but I would say particularly this one, is very hostile to any progressive or revolutionary regime."[38] On the other hand, the Reagan administration's aversion to any negotiations meant that other interests—for example, preventing the airport's use by the Cubans—were not pursued.

Comparing Revolutions: The Role of Process

In its relations with revolutionary regimes in Cuba, Grenada, and Nicaragua, U.S. policy evolved from tentative cooperativeness to cool distance to tense confrontation, and the regimes invariably moved from pledging democratic elections to repressing political opponents, from professing an interest in good relations with the United States to forging a close alliance with its enemies. The revolutionaries viewed Washington as bent on controlling and undermining their revolutions. The United States viewed these governments as Marxist-Leninist efforts to expand Soviet influence in the hemisphere. Each exaggerated negative and discounted positive information; by a mutually reinforcing process, the preconceptions, which were not originally accurate, became true. The self-fulfilling prophecy works most effectively when it works both ways. Richard Welch referred to this dynamic as the "cross fertilization of animosity."[39]

But the preconceptions were flawed in underestimating the possibility of political change over the long term. Even Fidel Castro acknowledged that his conversion to communism occurred as a result of a complicated and prolonged mental and political process, and U.S. actions influenced that process.[40] The question of who pushed first is the wrong one: Each side viewed the other as rebuffing initiatives and causing the hostility, and both were right.[41]

With the disintegration of the Soviet Union, the fear that revolutionaries will invite our global adversary has disappeared, and Cuba is no longer a threat. But revolutionaries in the western hemisphere have always been moved more by nationalism and its correlate anti-Americanism than by ideology. The relevance of the issues raised in this chapter derives from the fact that nationalism remains a potent force, and the possibility that the United States will lock horns with a stridently nationalistic regime remains. These past cases therefore yield three valuable lessons.

First, the United States must understand that a confrontational approach to a nationalistic regime is a mistake. It should concentrate on interests rather than rhetoric, and those interests relate to the use of hemispheric territory by a foreign adversary (even a middle-level power) and the preclusion of subversion.

Second, instead of searching for the similarities among nationalistic revolutions, U.S. policymakers ought to try to locate the differences. President Reagan bunched the revolutionary leaders of Cuba, Nicaragua, and Grenada in one package that permitted him to maintain his stereotypes. Obviously, these leaders had much in common, but their differences shed more light on the capacity of each to change. The Sandinistas were the most pragmatic; Castro, the most dogmatic; and the NJM floated somewhere in between. By looking for nuances and changes, the United States would be better able to nurture policies that it views as positive.

Third, the way to preclude a hostile relationship is to recognize the shared responsibility of both sides. Each can retain a policy that exaggerates the negative and provokes the worst in the other, or each can try to bring out the best. Fidel Castro, for example, told a reporter that "we always try to create the worst opinion of everything there is in the United States" by rarely mentioning good things and frequently emphasizing negative aspects of the United States.[42] The mirror image was captured in testimony before Congress in 1963 by Assistant Secretary of State Edwin Martin. He acknowledged that U.S. policy had failed to dislodge the Cuban regime, but he took comfort that, at least, "we are getting under the Castroites' skin."[43] The only way to break loose from this counterproductive relationship is to stop trying to get under the other's skin and start trying to get into the other's shoes.

Notes

1. Shridath Ramphal, "Options for the Caribbean," Address to the Institute for International Relations, University of the West Indies, St. Augustine, Trinidad, May 13, 1985, p. 16.

2. For a systematic analysis of the pattern of U.S. relationships with revolutionaries, see Cole Blasier, *The Hovering Giant: U.S. Responses to Revolutionary Change in Latin America* (Pittsburgh: University of Pittsburgh Press, 1985); and Anthony Lake, "Wrestling with Third World Radical Regimes," in John W. Sewell et al., eds., *U.S. Foreign Policy and the Third World: Agenda, 1985–1986* (New Brunswick, N.J.: Transaction Books, 1985), pp. 119–145.

3. In addition to the Grenadian documents, I will draw on my interviews with Prime Minister Maurice Bishop and Deputy Prime Minister Bernard Coard, October 25–27, 1982; with Coard and members of the Central Commmittee, January 13–15, 2000; and with members of the Carter and Reagan administrations. As an NSC staff member from 1977 to 1981, I participated in all of the key decisions on U.S. policy toward Grenada during that period.

4. V. S. Naipaul, "An Island Betrayed," *Harper's Magazine* (March 1984): 63.

5. In 1985, in the course of doing research on Grenada, I found an article in the *Washington Post* by Timothy Robinson ("Two at Grenada Embassy Accused of Gun-Running," September 1, 1979, pp. C1, 2) that seemed to offer some confirmation of what Bishop and Coard had told me on October 25–27, 1982, about an investigation of their party that led them to undertake the coup. Subsequent interviews and a letter by Ambassador Frank Ortiz helped in assembling this bizarre tale of the treasury agents' role. Ortiz, letter to the *Journal of InterAmerican Studies and World Affairs* 28 (Winter 1986–1987): 198.

6. Interviews with Bishop and Coard, October 25–27, 1982. In announcing Grenada's liberation the next day, Bishop said that Gairy had "fled the country, leaving orders for all opposition forces, including especially the people's leader [Bishop] to be massacred."

7. In his introduction to *Bishop's Speeches* ed. Chris Searle (London: Zed Books, 1984), Richard Hart disclosed the details of the vote, but he did not identify all those who voted (p. xxiii).

8. Interview with Tom Adams, December 2, 1981, Washington, D.C. Adams also discussed these events in the Barbados House of Assembly debates (official report), 2d sess., November 15, 1983.

9. The two communiqués issued at the end of the meetings of the leaders from the six Caribbean nations on March 14 and 15, 1979, are reprinted in *Caribbean and Central America,* the fifth report from the (United Kingdom) House of Commons Foreign Affairs Committee, session 1981–1982 (London, October 21, 1982), pp. 287–288.

10. Karen DeYoung, "Grenada Coup Wins Cautious Acceptance," *Washington Post,* March 24, 1979, p. A18.

11. Lawrence Rossin, "U.S.-Grenada Relations Since the Coup: A Background Paper" (January 1983), pp. 8–11.

12. Ibid., p. 15.

13. There are several accounts of the crucial meetings between Ortiz, Coard, and Bishop on April 10: Bishop presented his view in a speech on April 13, "In Nobody's Backyard" (reprinted in *Bishop's Speeches,* pp. 9–14); Ortiz's version is in his letter to the editor of the *Atlantic Monthly,* June 1984, pp. 7–12; and Bishop and Coard gave me a detailed account in October 1982.

14. After Bishop cited and criticized this point, the State Department on April 16 issued a clarifying statement that Grenada's relationship with Cuba was not the principal issue from the U.S. perspective: "We would be concerned [however] about the development of close military and security ties." Henry Trewhitt, "U.S. Cautions Grenada on Cuban Military Ties," *Baltimore Sun,* April 17, 1979, p. A4.

15. Interview with Bernard Coard, January 14, 2000, Richmond Hill Prison, Grenada.

16. For a description of British policy toward the PRG, see *Caribbean and Central America,* pp. 280–281.

17. Karen DeYoung, "U.S. vs. Cuba on Caribbean Isle of Grenada," *Washington Post,* April 27, 1979, p. A27. Although the article noted that a Cuban plane had arrived before the demarche, it gave more weight to the demarche as the cause of tensions.

18. In his famous secret "Line of March" speech to his NJM cadre on September 13, 1982, Bishop acknowledged that at the beginning of the revolution he and the leadership of the NJM took such steps as an alliance with the bourgeoisie to reassure everyone, "so that imperialism would not get too excited, and would say, 'well, they have some nice fellas in that thing; everything is alright.' And as a result wouldn't think of sending in troops." See p. I–19 of that speech, in U.S. Departments of State and Defense, *Grenada Documents* (Washington, D.C., September 1984).

19. Interview with Bernard Coard, January 14, 2000, Richmond Hill Prison, Grenada.

20. Details of this April 1979 delivery are in U.S. Department of State/Department of Defense, *Grenada: A Preliminary Report,* December 16, 1983.

21. Testimony of Ambassador Sally Shelton to the House Foreign Affairs Committee, *U.S. Military Actions in Grenada: Implications for U.S. Policy in the Eastern Caribbean,* 98th Cong., 1st sess., November 3, 1983, pp. 62–63.

22. John M. Goshko, "U.S. Rebuffed in Move to Bar Aid to Grenada," *Washington Post,* June 23, 1981, p. A9. United States aid to the Caribbean through the

Caribbean Development Bank had increased from $7.2 million in 1977 to $45.1 million in 1980, but in 1981 the Reagan administration refused to make any contributions to the organization. See General Accounting Office, Report to the Administrator of AID, GAO/ID–83–50, July 22, 1983, pp. 6–19.

23. Report of Secretary of Defense Caspar W. Weinberger to the Congress on the FY 1983 Budget, 97th Cong., 2d sess., February 8, 1982, p. II–26.

24. Conversations in October and November 1982 with Foreign Ministry officials in Barbados, Prime Minister Eugenia Charles of Dominica, Foreign Minister Lester Bird of Antigua, and Bishop and Coard of Grenada.

25. "Bishop Denounces U.S. in Anniversary Speech," *Foreign Broadcast Information Service (FBIS),* March 15, 1983, pp. S1–S4.

26. *FBIS,* March 15, 1983, pp. S10–S11; his speech on March 23, "Every Grain of Sand Is Ours!" in *Bishop's Speeches,* pp. 220–227.

27. For this reference and several other interesting PRG confidential documents on Bishop's visit, see Paul Seabury and Walter A. McDougall, eds., *The Grenada Papers* (San Francisco: Institute for Contemporary Studies, 1984), pp. 151–180.

28. John M. Goshko, "U.S. Offered Reassurance by Grenada," *Washington Post,* June 1, 1983, p. A18.

29. Ronald Reagan, *An American Life* (New York: Simon & Schuster, 1990), pp. 449–458. For an analysis of the administration's justification at the time, see Robert Pastor, "The Invasion of Grenada: A Pre- and Post-Mortem," in Scott B. MacDonald, Harald M. Sandstrom, and Paul B. Goodwin, eds., *The Caribbean after Grenada: Revolution, Conflict, and Democracy* (New York: Praeger, 1988), pp. 87–105.

30. These conclusions were confirmed in long conversations I had on January 14-15, 2000 with Bernard Coard and the other members of the Central Committee, who have been in prison in Grenada since 1983. The Coard group believes that Bishop had requested Cuban intervention to prevail in the internal debate, and this fear probably led to his execution. After that, the remnants of the NJM knew that they were isolated and vulnerable because neither Cuba nor the Soviet Union would assist them.

31. Interview with Bernard Coard, January 14–15, 2000, Richmond Hill Prison, Grenada.

32. The following account is based on interviews with Calliste Layne, Bernard Coard, and other members of the Central Committee, January 13–15, 2000, Richmond Hill Prison, Grenada.

33. Fidel Castro, interview granted to Jeffrey Elliot and Mervyn Dymally, *Nothing Can Stop the Course of History* (La Habana: Editora Politica, 1985), pp.

120–122. In the same interview, Castro claims that he would not have intervened even if he had time, and that he would have withdrawn the Cuban construction workers if U.S. ships hadn't been steaming to Grenada for the invasion.

34. Richard Hart, "Introduction," in *Bishop's Speeches,* p. xiv.

35. See, in particular, the report summarizing Grenada-Soviet relations written by Grenada's ambassador, W. Richard Jacobs, in July 11, 1983, in Seabury and McDougall, eds., *Grenada Papers,* pp. 196–216.

36. An economic report in 1984 noted that the "tourism industry was declining rapidly" during the period of PRG government. Government of Grenada and the Caribbean Development Bank, *Economic Memorandum on Grenada, Volume I,* February 1984, p. 22.

37. Jay R. Mandle, *Big Revolution, Small Country* (Lanham, Md.: North-South Publishing Company, 1985), chap. 2. The decision to give tourism the highest priority is all the more incomprehensible because the NJM already believed the United States was undermining tourism and because the PRG would have needed to negotiate a civil aviation agreement with the United States before U.S. airlines could land at Grenada's new airport.

38. "We Have the Right to Build Our Country after Our Own Likeness," in *Bishop's Speeches,* p. 251.

39. Richard E. Welch Jr., *Response to Revolution: The United States and the Cuban Revolution, 1959–1961* (Chapel Hill: University of North Carolina Press, 1985), p. 24.

40. In response to a question as to whether he was a Marxist-Leninist at the beginning of the Cuban revolution, Fidel Castro said: "Nobody can say that he reaches certain political conclusions except through a process," and that takes "a lot of time." Quoted in Lee Lockwood, *Castro's Cuba, Cuba's Fidel* (New York: Random House, 1969), pp. 254–255.

41. On the U.S.-Nicaraguan relationship, see Robert A. Pastor, *Condemned to Repetition: The United States and Nicaragua* (Princeton: Princeton University Press, 1987). The literature on the U.S.-Cuban relationship is vast, but the best analytical synthesis is Richard E. Welch Jr., *Response to Revolution.*

42. Quoted in Lee Lockwood, *Castro's Cuba, Cuba's Fidel* (Boulder, Colo.: Westview Press, 1990), p. 113, based on interviews conducted in 1965.

43. Statement of Edwin M. Martin to the Latin American Subcommittee of the House Foreign Affairs Committee, 88th Cong., 1st sess., February 1963, mimeograph, p. 9.

10

PROMOTING DEVELOPMENT: THE MARSHALL PLAN REFLEX

First, we do not want to take them [Latin American nations] for ourselves. Second, we do not want any foreigners to take them for themselves. Third, we want to help them.[1]

—ELIHU ROOT, SECRETARY OF STATE, 1905–1909

In June 1947, when Secretary of State George Marshall proposed a plan to help Europe recover from World War II, the situation there was grim. Millions faced starvation, and Communists seemed on the verge of taking power in a number of friendly, democratic nations. By 1952, when Marshall's plan was completed, Europe's economy had recovered, democracy was stronger, and the region had become the cornerstone of America's alliance against the Soviet Union. The Marshall Plan not only accomplished its goals, but it did so at a cost $4 billion below the original budget. Is it any surprise that someone proposes a new "Marshall Plan" whenever a crisis or problem emerges, whether in Central America, depressed cities, or the Middle East?

The Marshall Plan reflex rarely leads to a program, but when it does, the new initiative tends to follow the pattern of the original. Each is justified on humanitarian grounds. "Our policy," George Marshall said in June 1947, "is directed not against any country or doctrine but against hunger, poverty, desperation, and chaos." Similar statements were made by John F. Kennedy when he announced the Alliance for Progress and by Ronald Reagan when he proposed the Caribbean Basin Initiative. But if the purpose was to address hunger and promote development, then why was Europe chosen in 1947, Latin America in 1961, and the Caribbean Basin in 1982? At each moment, there were needier regions in the world.

In Latin America as in Europe, the driving motive was security. This does not mean that the United States has been indifferent to Latin America's development or that U.S. economic interests were of no concern to U.S. policymakers. These interests—Latin American development and U.S. trade and investment—reside in the house of American interests, but historically, the pursuit of these interests by the United States in a comprehensive program has generally occurred after a revolution, to preclude a revolution, or in response to criticism that the United States reacts only to revolutions rather than to the long-term social conditions that give rise to them. United States interests in helping Latin America to develop have taken, in Elihu Root's formulation, third place; they are derivative, not central.[2] The principal reason Congress transferred American taxpayers' money abroad or provided one-way trade preferences was to defend U.S. security. When the risk was distant, Congress was uninterested or stingy. The amount and duration of U.S. aid varied in direct relation to the intensity and the nature of the threat.

Although the United States has responded to Latin America primarily for security reasons, its policies have affected the region's development. Since independence, Latin American nations have experienced more economic failures than successes, but in the 1960s the region attained annual growth rates of 5.5 percent, which increased to 6.5 percent in the early 1970s, among the highest in the world at the time. That growth coincided with the first real effort by the United States to promote the region's development. This chapter traces the evolution of U.S. foreign economic policy toward Latin America during the twentieth century and examines the answers offered by the United States to the question of how to promote the region's development.

Of Big Sticks, Heavy Debts, and Good Neighbors

American entrepreneurs, like Minor Cooper Keith, who built railroads and the United Fruit Company, invested in Latin America and helped modernize the region's economy, but the U.S. government saw little role for itself until some American leaders proposed a customs union at the end of the nineteenth century. This idea did not prosper then. Only after the United States began to fear extra-hemispheric—primarily German—intervention in the Caribbean Basin at the turn of the century did the U.S. government begin to connect its security with the region's economic development.

The initial motive for European intervention was to compel the nations in the region to pay their debts, so the United States turned its attention to preventing its neighbors from becoming insolvent. Theodore Roosevelt answered with a message to Congress on December 6, 1904, that became known as his "corollary" to the Monroe Doctrine. "Chronic wrongdoing, or an impotence, which results in a general loosening of the ties of civilized society," he wrote, would compel the United States to act as an international policeman in the hemisphere.[3]

Preemptive intervention by the United States succeeded in keeping out the Europeans, but it was no solution to the region's debt problem. To address that problem, the United States compelled the Dominican Republic, Haiti, Nicaragua, and Honduras to accept "customs receivers," Americans who would manage the customs house, the principal source of revenue, and allocate the proceeds to pay the country's debts. Servicing a nation's debts kept it solvent but did not promote its economic development or assure political stability.

Theodore Roosevelt's "Big Stick" policy was denounced for relying on force and failing to address the region's underlying problems. In response to that criticism, President William Howard Taft decided to "substitute dollars for bullets," distinguishing his long-term, fiscally sound policy from his predecessor's. Taft viewed his policy as modern, appealing "to the dictates of sound policy . . . and legitimate commercial aims."[4] Philander Knox, Taft's secretary of state, defended the policy as the best way to get at the root of the problem: "True stability is best established not by military but by economic and social forces."[5] This may have been the first time that the U.S. government defined one of its goals in the region as promoting development. Taft implemented his "dollar diplomacy" idea by using American banks. "The aim," Taft told Congress, "has been to help such countries as Nicaragua and Honduras to help themselves." But the United States would also benefit, he wrote, because it was essential

> that the countries within that sphere [near the Panama Canal] should be removed from the jeopardy involved by heavy foreign debt and chaotic national finances and from the ever-present danger of international complications due to disorder at home. Hence the United States has been glad to encourage and support American bankers who were willing to lend a helping hand to the financial rehabilitation of such countries because this . . .

> would remove at one stroke the menace of foreign creditors and the menace of revolutionary disorder.[6]

To persuade banks to set up offices in such unpromising locations, the U.S. government had to provide security and sometimes fiscal and administrative authority. In Nicaragua, American banks nominated the collector general of the customs and directed the Nicaraguan railroad and national bank. The American collector managed all the nation's finances, even to the point of refusing to reimburse the Nicaraguan president for his expenses ($446) in hosting a reception that the American thought extravagant.[7]

Americans saw their efforts as sensible and altruistic, but most Latin Americans regarded them as arrogant, if not imperialistic. This criticism found its way into the American debate. Just as Taft dismissed Roosevelt's Big Stick policy, Woodrow Wilson criticized Taft's amoral dollar diplomacy. During the presidential campaign of 1912, Wilson chided Taft for taking more interest in "the progress of this or that investment" than in "the maxims of justice and . . . goodwill [and] the advancement of mankind."[8]

William Jennings Bryan, Wilson's secretary of state, took Wilson's comment seriously and proposed that the U.S. government become a "modern good Samaritan." European banks were charging Latin American nations exorbitant interest rates (18–48 percent); Bryan suggested that the U.S. government replace these with loans at 4.5 percent. He argued that this would constitute a kind of aid, and it would relieve Latin America of its debts and allow investment in infrastructure. In addition, the plan "would give our country such an increased influence . . . that we could prevent revolutions, promote education, and advance stable and just government."[9] Foreign aid was an idea of vast promise, but Wilson was not persuaded that its time had arrived.

After World War I, the United States recalculated the costs of intervention and decided on gradual military disengagement from the region. Economically, however, this was a period when U.S. trade with and investment in the region surpassed that of the Europeans. At the same time, the U.S. economic presence sometimes collided with "economic nationalism," the desire by Latin American governments to control communications and major resources in their countries.[10] The Republican administrations through the 1920s defended U.S. businesses and helped them to expand. Franklin D. Roosevelt changed this policy. He refused to intervene even though virtually every government in Latin America defaulted on its debts. When Mexican President Lázaro Cárdenas expropriated U.S. and other foreign oil companies in March 1938, the companies lobbied the U.S. government to take strong actions against Mexico. Ambassador Josephus Daniels, however, was more sympathetic to the goals of the Mexican revolution than to the companies. He cabled the president:

> I fear the State Department lawyers see nothing except from the standpoint of creditor-and-debtor, and would like to see the Big Stick used to force payment. They see none of the social implications growing out of the Revolution and the absolute necessity for educating the people and breaking up the big haciendas if Mexico is to be freed from feudalism. And besides, to demand the whole amount [of compensation] in the thirty months of Cárdenas' term is to try to extract blood from a turnip. The Mexicans were wrong in expropriating without arranging payment, and we should do everything we can short of Dollar Diplomacy and the use of the Big Stick to secure payment for our nationals. The Good Neighbor Policy forbids our going further.[11]

President Roosevelt agreed, especially because he did not want to get stampeded into a conflict with Mexico on the eve of a European war.

During the Roosevelt administration, trade replaced marines and dollars as the central component of U.S. policy toward the region. Cordell Hull, FDR's secretary of state (1933–1944), was a disciple of free trade and persuaded Congress to approve the Reciprocal Trade Agreements Act (RTAA) of 1934. This was a landmark event in U.S. trade policy. Prior to this law, Congress set high tariffs on thousands of products. With the RTAA, Congress delegated to the president the authority to negotiate bilateral agreements aimed at reducing tariffs, and Hull concentrated on Latin America. Of twenty-eight agreements negotiated by 1945, sixteen were with Latin American countries. These reduced tariffs from an average of 59 percent in 1932 to 28.2 percent in 1945. The reduction of trade barriers promoted the region's development and strengthened inter-American relations.

Promoting Development by Foreign Aid

During World War II, the United States and Great Britain began negotiating the outlines of a new global economic order. Determined to avoid

Woodrow Wilson's mistake, Roosevelt built support in Congress for the idea of U.S. leadership in the new world. The new global structure would include the International Monetary Fund (IMF) to serve as a financial clearinghouse, the World Bank to facilitate reconstruction in Europe and development in the rest of the world, and the General Agreement on Tariffs and Trade (GATT) to reduce trade barriers in the world. The premise undergirding the World Bank and the Marshall Plan was that public resources and planning would help countries to develop. This idea turned imperialism on its head: Instead of extracting wealth from the poorer countries, development aid transferred it from the richer countries. It also departed from laissez-faire theory, which argued that countries could develop only if governments left businesses alone. World War II had tolled the end of imperialism, and the Great Depression and the New Deal impugned the market's magic, although that wand continued to be waved at periodic intervals by the United States.

In 1948, at the Conference of Bogotá, which established the Organization of American States (OAS), Latin American leaders complimented Marshall for his plan but advised him that it would be better applied to Latin America than to Europe. Poorer than Europe and supportive of the U.S. effort in World War II, Latin Americans felt that they deserved help and that the United States owed it to them. Marshall, though sympathetic, explained that the communist threat was urgent in Europe and remote in Latin America. When he returned to Washington, however, Marshall persuaded President Harry Truman to provide some aid to Latin America and the developing world. In his inaugural address on January 20, 1949, Truman used the last of four points—the "Point IV" program—to describe a $45 million technical assistance program for the entire developing world.

Despite the meagerness of Truman's Point IV program as compared to the $17 billion, four-year plan for Europe, Latin American interest in a new plan did not diminish. During his presidential campaign, Dwight Eisenhower raised some hopes when he criticized Truman for neglecting Latin America. When Secretary of State John Foster Dulles arrived in Caracas in March 1954 for the Tenth Inter-American Conference, Latin American foreign ministers hoped he had brought an Eisenhower plan with him. Instead, he brought the Cold War. But to obtain a declaration that communism was "incompatible" with the inter-American system, Dulles had to promise that the United States would participate in an inter-American economic conference and expand loans by the Export-

Import Bank.[12] This was the essence of the postwar bargain: In exchange for supporting U.S. Cold War objectives, Latin Americans would receive economic help.

Dulles did not violate his agreement, but neither did he deliver in the manner the Latin Americans wanted. During the 1950s, Cold War priorities assigned most of the $50 billion in U.S. foreign aid to countries nearer the Soviet Union than the United States. A second impediment to a more responsive policy toward the region was ideology. Secretary of the Treasury George Humphrey and Assistant Secretary of State Henry Holland were conservative businessmen who believed that foreign investment was the only way to develop Latin American economies. Humphrey led the U.S. delegation to the economic conference in Rio de Janeiro in late 1954 and made sure that no U.S. aid was promised.

Eisenhower made an exception to this laissez-faire foreign economic policy in Bolivia. Between 1953 and 1961 Bolivia received $192.5 million in aid, more per capita than any nation in the world. Two reasons explain this exception. First, the Bolivian revolution had begun a dramatic social restructuring, and the Eisenhower administration was eager to prove that it had opposed the Guatemalan revolution because of communism, not reforms. Second, Milton Eisenhower, the president of Johns Hopkins University, had become an important adviser to his brother on Latin America, and he believed the Bolivian experiment was important for the region and for U.S. policy.[13]

After Humphrey and Holland retired and Milton Eisenhower's influence increased, the administration's positions began to change. The turning point probably occurred as a result of Vice President Richard Nixon's trip to Latin America in May 1958. The attacks on him in Caracas woke up the administration to the dangers of social unrest. Also important was the letter sent by Brazilian President Juscelino Kubitschek to Eisenhower in June asking for a $40 billion, twenty-year aid program called "Operación Pan America." Eisenhower rejected that idea and the amount, but he accepted a number of other proposals. In August 1958 he announced support for a regional development bank, and in April 1959 the Inter-American Development Bank (IDB) was established with $1 billion in capital, of which the United States supplied 45 percent. Eisenhower also signed an international coffee agreement in September 1959.

These new policies laid the foundation for the Alliance for Progress, but the real impetus for John F. Kennedy's initiative was the Cuban revolution and the fear that it would spread. In March 1961 Kennedy unveiled the Alliance, the closest approximation to the Marshall Plan that Latin America would ever get. Congress was asked to provide half of a $20 billion commitment to the economic, social, and political development of Latin America over a ten-year period. Corporations in the United States were expected to invest an equal amount. Kennedy stressed the importance of private investment because "there isn't enough public capital to do the job."[14] The extent to which the Kennedy administration committed itself to helping U.S. business is a matter of debate. J. P. Morray argued that the Alliance represented "the use of U.S. public funds in the battle to reopen Latin America to U.S. investors."[15] Arthur Schlesinger disagreed, viewing the main focus of the Alliance as support for democracy and social change; private enterprise should play a role, but it should not be "the determining principle or sole objective."[16]

The Alliance was made multilateral at Punta del Este in August 1961, when U.S. and Latin American leaders agreed on a declaration of ninety-four specific economic and social objectives, ranging from raising per capita income by 2.5 percent a year to increasing life expectancy by "a minimum of five years" in the decade. One of the program's purposes was to infuse Latin American elites with a developmentalist attitude, and the administration placed great emphasis on national planning and self-help. Latin Americans were expected to multiply the U.S. investment, and this occurred. By the second half of the 1960s, 91 percent of the region's investment for development came from domestic savings.

The Alliance raised expectations, and Arthur Schlesinger, one of its authors, acknowledged that it "accomplished far less than its founders had hoped." Evaluations of the program are mixed: Some observers suggest that it was well intended but "lost its way"; others argue that it never came to grips with the structural problems; still others regard it as a success.[17] In terms of aid levels, the Alliance did not approach the Marshall Plan, but because Latin America had neither the physical nor the technical infrastructure to utilize the capital, the two plans should not be directly compared. Nevertheless, the Kennedy and Johnson administrations and private investors met their $20 billion pledge during the decade.

President Lyndon Johnson, however, gave less emphasis to social change and democracy than to economic development. This shift was due both to the diversion of his energies and resources to Vietnam and to the realization that social and political goals in Latin America were, in the words of President Kennedy shortly before his death, "a far greater task" than the Alliance had originally envisioned. To succeed, Kennedy said, "will require difficult and painful labor over a long period of time."[18]

Presidents Richard Nixon and Gerald Ford also focused on other regions and problems, but Latin America did not need to wait for the return of the U.S. president's attention. Loans and advice from the World Bank and the IDB gradually came to supplant U.S. aid. In 1961 U.S. bilateral aid to Latin America was more than three times the total from the World Bank and the IDB; one decade later, loans from the banks were about three times the amount of U.S. aid. International civil servants replaced U.S. officials as the source of advice and capital, and the paternalism in U.S.-Latin American relations was reduced.

As Latin America developed, private banks began to lend. When oil prices soared in the 1970s, the demand for money, and also the supply, increased. Many Latin American governments borrowed excessively. By 1975, more than two-thirds of the total external financing to Latin America was provided by banks. The stage was set for a massive debt crisis when interest rates rose in the 1980s and oil prices declined.

A third trend was the increasing importance of trade in promoting Latin American development. Trade expanded faster than domestic production, and the region's leaders shifted their attention from requesting aid toward negotiating market access. Latin America pursued this agenda globally. Instead of seeking a regional trade preference scheme from the United States, the region's leaders asked all of the industrialized countries to adopt a generalized system of tariff preferences (GSP) for all the developing countries. What Latin America wanted was development without dependence. By increasing trade with Europe and Japan, Latin America expanded and diversified its economic opportunities. Because of its stake in the global trading system, the United States also decided to provide global rather than regional trade preferences. The Trade Act of 1974 implemented the proposal.

The Carter administration accepted Latin America's desire for global trade preferences and the North-South dialogue, and it expanded U.S. contributions to the international development banks. However, it also developed some new ideas for the region. Reflecting the region's more advanced needs, the Agency for International Development (AID) developed a special program on science and technology for Latin America. Second, Carter gave more concentrated attention and resources to the

Caribbean Basin. In 1977 he took the lead in establishing the Caribbean Group led by the World Bank, which quadrupled external aid to the region. Three years later, he encouraged the establishment of a nongovernmental group, the Caribbean/Central American Action (C/CAA), composed of business, labor, academic, religious, and community-based organizations—a veritable mirror of U.S. pluralism—to foster development at the grassroots level.

President Ronald Reagan viewed the threat of Soviet-Cuban influence in the region as grave, and U.S. aid to Latin America in the 1980s was commensurate with this assessment. Of total U.S. aid, 10–15 percent went to the region—a figure exceeded only during the 1960s. The total amount of aid to Latin America in the Reagan years was, of course, much lower in real terms than during the Alliance, and it was heavily concentrated in just two countries, El Salvador and Honduras.[19]

In addition to increasing aid, Reagan shaped trade preferences around his security concerns. In response to a proposal by Edward Seaga, Jamaica's prime minister, for a mini-Marshall Plan for the Caribbean, Reagan offered a bold one-way free trade program that became the Caribbean Basin Initiative (CBI). In making the political case for the CBI in 1982, Reagan warned: "A new kind of colonialism stalks the world today and threatens our independence. It is brutal and totalitarian. It is not of our hemisphere, but it threatens our hemisphere and has established footholds on American soil for the expansion of its colonialist ambitions."[20] Approved by Congress, the CBI permitted nations in the Caribbean Basin to export some products duty-free to the United States.

The Reagan administration used a new phrase, "supply-side economics," to preach an old laissez-faire formula for development. Its principal goal was to reduce taxes and the power of the state, and it pursued this policy with equal vigor at home and abroad. The administration initially viewed the international development banks as agents of state socialism, and, breaking with a trend begun in the Johnson years, it initially reduced U.S. support for these institutions.

Reagan tried to avoid the region's main economic preoccupation, debt. However, when the Mexican minister of finance announced in August 1982 that his government could no longer service its debt, the United States realized the extent to which the two countries' economies had become intertwined. A default by Mexico would have dragged down most of the major banks of the United States, with dire implications for the entire economy. The United States therefore helped Mexico to reschedule its debt.

Beyond Mexico, however, the Reagan administration viewed Latin America's debt crisis as a problem between the region's governments and the banks. After rumors spread of a debtors' cartel, Secretary of the Treasury James Baker rediscovered the utility of the international development banks and announced a plan in September 1985 that would use them to provide more loans to the region. This proposal helped to divert attention away from the United States, but it had little effect on the debt crisis, which dragged the region down into its worst depression since the 1930s. In 1989 Secretary of the Treasury Nicholas Brady finally accepted Latin America's need for debt relief, and the next year President George Bush proposed reductions on the $12.3 billion worth of U.S. government debt throughout the region.

From the end of World War II, U.S. trade policy aimed to knock down barriers to a single world trading system. When Washington deviated from that principle with the CBI in the mid-1980s, there were few objections because the Caribbean Basin was economically insignificant and the strategic motive was evident. This situation changed, however, when the United States moved toward a North American Free Trade Area that included Canada and Mexico. Bush then promised the whole of Latin America the prospect of a hemispheric economic community if each nation implemented market-oriented economic reforms and reduced trade and investment barriers. Within one year of the announcement of this idea on June 27, 1990, thirty Latin American and Caribbean governments had signed preliminary agreements to reduce trade and investment barriers.

After completing NAFTA and securing its approval by Congress, President Bill Clinton hosted the Summit of the Americas, and all thirty-four leaders pledged to establish a Free Trade Area of the Americas by 2005. Latin America's embrace of free trade with the United States brought the region around full circle: from extreme dependence on the U.S. market and aid (1945–1965) to a demand for a North-South dialogue and reduced dependence on the United States (1965–1985) to a new regional partnership. The changes in objectives reflected changes in trade patterns. Emerging from World War II, Europe reduced its presence precipitously, and the United States accounted for about 50 percent of Latin America's trade. By 1970, the U.S. share had diminished to about one-third, and that declined to 30 percent by 1980. By then, Latin

America looked to Europe and Japan, but Europe was preoccupied by deepening and enlarging the EU, and Japan was cautious. Then, when the debt crisis forced a contraction of imports, the intra–Latin American market went down. To service its debt, the region had to expand exports, and there was only one market open; the United States increased its imports from the region by more than 70 percent. By 1988, the United States accounted for more than 40 percent of Latin America's trade, with the amounts higher for those nations closer to the United States and lower for those farther away.[21] In the 1990s, Latin America lowered its barriers to trade and investment, and it expanded its trade within the region and with the United States faster than with the rest of the world.

The Impact on Development

Since the beginning of the twentieth century, the United States has recognized that its security depends in part on the economic development of Latin America. The premise was that poverty led to instability, which created opportunities that America's rivals could exploit. When threats to U.S. security in the hemisphere seemed imminent, U.S. policymakers forged a strategy that included an economic component aimed at dealing with the roots of the crisis. The national interests of the United States are most clearly visible in the similarity of U.S. responses, particularly in the motive, timing, and explanation of the initiative.

Variations in the level of foreign aid reflect Washington's assessment of the security threat in the region. Aid to Latin America as a proportion of total U.S. aid worldwide remained low (about 7 percent) in the postwar period, but in the two decades when the Cold War intruded into the hemisphere, U.S. aid soared. In the 1960s, U.S. aid to the region averaged 15.4 percent of total U.S. aid; in the 1980s, 12.4 percent. Between World War II and the end of the Cold War in 1990, more than 70 percent of all foreign aid to Latin America was allocated between 1960 and 1980 (see Figure 10.1). (The rise in the percentage of aid to Latin America in 1975 was due to the sharp decline in total U.S. aid as a result of the withdrawal from Vietnam in that year.) Absolute levels of aid reflected the same calculus, with an average of $3 billion a year during the 1960s (in constant 1989 dollars), $1.7 billion in the 1980s, and less than $1 billion in the other periods. With the end of the Cold War, the total level of foreign aid to Latin America plummeted.

FIGURE 10.1 U.S. Aid to Latin America as a Percentage of Total Foreign Aid, 1946–1997

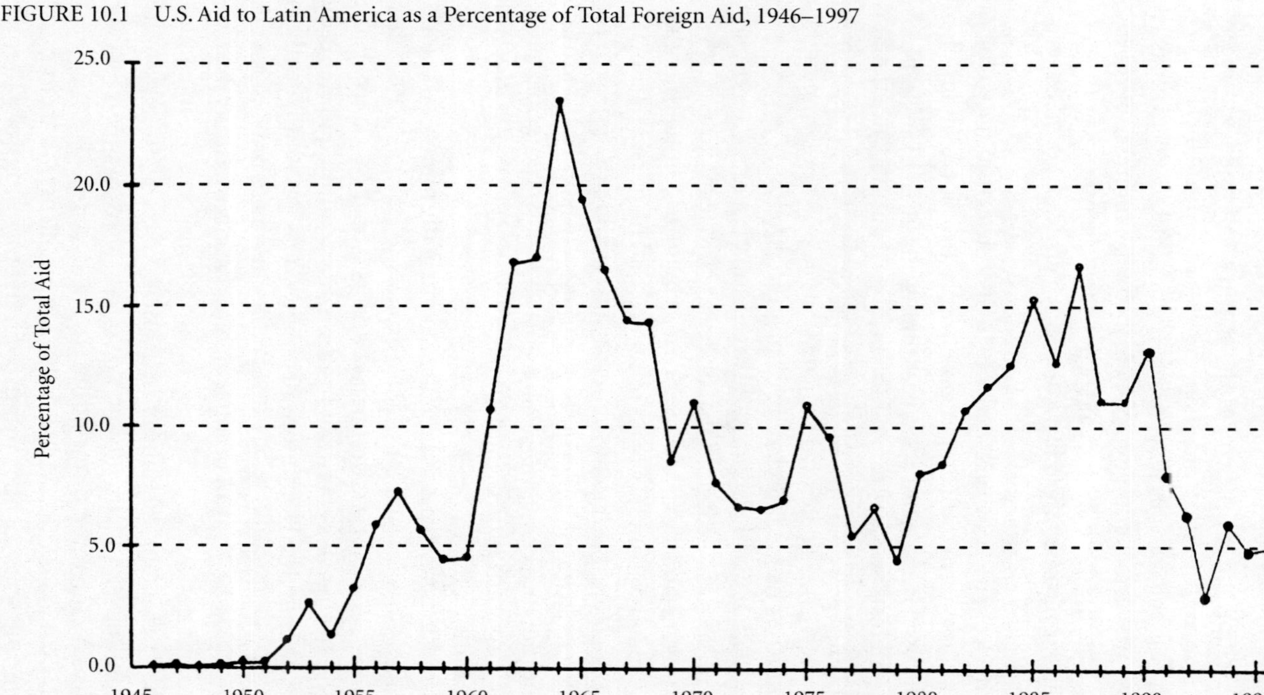

SOURCE: Congressional Research Service, Library of Congress, *Foreign Aid Data Base* (Washington, D.C.: Library of Congress, 1991); U.S. Agency for International Development, *Latin America and the Caribbean Databook* (Washington, D.C., 1999); U.S. Census Bureau, *Statistical Abstract of the United States, 1999* (Washington, D.C.: Government Printing Office, 1999).

There were two important exceptions to this trend. Counter-narcotics funding climbed in the 1990s, particularly in response to the crisis in Colombia, but most of the funding was for police and military aid, not economic development. By the end of the century, Colombia was receiving more police and military aid than the rest of Latin America combined, and it was the third largest recipient of grant U.S. security assistance in 1999, after Israel and Egypt. Then, in 2000, Congress approved a two-year package of $1.3 billion in aid. The other exception was the generous and rapid response after Hurricane Mitch struck Central America in October 1998.

Overall, the security motive was the principal determining factor of the foreign aid program. Still, its purpose was to promote development by its public investment and by encouraging private investment. At times, these interests seemed to collide, such as when the United States reduced aid to protest expropriations of U.S. investments. But in those cases, U.S. policymakers defended the sanctions as pro-development because the countries needed foreign investment to develop.

American leaders used similarly disingenuous language to explain their grand initiatives. George Marshall declared that his program was aimed at "hunger," and he asked the Soviet Union to join, although it was really intended to contain Soviet influence, and he hoped the Soviets would not participate. He said the United States would not approach the task "on a piecemeal basis" and would encourage self-help, but U.S. leadership was dominant. The options were portrayed in stark terms: either approve the program and defend freedom or reject it and lose our friends to communism.

Kennedy and Reagan repeated the arguments with minor variations. Kennedy "called on all people of the hemisphere to join . . . a vast, new ten-year plan . . . [to] attack the social barriers which block economic progress." The struggle was between freedom and tyranny, and Kennedy hoped that Cuba and the Dominican Republic would be "uniting with us in common effort," although he obviously did not expect or want that to happen. Like Kennedy, Reagan began by telling Latin Americans that "we share a common destiny. . . . " He called for "a long-term . . . integrated program that helps our neighbors help themselves." The goals were democracy and development, and he promised "to exclude no one," although he had no intention of including Nicaragua, Grenada, or Cuba.

The similar language of these very different presidents was neither artificial nor unimportant. The words explain the way Americans wanted to view themselves addressing the region's problems. The United States is uncomfortable with just a military response to a crisis; it understands that political problems have social and economic roots and that the United States alone cannot solve these problems. But if the region's development were in the long-term interest of the United States, then aid would have steadily increased instead of leaping after a crisis and then drifting downward.

Large-scale aid programs to Latin America began in the last year of the Eisenhower administration and started to have an impact during the second year of the Alliance. From 1946 to 1997, the United States transferred nearly $37.5 billion in economic and military aid to Latin America. Ninety-six percent of that was provided after 1962. Of the total aid, 87 percent was economic and 13 percent military assistance.[22]

In the early 1970s, the United States quickened the pace of multilateralizing U.S. foreign aid policy. The World Bank and the Inter-American Development Bank became the principal vehicles for promoting development in Latin America. This was a stroke of genius for financial and political reasons. Although the United States was the largest contributor to the banks, it paid a small proportion directly, and the multiplier effect was enormous. From 1946 to 1997, the international development banks made loans totaling $208 billion to Latin America and the Caribbean, with the World Bank accounting for 57 percent and the IDB 40 percent.[23] This represented five times the amount of U.S. aid. Moreover, all external aid mobilizes significant domestic investment. For example, between 1960 and 1998 the IDB approved 1,864 loans to Latin America that amounted to $95.7 billion but generated a total investment of $240 billion.[24]

Politically, the growing role of the international development banks permitted U.S.–Latin American relations to begin to break loose from the paternalism that was endemic in a bilateral aid relationship. "The crucial difference between bilateral and international aid," wrote J. William Fulbright, "is the incompatibility of bilateralism with individual and national dignity. Charity corrodes both the rich and poor, breeding an exaggerated sense of authority on the part of the donor and a destructive loss of self-esteem on the part of the recipient."[25] The United States always used its aid as leverage to pursue particular interests, although these varied by administration. Not surprisingly, Latin America preferred more aid and fewer strings, whereas the United States wanted to give less and gain more influence. This tension was unavoidable so long as bilateral aid remained the most important instrument of the relationship. The paternalistic dimension is exacerbated by the interbranch process in the United States. Congress always presses the president to use aid to support other foreign policy goals and to do so publicly, thus adding insult to private pressure. The multilateralization of aid has been a positive trend in that it has permitted an increase of funds and reduced overt attempts by the United States to influence internal policies.

From 1990 to 1997, U.S. aid declined significantly while multilateral aid and bilateral aid from Europe and Japan increased, so that by 1997, only about 10 percent of the foreign aid to Latin America and the Caribbean came from the United States. More significant was the increase in private capital flows, which dwarfed all foreign aid. From 1990 to 1997, U.S. aid as a percent of total capital flows to the region declined from 14.5 percent to .5 percent (see Table 10.1). With private capital flows increasing twelve-fold from 1990 to about $116 billion in 1997, the capacity of the U.S. government to address the region's need for capital declined proportionately.

Every president promoted and tried to protect U.S. businesses in Latin America, but the tie connecting the U.S. government to its businesses overseas has been more intimate during Republican administrations than during Democratic ones. Democrats preferred to support national planning, multilateralism, and social reforms more than Republicans, who more often stressed private investment, "the magic of the marketplace," removal of the state from the economy, and unilateral approaches.

The contribution of U.S. foreign economic policy toward Latin America's economic development was negligible until the 1960s. Since then, the United States has relied on a package of bilateral aid, loans from multilateral development banks, private investment, and trade concessions. Together, these elements have helped the region. Examining the growth in the region from the 1950s to the 1980s, David Baldwin wrote: "Never before have so many people experienced so much economic growth in so short a time span."[26] The 1980s was an unfortunate decade economically for Latin America. By 1998, however, per capita gross domestic product for the entire region was still almost twice what it had been in 1960, even though population had more than doubled.[27]

More impressive are the social advances in the region. Between 1960 and 1997, the rate of infant mortality per 1,000 live births dropped from

TABLE 10.1 U.S. Aid to Latin America as a Percentage Of Total Foreign Aid and Capital Flows to the Region, 1990–97

Year	*US Aid to LAC*	*Total Multilateral and Bilateral Aid to LAC*	*Private Capital Flows to LAC*	*US Aid to LAC as a % of Total Int'l Aid*	*US Aid to LAC as a % of Total Capital Flows to LAC*
1990	1,794.9	4,811	12,411	37.3	14.5
1991	1,423.9	5,390	22,846	26.4	6.2
1992	1,185.5	4,988	31,159	23.8	3.8
1993	1,178.9	5,126	60,122	23.0	2.0
1994	824.2	5,454	60,415	15.1	1.4
1995	604.6	6,227	62,814	9.7	1.0
1996	575.0	6,263	104,546	9.2	0.5
1997	575.9	5,426	115,738	10.6	0.5

SOURCE: United States Agency for International Development, *Latin America and the Caribbean Databook, 1999* (Washington D.C., 1999). (Millions of current dollars)

157 to 35. Average life expectancy for the entire region increased from 56 to 70 years. Adult literacy rates rose from 66 to 82 percent. By 1990, the region had four times as many scientists and technicians per 1,000 people as the developing world as a whole. Still, the population explosion and the shift from a rural populace (more than 50 percent in 1960) to an urban one (more than 73 percent in 1995) have resulted in massive poverty problems that have not yet been addressed by the region.[28]

Antonio Ortiz Mena, who was Mexico's minister of finance and subsequently president of the IDB, wrote that "the changes that have taken place in Latin America since 1961 are nothing short of revolutionary," and that they could not have occurred without the Alliance for Progress.[29] Development was the result of a change in Latin American attitudes and policies, stimulated initially by the Alliance and sustained by loans and advice from the international development banks.

The movement toward freer trade between the United States and the nations of the region offers greater promise both for the region's development and for more cooperative relationships. The United States will have a growing economic interest in trade with the region, which will compensate and perhaps substitute for the declining security interest. But one would be wise to hesitate before announcing a cure for the Marshall Plan reflex.

Notes

1. Quoted in Dana G. Munro, *Intervention and Dollar Diplomacy in the Caribbean, 1900–1921* (Princeton: Princeton University Press, 1964), p. 113.

2. See the excellent essay by Albert Fishlow, *The Mature Neighbor Policy: A New United States Economic Policy for Latin America* (Berkeley: University of California Institute of International Studies, Policy Papers no. 3, 1977).

3. "Annual Message from President Theodore Roosevelt to the U.S. Congress," December 6, 1904, reprinted in James W. Gantenbein, ed., *The Evolution of Our Latin-American Policy: A Documentary Record* (New York: Octagon Books, 1971), pp. 361–362.

4. "Message of President William H. Taft to Congress, December 3, 1912," *Papers Relating to the Foreign Relations of the United States, 1912* (Washington, D.C.: Government Printing Office, 1919), p. x.

5. Quoted in Harold Norman Denny, *Dollars for Bullets: The Story of American Rule in Nicaragua* (New York: Dial Press, 1929), pp. 3–4.

6. Taft, "Message to Congress, 1912," p. xii.

7. Dana G. Munro, *The United States and the Caribbean Republics, 1921–1933* (Princeton: Princeton University Press, 1974), pp. 159–166.

8. Quoted in Mark T. Gilderhus, *Pan American Visions: Woodrow Wilson in the Western Hemisphere, 1913–1921* (Tuscon: University of Arizona Press, 1986), p. 8.

9. Quoted in Samuel F. Bemis, *The Latin American Policy of the United States* (New York: Harcourt, Brace, 1943), p. 186.

10. Robert H. Swansbrough, *The Embattled Colossus: Economic Nationalism and United States Investors in Latin America* (Gainesville: University Presses of Florida, 1976); Michael L. Krenn, *U.S. Policy toward Economic Nationalism in Latin American, 1917–1929* (Wilmington, Del.: SR Books, 1990).

11. Personal correspondence to President Roosevelt, September 15, 1938, in Donald B. Schewe, ed., *Franklin D. Roosevelt and Foreign Affairs*, vol. 11, *August 11, 1938–October 1938* (New York: Clearwater Publishing Company, 1969), p. 177.

12. Stephen G. Rabe, *Eisenhower and Latin America: The Foreign Policy of Anticommunism* (Chapel Hill: University of North Carolina Press, 1988), pp. 47–53.

13. Ibid., pp. 77–83.

14. "News Conference," *Public Papers of the Presidents of the United States, John F. Kennedy, 1962* (Washington, D.C.: Government Printing Office, 1963), March 7, 1962, p. 75.

15. J. P. Morray, "The U.S. and Latin America," in Gustav Ranis, ed., *The United States and the Developing Economies* (New York: W. W. Norton, 1973), p. 301.

16. The quote is from a report that was written for Kennedy as the Alliance was being formulated. Arthur M. Schlesinger, *A Thousand Days: John F. Kennedy in the White House* (Boston: Houghton Mifflin, 1965), p. 196.

17. See Jerome Levinson and Juan de Onis, *The Alliance That Lost Its Way* (Chicago: Quadrangle Books, 1970). For a systematic and positive assessment, see L. Ronald Scheman, ed., *The Alliance for Progress: A Retrospective* (New York: Praeger, 1988), especially his first chapter. For a review of the various critiques, see Abraham F. Lowenthal, "Liberal, Radical, and Bureaucratic Perspectives on U.S.-Latin American Policy: The Alliance for Progress in Retrospect," in Julio Cotler and Richard Fagen, eds., *Latin America and the United States: The Changing Political Realities* (Stanford: Stanford University Press, 1974). Schlesinger has a chapter in the Scheman book and in one by Ronald Hellman and H. Jon Rosenbaum, eds., *Latin America: The Search for a New International Role* (New York: John Wiley & Sons, 1975), p. 69.

18. Address in Miami before the Inter-American Press Association, November 18, 1963, reprinted in *Public Papers of the Presidents of the United States: John F. Kennedy, 1963* (Washington, D.C.: Government Printing Office, 1964), pp. 872–877.

19. House Committee on Foreign Affairs, *Background Materials on Foreign Assistance,* 101st Cong., 1st sess., February 1989, pp. 151–152.

20. "Remarks on the Caribbean Basin Initiative to the Permanent Council of the Organization of American States," *Public Papers of the Presidents of the United States: Ronald Reagan, Book I, January 1–July 2, 1982* (Washington, D.C.: Government Printing Office, 1983), p. 213.

21. For the statistics up to 1980, see Sergio Bitar, "U.S.–Latin American Relations: Shifts in Economic Power and Implications for the Future," *Journal of Inter American Studies and World Affairs* 26 (February 1984): 3–31. For updates, see IMF *Direction of Trade,* various years; and "The Changing Patterns of Foreign Trade," *Latin American Special Report* (April 1990): 1–12.

22. *U. S. Overseas Loans and Grants and Assistance from International Organizations* (Washington, D. C.: Agency for International Development, July 1, 1945–September 30, 1997), p. 83. (These data are in 1997, not constant, dollars.)

23. Ibid., p. 251.

24. Inter-American Development Bank, *Annual Report, 1998* (Washington, D.C.: Inter-American Development Bank, 1998), pp. 36, 38.

25. J. William Fulbright, *The Arrogance of Power* (New York: Vintage Books, 1966), p. 225.

26. Baldwin reviews various assessments in the literature on the role of foreign aid and other policies in achieving such high levels of development for much of the developing world. See his *Economic Statecraft* (Princeton: Princeton University Press, 1985), pp. 319–335.

27. Inter-American Development Bank, *Annual Report, 1998*, pp. 145–146. Population increased from 207 million in 1960 to 415 million in 1998; per capita GDP (in constant 1988 dollars) increased from $1,587 in 1960 to $3,069 in 1998. It had declined from $2,512 in 1980 to $2,336 in 1988.

28. United Nations Development Programme, *Human Development Report, 1991* (New York: Oxford University Press, 1991), p. 34; Scheman, ed., *The Alliance for Progress*, pp. 130, 162; Inter-American Development Bank, *Economic and Social Progress in Latin America: 1991 Report* (Washington, D.C., 1991), p. 272; U.S. Agency for International Development, *Latin America and the Caribbean: Selected Economic and Social Data, 1998* (Washington, D.C., 1998), pp. 3–9.

29. Antonio Ortiz Mena, "Overcoming the Inertia," in Scheman, ed., *The Alliance for Progress*, p. 130.

11

PROMOTING DEMOCRACY: PUSHING ON THE PENDULUM

We are firmly convinced, and we act on that conviction, that with nations, as with individuals, our interests soundly calculated, will ever be found inseparable from our moral duties.

—THOMAS JEFFERSON

I know nothing stays the same,
But if you're willing to play the game,
It will be coming around again.

—CARLY SIMON, "COMING AROUND AGAIN"

A rarely questioned political axiom in the United States is that democracy is the best form of government, not just for Americans, but for everyone. Beyond that consensus, however, Americans are divided on their answers to four questions that have swirled around the issue of democracy in Latin America: (1) whether democracy is possible or sustainable in Latin America, (2) whether democracy is an effective instrument to prevent instability and revolution in Latin America, (3) whether the United States should promote democracy *or* respect the right of other states to choose their own political systems, and (4) what are the best ways to promote democracy. The trigger for debating these questions has often been the perception of a security threat in the region, but the issues remain long after the threat has disappeared.

If its closest neighbors to the south had followed a path of political development similar to that of the United States, then the question of whether—and if so, how—to influence Latin America's political system would not have arisen. But the paths could not have been more different. The divergence was evident from the beginning, even though its causes have been the subject of varying interpretations. In a letter to John Adams in 1818, Thomas Jefferson predicted that the people of Latin America would attain independence but were unlikely to become democratic. "The dangerous enemy," wrote Jefferson, "is within their own breasts. . . . Ignorance and superstition will chain their minds and bodies under religious and military despotism."[1]

Woodrow Wilson initially denied Jefferson's conclusion, believing that Latin Americans could be taught constitutional government. Numerous frustrating experiences caused Wilson to modify his views. Future presidents, particularly Democrats, learned Wilson's lessons the same hard way. Americans were proud of their ability to solve problems, but they were repeatedly discouraged by their failure to implant, without rejection, their democratic hopes into Latin America's body politic.

The Monroe Doctrine was the first official statement by the U.S. government about the independence movements in Latin America. It was also the first occasion for U.S. policymakers to consider the proper place of democracy in U.S. foreign policy. The principal question the Monroe Doctrine aimed to answer was whether the United States should join with Great Britain to warn other European powers not to recolonize Latin America, but the broader issue was whether the United States should be guided by its idealism or by a realistic calculation of its interests. Henry Clay, Speaker of the House, urged President James Monroe to use the occasion to endorse democratic revolution throughout the world. Secretary of State John Quincy Adams feared that Clay's idea could lead the United States to dissipate its scarce resources in faraway conflicts, while inviting European interference in U.S. affairs. He advocated a more limited, realistic warning to Europe to stay out of Latin America. Adams also believed that Latin America was unlikely to become democratic; the United States therefore could not base defense of the region on a common interest in democracy. Monroe concluded the debate by weaving the two arguments together into a "doctrine of the two spheres." His goal was to exclude the Europeans from the hemisphere, but his rationale was that the hemisphere was distinct and better—although not necessarily more democratic—than Europe.

Jefferson and Adams were right. With few exceptions, most Latin American governments have been undemocratic throughout most of their history. The United States, preoccupied by sectional problems and continental opportunities, remained largely uninterested in the region's internal politics until the twentieth century. Since then, "democracy" has been a leitmotif in the debate on U.S. policy toward the region because it is morally correct, *and* it has served other interests. Americans have defined democracy as free elections rather than seeing elections as a necessary, but not sufficient, condition for democracy. Until the last decade of the twentieth century, there was no consensus among Americans as to how and when to promote elections or how to relate them to other U.S. interests. To a great extent, U.S. policy on democracy in Latin America has ricocheted between different interpretations of America's proper role abroad and Latin America's pendulous swings between weak democracies and militant dictatorships.

The Rise and Decline of a Democracy Policy, 1901–1944

Democracy was not the reason Theodore Roosevelt and William Howard Taft intervened so often in the Caribbean Basin. However, after intervening, democracy became part of their strategy for solving the crisis and withdrawing. During the protectorate era, free elections were an instrumental goal of the United States, aimed at locating the leader with the most popular support and using him to restore a modicum of stability. Woodrow Wilson was not content to view elections as just a means to pursue other ends; he wanted the United States to be the "champion" of constitutional government in Latin America. To Latin American despots, he sent a warning: "We can have no sympathy with those who seek to seize the power of government to advance their own personal interests or ambition."[2]

Wilson's approach was first applied to Mexico. One month before Wilson's inauguration, Mexican President Francisco Madero was overthrown by General Victoriano Huerta. Determined to help restore constitutional government in Mexico, Wilson refused to recognize Huerta and dispatched marines to Veracruz to stop a shipment of arms to his regime. Lorenzo Meyer, a Mexican scholar, wrote that it was "impossible to deny" that Wilson helped in the overthrow of the Huerta regime, although most Mexicans are reluctant to give him credit for it.[3] Wilson himself was dissatisfied because the revolution failed to follow the orderly, democratic path he had hoped for it.

Nonetheless, Wilson persisted in his pursuit of liberty in the hemisphere. He blocked electoral fraud in the Dominican Republic; encouraged free elections in Nicaragua, Cuba, and Haiti; and proposed to make his approach multilateral with a "Pan American Liberty Pact." Some thirteen nations in the hemisphere expressed interest in the idea, but Mexico, Argentina, and Chile successfully blocked the initiative by redefining the issue from a question of how to support democracy to how to stop U.S. intervention in Latin America's internal affairs.[4]

After World War I, the United States came to recognize the rising costs and declining benefits of intervention. The government learned that it was not easy, and perhaps not possible, to graft elections and a nonpartisan national guard onto an authoritarian political landscape. Washington withdrew from the region, but old attitudes reasserted themselves and the new institutions were used to create modern dictatorships.

To extract itself from the region's politics, Franklin Roosevelt's administration swung the pendulum from the extreme of interventionism to absolute silence on internal political issues. For example, in the mid-1930s Anastasio Somoza García began to use his control of the National Guard of Nicaragua to undermine the elected president. The U.S. minister to Managua asked for permission to denounce Somoza publicly, but Secretary of State Cordell Hull disapproved, explaining:

> It has for many years been said that the United States has sought to impose its own views upon the Central American states, and that to this end, it has not hesitated to interfere or intervene in their internal affairs . . . particularly in regard to our relations with Nicaragua. We therefore desire not only to refrain in fact from any interference, but also from any measure which might seem to give the appearance of such interference.[5]

Somoza filled the vacuum created by American withdrawal. The U.S. minister persisted and finally convinced Hull to allow him publicly to reject Somoza's insinuations that the United States actually approved of his actions. The State Department opposed the dismantling of Nicaragua's democracy, and it knew that its inaction might permit that outcome. However, according to Joseph Tulchin and Knut Walter, "getting Somoza to behave in a genuinely democratic fashion would have required more than idle threats. It would have sucked the United States deep into the vortex of Nicaragua politics."[6] Americans were tired of military adventures, and many policymakers were dubious that another occupation could build democracy in Nicaragua. Without U.S. opposition, National Guard leaders in the Dominican Republic and Cuba also were able to seize power. Tragically, many moderates in these countries misinterpreted U.S. passivity as support for dictators. That was the effect but not the intent of U.S. policy.

As the war in Europe approached, and Latin democracy receded further, Roosevelt sought to strengthen bonds of collaboration with all the governments of the region, including the dictators. Victor Haya de la Torre, a great Peruvian democrat, criticized Roosevelt for a double standard: The president criticized Europe's dictators but had "pleasant words" for Latin America's despots. Roosevelt defended his approach by referring to the principle of nonintervention, but Bryce Wood wrote that FDR would have been more honest if he said that the United States "could hardly denounce" Latin dictators when it needed their support in the war and when "the list of those denounced might well be a long one."[7]

Roosevelt was aware of the moral dilemma, and he offered an idea for reconciling the contradictory principles of nonintervention and democratic governance: "The maintenance of constitutional governments in other nations is not a sacred obligation devolving upon the United States alone." He hoped that obligation would "become the joint concern of the whole continent," but he realized that would occur only if "conditions in that nation affected other states."[8] This formula would later become the collective action concept in the charter of the Organization of American States (OAS).

Democracy suffered numerous setbacks in the 1930s, but Roosevelt was revered by Latin democrats for his commitment to nonintervention, his willingness to distance U.S. policy from U.S. businesses in the region, his leadership in the struggle for social justice, and his struggle against fascism.

The Pendulum and the Policy

The "four freedoms" that Winston Churchill and Franklin Roosevelt articulated as the rationale for fighting fascism inspired Latin America, and the last year of the war witnessed an unprecedented flowering of democracy in the region. Free elections brought civilian governments to power in Ecuador, Cuba, Guatemala, Venezuela, Peru, and Bolivia, and the roots of democracy deepened in Costa Rica, Colombia, and Chile. Leslie Bethell attributed this transformation primarily to the "victory of the allies."[9]

As Latin America changed, the State Department reassessed its rigid interpretation of nonintervention. The first issue was how to avoid being identified with brutal dictators like Rafael Trujillo of the Dominican Republic without intervening. United States Ambassador Ellis O. Briggs suggested in July 1944 that "we should decline to endorse Trujillo's dictatorship, or to permit ourselves through misinterpretation of our policies to become identified with it." State Department officials called this new posture toward dictators "aloof formality." The second step, proposed a few months later, was to have "a greater affinity, a deeper sympathy and a warmer friendship" for democracies.[10] The third step was to demonstrate these intentions with specific decisions, as the administration did in rejecting Trujillo's request for arms.

Step by step, even while genuflecting toward the nonintervention principle, the Truman administration increased pressure on dictators to permit free elections. On August 1, 1945, the assistant secretary of state met with the Nicaraguan ambassador and asked him to inform Somoza that if he chose to run for reelection, "it might create difficulties for him which would seriously affect relations between the two countries." This message was placed in a file that captured the policy's ambiguity, "Efforts to Discourage President Somoza's Bid for Re-Election in 1947, While Maintaining a Policy of Non-Interference in Nicaragua's Internal Affairs."[11]

A few analysts in the department, including Spruille Braden, argued that intervention was a false issue: "Whatever we refrain from saying and whatever we refrain from doing may constitute intervention, no less than what we do or say."[12] As ambassador to Argentina in 1945, Braden openly campaigned against presidential candidate Juan Perón, who accepted the challenge and ran a fervently nationalist campaign against the U.S. ambassador. Perón won.

From the end of the war until 1947, U.S. ambassadors in Nicaragua, Paraguay, Bolivia, and Brazil also pressed vigorously for free elections. In Brazil, the U.S. ambassador told President Getulio Vargas that any attempt by him to extend his term would be contrary to the Brazilian constitution and unacceptable to the United States. In Nicaragua, the United States broke relations with Somoza in 1947 after he replaced the elected president. The Truman administration intensified the pressure by withdrawing the chief of the U.S. military mission in Nicaragua, recalling the American director of the military academy, and demanding the return of all ammunition belonging to the military mission. U.S. diplomats then hinted to influential Nicaraguans that Somoza's departure would improve relations between the two countries.

The days of muscle flexing for democracy did not last long. Both democracy and U.S. support for it in the hemisphere peaked in 1947, the year of the Truman Doctrine. The military and the dominant classes in Latin America began to retake power from the working and middle classes that had floated in with the first wave of postwar democratization. The wealthy often used the Cold War as an excuse to disenfranchise the middle class and labor unions. Truman and Secretary of State George Marshall were not fooled, but they failed to fashion a strategy to prevent democracy's demise.

The State Department expected the right-wing Latin American governments to propose anticommunist resolutions at the conference held in April 1948 to establish the OAS. Before the conference, the department reviewed the communist threat and concluded that communism represented "a potential danger, but that, with a few possible exceptions, it is not seriously dangerous at the present time."[13] The department was more concerned that anticommunist resolutions would be introduced that were "so drastic in nature that they would . . . give dictatorial governments . . . a means of attacking all opposition, and might even infringe constitutional liberties in the United States."[14] The department viewed the anticommunist forces—including the Catholic Church, the army, and large landowners—as capable of the same "totalitarian police state methods" as the Communists, but more powerful than them. The Truman administration decided not to cooperate with these groups but to continue monitoring the communist threat.

In the spring of 1950, as the Cold War grew hotter in Europe and Asia, the "father of containment," George F. Kennan, toured Latin America. He concluded that communism had become "our most serious problem in the area." Kennan did not have Marshall's reservations about allying with right-wing forces. He believed "harsh government measures of repression may be the only answer" for dealing with communism.[15] Secretary of State Dean Acheson rejected the report, and when he learned that the CIA was plotting with the United Fruit Company to overthrow the leftist regime in Guatemala, he convinced Truman that the threat there did not warrant U.S. subversion of a democratically elected president.

Anticommunism was running rampant both in Latin America and in the United States. Between 1948 and 1954, six democratic regimes in Latin America were overthrown by the military. Only four remained: Uruguay, Brazil, Chile, and Costa Rica. In the United States, the Democrats were under assault by Senator Joseph McCarthy for "losing" China and for collaborating with Communists.

Eisenhower assessed the threat in the hemisphere and elsewhere to be much more serious than Truman had judged, and his response was more militant. On March 18, 1953, the National Security Council approved NSC 144, "U.S. Objectives and Courses of Action With Respect to Latin America." The paper reeked of the Cold War and lacked any reference to democracy.[16] Before the end of the year, Eisenhower had approved a CIA plan to overthrow the Guatemalan government. Prior to the invasion in June 1954, Secretary of State John F. Dulles sought OAS support for a resolution aimed at Guatemala. To assure a majority of votes, he later admitted, he had to make "embarrassing" alliances with unsavory military regimes.[17]

The Communist party of Guatemala had substantial influence over the government of Jacobo Arbenz, but it did not have control and, given the power of the army, was unlikely to ever gain it.[18] The United States prevented the regime from obtaining arms to defend itself, and when Arbenz received a shipment of arms from Eastern Europe, Dulles used that as proof of Soviet influence. Because communism was incompatible with and, indeed, a threat to democracy, Eisenhower did not view the decision to help overthrow the regime as undemocratic. It was precisely that, however, and it also undermined democracy's prospects in the region by emboldening the right wing to block needed reforms and by convincing leftists that they had no avenue to power but by violent revolution.

In an astonishingly revealing NSC meeting in February 1955, Eisenhower and his Cabinet debated the issue of whether the U.S. government should support democracy in Latin America. Like most issues of concern to the Eisenhower administration, this one was approached via a discussion of the threat of communism. Secretary of the Treasury George Humphrey argued that "the U.S. should back strong men in Latin American governments" because "wherever a dictator was replaced, Communists gained." Nelson Rockefeller, then a special assistant to the president, countered: "It is true, in the short run, that dictators handle Communists effectively. But in the long run, the U.S. must encourage the growth of democracies in Latin America if Communism is to be defeated in the area." The discussion wandered, with Humphrey recalling a conversation with General Marcos Pérez Jiménez of Venezuela, who emphasized the importance of the army in Latin America, and Eisenhower mentioning a conversation with Portuguese dictator Antonio Salazar, who stated that "free government cannot work among Latins." But Ike completed the discussion with a clear statement that he agreed with Rockefeller: "In the long run, the United States must back democracies."[19]

This was not a public statement to disguise a secret policy aimed at bolstering dictators. Eisenhower made this remark in a secret meeting with his senior advisers, and the results were written in a memorandum that remained classified for more than thirty years. In the same meeting there was a brief mention of the coup in Guatemala six months before, but no one noted that the United States had overthrown a democracy or that its actions in Guatemala betrayed the intent of the president's final comment. Nor was Eisenhower's decision to "back democracies" translated into new guidance for ambassadors in Nicaragua, Venezuela, and Cuba, who continued to help and defend cruel dictators. Indeed, Eisenhower himself presented an award to the Venezuelan dictator Pérez Jiménez in 1954. Vice President Richard Nixon, who visited the region after the NSC meeting, publicly complimented and embraced Rafael Trujillo and Fulgencio Batista, and urged these tyrants to "guard against Communism" rather than protect civil liberties.[20]

Despite the administration's support for them, dictators began to fall with the second swing of the pendulum in the postwar period. In 1955, Perón of Argentina was toppled; the next year, Anastasio Somoza of Nicaragua was assassinated. By 1959, Gustavo Rojas Pinilla of Colombia, Pérez Jiménez of Venezuela, Manuel Odría of Peru, Getulio Vargas of Brazil, and Batista of Cuba had been overthrown. "The long age of dictators in Latin America is finally in its twilight," wrote Tad Szulc, in a sensational overstatement. "Democracy, so late in coming and still taking its first shaky and tentative steps forward, is here to stay in Latin America."[21]

Not only had the Eisenhower administration failed to contribute to this development, it was very slow to adjust to it. Nixon visited Venezuela in May 1958, shortly after Pérez Jiménez was overthrown. Instead of being hailed as a leader of the Free World, as he expected, Nixon was assaulted by crowds who condemned him for the intimate relations the United States had maintained with the despised dictator. Nixon attributed the demonstrations to communist agitation, and he reported to Eisenhower that "the threat of Communism in Latin America is greater than ever before." The president agreed.[22]

The Cuban revolution, of course, focused U.S. attention on Latin America with an intensity not seen for many years. Eisenhower, who had gradually modified his economic policies toward the region in response to advice from his brother Milton, now reviewed political matters. In February 1959, the month after Castro's takeover, Eisenhower instructed his Cabinet at an NSC meeting to give "special encouragement" to representative government in the hemisphere as a way to counter Castro's message of revolution.[23]

Because of Cuba, Latin America became an important issue in the presidential campaign of 1960. One month before the election, John F. Kennedy promised an Alliance for Progress to lift Latin America from its poverty and tyranny: "Political freedom must accompany material progress." Whereas some policymakers in Eisenhower's administration regarded dictators as a source of stability, Kennedy and his team spoke of them as a source of instability. In an influential book on the developing world, John Davies Jr. disagreed with Kennedy's view that democracy was a bulwark against communism. "The basic issue," he argued, "is not whether the government is dictatorial or is representative and constitutional. The issue is whether the government, whatever its character, can hold the society together sufficiently to make the transition."[24] Davies thought that military order should precede democracy. The New Frontiersmen thought otherwise.

The Alliance for Progress singled out Venezuela, Costa Rica, Colombia, and Chile as showcases to demonstrate that democracy offered the best road to development and social justice. Kennedy described Venezuela's Social Democratic president, Rómulo Betancourt, as "all that we admire in a political leader."[25] To prevent tyrants like Batista from being overthown by revolutionaries like Castro, Kennedy pressed dictators to hold elections or give up power.

Kennedy's policies exhibited more realpolitik than his eloquent statements about democracy would have led one to suspect. To help Cuban exiles prepare for an invasion of the island, Kennedy collaborated with the right-wing despots of Guatemala and Nicaragua. After the assassination of Trujillo in May 1961, Kennedy supported a conservative provisional regime, as Davies had recommended, to make the transition to democracy, because he believed "the anti-Communist liberals aren't strong enough."[26] Kennedy preferred democracy, but he also believed that right-wing options should not be discarded so long as a leftist regime was possible. Of course, one could argue—as conservatives have—that left-wing options are *always possible.*

Kennedy, who had attached his policy's fate to democracy in Latin America, had the misfortune to be in office when the pendulum began to move back toward dictatorship. In March 1962 Argentine President Arturo Frondizi was overthrown. The U.S. ambassador recommended recognizing the new regime based on the apathetic reaction of the Argentine people to the coup. Kennedy reluctantly agreed. A few months later, when Peru's military disliked the outcome of the presidential elections and seized power, Kennedy took a stronger position, suspending diplomatic relations and aid: "We are anxious to see a return to constitutional forms in Peru. . . . We feel that this hemisphere can only be secure and free with democratic governments."[27] Perhaps the pressure helped. One year later, new elections were held, but three years after that, the new president was overthrown.

In 1963, coups occurred in Guatemala, Ecuador, the Dominican Republic, and Honduras. In the first two cases, the Kennedy administration acquiesced; in the latter two, it protested. Kennedy's policy on military coups, as Theodore Sorenson acknowledged, "was neither consistently applied nor consistently successful."[28] By late 1963, Kennedy had accepted the need to work with military regimes, recognizing the formidable obstacles to Latin American political and economic development.

Two months after Kennedy's death, in January 1964, Brazil's military stepped into an increasingly chaotic situation, and the United States welcomed the coup. The Alliance reduced the priority it attached to social reform and democracy, and some observers attributed the shift to the change from Kennedy to Lyndon Johnson. In fact, the United States was adjusting to another swing of the pendulum toward dictatorship. Johnson decided to rely on the one element of the Alliance—economic aid—that was within his control.

Realists argue that a state should define its policies according to its interests, not according to how other states treat their citizens. A classic realist, President Richard Nixon paid attention to only two Latin American issues: Soviet naval facilities in Cuba and the election of a Marxist president in Chile.

On September 4, 1970, Salvador Allende won a plurality of votes for the presidency of Chile. Nixon authorized the CIA to prevent Allende's election in the Chilean Congress by purchasing the votes of some congressmen. This attempt failed, and Allende was elected. The CIA's next instructions were to "make the Chilean economy scream." Within three years, owing to U.S. pressure and Allende's inability to manage his heterogeneous leftist coalition, the country had polarized, and the military overthrew him. For the second time in the postwar period, the United States had contributed significantly to undermining a democracy in Latin America because the incumbent was a leftist.

As in Eisenhower's first term, Nixon's envoys cultivated anticommunist dictators. The U.S. ambassador to Nicaragua, Turner Shelton (1969–1975), acted as if U.S. national interests coincided with those of the Somoza dynasty. He refused to meet opposition leaders and was so close to the Somozas that they put his picture on a postage stamp. When an earthquake shook Managua and Anastasio Somoza's regime, Shelton solicited a massive amount of aid to steady the dictator instead of using the leverage to gain assurances for a free election. Similarly in El Salvador, when the military annulled an election won by Christian Democratic leader José Napoleón Duarte in 1972, the Nixon administration was silent. The seeds of revolution were sown in both countries in those years, and the silent realism of the Republicans evoked the righteous indignation of congressional Democrats.

Jimmy Carter inherited the Wilson-Kennedy democratic tradition with a born-again twist. Human rights, he announced, would be the "soul" of his foreign policy. "You will find the United States," he told the OAS in 1977, "eager to stand beside those nations which respect human rights and promote democratic ideals." Carter reshaped U.S. relations with Latin American governments according to whether they respected human rights. He denied that there was a dichotomy between realism and idealism: "To me, the demonstration of American idealism was a practical and realistic approach to foreign affairs, and moral principles were the best foundation for the exertion of American power and influence."[29]

The countries chosen for Rosalynn Carter's trip to Latin America reflected the administration's agenda on democracy. She visited social democratic governments in Jamaica, Costa Rica, and Venezuela, and military governments that had pledged to begin a transition to democracy in Ecuador, Peru, and Brazil. In the latter countries, she encouraged progress toward democratization, and at crucial moments the administration used its leverage to reinforce the process. The pendulum began to move toward democracy with free elections in Ecuador, Peru, and the Dominican Republic, but the process was not always straightforward. In Central America, a small political opening led to violent revolution. Jeane Kirkpatrick echoed the argument made by Davies in the 1960s: Latin America's centralist tradition made democracy a weaker reed than authoritarian government when confronting Marxists.[30] Ronald Reagan agreed.

As president, Reagan invoked "democracy" as the goal of many of his policies in the region. In a perceptive analysis, however, Thomas Carothers showed how the rhetoric concealed four kinds of policies: (1) fostering democratic transitions in Central America; (2) imposing democracy by force in Nicaragua and Grenada; (3) applauding the spread of democracy in South America; and (4) using pressure in Chile, Paraguay, Panama, and Haiti. The fourth policy was developed in Reagan's second term and represented the most dramatic change from his initial approach. Carothers discerned a "clear evolution . . . [during the second term] away from the Kirkpatrick doctrine. The policy of pressure [on rightist regimes] entailed the very sort of public criticism and pressure on anti-communist, pro-U.S. governments for which the Reagan Administration had initially lambasted the Carter Administration."[31]

There are several reasons for this evolution. First, the swing toward democracy begun in the late 1970s continued, and Reagan rushed to take credit for the new democracies. Second, the administration increasingly tried to justify its support for the contras "in the name of democracy," but critics in Congress insisted that Reagan's credibility depended on pressuring right-wing dictators as well as those on the left. The most obvious opportunity was Chile, where Harry Barnes, a career ambassador, played a significant role in the success of the democratic transition. Finally, the rhetoric took on a life of its own, much as it had at the beginning of the century, and the institutions that Reagan helped to establish to promote democracy, including the National Endowment for Democracy and the party institutes, maintained the momentum. These organizations provided needed funds and advice for political parties and electoral institutions.

Presidents George Bush and Bill Clinton continued the policy of supporting elections, and collectively, the Americas had some success in discouraging or reversing military coups, although less in deepening democracy. Overall, the Latin American movement toward democracy was breathtaking, with competitive elections in every country in the region except Cuba. The breadth of democracy was wide, but in most cases it was not deep. The social problems beneath the electoral veneer were so profound and the political institutions so fragile that one should pause before applauding.

Trade-offs: Rights, Wrongs, and Principles

Gordon Connell-Smith argued that the gap between America's pro-democracy rhetoric and its actual policies was filled with hypocrisy. In his view, the issue of whether the United States should support democracy is "essentially an academic exercise—remote from reality—since the United States traditionally has supported co-operative dictators until they have outlived their usefulness and, notwithstanding all the rhetoric suggesting otherwise, has pressed for elections only when these have served its particular policy objectives."[32]

History certainly provides examples of U.S. support for dictators, and no one seriously disputes that Washington has been more relaxed and acquiescent with right-wing dictators than with leftist governments. But a full reading of the history does not sustain Connell-Smith's cynical conclusion. The United States has undermined democracy in two cases, Guatemala in 1954 and Chile in 1973. At both times, the Republican administrations believed that Communists, the enemies of democracy, had either captured the government or would soon do so. Their perceptions were not without foundation, although their policies were shortsighted and mistaken. The cases were also exceptional. More often, Americans have searched for the best way to translate U.S. interests in democracy into policy, and overall, the policy has had a positive, albeit a marginal, influence.

United States policy on democracy in Latin America has ranged so widely that no map has been able to chart its course. The problem has been that U.S. policymakers and scholars have searched for a single map when in fact there are two—one in the United States, the other in Latin America—which respond to different logics. Each map has touched, occasionally influenced, but rarely determined, the contours of the other.

One map surveys a debate within the United States between realism and an idealism that has been torn between competing visions. The realistic perspective believes, first, that Latin America cannot sustain democracy and, second, that the United States has more important interests at stake in the hemisphere than a quixotic pursuit of an impossible dream. The two visions of idealism were represented by Woodrow Wilson, who believed that democracy is possible everywhere and that the United States should try to make democracy succeed, and by Franklin Roosevelt, who believed that Latin America could learn democracy only by making its own mistakes without U.S. interference.

Latin America's map contains numerous swamps and cul-de-sacs, but two key landmarks reflect the traditions of authoritarianism and constitutionalism. For most of its history, Latin America has been ruled by military dictators who gave up power to democrats rarely, reluctantly, and, until quite recently, for relatively short intervals. The region is also filled with democratic aspirations and a tradition of constitutionalism that has influenced law and politics. The dual traditions explain the swing of the pendulum.

Many theories and arguments attempt to explain each swing. History, culture, and religion have been held responsible for past despotism. Some analysts have suggested that a minimum level of education, economic development, and political institutionalization are preconditions for democracy.[33] Yet these arguments fail to explain the most recent and convincing swing of the pendulum toward democracy. In this regard, Samuel Huntington offered a crucial insight: Developing countries that attain a certain threshold of income and education enter a "zone of transition" where the probabilities increase that they *can* become democratic. But there are no guarantees. In this zone, leaders and choices determine whether democracy prevails.[34]

The failure to recognize that there are two maps, not one, has led some observers to confuse cause and effect. North Americans have thought that their support for democracy caused Latin American swings in that direction, and Latin Americans have thought that U.S. support for dictators pushed the Latin pendulum in that direction. (Each side has wanted to take credit for the democratic swing and blame the other for the swing toward dictatorship.) In fact, each side has responded more to the logic of its internal debate than to the policies of the other. The pro-democracy policies of Woodrow Wilson and Jimmy Carter were more a reaction to the undemocratic policies of their predecessors than to developments in Latin America. Similarly, most military coups in Latin America were responses to a country's politics rather than to the oscillations of U.S. policy.

Nonetheless, paths on the two maps have intersected at times. Because the issue is Latin American politics, events in the region have influenced the U.S. debate more than U.S. policy has determined whether dictators or democrats prevail. The first swing toward democracy in the postwar period led Truman to reassess Roosevelt's nonintervention policies. The second swing a decade later awoke the Eisenhower administration from its siesta with dictators. The position of Latin America on the pendulum also affected U.S. policy. A swing toward dictators discouraged U.S. policymakers and led to either a Rooseveltian preference for nonintervention or a Nixonian realism, depending on whether the Democrats or Republicans were in office.

American foreign policy has helped and harmed Latin American democracy. On balance, it helped more. Over the long term, however, no specific policy has been as influential as the stability and success of U.S. democracy. The model of the U.S. political system has exerted a gravitational pull on Latin American democrats. Even their expressions of disappointment with U.S. policy can be viewed as efforts to elicit policies more consistent with their hopes.

Few presidents have neglected democracy as an important interest of the United States, and public criticism has compelled those few to modify their positions. Security considerations have dominated, but the debate between security and democracy is seldom resolved with a neat answer. Eisenhower and Nixon believed that they defended U.S. security *and* promoted democracy in confronting leftist regimes in Guatemala and Chile.

The question of whether democracy is the best way to prevent instability and revolution in Latin America has yielded different answers at different times. John Davies in the 1960s and Jeane Kirkpatrick in the 1980s thought that the transition toward democracy was so tenuous that the United States should be patient with right-wing repression, lest left-wing revolution result. John F. Kennedy rebutted this argument: "Those who make peaceful evolution impossible make violent revolution inevitable." But his actions and some of his other words contradicted this point. Kennedy opposed Trujillo, but he believed that Joaquín Balaguer's quasi-dictatorship in the Dominican Republic was more stable than Juan Bosch's democracy there.

The hardest trade-off was between the principle of nonintervention and the right of democracy. No one wrote more eloquently on behalf of democracy than Thomas Jefferson, and yet he also wrote that Latin

Americans "have the right, and we none, to choose" their political system.[35] The members of the OAS enshrined both rights in their charter. Several administrations searched in vain for the recipe for defending democracy without violating the principle of nonintervention. The Truman administration tried to reconcile the two contradictory rights: It promised not to intervene, but at the same time warned that bilateral relations would be adversely affected if a country did not move in a democratic direction. Of all the postwar presidents, Carter faced the conflict between the principle of nonintervention and the right to democracy most squarely, during the Nicaraguan revolution. His administration believed that the longer Anastasio Somoza remained in office, the more likely were the Sandinistas to take power in a violent, anti-American, undemocratic revolution. The question was how far the administration should go in defining and imposing a democratic transition on an intransigent dictator. Carter was initially reluctant to mediate or arbitrate the political conflict, but he also let Somoza know that U.S. relations would be adversely affected in the absence of a democratic solution. This formulation was inadequate to the magnitude of the crisis.

After considerable soul-searching, the administration proposed a new way to slice through the problem of conflicting principles: *collective mediation.* Just as the pursuit of human rights could not be considered intervention because it was a treaty obligation, the mediation of an internal conflict in Nicaragua was not intervention because the OAS approved it as a legitimate response to a threat to international peace. This approach failed in 1979, but it succeeded a decade later when international statesmen were invited by the government and opposition in Nicaragua to mediate an electoral process. The question (addressed in the final chapters of this book) is whether the concept, which was first outlined by Franklin Roosevelt, can be made to work.

Collective mediation has proven more awkward and frustrating than unilateral policies, and President Bush, like several of his predecessors, decided to violate the principle of nonintervention unilaterally by invading Panama in December 1989. One of his justifications was to restore democracy, but he found it easier to capture Noriega than to install democracy. Unilateral intervention failed in Cuba in 1961 and in Nicaragua from 1982 to 1988. Even when intervention "succeeded" in Guatemala in 1954, democracy failed to emerge for nearly three decades. Collective intervention, however, in the Dominican Republic in 1965 and in Grenada in 1983 was more successful in establishing democracy, although it took years to consolidate the gains.

Thus, we have seen a wide range of policies undertaken by different U.S. presidents in pursuit of democracy. Some have helped Latin American democracy; others have undermined it. The issue is whether the twin logics of U.S. policy and Latin American politics can be managed in a way that will reinforce democracy and isolate and undermine dictatorship. Dean Acheson wrote that the primary U.S. national interest is to promote "as spacious an environment as possible in which free states might exist and flourish."[36] The hope for the twenty-first century is that the OAS will create a system to guarantee the permanence and deepening of democracy in this hemisphere.

Notes

1. Quoted in Robert W. Tucker and David C. Hendrickson, "Thomas Jefferson and Foreign Policy," *Foreign Affairs* 69 (Spring 1990): 153.

2. Quoted in Mark T. Gilderhus, *Pan American Visions: Woodrow Wilson in the Western Hemisphere, 1913–1921* (Tucson: University of Arizona Press, 1986), pp. 11–12. For a good review of U.S. policy in elections in the first three decades of the twentieth century, see Theodore P. Wright Jr., "Free Elections in the Latin American Policy of the United States," *Political Science Quarterly 74* (1959): 89–112.

3. Lorenzo Meyer, "Mexico: The Exception and the Rule," in Abraham F. Lowenthal, ed., *Exporting Democracy: The United States and Latin America*, 2 vols. (Baltimore: Johns Hopkins University Press, 1991), 2: 102.

4. Paul W. Drake, "From Good Men to Good Neighbors: 1912–1932," in Lowenthal, ed., *Exporting Democracy*, 1: 14.

5. Secretary of State to the Minister in Nicaragua [Lane], February 26, 1934, in U.S. Department of State, *Foreign Relations of the United States* (hereafter *FRUS*) (Washington, D.C.: Government Printing Office, 1934), vol. 5, pp. 538–39.

6. Joseph Tulchin and Knut Walter, "Nicaragua: The Limits of Intervention," in Lowenthal, ed., *Exporting Democracy*, 2: 123.

7. Bryce Wood, *The Making of the Good Neighbor Policy* (New York: Columbia University Press, 1961), pp. 152–153.

8. Ibid.

9. Leslie Bethell, "From the Second World War to the Cold War, 1944–1954," in Lowenthal, ed., *Exporting Democracy*, 1: 47.

10. See ibid., pp. 49–50. See also Steven Schwartzberg, "Romulo Betancourt: From a Communist Anti-Imperialist to a Social Democrat with U.S. Support," *Journal of Latin American Studies* 29 (1997): 613–665.

11. *FRUS*, 1945, vol. 9, p. 218.

12. Quoted in Stephen G. Rabe, *Eisenhower and Latin America: The Foreign Policy of Anticommunism* (Chapel Hill: University of North Carolina Press, 1988), p. 14.

13. The Secretary of State to Diplomatic Representatives in the American Republics, "Policy of the United States Regarding Anti-Communist Measures Within the Inter-American System," secret telegram, June 21, 1948, reprinted in *FRUS*, 1948, vol. 9, p. 196 (entire memo is pp. 193–201).

14. Ibid., p. 195.

15. Quoted in Bethell, "From the Second World War to the Cold War," p. 65.

16. *FRUS*, 1952–1954, vol. 4, pp. 6–10.

17. In executive testimony before a congressional committee, Dulles acknowledged that he was embarrassed by the kinds of regimes with which he had to collaborate to pass the resolution. See Stephen Rabe, *Eisenhower and Latin America*, pp. 52–53.

18. See Piero Gleijeses, *Shattered Hope: The Guatemalan Revolution and the United States, 1944–1954* (Princeton: Princeton University Press, 1991).

19. "Memorandum of Discussion at the 237th Meeting of the National Security Council, February 17, 1955," *FRUS*, 1955–1957, vol. 6, pp. 4–5.

20. Rabe, *Eisenhower and Latin America*, pp. 87–88.

21. Tad Szulc, *Twilight of the Tyrants* (New York: Henry Holt, 1959), p. 3.

22. In his memoirs, Eisenhower described Nixon's report as "clear truth." Dwight D. Eisenhower, *Waging Peace, 1956–61* (New York: Doubleday, 1965), p. 520.

23. Rabe, *Eisenhower and Latin America*, p. 104.

24. John Paton Davies Jr., *Foreign and Other Affairs* (New York: W. W. Norton, 1964), pp. 57–58. For a rebuttal to Davies, who articulated his argument in Washington years before this book was published, see Arthur M. Schlesinger Jr., *A Thousand Days: John F. Kennedy in the White House* (Boston: Houghton Mifflin, 1965), pp. 197–198.

25. Schlesinger, *A Thousand Days*, p. 768.

26. Ibid., p. 769.

27. Ibid., p. 787.

28. Theodore C. Sorenson, *Kennedy* (New York: Bantam, 1965), p. 603.

29. Jimmy Carter, *Keeping Faith: Memoirs of a President* (New York: Bantam, 1982), p. 143.

30. Jeane Kirkpatrick, "U.S. Security and Latin America," *Commentary* 71 (January 1981): 29–40.

31. Thomas Carothers, "The Reagan Years: The 1980s," in Lowenthal, ed., *Exporting Democracy,* 1: 109. See also Carothers, *In the Name of Democracy: U.S. Policy toward Latin America in the Reagan Years* (Berkeley: University of California Press, 1991).

32. See Connell-Smith's review of a book by John Martz in *Journal of Latin American Studies* 21 (October 1989): 618.

33. For a review of some of this literature, see Robert A. Pastor, ed., *Democracy in the Americas: Stopping the Pendulum* (New York: Holmes and Meier, 1989), chap. 1.

34. Samuel P. Huntington, "Will More Countries Become Democratic?" *Political Science Quarterly* 99 (Summer 1984): 193–218.

35. Quoted in Tucker and Hendrickson, "Thomas Jefferson and Foreign Policy," 153.

36. Dean Acheson, *Present at the Creation* (New York: Signet, 1970), p. 923.

Part 3

EXIT

Angelic impulses and predatory lusts divide our heart just as they divide the heart of other countries.

—WILLIAM JAMES

The questions that have preoccupied Americans who have formulated policy toward Latin America have a repetitive quality. The answers also bear the signs of history's weight. Our purpose in reviewing the past has been to identify the landmarks that can permit us to map an exit.

Five conditions have determined the contours of the whirlpool that has drawn the United States and the countries of the region into recurring cycles of unproductive and often violent relationships: different interpretations of history, the disparity in power and wealth, chronic instability and proximity to the United States, the impact of international rivalries on local conflicts, and divergent perceptions.

Some of these conditions can be changed; others are more enduring. We cannot change history, but by studying it closely, we can try to avoid repeating past mistakes. The differences in wealth and power that separate North from Latin America will not be narrowed easily or soon, although we have learned that some economic strategies and international trade policies are more productive than others. International rivalries can be muted or ended, but this will not necessarily end local conflicts. Democracy is the best path toward preventing the internationalization of civil conflicts. One condition that can be changed, often just by the illumination of self-awareness, is perceptions.

Of course, perceptions are not detached from the world; they are the product of the other conditions. But if perceptions lead to inaccurate definitions, a problem becomes difficult, perhaps impossible, to solve. Conversely, if nations perceive problems in similar terms or emphasize common interests, such perceptions would facilitate collective problem solving. Unfortunately, the psychological baggage amassed during decades of distrust has made cooperation difficult.

To understand how perceptions can change and what that might portend, we need first to understand why they rarely do—why, in brief, the relationship tends to get stuck in the whirlpool. I first seek clues to the exit in the psychology of U.S.–Latin American relations (Chapter 12). I then analyze how the concept of "sovereignty" has been used to impede inter-American cooperation and why its redefinition by two of the region's most nationalistic regimes leads to the exit out of the whirlpool. The last chapter offers specific policies that can invigorate the inter-American system and permit the establishment of a new, prosperous democratic community in the Americas.

12

THE PSYCHOLOGY OF INTER-AMERICAN RELATIONS

ESTRAGON: *Wait! I sometimes wonder if we wouldn't have been better off alone, each one for himself. We weren't made for the same road.*
VLADIMIR: *It's not certain.*
ESTRAGON: *No, nothing is certain.*
VLADIMIR: *We can still part, if you think it would be better.*
ESTRAGON: *It's not worthwhile now.*
VLADIMIR: *No, it's not worthwhile now.*
ESTRAGON: *Well, shall we go?*
VLADIMIR: *Yes, let's go.*
(THEY DO NOT MOVE).
(CURTAIN.)

—**SAMUEL BECKETT, *WAITING FOR GODOT***

For some in Latin America, "Puerto Rico" is not an island; it is an insult to hurl at a political adversary who proposes close relations with the United States. Those Mexicans who take pride in being *distant* from the United States often relish a comparison with Puerto Ricans, a people who, to their minds, gave up dignity for food stamps. Fidel Castro used more colorful language to condemn U.S. imperialism and Puerto Rican subservience. It is easy to dismiss the argument that the United States is a colonial power when Fidel Castro is the accuser. It is more difficult when Castro's charge is made by Carlos Romero Barceló, who served as a pro-statehood governor of Puerto Rico for two terms, and was subsequently elected Resident Commissioner in Washington. "The United States," he insists, "is the only nation in the hemisphere with a colony."[1]

Every president since Eisenhower has pledged to accept whatever status a majority of the people of Puerto Rico choose. If Puerto Ricans have the right to choose independence, statehood, or commonwealth, how can the relationship be described as "colonial?" Puerto Ricans answer this question by saying they need to know what status Washington will grant before they can choose. Puerto Rico and the United States each wait for the other to take the first step. What explains the deadlock? And given the unique circumstances of Puerto Rico, what is its relevance to inter-American relations?

The United States and Puerto Rico are caught by their own embrace in the vortex of the same whirlpool that has bedeviled the United States and Latin America. The difference between the two predicaments is that Puerto Rico's is cast in sharper relief. To sketch the outline of the Puerto Rican dilemma is to better understand Latin America's. Given the political gulf between independent Latin American states and the quasi-colony of Puerto Rico, it is not surprising that few observers in Latin America have looked for any connection, let alone noticed one. One who did was Carlos Rangel, a Venezuelan journalist who wrote a perceptive psychological inquiry into inter-American relations. Rangel observed that Latin America benefited economically from proximity to the United States and politically from its example. This insight, of course, runs counter to the view articulated by dependency theorists, that the United States reaps the gains of its relationship, and Latin America pays the bills.

Rangel put an interesting spin on his novel thesis by suggesting that the relationship with the United States has bestowed both benefits and costs on Latin Americans. To the extent that the "most basic need of any society is probably the ability to live with itself, and to accept its position with respect to the rest of the world," Latin America suffers because of the example and the proximity of the United States. Puerto Rico, Rangel realized, "suffers from an acute case of the Latin American complex." It admires the United States and profits from a close relationship, but it also has to face the indigestible realization that it cannot, perhaps ever, measure up to its neighbor.[2]

Feelings of persistent inferiority can and have evoked several kinds of reactions in Latin America: depression, indecision, internal rage, and violent manifestations of anti-Americanism. Attacks on the United States, such as those in Caracas against Nixon in 1958 or in the Canal Zone in 1964, usually occur as a result of a specific event or decision by the United States that detonates deep-seated negative feelings. Washington has not understood the kinds of emotions that have led to such attacks. Americans believe that the path to development is self-improvement. When faced with a region that has been unable to compete, the United States has behaved with insensitivity, arrogance, or lack of interest. The U.S. attitude often provokes the Latin response, which has ranged from an unproductive defiance of the United States to a fruitful humiliation.

The central issues that tug at inter-American relations are thus similar to those that entangle Puerto Rico. For Latin America, the issues have been how to develop economically while increasing its autonomy from the United States, how to develop politically without permitting the United States to interfere in its internal affairs. Some U.S. presidents, including Franklin Roosevelt and Jimmy Carter, have wanted to enhance the region's autonomy, but most have promoted a narrower definition of U.S. interests with little or no concern about the way it might diminish the region's autonomy or sense of itself as an important actor on a wider stage.

On one end of the continuum, Fidel Castro and Daniel Ortega reaped the political dividends of defying the United States, but their countries paid an exorbitant price. Puerto Ricans sit at the other end of the continuum, with the highest standard of living in Latin America, but with "bitterness and resentment."[3] First, I seek to explain the stalemate in Puerto Rico and then extrapolate insights that could help us understand and deal more effectively with the dysfunctional relationship between the United States and Latin America.

Origins of the Stalemate

When President William McKinley succumbed to the pressures within his party to go to war against Spain in 1898, American attention was focused on liberating Cuba. To prove that U.S. motives were purer than those of European imperialists, Congress added to the declaration of war the Teller Amendment, which denied any intention to annex Cuba, the main prize of war. Nothing was said about Puerto Rico because, at the time, the island was less known to the United States than Madagascar.[4]

On July 25, 1898, American soldiers went ashore on Puerto Rico, and the conquering General Nelson Miles promised "to give to the people of your beautiful island the largest measure of liberty . . . [and] to bestow upon you . . . the liberal institutions of our government." Instead of demanding independence, Puerto Ricans welcomed the Americans' promise of liberty, but the promise was fulfilled slowly, grudgingly, and never completely.

The basic structure of the relationship was established with the Foraker Act of 1900. The United States would defend—nationalists would say "occupy"—Puerto Rico and provide its currency, but Congress was not willing to consider the island a potential state or an actual colony. A new term was coined, "unincorporated territory." Puerto Rico would belong to, but not be part of, the United States. In 1917 Puerto Ricans became U.S. citizens, eligible to enlist in the army. However, those living on the island could not vote for Congress or the president and did not have to pay federal taxes.

Some Puerto Ricans see a cord of colonialism connecting almost every U.S. decision on the island,[5] but Raymond Carr offered embarrassing proof that there was nothing inevitable or even planned in the way that the United States acquired and governed the island.[6] At every decision point, there were those in Congress and among the public who argued for self-government and those who felt—for reasons that evolved over time—that U.S. stewardship or "tutorship" was essential. At the beginning, McKinley asked the Reverend Henry Carroll to visit Puerto Rico and advise him on the proper course. Carroll concluded that the only way Puerto Ricans would learn self-government was "by having its responsibilities laid upon them" and by learning from their blunders. Neither McKinley nor Congress accepted Carroll's wisdom, believing, as President Calvin Coolidge later did, "that, far from meriting more self-government, the Puerto Ricans already possessed more self-government than was good for them."[7]

In 1941 Franklin Roosevelt sent Rexford Tugwell, one of his "brain trust," to Puerto Rico as governor. Until then, U.S. governors had been insensitive, uninterested, or insulting to the local people. When Tugwell arrived, per capita income was less than $150, and life expectancy was forty-six years. Tugwell forged a partnership with a young politician, Luis Muñoz Marín, who had studied in the United States and returned in the 1930s to build a political party. Together, they brought the New Deal to the island, using the state to promote development. In 1948, Muñoz Marín became the first elected governor of the island, and he dominated politics for the next two decades. His statist economic program modernized the island. From a depressed agrarian economy, one of the poorest in the hemisphere, Puerto Rico was transformed into a service-based industrialized island with the highest per capita income and literacy rate in Latin America.

An advocate of independence in his youth, Muñoz soon learned that his people cared more about food and jobs than political status. In the aftermath of World War II, however, some form of decolonization was necessary. Muñoz therefore conceived of a new status, which he called "Estado Libre Asociado." Although the term translates as "free associated state," he used a different word, "commonwealth," as the English translation. The Spanish name was an exquisite compromise that combined the key word from each of the status options. The commonwealth formula pushed the status issue off the agenda for a generation, and during that time Puerto Rico did so well that its development policies were used as a model for the Alliance for Progress.

The postwar period also witnessed massive emigration from every island in the Caribbean to the United States. Puerto Rico, sharing citizenship, naturally sent the largest numbers. By the mid-1970s, two of every five Puerto Ricans lived on the mainland (roughly 2.2 million of 5.5 million people). This familiarity, together with the rising living standards on the island, enhanced the credibility of the pro-statehood New Progressive Party (PNP). The retirement of the charismatic Muñoz in the mid-1960s gave the PNP an opening, and the economic slowdown gave it an argument: that the commonwealth idea was exhausted. Support for statehood grew steadily, and it slowly overtook the commonwealth option in popularity. In the 1967 referendum, 60.4 percent of the voters chose commonwealth; 38.9 percent, statehood; and 0.6 percent, independence. A 1990 poll showed that 48.3 percent preferred statehood; 40.6 percent, commonwealth; and 5 percent, independence.[8]

Although Puerto Rican leaders have a reputation in Latin America for being deferential to Washington, they have always been among the most skilled and effective lobbyists, particularly for discrete benefits. Turning their attention to the status issue, statehooders drew from a deep quiver of tactics. They lobbied the White House and Congress; they condemned U.S. colonialism at the United Nations in the hope of provoking Washington to change the status; and they used presidential primaries on the island to influence candidates. Some of their efforts worked. In 1976 President Gerald Ford endorsed statehood. President Carter, however, pledged to "support, and urge the Congress to support, whatever decision the people of Puerto Rico reach." Presidents Ronald Reagan and George Bush both endorsed statehood, but also said that they would "accept whatever choice is made by a majority of the island's population."[9]

Despite all these presidential promises, the status of Puerto Rico remained the same. Why? The day after Ford's endorsement, Carter answered: "Until the Puerto Rican people themselves express a preference for statehood . . . the Congress should not take the initiative."[10] The United States was waiting for Puerto Rico to take the first step.

Why did Puerto Rico not take it? Just barely below the surface, Puerto Ricans remain deeply ambivalent on the issue of political status, torn by psychological, political, cultural, economic, and familial ties that pull them in several directions simultaneously. On the surface, statehooders want *equality*: the same rights and responsibilities as all U.S. citizens. Independentistas want *dignity*: the legitimacy of being a Latin American nation. And commonwealth supporters want *both*. All sides agree that the current status is imperfect, but repeated polls suggest that the status issue is near or at the bottom of their concerns.[11] In 1980 Carlos Romero Barceló, a popular governor then, declared that if he won reelection he would call for a referendum on statehood. He nearly lost and dropped the idea.

One conclusion that could be drawn from the survey data and election campaigns is that the Puerto Rican people do not want or are not yet ready to make a definitive choice on status. Indeed, the success of the commonwealth candidate for governor in the elections of 1984 and 1988 might be attributed to the fear that the island was slipping toward statehood. Because most Puerto Ricans want something of each status, their strongest statement has been to avoid a commitment. Their leaders, on the other hand, are frustrated by the uncertainty and so have aimed their appeal to Washington to untie the Gordian knot.

The psychology of indecision is also shaped by the distribution of power. As Maurice Ferré, the Puerto Rican-born former mayor of Miami, put it: "The question is not what the people of Puerto Rico want; it's what the Congress will concede."[12] Any change in the status of Puerto Rico requires the approval of Congress and the president. Few leaders in Puerto Rico want to commit themselves fully when they know the decision rests in Washington. For the United States to demand a decision first, and to leave them uncertain whether that decision will be accepted, is to allow no margin of error, no *dignidad*. And frankly, from a U.S. perspective, that is also the worst approach: If Puerto Rico were to make a decision, and then Washington either rejected it or fundamentally altered the terms, the United States would unwittingly transform a family member into a very resentful and angry neighbor.

Throwing the Ball into the U.S. Court

The reason that the United States has not taken the lead in resolving the status issue is fundamentally the same one that explains the Puerto Rican stalemate: ambivalence. From the time that U.S. soldiers arrived in 1898 through today, the United States as a nation has always had a clearer idea of what it does not want in Puerto Rico than what it does want. In the beginning, the United States did not want to behave or be perceived as an imperialist, but it also did not want to grant the island real equality. Over time, it ceded sufficient powers to stunt an independence movement, and it was responsive to enough of the island's concerns to keep its politicians bargaining endlessly with Washington.

Today, Americans remain as ambivalent on the three status options as Puerto Ricans. Republicans are more outspoken in their ambivalence, endorsing statehood and yet blocking any plebiscite bill for fear that statehood would mean more Democrats in Congress. Democrats have always felt more of an affinity with the commonwealth politicians on the island, but they suspect that, of the three options, the "enhanced commonwealth"—which combines the attributes of sovereignty with larger transfer payments from the mainland—may be the least realistic option politically.

Some Americans would like Puerto Rico to be a state, provided that it accepts English as an official language, which is not a negotiable point in Puerto Rico. They would like to remove the financial burden by giving the island independence, but they do not want to lose the military bases or pay to keep them. Because they cannot have both, the logic brings them back to the status quo.

Ronald Reagan's short journey from urging statehood to dropping the issue—in less than two years—is a graphic illustration of this vacillation. During the 1980 presidential campaign, Reagan promised to initiate statehood legislation if elected, and in September 1981 he sent Vice President Bush to San Juan to promise "Statehood Now!" in a rousing speech. Yet, by the time a delegation of statehooders visited him in the White House in January 1982, Reagan apparently was having second thoughts. Instead of receiving a statehood bill, the Puerto Ricans were offered a bland White House announcement that reaffirmed Reagan's preference for statehood but also expressed willingness to accept whatever the people of Puerto Rico decided. In his meeting, Reagan dwelled on the assassination attempt against him the previous March, "implying," according to a Puerto Rican analyst, "that the Puerto Rico issue could provoke another." The visitors later learned that the Secret Service had found a letter bomb to the president the month before the meeting, and it was postmarked Puerto Rico.[13]

The leaders of Puerto Rico's political parties waited until after the 1988 U.S. elections before trying another approach to Washington. On January 18, 1989, Governor Rafael Hernández Colón of the Commonwealth party (PDP), Rubén Berríos of the Independence party (PIP), and Baltasar Corrada of the pro-statehood PNP signed a joint declaration asking President Bush and Congress to enact legislation to hold a plebiscite in Puerto Rico in 1991—*and to honor the results.*

The U.S. Congress, under the leadership of Senator J. Bennett Johnston of the Senate Energy and Natural Resources Committee, took up the issue in an agonizing two-year review. The Senators listened to the proponents of each status option describe in some detail what they expected if they won the plebiscite. Then, the senators dismissed virtually every proposal. Senator Johnston rejected seventeen out of twenty ideas recommended by the governor, including his proposal for sharing sovereignty. The Republicans criticized the statehooders for thinking that they could have Spanish as the official language, and all the Senators ridiculed the "independentistas" for thinking they could retain citizenship if they chose to be a separate country. The bill never even emerged from the Committee.

Senator Johnston actually tried to implement a modest variation of a proposal for "mutual determination" that I had offered,[14] but it failed for the same reason that mine did. Trying to resolve the Puerto Rican status issue is roughly equivalent to ratifying the Canal treaties; it would require a huge expenditure of political capital. As long as there is so little clarity on the preferred status on the island, a president is unlikely to want to use that capital. Despite his rhetorical endorsement for statehood, Bush clearly decided not to invest his time and prestige to break the deadlock.

The Puerto Ricans had tossed the ball into Washington's court, and Congress tossed it back. With their exit blocked, Puerto Rican leaders returned to their old habits. Hernández Colón tried to outmaneuver the statehooders with a referendum on December 8, 1991, that would have prevented any future yes-no vote on statehood and made permanent six rights, including language and separate sports teams. The vote was interpreted as an attempt by the governor to make difficult, if not impossible, any future decision on statehood. By 53 to 45 percent, the people of Puerto Rico rejected the referendum.

Eight years later, on December 13, 1998, one hundred years after the island had become the "unincorporated territory" of the United States, the leaders tried again. This time, the referendum was described on the ballot as a petition to the U.S. Congress to end "one hundred years of political servitude." Four options were listed: Commonwealth, statehood, free association, and independence. The Puerto Rican Supreme Court mandated a fifth option: "none of the above." Guess which won? Forty-six percent voted for statehood, but the majority (50.2 percent) voted for the last option—none of the above! Again, the people confounded the pundits, who thought the vote would be a turning point, reminding the politicians of the immortal wisdom of Luis Muñoz Marín: "When you are on a circle, every point is a turning point."

The Metaphor, Writ Large

During a distinguished career, Arturo Morales-Carrión had the opportunity to examine his island's quandary from three vantage points: the Puerto Rican government, the State Department, and the Organization of American States. His memoir evinced more sadness than impatience with the often accusatory language exchanged by North Americans and Puerto Ricans, but the lesson he drew from the history was this: "Puerto Rican contradictions are matched by American contradictions."[15] Governors appointed by the United States accused Puerto Rican leaders of corruption even while they themselves obtained their jobs through campaign contributions. North Americans charged Puerto Ricans with "petty factionalism" in the 1930s, but Morales-Carrión's unemotional account of bureaucratic politics in Washington during the same period demonstrates that the term applies as much to the accuser as the accused. It is not just that Puerto Ricans are divided and confused by a mix of interests, but that the United States is as well. Puerto Ricans are "caught in a century-old dilemma," Morales-Carrión writes, torn between their economic ties and their "cultural nationality." The United States has also been torn between its idealistic vision and its parochial reflex not to disturb the status quo.

A mirror image of ambivalence defines the psychological interior of the inter-American dilemma. In viewing the other, Latin America couples admiration with bitterness; the United States, sympathy with paternalism. The ambivalence is manifested in contradictory postures, which have been pounded deep by history: Latin America wants equality but expects special treatment; the United States wants friendship but expects support.

A first step in understanding U.S. policy toward the region is to recognize the parallel nature of perceptions and behavior patterns. But the force that draws the United States and Latin America into the whirlpool is not the result of mirror images. Rather it derives from *the way that perceptions connect and interact.* Divisions within Puerto Rico inhibit U.S. decisions on the island's status, and those decisions reinforce Puerto Rico's divisions. In a similar dynamic, when the United States confronts an unfriendly regime, or even just withholds aid, it can strengthen hostile elements within a country, who in turn take actions that confirm the worst suspicions of hard-liners in the U.S. government. And, of course, we have learned that Cuban hostility provokes U.S. belligerence and leads both sides down a descending spiral. *Neither side has found the exit because both are still looking in the wrong direction.* In an exercise in futility, each side blames the other rather than trying to understand how each justifies the other.

Glimmers of self-awareness and understanding are discernible in the region as well as in the United States, and these offer hope of finding a way out of the whirlpool. Octavio Paz, the late Mexican philosopher, observed that Latin Americans need to accept their responsibility for political instability just as Americans should accept their share:

> It is true that the fragmentation of our countries, our civil wars, militarism, and dictatorships were not the invention of the U.S. But that country has a fundamental responsibility for this state of affairs, because it has taken advantage of it to materially improve its own situation and to dominate.[16]

Throughout Latin America and the Caribbean, the power and the presence of the United States have shaped values and perceptions. Some in the region admire the achievements of the United States and look to it for answers; others see the United States as the region's biggest problem and want to eliminate its influence. Attitudes are most intense in countries closest to the United States and on issues related to intervention, but anti-American feelings have demonstrated strength and durability all the way down to Argentina and Chile. American interventions generally have been viewed in the region as unwanted projections of U.S. hegemony, whereas the United States has tended to regard them as necessary responses to an invitation or a provocation. The United States not only fails to reciprocate the region's strong feelings, both positive and negative; it has difficulty understanding the basis of those feelings and attributes them to some character flaw or to the region's inability to deal with its own problems. Whereas many Latin Americans exaggerate the adverse and minimize the positive impact of certain U.S. policies, Washington does the opposite.

Sir Eric Williams, the scholar and long-serving prime minister of Trinidad and Tobago, ends his epic history of the Caribbean with contradictory conclusions that reflect these two perceptions. "The whole history of the Caribbean so far can be viewed as a conspiracy to block the emergence of a Caribbean identity—in politics, in institutions, in economics, in culture, and in values." And yet, Williams also concludes, "In the last analysis, dependence is a state of mind," suggesting that underdevelopment is a function not just of foreign conspiracies but of internal inadequacies as well:

> A too-long history of colonialism seems to have crippled Caribbean self-confidence and self-reliance, and a vicious circle has been set up: psychological dependence leads to an ever-growing economic and cultural dependence on the outside world. Fragmentation is intensified in the process. And the greater degree of dependence and fragmentation further reduces local self-confidence.[17]

Jean-Paul Sartre wrote of the "split personality" of Third World people, who are born with "a nervous condition introduced and maintained by the settler among colonized people with their consent."[18] *With their consent*—could that be the point? The clue to the psychological relationship between the United States and Latin America lies in the intersection between the concepts of free will, so deeply ingrained in the United States, and dependency, so popular in Latin America and the Third World. Whereas the United States believes Latin America to be responsible for its own instability and underdevelopment, many in the region stress the structural impediments placed in their way by U.S. power.

Both perceptions are valid, and the truth is in their merger. The region is vulnerable to outside forces in ways the United States will never be, but it also has considerable room and choice to reduce its dependence. The path toward greater autonomy lies between those who prefer to pay the price of defiance and those who would reap the rewards of subservience. Ironically, those who have struggled hardest to sever the ties of dependence have found themselves more dependent than those who have taken a moderate course. Fidel Castro made his country more dependent on outside aid with a confrontational policy, whereas Omar Torrijos succeeded in recapturing his nation's independence with a moderate strategy. Perceptions can either impede or facilitate the journey toward greater autonomy.

The United States needs to appreciate the perspective of a country that sits on the receiving end of U.S. policy or of a traumatic external shock, like a hurricane or the declining price of sugar, over which a nation has no influence, let alone control. In turn, the region needs to accept that it has at least as much responsibility for its problems as does the United States. As we see in the last chapters, old perceptions are changing, and as that occurs, the prospects for cooperation improve.

Because the United States shares in the consequences of the region's instability and underdevelopment, it has a stake in assisting the region to become more developed and less vulnerable. The United States should promote regional unity even at the cost of reducing its leverage over individual nations, and the region needs to look more to its neighbors to solve problems and less to Washington.

Puerto Rico straddles the intersection between the domestic and the international and between the United States and Latin America. The case for breaking the deadlock on political status is a simple but compelling one: It runs against the grain of the American character to have a permanent underclass or privileged class. Puerto Rico is a combination of both, and many Puerto Ricans feel awkward at the generous but unequal treatment. All Americans should share that sense of awkwardness; it is a testament to the distance of Puerto Rico and the insensitivity of Americans that so few do. The United States will have taken an important step out of the Latin American whirlpool when it demonstrates the political will and the respect necessary to resolve the status issue with the people of Puerto Rico.

Notes

1. Quoted in Alan Weisman, "An Island in Limbo," *New York Times Magazine*, February 18, 1990, p. 34.

2. Carlos Rangel, *The Latin Americans: Their Love-Hate Relationship with the United States* (New York: Harcourt Brace Jovanovich, 1977), p. 50.

3. Ibid.

4. Arturo Morales-Carrión, *Puerto Rico: A Political and Cultural Odyssey* (New York: W. W. Norton, 1983), pp. 130–132.

5. See, for example, Juan M. García-Passalacqua, *Puerto Rico: Equality and Freedom at Issue* (New York: Praeger, 1984).

6. Raymond Carr, *Puerto Rico: A Colonial Experiment* (New York: New York University Press, 1984).

7. Carroll's advice is quoted in Carr, *Puerto Rico,* p. 34; see p. 57 for a summary of the views of Coolidge and others.

8. "Poll Shows 48.3% of Puerto Ricans Favor Statehood," *Miami Herald,* July 25, 1990, p. 4A.

9. For Ford's statement, see *The New York Times,* January 1, 1977, p. 1. For Carter's proclamation, see *Papers of the Presidents of the United States: Jimmy Carter, 1978* (Washington, D.C.: Government Printing Office, 1979), July 25, 1978, p. 1336; for Reagan's, *Papers of the Presidents of the United States: Ronald Reagan* (Washington, D.C.: Government Printing Office, 1983), January 12, 1982; for Bush's, see his State of the Union address to Congress, reprinted in *Congressional Record,* February 9, 1989, p. H268.

10. *The New York Times,* January 2, 1977, p. 2.

11. For two polls six years apart showing the low priority of the status issue, see *El Nuevo Dia* (San Juan, Puerto Rico), June 2, 1983, p. 2; and February 21, 1989, p.4.

12. Interview with Maurice Ferré, April 27, 1983, Miami.

13. García-Passalacqua, *Puerto Rico,* p. 160. For previous comments by Reagan and Bush, see Ronald Reagan, "Puerto Rico and Statehood," *Wall Street Journal,* February 12, 1980; Robert Friedman, "Bush, at San Juan Rally, Calls for 'Statehood Now,'" *San Juan Star,* September 28, 1981, p. 1.

14. See Robert Pastor, "The United States and Puerto Rico: A Proposal," *Washington Quarterly 7* (Summer 1984): 56–66.

15. Morales-Carrión, *Puerto Rico.*

16. Octavio Paz, "Latin America and Democracy," in *Democracy and Dictatorship in Latin America* (New York: Foundation for the Study of Independent Social Ideas, n.d.), p. 9.

17. Eric Williams, *From Columbus to Castro: The History of the Caribbean* (1970; reprint, New York: Vintage Books, 1984), 502–504.

18. Jean-Paul Sartre, preface to Frantz Fanon, *The Wretched of the Earth* (Harmondsworth, England: Penguin, 1967), p. 17.

13

THE REDEFINITION OF SOVEREIGNTY: THE NICARAGUAN PRECEDENT AND THE MEXICAN MODEL

Historically, nationalism has been the answer to any external challenge. Now the big challenge is not being left out of the great integrationist efforts and the great exchange of resources.[1]

—CARLOS SALINAS, PRESIDENT OF MEXICO, 1991

No country in Latin America has been sucked into the center of the whirlpool more often and with more adverse consequences than Nicaragua. And no country has been more zealous in defending its sovereignty and the principle of nonintervention than Mexico. Yet, in 1990, both countries redefined their traditional positions on "sovereignty" and tossed away the shield they had so long used to defend themselves from foreigners. Both opened their sovereign doors to the international community and discovered the counterintuitive truth of the modern world: that they could liberate themselves and enhance their capacity more without the walls than within them. With this fundamental redefinition of sovereignty, Nicaragua and Mexico also mapped the exit from the whirlpool and made possible the modernization of U.S.–Latin American relations.

The traditional conception of sovereignty had been the defining element of the national psychology of these two countries and most of Latin America, and it was embedded in the Charter of the Organization of American States. Article 18 of the Charter prohibits member states from any direct or indirect interference "for any reason whatever in the internal or external affairs" of any state. The Charter also proclaims the sanctity of human rights and democracy, but fails to explain how human rights could be promoted if all countries are barred from pursuing them within the national jurisdictions in which they are most affected. F. Scott Fitzgerald once wrote that the test of a first-rate mind is the ability to hold two contradictory thoughts at the same time. Did the government officials who wrote and signed this charter pass that test? Did they display a lack of seriousness or a trace of hypocrisy?

The conceptual boundary that has separated sovereign rights from human rights has often been defined by the most nationalistic regimes. The reasons are not hard to divine. In Mexico's case, the loss of more than one-third of its territory to the United States in the middle of the nineteenth century, a 1,950-mile border with a superpower, the resentment of being overtaken by a less-cultured country, and the fear of being overwhelmed by the U.S. economy and its consumer culture all led Mexico to build walls to keep the United States from interfering or even influencing its internal affairs. Mexico's diplomats have used international law as one more instrument to keep the world at bay. Yet it was Mexico's president in the spring of 1990 who proposed a free trade agreement with the United States. That initiative displaced the economic nationalism of the past.

In a similar fashion, the nationalistic Sandinista government in Nicaragua redefined political sovereignty in its precedent-setting invitation to the international community—the United Nations, the OAS, and the Council of Freely-Elected Heads of Government, based at the Carter Center—to observe its elections in February 1990. These international groups did much more than just observe the elections; they mediated the rules of the political game. The opposition did not trust the government or the electoral process, and the government did not trust the opposition, but both trusted the international mediators to ensure a fair election or to denounce a fraudulent one. So the observers became the surrogates for the election officials and a free process. They assisted all parties, despite their deep suspicions, to participate in the election and to accept the results, permitting the first peaceful transfer of power in the nation's history.

Nicaragua's true distinction, then, was not as the victim of the whirlpool, but as the first to escape its control. Condemned to repeat a tragic pattern of authoritarianism and instability for 160 years,

Nicaragua finally broke loose from its history in the election of February 25, 1990. In this chapter, I describe the events leading to the Nicaraguan precedent of redefining political sovereignty and the Mexican model of redefining economic sovereignty, then explore the significance of the two cases for the emerging inter-American community.

Nicaragua's Travails and the Arias Alternative

Suspicion has dominated Nicaragua's political history. The government and its opposition have always believed the worst of each other and repeatedly acted in ways that made those beliefs come true. Hostility bred belligerence. Conciliatory gestures were dismissed as tricks or signs of weakness. Extremism prevailed over compromise.

"Peaceful changes between different factions of the ruling classes, which have been rather frequent in other Latin American countries, have not taken place in Nicaragua," wrote Carlos Fonseca Amador, the founding father of the Sandinista National Liberation Front (FSLN). "This traditional experience predisposed the Nicaraguan people against electoral farces and in favor of armed struggle."[2] The government traditionally viewed the opposition as weak, fragmented, and ineffectual and did everything possible to keep it like that. The opposition viewed the government as coercive and corrupt. A few opposition groups would participate in elections; others boycotted, lest they provide a veneer of respect to an illegitimate regime.

Prior to 1990, no Nicaraguan election was judged free by all parties and observers, and only three were viewed as fair by some observers. The elections of 1928 and 1932 were regarded as fair, but because both were supervised by U.S. Marines, they can hardly be considered ideal examples of self-determination. Many observers judged the election of 1984 as fair, but several opposition parties, encouraged by the Reagan administration, withdrew before the election, protesting government harassment.

This tragic, repetitive pattern of government coercion and opposition abstention, so well analyzed by the father of modern Sandinismo, reached its culmination under their rule. The FSLN accused the opposition of being disloyal pawns of the United States; the opposition characterized the FSLN as repressive, Marxist-Leninist surrogates of Cuba and the Soviet Union. Accusations substituted for communication. The Reagan administration helped each side's perceptions of the other come true. The contras—first the means and then the ends of U.S. policy—justified the militarism of the Sandinistas and deepened the regime's dependence on the Soviet Union and Cuba even while rendering the internal opposition impotent.

Costa Rican President Oscar Arias offered both sides a possible exit. In August 1987, Arias persuaded Daniel Ortega and the other Central American presidents to accept his proposal to end conflicts in the region by democracy, national reconciliation, and an end to insurgencies. By making each country responsible for securing democracy in all five, the plan offered a way to cut the cord that had tied internal conflict to external intervention.

As part of the accord, Arias and the other presidents asked the United States to stop providing arms to the contras. Reagan called the plan "fatally flawed" and insisted that the Sandinistas would never accept democracy unless Congress approved military aid to the contras.[3] Congress rejected Reagan's argument and was proven right. With the political space permitted by a suspension of aid to the contras, President Ortega called for elections on February 25, 1990. He believed that a free election would return him to power, and by proving he was genuinely democratic, would also unlock aid from Europe, lift the U.S. embargo, and end the contra war.

The opposition had learned two lessons from the 1984 election: unite and stay in the race. Invigorated by returning exiles like Alfredo Cesar, encouraged to participate by the Bush administration, and convinced that the economy's collapse, the Sandinistas' militarism, and the spread of democracy in Latin America all favored them, the opposition felt it could win *if* there were a free election.

One of the reasons that the mediation in Nicaragua in 1978 failed to produce agreed-upon rules for a plebiscite is that both Somoza and the moderate opposition each feared that *the other might win.* (The opposition believed that Somoza would manipulate the election, and Somoza feared he might not be able to do that.)[4] The more promising climate of 1989–1990 could be attributed to the fact that the FSLN and the National Opposition Union (UNO) each thought *it would win.* These favorable conditions, however, still had to contend with Nicaragua's historical burdens. The Sandinistas were committed in principle to a free election, but in practice this meant reducing their control over the state and the media and negotiating with the opposition on the terms that would give the latter confidence in electoral procedures. This was not the FSLN's style. It preferred to hand down election rules (for example, the decree on electoral reform in April 1989), and the opposition's style was to boycott (for example, by not proposing candidates to the regional electoral councils in 1989).

On September 2, 1989, the fourteen disparate groups that had united to become UNO nominated Violeta Barrios de Chamorro as their presidential candidate and Virgilio Godoy, the leader of the Independent Liberal party (PLI) as vice president. Doña Violeta was the widow of Pedro Joaquín Chamorro, Somoza's long-standing rival, whose assassination on January 10, 1978, was the catalyst that bonded Nicaragua's middle class to the Sandinistas and ensured their military victory on July 20, 1979. She had served on the first junta but resigned in the spring of 1980, upset over the direction in which the Sandinistas were taking the country.

Mediating the Terms of the Election

During the campaign, UNO complained repeatedly of abuses by the FSLN. Many of their charges reflected legitimate concerns, but UNO rarely pursued them by documenting incidents and appealing to the Supreme Electoral Council (SEC). Instead, UNO leaders preferred to use the charges to prove that the Sandinistas were not serious about a free election. The FSLN responded by accusing UNO of trying to discredit the election because it knew it would lose. The U.S. State Department echoed UNO, insisting that FSLN behavior "raises grave questions as to whether there can be truly free and fair elections in Nicaragua."[5]

The Sandinistas also raised legitimate concerns about UNO's constant attacks on the SEC, but their primary concerns were the contras and U.S. policy. President Ortega was willing to permit the United States to fund UNO overtly, but he promised to make the CIA the central campaign issue if there were any covert aid. The Bush administration decided against covert aid but would not assure Ortega of this. In an effort to remove the covert funding issue from the campaign, Jimmy Carter asked Ortega if he would accept his promise that there would be no covert funding if Carter could get assurances from the Bush administration and the congressional intelligence committees. After discussions with both governments, Carter conveyed those assurances to Ortega in a letter on September 22, 1989, and the covert funding issue, which had been an important FSLN negative issue in September and had threatened to poison the campaign, disappeared.[6]

The Sandinistas asked the Bush administration to accept the Central American Accords and channel U.S. funds through a UN-OAS operation to demobilize the contras. Although the contras disrupted the electoral process, the administration rejected this and every opportunity to resolve the contra problem before the election, even a proposal in December to demobilize the contras between the date that the election was certified as fair and the inauguration.[7] Bush also refused to exchange ambassadors, expand diplomatic personnel, or pledge to accept the results if the three main observer groups certified the election free and fair. Although Bush would not try to improve relations, at least he did not deliberately try to undermine the election, as his predecessor had done in 1984, and he did encourage the opposition to participate.

The most positive element of the Bush administration's policy was that it offered space for others to negotiate the rules for a free election in Nicaragua. Among the many precedents established in the Esquipulas Accord of 1987, perhaps the most significant was the invitation by the five Central American presidents to the OAS and the UN "to send observers to verify that the electoral process has been governed by the strictest rules of equal access for all political parties."[8] On past occasions, when invited to elections, the OAS had sent a few passive observers on the day of the vote. The UN had never before monitored an election in a sovereign country. With considerable reluctance and hesitation, the UN Secretary General finally agreed to send a mission, because the request had come from five countries and because it was directly related to resolving an international conflict.

In May 1989 Jimmy Carter and Gerald Ford observed the elections in Panama under the auspices of two U.S. party institutes and the Council of Freely-Elected Heads of Government, a group of leaders chaired by Carter. When Panamanian General Manuel Antonio Noriega tampered with the results, Carter denounced him. Carter sent me to Managua in July 1989 to meet with Ortega, Vice President Sergio Ramirez, and leaders of the opposition and to describe how the council had monitored the elections in Panama. I told Ortega and Ramirez that their defense of Noriega in the OAS had been interpreted by some in the United States as a sign that they wanted to rig the elections as Noriega had done. One way to disprove that charge would be to invite the man who had denounced the election fraud in Panama. The FSLN was interested, and the opposition enthusiastic, to invite Carter, but I told them that Carter would accept only if invited by both sides.

In early August 1989 Carter, as chairman of the council, received invitations from Ortega, UNO, and the SEC to observe the electoral process "from beginning to end." Ortega promised Carter "unrestricted access to all aspects of the process." Carter accepted, promising to be partial to the democratic process but "meticulously impartial" with respect to competing candidates and parties. The invitations gave Carter and the council leverage to mediate, as neither side wanted to be blamed for problems.

In the end, the Nicaraguan election was watched by more foreign observers and correspondents (four thousand total) than any independent country had ever hosted. Each of the three main observer groups—Carter's, the OAS, and the UN—played a slightly different role. Both the OAS and the UN had the funds and the personnel to assemble large missions. The OAS helped resolve problems at the regional level. The UN team's strength was in its analytical skills and its diplomatic approaches at the middle levels in Managua. Carter's high-level group tried to resolve the main problems by dealing directly with Ortega and Chamorro.

Four lessons were drawn from the Panamanian experience. First, the delegation needed to monitor the process for at least six months before the election. Second, it was essential to retain the confidence and trust of both sides, but particularly of President Ortega so as to ensure that if any problems arose during the election or counting, Carter would have access to him. Third, the delegation had to ensure that the vote would be secret and convince Nicaraguans of that. The best way to detect, and hopefully deter, any tampering with the vote count was a parallel "quick count" run by the international monitors.[9] The fourth lesson from Panama was to avoid being diverted by minor issues or by reports of conspiracies to fix the vote. The many reports that Noriega had an intricate plan to steal the election were false. He was taken by surprise and had to improvise so crudely that the fraud was easily detected. The climate was far more repressive in Panama than in Nicaragua, and there were fewer international observers, yet the observers in Panama were enough to give confidence to the voters, who turned out in large numbers and voted overwhelmingly against the government.

Nicaragua's history also provided lessons. The most important was to keep the opposition in the electoral game and the government from intimidating the opposition. To do this, the international observers patrolled and sought to expand the boundaries of civility. The three groups listened to UNO's charges, distilled the hundreds of complaints down to the few that were most serious, and then raised them directly with Ortega. In virtually every case, Ortega responded—not as quickly or as fully as UNO wanted—but almost every issue was resolved. He ended confiscations of lands; ceased recruiting UNO activists into military service; released most of the political prisoners; permitted Brooklyn Rivera, an Indian leader, to return; ensured a fair registration process that Chamorro applauded; accepted a decree to prevent campaign violence; ended intimidation and harassment of UNO candidates and poll watchers; and released funds to UNO.[10] By the end of these negotiations, UNO had a stake in the process, and the FSLN had begun learning the benefits of compromise.

As the election approached, the Sandinistas were so confident that they tried to divert the media to the issue of normalizing relations with the United States after their victory. Chamorro's advisers were equally confident but much more cautious. Ironically, American conservatives and UNO hard-liners believed the FSLN and tried to persuade the media to dismiss both the election and the international observers. Two days before the election, Elliott Abrams, former assistant secretary of state in the Reagan administration, told a Stanford audience that the Sandinistas would win a fraudulent election and that Carter would foolishly certify it as fair: "It is obviously going to be a very crummy election in Nicaragua. President Carter will have the unique historical opportunity to lose Nicaragua twice.[11] Other conservatives wrote that the Sandinistas would "fix" the results.[12]

There were few incidents or problems on the day of the election. UNO had poll watchers at almost every voting site. Turnout was high: 1.5 million people, 86 percent of those who had registered. Nicaraguans were surprisingly somber, quiet, uncertain, perhaps afraid. Few volunteered their preferences; several would sheepishly raise a single finger, signifying UNO. Confidence in the secrecy of the vote had been bolstered by appeals and assurances of Cardinal Obando y Bravo and Jimmy Carter, who gave a brief statement in Spanish encouraging people to vote "and be confident that your vote will be secret and will count. We are here to make sure of that."

The OAS fielded 435 observers who visited 3,064 voting sites (70 percent of the total), and the UN had 237 observers who monitored 2,155 sites (49 percent).[13] Woody Allen once said that 90 percent of life is just being there, and on election day, that was the case for international observers. Just being there—actually, almost everywhere—imparted tranquillity and confidence to the voters.

At 10:00 P.M., Carter was informed that slightly more than one-third of the UN sample had been received and that Chamorro was decisively winning by a margin of about 56 to 40 percent. The margin was so great, and the returns coming in so consistent, that there was no question she would win. The counting center was not announcing results, but at 11:30 P.M., after repeated requests by Carter for a meeting, President Ortega invited Carter, UN Representative Elliott Richardson, and OAS Secretary General Joao Baena Soares—the three "wise men"—and their senior aides to meet with him at the FSLN campaign headquarters. The meeting began at 12:20 A.M. and ended fifty minutes later.

The Sandinistas looked shocked and ashen-faced. Ortega admitted that he was losing the election, but he would not concede. He claimed that the margin of difference was 5–6 percent, and said "I still think it might be possible to reverse the trend."[14] Whether Ortega believed this, or was trying to gain time or some room to assess his options, Carter and Richardson left him no space. They said that the quick count was stable and definitive and that the margin was wider. Ortega reaffirmed that he would respect the popular will if UNO won, and after an extended discussion he sought their advice on how the transition could be handled peacefully.

Carter moved to reassure Ortega: "I have won a Presidential election and lost one, and losing wasn't the end of the world." Rosalynn Carter then interjected: "I thought it was." Her comment punctured the tension, releasing the emotion that the Sandinista leaders were trying to hold back. The Sandinistas burst out with a laugh, their first and undoubtedly their last of the evening. Carter then described Ortega's accomplishments, from defeating Somoza to holding a free election. As he spoke, Ortega listened intently, and his concession speech the next morning reflected the points that Carter made about why the Sandinistas should feel proud rather than defeated.

Ortega asked if the observers could persuade Chamorro not to give a victory statement until the SEC, which had delayed publicizing the results, could release some, and until he had time to prepare his followers. The three observers then met with Chamorro at her home, and she agreed to delay her statement and make it conciliatory. Within an hour, about 3 A.M., 30 percent of the returns were released, indicating that she was winning, and she made her statement. Three hours later, after 60 percent of the returns were announced, Ortega announced on television that he would respect the results, and his face announced that he had lost. The next afternoon, he asked the three wise men to accompany him to Chamorro's house, where he congratulated her and agreed to work together to assure a smooth transition.

The final results showed Chamorro winning 54.7 percent of the vote and Ortega 40.8 percent. Although many American conservatives feared that the FSLN's control of the government would tilt the playing field in its favor, the burden of incumbency—of governing during ten years of war and economic decline—was decisive.

Transfer of Power

The indirect exchange between Ortega and Chamorro in the early hours of February 26 was the first time in Nicaraguan history that the government and the opposition had sought ways to reassure each other and the nation. Both sides soon agreed on virtually every step that each would take during the next week, and this orchestrated process served to build trust where none had existed before.

Both Ortega and Chamorro asked the three observers to remain, monitor, and guarantee the transition, and on February 27, the leaders of the two transition teams—Humberto Ortega for the FSLN and Antonio Lacayo for UNO—met at the Carter Center's Managua office. Within two hours, the parameters of the transition were defined. Both sides agreed that Chamorro would assume full power on April 25 and would name all her ministers. Second, they agreed there would be no retribution, and each side would need to be sensitive to the main concerns of the other. Chamorro would respect "the integrity of the armed forces as an institution" and appoint ministers of defense and interior who would not be viewed as enemies by the Sandinistas. This meant that she would give Ortega the opportunity to express his views on her nominees.

Third, both sides agreed to call for rapid and immediate demobilization of the contras and to work toward that end. This would make it easier to implement Chamorro's campaign promise to reduce the army. UNO confirmed its commitment to the land reform, and both agreed to deal with the problems of expropriated property within the existing law. Any changes in the law before the inauguration would have to be approved by Chamorro, or the FSLN would risk a repeal of the laws after UNO took power.[15]

In a press conference on April 5, Antonio Lacayo, who was named minister of the presidency, said that the new Chamorro government would try "to break the violent cycle" of Nicaragua's past by respecting "the 41 percent minority," the Sandinistas. He was criticized by members of his own coalition for being too solicitous of the FSLN, but he insisted that the only way for democracy to take root was by national reconciliation.[16] This was the theme of Chamorro's inaugural address on April 25, 1990, and of her government, but overcoming a decade of polarization would take time.

The most dangerous issue during the transition was the demobilization of the contras. The Sandinistas were worried about the delay in negotiating the contras' disarmament, and Chamorro felt compelled to appoint Humberto Ortega as chief of the army. She paid a high price for that decision. The contras further delayed demobilization, many in UNO were alienated, and the Bush administration was angry. Ironically, General Ortega's presence in Chamorro's government proved helpful in bridging the differences between the two groups and in bringing the FSLN to understand that Nicaragua would not be worth inheriting in 1996 if she was unable to restore the economy. In 1990 the economy had fallen to the level of 1960.[17]

In Chamorro's first year, the war ended, and 22,000 contras were demobilized and reintegrated into the country. The military under Humberto Ortega was reduced by two-thirds and retired five thousand officers. In the second year, the government tamed hyperinflation.

The Nicaraguan Precedent and the Collective Defense of Democracy

Until the last decade of the twentieth century, Nicaragua had been a model that no country would want to emulate: a small, impoverished, authoritarian country, subject to chronic instability and foreign intervention. This image changed in 1989 and 1990 as Nicaraguans struggled to make an election credible and fair.

A strategy based on respect prevailed, and for the first time in Nicaraguan history the cynics found themselves on the margins of events. Those like President Reagan who said that the Sandinistas were Communists who would never have a free election and would never give up power were proven wrong. This appraisal, however, was not outlandish. If Reagan had been president and had discouraged the opposition from participating in the election, his prediction would have come true.

No doubt, one of the reasons the process worked and political space opened was that Ortega was confident of winning the election. But the more enduring point is that the campaign transformed both parties and Nicaragua's politics. Ortega began to respond to the public temper, and the public responded to him too. The 41 percent of the vote that he won is evidence of that. Outsiders were welcomed by both sides and played a pivotal role in helping to modify the country's political habits. Both sides staked so much on the judgment of these outsiders that, by election time, it was difficult to break faith. Daniel Ortega could have stolen the election, but he was not as cynical as some critics alleged. In a place where distrust was the currency of politics, both government and opposition decided to alter that history and peacefully exchange roles.

In the process, Nicaraguans redefined the boundaries of political sovereignty and developed a new model for the Americas that offers promise of making democracy sturdier and possibly permanent. The idea that a defiantly nationalistic regime that fought the United States to a stalemate should open its gates to Americans to judge an election is certainly ironic. But that was the essence of the Nicaraguan formula: to invite the international community to help make democracy work within a sovereign state.

One month after the Nicaraguan election, Ertha Pascal-Trouillot, the provisional president of Haiti, invited the OAS and the UN (and later Carter's council) to observe her country's elections. Haiti's problem was different from Nicaragua's. The incumbent was not seeking office; in fact, she was fleeing it, eager to return to the solitude of the Supreme Court. Haiti's problem was a lack of security, and Trouillot asked the UN Secretary General to send security advisers. There was no consensus in the UN about observing the Haiti election, and the UN did not want to set a precedent by sending security advisers. An old conception of sovereignty was the roadblock. Only after intensive lobbying by Venezuelan President Carlos Andrés Pérez, various Caribbean leaders, and Carter did the UN finally accede to the request on October 10, 1990.

On election day, December 16, 1990, the presence of all three groups—the UN, OAS, and the Council—was decisive in providing the Haitian people with a sense of security, but it also provided the results. Because Haiti's Electoral Tribunal did not finish its counting for weeks, and even then lost as many as 25 percent of the ballots, the UN/OAS quick count, which was completed on the evening of the election, was viewed as the final word.[18]

The Nicaraguan precedent thus expanded in Haiti, but it was also extended to Suriname, where a coup in December 1990 was condemned by the OAS. Fear of isolation compelled the coup leaders to invite the OAS to send observers to monitor an election in May 1991, and the OAS stayed to observe the transition to civilian leadership. At the same time, Guyana invited the Council of Freely-Elected Heads of Government to observe its electoral process, and council leaders mediated fundamental electoral reforms over a two year period.

In all of these cases, the pattern of mistrust among opposing political parties was similar to that in Nicaragua. Each group accused the other of duplicity and saw conspiracies in election-related problems where incompetence or miscommunication would have been far better explanations. Still, each country faced a distinct challenge, and the effectiveness of the international monitors depended on whether they were able to adapt their model to the specific needs of a country. The measure of what a change had occurred in the international system was the establishment by the OAS and the UN of Election Units, a subject that was outside the purview of both organizations in the days when the principle of noninterference was zealously guarded.

Nicaragua opened the door, but the reason that the nations of the hemisphere entered can be found in the region's breathtaking political transformation. In the mid-1970s some Latin Americans argued that true democracy should be judged by mass participation rather than by the choices people face in the privacy of a voting booth. The spread of Latin governments based on popular consent settled the debate on the definition of democracy and vanquished the idea that elections are an ethnocentric North American invention, alien to the Latin cultural tradition. Latin Americans still tend to attach a wider social and economic meaning to democracy than do most North Americans. Yet democrats in both regions agree that, at bottom, democracy means choice—free elections, free press, freedom to organize—and that the argument that health and development should precede democracy masks a self-serving effort to perpetuate dictatorship.

The consensus on norms facilitated the observation and mediation of elections, which in turn began to instill in the region's leaders a sense of collective responsibility for the maintenance of democracy. The next step for the hemispheric community was to translate a shared responsibility into a framework of collective defense. The occasion was the OAS General Assembly meeting in Santiago, Chile, in June 1991. The Venezuelan delegation proposed the "Betancourt Doctrine," named after its first president after the overthrow of General Marco Pérez Jiménez in 1958. The doctrine recommended automatic suspension from the OAS and isolation of any regime that overthrew a democratically elected president. Betancourt's idea was unrealistic in the early 1960s when the OAS was dominated by military regimes, but in the 1990s it became feasible. The Mexicans, however, opposed the idea. Sergio Gonzalez Galvez, the deputy foreign minister, said: "Mexico has never regarded the OAS as a mechanism to supervise democracy, and we're not going to allow this to happen."[19]

Nonetheless, the members reached a consensus on "The Santiago Commitment to Democracy and the Renewal of the Inter-American System." All thirty-four nations declared "their firm political commitment to the promotion and protection of human rights and representative democracy" and the recognition that the OAS has a major responsibility in the area. The coup in Haiti provided the first test for the OAS to apply this general statement of support for democracy, and we have discussed how the organization wrestled with the issue before the UN finally approved its members using force to restore constitutional government. The involvement of the OAS in this crisis represented one more step on the road to establishing a collective support mechanism for democracy in the hemisphere, but the journey was only beginning. In the next chapter, I offer some specific recommendations on the next steps for the OAS.

Nicaragua led the way into the whirlpool and finally out. The contra war froze Nicaragua's major players into stereotypes of Marxist tyrants and imperialist surrogates. The electoral process melted these images and permitted Nicaraguans to evolve into quasi-democrats. The events in Nicaragua had a wider significance for the hemisphere and the world. One of the most nationalistic regimes in Latin America redrew the traditional boundaries of political sovereignty. With the advice and active mediation of international statesmen, Nicaraguans designed a new political map, one that identified the dangerous, shallow waters so that the United States and Latin America could exit from the Latin American whirlpool without smashing onto rocks. That new map could point the way to the establishment of a new community of democratic nations in the western hemisphere. It is Nicaragua's gift to the Americas for the twenty-first century.

Mexico's Walls and The Salinas Postrevolutionary Opening

Over many years, Mexico's leaders constructed walls around the country that were held up by four pillars, each serving a different role. Its state-managed protectionist economic strategy protected Mexican businesses from competition and produced and sustained growth for a remarkably long period. But by the mid-1980s, the pillar was weakening, and Mexico's economy suffered its worst recession since the 1930s. The second pillar kept the opposition on the defensive and shielded the governing Institutional Revolutionary Party (PRI) from defeat. But by the mid-1980s, the opposition to the PRI had begun to grow. Indeed, in reaction to economic reforms, the son of one of Mexico's most revered presidents and the PRI governor of the state of Michoacan, Cuauhtémoc Cardenas, defected and contested the PRI for the presidency. The third pillar protected the privileged from the poor, darker masses, and it did so by government subsidies, party and corporatist organization, and a revolutionary mystique. The Mexican revolution, it should be recalled, was the twentieth century's first attempt to change fundamentally its social and economic relationships; this gave Mexico a mystique among intellectuals that continued long after the revolution had ossified. Mexico sought to retain the aura by its defense of the Cuban revolution and leftist movements in Latin America. Finally, the last pillar kept its northern neighbor at bay. Mexico defined the "limits to friendship" with the United States to prevent the U.S. from interfering in its affairs.

These four pillars—a statist development strategy, a dominant-party regime, a revolutionary mystique and a rigid social order, and anti-Americanism—composed the Mexican system. Despite Mexico's aloofness from Latin America, its system influenced the tone of inter-American relations. More than that, Mexico's relentless opposition to U.S. foreign policy defined the psychological, diplomatic, and economic boundaries separating the United States from Latin America.

Carlos Salinas de Gortari was elected president in July 1988, by a bare majority of 50.4 percent, amid credible charges of fraud. In a poll taken one year later, 73 percent of the Mexican people said they doubted the 1988 election had been fair.[20] Despite a weak mandate, the young president moved quickly after his inauguration to dismantle two pillars holding Mexico's walls: the old economic strategy and anti-Americanism. He moved more slowly and equivocally toward redefining the revolutionary mystique and modifying the political system.

With a doctorate from Harvard University's Kennedy School of Government, Salinas was one of a new generation of Latin American leaders, who came to power after years of economic failure. By the time of his election, Mexico had suffered seven consecutive years of economic decline. Real wages had dropped by 40 percent. His predecessor, Miguel de la Madrid, had begun to change Mexico's economic direction, from a closed, import-substitution-industrialization strategy into one that was more export-oriented, but he was a cautious man, who slowed his reforms as opposition built within his party.

In his first hundred days, Salinas moved swiftly and with authority. He sent the army to arrest the corrupt boss of the oil workers' union. Then he moved with equal vigor to arrest businessmen for illegal trading or for not paying their taxes, well-known drug traffickers for controlling local or state governments, and a senior government official for the murder of a controversial journalist.

Salinas's economic priority was to reduce his country's external debt, and he negotiated an agreement with U.S. Treasury Secretary Nicholas Brady that saved Mexico about $4 billion in annual debt service.[21] Salinas raised revenues 13.4 percent by enforcing the tax laws and slashed the fiscal deficit from 11.7 percent of gross domestic product in 1988 to a surplus in 1991. By 1992, 80 percent of the state's corporations had been privatized, and deregulation permitted businesses to respond to the market rather than to bureaucrats. Trade barriers were lowered so sharply that Mexico went from being one of the most protected markets in the world to one of the most open. Manufacturing exports surged.

Salinas not only changed policies, he also tried to change the way Mexicans thought about the role of the state. In his first state of the nation report on November 1, 1989, he criticized the "outmoded view that confuses being progressive with being statist. . . . In Mexico, a larger state has resulted in less capacity to respond to social demands."[22] Salinas then confronted the "untouchables." He revised the rules on foreign investment,[23] and he announced that Mexico's eighteen largest banks, which had been nationalized in 1982, would be privatized.

The one element of the new Mexican approach that would have the greatest influence on Latin America was not even a part of the original strategy: the proposal for a free trade agreement with the United States. For some Americans, it seemed logical to extend the U.S.-Canadian Free Trade Area to include Mexico, but Mexicans were worried that they could not compete. As late as October 1989, Salinas visited Washington and dismissed the idea of a free trade agreement, but in June 1990 he returned and proposed the idea to Bush. Why did he change his mind?

"Two elements," he told me later in an interview. "First, we opened the economy to reduce inflation." Because Mexico no longer protected its market, its challenge was to secure access to the U.S. market. "Secondly, the changes in Europe and East Asia and an apparent reliance on blocs convinced me that we should also try to be part of an economic trading bloc with the United States and Canada." But, he insisted, "we do not want this bloc to be a fortress. We want it to strengthen our ability to be part of Asia, Europe, and especially Latin America."[24] Salinas would have preferred to attract new investments from other regions, but he found the Japanese cautious and the European Community preoccupied by Eastern Europe. On June 12, 1991, in Toronto, the trade representatives from the United States, Canada, and Mexico officially launched the NAFTA negotiations.

Salinas had to defend himself against charges of embracing the United States: "Relations with such a powerful neighbor, with . . . a history burdened by acts of extreme aggression, will never be easy. Nevertheless, there is no reason for our relations always to be bad or tense. The cordiality that exists today is understandable because matters of common interest require concerted actions."[25] The language of "common interests" is hard for some Mexicans to accept; Jorge Castañeda, my coauthor on another book, rejected the phrase in the only chapter of the book that we wrote together. Castañeda accused Salinas of abandoning Mexico's "one distinct trademark": a foreign policy that differs from that of the United States.[26] Cárdenas also criticized Salinas for a "dangerous [and] unprecedented subordination of Mexico's national interests to American preferences."[27]

On the political front, Salinas improved on his predecessors, but his electoral record did not reach democratic standards. In July 1989, for the first time, an opposition party won a governorship, and it was in a border state. At the same time, the PRI stole elections in another state. Salinas negotiated an electoral reform law with the conservative PAN, but Cárdenas's supporters and some PANistas opposed it because the government would retain control of the new federal electoral institute. A new registration list was compiled for the midterm elections of 1991, but it had flaws.

Salinas and the PRI recovered support because the economy improved, and he founded a program he founded to help poor communities. However, people still lacked confidence in the electoral system; only 42 percent in 1991 believed their vote would be respected. That was an improvement over 1988, when only 23 percent answered that way, but it fell short of a democratic system.[28] This was deliberate; Salinas believed that economic reforms should precede political reforms. Contrasting his strategy with Gorbachev's, which moved in the opposite direction, he quipped: "I believe in glasnost, *not* glasses that break," he said.[29]

Of course, Salinas's glass broke. Within three weeks of his leaving office on December 1, 1994, the Mexican peso crashed. Soon after, his brother, Raul, was arrested for so much corruption that even Carlos Salinas blanched. Raul was also charged with complicity in the assassination of the secretary general of the PRI, and many believed he was involved in the assassination of the PRI candidate, Donaldo Colossio. Salinas was blamed for all of these problems and crimes, and he was so vilified that he moved to Ireland. The failure to undertake serious political reforms had left the old Mexican system weakened and illegitimate, and Salinas, the leader who had dismantled the economic walls, was held accountable for the pillars he left untouched.

The Mexican Model and Regional Integration

Nonetheless, Mexico's gift to the hemisphere's economic future was as important as Nicaragua's to its political future. Since its revolution in 1910, Mexico had defined "economic nationalism" in defensive terms: expropriating foreign investments and excluding foreign goods and services. President Salinas redefined economic nationalism in a manner that opened Mexico and Latin America to new economic relationships and to a concerted process of managing integration. "Sovereignty," Salinas told his people, "does not imply self-sufficiency or autarky. . . . Interdependence does not necessarily threaten sovereignty."[30] "Our country is modernizing to make our economy viable within an international context of strong competition. . . . Those nations that do not adapt themselves creatively will not be able to maintain their integrity." Argentine President Carlos Menem agreed: "Argentina and the United States were in opposite camps because of a false [Argentine] concept of what sovereignty is. We isolated ourselves from practically all the world. . . . We are living in another Argentina now."[31]

Previous initiatives by Latin Americans to seek closer relations with the United States had often provoked Mexican opposition. In a region looking for its identity under the shadow of a superpower, the Mexican objection often translated into a veto. Carlos Salinas's proposal for NAFTA transformed the Mexican veto into an affirmation. Fearing marginalization, the rest of Latin America requested a similar deal. On June

27, 1990, President Bush offered his Enterprise for the Americas Initiative (EAI), promising free trade agreements to governments in the hemisphere that implemented market reforms and deepened subregional integration schemes.

Latin America embraced Bush's proposal and Salinas's example. Most implemented reforms. Latin America had always valued regional integration in its rhetoric, but the reality spoke of national priorities. NAFTA stirred a rejuvenation. The Andean Pact accelerated the integration process to establish a free trade zone and a common external tariff in 1992. Brazil, Argentina, Uruguay, and Paraguay signed a common market treaty in March 1991 to establish a single trade area called Mercosur, with a common external tariff by 1995. The Central American Common Market and the Caribbean Community also took steps to reduce their internal trade barriers and establish common external tariffs. The Bush proposal did not prosper, but it reemerged in a few years in another guise. President Bill Clinton hosted the Summit of the Americas, and the thirty-four governments all pledged to establish a Free Trade Area of the Americas (FTAA) by 2005.

This is not to say that there was unanimity in Latin America on the benefits of privatization, freer trade, and foreign investment. In fact, the *Latinobarometer* survey of January–March 1998 found public opinion in the region evenly divided (34 percent to 34 percent) on the question of whether privatization benefits or harms their economies. But traditional economic nationalism definitely declined: 57 percent believe that foreign investment is beneficial and only 25 percent fear that it gives foreign countries too much influence. The vast majority (78 percent) of Latin Americans favor freer trade, although fewer believe that it has improved jobs, wages, or their own family's economic conditions.[32] In almost every country in the Americas, there are leaders who distrust the "neo-liberal model," and if the economies fail, they might be tempted to restore trade and investment barriers, but they will be constrained from returning to the past because of regional trading agreements and a global financial and trading market.

The last decade of the twentieth century witnessed a remarkable proliferation of free trade agreements among the countries of the Americas and between them and other areas. Trade and investment barriers continued their decline, and trade and investment soared. From 1990 to 1998, the hemisphere's exports grew at the annual average rate of 8 percent, more than twice as fast as its domestic product, and the average annual rate of growth of exports within the Americas was 11 percent.[33] What this means is that trade within the region was growing much faster than the countries' economies and their trade with the outside world. The bonds connecting the nations of the Americas were becoming thicker.

Preparations for negotiating the FTAA also began after the Santiago Summit in 1998. The preliminary work involved cataloguing existing trade restraints of each country in each of the eleven categories that would define the parameters of the negotiations. No government, however, wants to make the very hard decisions that would be required to make the FTAA a reality unless and until the United States—the market for about 75 percent of the goods of the hemisphere—demonstrates a commitment to the negotiations, by gaining Congress's approval of fast-track negotiating authority.

Free trading schemes do not represent fixed agreements; rather they are the beginning of a process of harmonizing domestic policies and of negotiating a wide swath of issues that had been previously considered wholly domestic. Any domestic policy that confers an unfair advantage on a country's exports or a disadvantage on imports can be considered a trade issue. This includes sales taxes and safety and environmental laws that increase the cost of investment in one country and thus may encourage relocation. It means that labor rights and workmen's compensation in one country become a legitimate issue in the other. As integration proceeds, the line that separates internal and external issues blurs. The range of the debate widens. The ability of each government to control the flows of capital, goods, and labor declines, much to the frustration of each president.

Social integration is already well advanced, particularly in the southwest of the United States and the north of Mexico, due to the heavy migration and the ease of communications and travel. Like economic integration, social interchange produces both benefits and tensions. The process will not be easy, and new procedures will be needed to keep the dialogue fruitful. The United States should conduct periodic "double-standard tests." Before telling Mexico or another Latin American government how to manage its affairs, it should consider how it would respond to a similar message. The United States had long pressed Latin America to accept foreign investment treaties that many in the region viewed as threats to sovereignty. In the late 1990s, the U.S. government promoted such a model treaty to the twenty-four advanced members of the Organization of Economic Cooperation and Development (OECD) until opposition grew in the United States against the Mutual Agreement on Investment (MAI) for the very reasons that Latin Americans had previously raised.

Freer trade in the hemisphere benefits all nations, but it does not benefit them equally, and it does not benefit all groups within a nation equally. Some American workers, for example, lose jobs to Mexicans, even while American industry becomes more competitive. Unfortunately, the loss of jobs due to cheaper imports is more visible and painful than the gains to trade resulting from increased exports. This basic inequality has obvious political consequences. New programs and institutions are needed to redistribute the gains of trade to those who lose and to help those backward regions in both the United States and Latin America connect with the modern economy.

These ideas are devices to cope with the redefinition of sovereignty and the anticipated tensions of interdependence. A freer trade regime in the hemisphere will lead to more trade disputes, not fewer, because as trade increases, more businesses and workers will become more dependent on the new flow of goods. Workers who lose their jobs by a "surge" in imports will find many reasons—some justifiable—why trade was unfair. To contain and eventually resolve those problems while expanding the boundaries of sovereignty requires a framework that will give confidence to all parties in the system.

A Higher Plateau

The Nicaraguan precedent and the Mexican initiative have permitted inter-American relations to move to a higher plateau. The disparities in power and wealth remain so huge that it would not be accurate to characterize the relationship between the United States and Latin America as equal or even remotely comparable to the relationship between the United States and Europe. And yet something fundamental changed in the last decade of the twentieth century, and it can be seen in the nature of the communication and the agenda. No doubt the end of the Cold War facilitated a change, but there were two more important explanations.

Sandinista Nicaragua invited the international community to monitor and guarantee its electoral process. By that act, the frigid Article 18 of the OAS Charter that prohibited any interference in the internal affairs of a member state began to melt. The left and the right in Latin America, which had used the principle of nonintervention to protect each other from their people's right to vote, found themselves on the defensive. The Nicaraguan precedent was a ringing affirmation that legitimacy was derived not from revolution or counterrevolution, but from the consent of the governed, and everyone in the Americas had a voice on the issue. Suddenly, the inter-American system began to come to grips with the question of what it should do to defend and reinforce democracy. No other regional organization in the developing world had even contemplated such a question, let alone tried to answer it.

The other cause of the change emerged from Mexico. Disregarding its ideology and unhappy history, Mexico dismantled its walls and embraced its northern neighbors. Mexico realized that true "sovereignty" required development, and in the modern world, that meant an open economy, not a closed one. The result is a North American entity that has a larger market than the European Union and greater promise.

These were two compelling but counterintuitive ideas: that the best defense of a country's political and economic system is to open it to freedom and commerce. The political and economic openings were also mutually reinforcing. When the U.S. Congress debated NAFTA, some argued that it would entrench the ruling oligarchy in Mexico. Jimmy Carter, among others, argued the opposite: that rejecting NAFTA would reinforce authoritarianism; accepting it would raise the cost of electoral fraud. It would be very difficult to keep the political system closed if the economic system was opening. Of course, that is exactly what happened.

Mexican President Ernesto Zedillo, who served from 1994 to 2000, negotiated a series of electoral reforms that gradually permitted the Mexican electorate to choose their leaders in a secret ballot without fear of intimidation or manipulation. On July 2, 2000, the people did just that, and Vicente Fox, the leader of the National Action Party (PAN), defeated the PRI candidate for president, the first time an opposition party had won a presidential election in Mexico since the revolution.

As democracy takes root, and each government faces a similar agenda—trade, jobs, crime, drugs, education—the debates in each country may sound similar because people everywhere want better lives. Latin Americans want U.S. foreign investment, but some also fear the influence that accompanies such investment. It's now clear, courtesy of *Latinobarometer* surveys, that Americans share the same fears—only worse! A higher percentage of Americans disapprove of foreign investment (48 percent) than do Latin Americans (25 percent), and more

Americans disapprove than approve of it, whereas the opposite is the case in Latin America. In other words, those in the United States who are concerned about Latin American nationalization of U.S. investment ought to recognize that there is stronger sentiment for such actions in the United States today than in Latin America.[34] It was not a long time ago that Latin Americans were much more suspicious about free trade with the United States. Now Americans are more fearful than their Latin American counterparts. Only half of all Americans support the FTAA, whereas 70 percent of Latin Americans favor it. Moreover, the opposition to freer trade is twice as strong in the United States as it is in Latin America. Those Americans who would lecture Latin America on free trade should consider another form of communication.

Both the United States and Latin America should merge their complementary qualities to become more competitive internationally. A century-old dream—a democratic community of the Americas—could combine the technology, skills, and capital of the north with the market, resources, and labor of the south to create a formidable new economic and democratic giant. The pragmatic pursuit of the regionalist option could produce, however unintentionally, not only a better hemisphere, but also a more open international trading system by encouraging Europe and Japan to open their markets or risk the closure of the western hemisphere market.

The challenge that awaits the nations of the Americas is part of a broader phenomenon of coping with the consequences of globalization. The forces of geography and the efficiencies of an international market are drawing countries closer together in new regional agreements, but traditional political insecurities continue to push them apart. That is why the Nicaraguan and Mexican precedents are so important: They demonstrate a recognition that the future of the Americas will depend on a willingness to remain engaged globally. It is thus a very positive sign that the contours of a future American system were defined by the two least likely regimes. The basis for constructing a genuine community in the Americas now exists.

Notes

1. "State of the Nation Address by Carlos Salinas," November 1, 1991, reprinted in *Foreign Broadcast Information Service (FBIS)*, Latin America, November 13, 1991, p. 14.

2. Carlos Fonseca Amador, *Nicaragua: Hora Cero,* first published in *Tricontintenal* 14 (1969); excerpts reprinted in Tomás Borge et al., *Sandinistas Speak* (New York: Pathfinders Press, 1982), p. 29.

3. Neil A. Lewis, "Reagan Sees Fatal Flaws in Central American Pact," *The New York Times,* September 13, 1987, p. A24. In a later address to the American people, Reagan said that if aid were cut to the contras, "the Sandinista Communists [would] continue the consolidation of their dictatorial regime and the subversion of Central America." Excerpts printed in *The New York Times,* February 3, 1988, p. A10.

4. Robert A. Pastor, *Condemned to Repetition: The United States and Nicaragua* (Boulder, Colo.: Westview Press, 1987).

5. John M. Goshko and Al Kamen, "U.S. Accused of Overstating Managua Election Offenses," *Washington Post,* January 25, 1990, pp. A29, 34.

6. Two years later a *Newsweek* article, "CIA on the Stump," October 21, 1991, alleged that the CIA secretly gave $600,000 to the contras to participate in the elections, and thus violated the assurances. Senator David Boren, chairman of the Senate Intelligence Committee, investigated the operation and reported in a letter to Carter on November 15, 1991, that the program was aimed at relocating individual contra leaders, not at influencing the elections. Carter and Boren concluded that the administration's assurances had not been violated, and Carter conveyed that to Ortega in a letter on November 20, 1991.

7. I was personally involved in these talks and the conveying of proposals between Ortega and the Bush administration. These are my assessments of the reasons why the proposals did not prosper.

8. For the complete reference, see the UN Secretary General's Report to the General Assembly, *Enhancing the Effectiveness of the Principle of Periodic and Genuine Elections,* November 19, 1991, p. 10.

9. In Panama, a group from the Catholic Church, led by Father Fernando Guardia, organized the quick count with the help of Larry Garber and Glenn Cowan, two election experts who worked with the National Democratic Institute for International Affairs. Their count permitted Carter to know by the early morning after the election that Noriega's candidates had lost by a ratio of 3 to 1.

10. For a full description of these issues, see Council of Freely-Elected Heads of Government, *Observing Nicaragua's Elections, 1989–1990* (Atlanta: The Carter Center of Emory University, 1990).

11. Quoted in *Stanford Magazine* (June 1990).

12. Quoted in Rochelle L. Stanfield, "Centralized Headache," *National Journal,* January 27, 1990, p. 189. See also Reed Irvine and Joe Goulden, "Carter's Rush to Appease," *Washington Times,* February 13, 1990, p. F4.

13. Organización de los Estados Americanos, *Quinto Informe Sobre La Observación del Proceso Electoral, Febrero 16 & Marzo 20* (Washington, D.C.: OAS, 1990), p. 12; UN Secretary General, *Fifth Report by the U.N. Observer Mission to Verify the Electoral Process in Nicaragua* (New York: UN General Assembly, 1990), A/44/927, p. 7.

14. Based on my verbatim notes of the meeting.

15. The Sandinistas changed some important laws on property. Antonio Lacayo approved some of them, but Alfredo Cesar, who became president of the Assembly, and UNO were not aware of these and later tried to revise them.

16. Ana Maria Ruíz, "Transición a la democracia: Sin Pactos ni Componendas," *La Prensa* (Managua), April 5, 1990, p. 1.

17. *Central American Report,* March 2, 1990, p. 64, citing an Inter-American Development Bank Report that also showed that Guatemala had sunk to the level of 1971, Honduras to 1973, Costa Rica to 1974, and Panama to 1982.

18. UN Secretary General, *Second Report of the United Nations Observer Group for the Verification of Elections in Haiti,* February 22, 1991, p. 15.

19. Quoted in "Plan on Reacting to Coups," EFE news service, reprinted in *FBIS,* Latin America, June 6, 1991, pp. 1–2.

20. *Los Angeles Times* Poll 192, Mexico. National poll conducted August 5–13, 1989, mimeo, p. 23.

21. U.S. Embassy, Mexico, *Economic Trends Report, February* 1992, pp. 3, 13–18.

22. Carlos Salinas de Gortari, *First State of the Nation Report,* November 1, 1989, printed by Embassy of Mexico, pp. 8, 14.

23. Mark A. Uhlig, "Mining Laws Are Eased by Mexico," *The New York Times,* September 28, 1990, p. D3.

24. Interview with President Carlos Salinas, July 24, 1990, Mexico City.

25. Carlos Salinas de Gortari, *First State of the Nation Report,* November 1, 1989, pp. 16–17.

26. Jorge Castañeda, "Salinas' International Relations Gamble," *Journal of International Affairs* 43 (Winter 1990): 407. See also Robert A. Pastor and Jorge G. Castaneda, *Limits to Friendship: The United States and Mexico* (New York: Alfred A. Knopf, 1988).

27. Cuauhtémoc Cárdenas, "Misunderstanding Mexico," *Foreign Policy* 78 (Spring 1990): 113.

28. Miguel Basañez, "Encuesta Electoral, 1991," *Este Pais* (August 1991): 6.

29. Interview with President Carlos Salinas, November 30, 1990, Mexico City.

30. Carlos Salinas de Gortari, "State of the Nation Address," November 1, 1990, p. 14.

31. Quoted in "Yanqui, Come Here," *Newsweek,* July 15, 1991, p. 28.

32. "Latinobarometer Survey of January–March 1998," *Wall Street Journal,* April 16, 1998.

33. Inter-American Development Bank, *Integration and Trade in The Americas, Periodic Note* (Washington, D.C., October 1999), Annex A, E.

34. "Latinobarometer Survey of January–March 1998."

14

THE CENTURY OF THE AMERICAS: A COMMUNITY OF DEMOCRACIES

For the first time in history, the Americas are a community of democratic societies. . . . We reaffirm our commitment to preserve and strengthen our democratic systems. . . . We resolve to conclude the negotiation of the Free Trade Area of the Americas no later than 2005.

—THE SUMMIT OF THE AMERICAS DECLARATION OF PRINCIPLES, 1994

A hopeful portent for the future of inter-American relations lies in the irony that Sandinista Nicaragua and PRIista Mexico were the two countries that dismantled the traditional nationalistic walls around Latin America—the walls that they had built and defended with such zeal. The Sandinistas invited the international community inside their political gates to help make their democracy credible to the world. The monitoring of the Nicaraguan election became a model that was repeated throughout the Americas, permitting the international community to reinforce democracy at the most delicate moment of transition. Similarly, Mexico's proposal for a free trade agreement with the United States also opened the doors for a hemispheric-wide free trade area.

Both initiatives were as liberating for the two countries and the hemisphere as the fall of the Berlin Wall was for Europe and the world. That all three walls—in Berlin, Managua, and Mexico—should come down at roughly the same time is one of those fortuitous occurrences that imbues history with drama. "Walls," the playwright Arthur Miller once wrote, "are an expensive investment in denial." Dismantling the walls was an affirmation of new vistas, an opportunity to reconfigure the international landscape.

Like import-substitution as an economic strategy, the traditional conception of political sovereignty served its original purpose well; it built the state and protected it from foreign interference, particularly from the United States. However, by the 1980s both the economic and the political strategies were exhausted and unproductive. The old strategies failed to reduce debt, promote development, secure peace, or assure democracy.

The experience of the 1980s contained a lesson for the United States as well. Whenever it forced an issue that impugned Latin America's sovereignty, Washington compelled Latin Americans to strengthen their defenses. "The determination to bind the North American giant," wrote one scholar, was "the most recurrent and central principle guiding the majority of the Latin American states in their formation of hemispheric policy."[1] The culmination of this sterile interaction occurred during the administration of Ronald Reagan. The most forceful, unilateral attempt to intrude in Latin America's affairs in decades met the stiffest resistance.

But the 1980s also witnessed three profound changes in Latin America that made possible the Managua and Mexico precedents. The debt crisis compelled a new generation of elected leaders to rethink and revise the old economic strategy and adopt a more outward and market-oriented, fiscally responsible, leaner state-based economic policy. By the time that Mexico proposed a free trade agreement with the United States, much of Latin America wanted to join. They had reduced their trade barriers to about 15 percent on average, and they could contemplate negotiations that could bring their barriers closer to the U.S. level of 4 percent.

Second, faced with an uncommunicative administration in Washington, Latin Americans turned to each other to address hemispheric concerns. As a result of the Contadora negotiations on Central America, summits on the debt crisis, the Rio Group, and the Esquipulas Accord, Latin Americans gained new confidence in their ability to address the inter-American agenda, but they also learned that they could not succeed without U.S. cooperation. The administration of George Bush also recognized—as its predecessor had not—that the United States needed Latin American cooperation to achieve its goals in the region, whether on Central America, drugs, or trade. To obtain this, Washington would need to modify its objectives and strategy.

Third, the pendulum that had begun the third swing toward democracy in Latin America in the mid-1970s continued to the point that every country but Cuba had elections judged free and fair by opposition leaders and international observers. The salient point, however, was not that democracy was wide, but that it was thin. Most leaders understood that the only way to keep the pendulum from swinging backwards toward dictatorship was by mutual support.

These three currents all came together in Miami in December 1994 when President Bill Clinton hosted the first Summit of the Americas. All the leaders were freely elected, and they pledged to support each other's democracy and to negotiate a Free Trade Area of the Americas (FTAA). They also agreed to make "concrete progress toward the attainment of this objective . . . by the end of the century." They succeed in defining a worthy goal, but they failed to make any progress by the end of the century on trade, and their record on democracy was mixed. Setbacks in Haiti, Peru, Ecuador, and Paraguay met with a very uneven, and sometimes equivocal, collective response.

With the onset of the twenty-first century, the promises of the Summit were unfilled, but the successful completion of Mexico's journey to democracy on July 2, 2000, offered hope that the twenty-first could be the century of all of the Americas, just as Henry Luce correctly predicted in 1941 that the twentieth would be America's century. Whether that occurs depends on leadership in the United States, Brazil, and throughout the Americas.

Before offering some ideas, let us first return to the original metaphor, the whirlpool, and summarize the clues we have gathered on how to escape from it. Then, I will recommend ways to build a hemispheric democratic community.

Whirlpool: Entrance and Exit

On February 25, 1990, 2,578 accredited foreign observers from 278 organizations and an additional 1,500 foreign correspondents were in Nicaragua to observe the election. All of the major U.S. newspapers and television networks had offices in Managua. One year later, Nicaraguan President Violeta de Chamorro invited everyone back to celebrate the anniversary of the election, and almost no one came. Even if they had come, few Americans would have known about it because the major newspapers and networks had closed their offices.[2] Nicaragua's problems remained, but America's attention had moved.

Resting on the lip of the Latin American whirlpool, a detached analyst would no doubt wonder why the United States cannot modulate and sustain its attention and energies—why, for example, it could not give less attention and resources to Nicaragua in the 1980s and more in the 1990s. There is, of course, an answer to that query. As a superpower, the U.S. government yields to the urgent demands of global crises, and no country or region can claim its undivided attention except at those moments. When the hour passes, Washington's attention shifts. For Latin America, which is permanently preoccupied with the United States, the lack of attention is disconcerting.

Attention, however, is not the issue; it is simply a barometer for measuring the difficulty of the relationship. The issue is whether the United States and Latin America can fashion a more evenhanded relationship that will benefit all the people of the Americas. The answer is not to give less attention to Nicaragua and more to Brazil, although that would make more sense, but for the United States and the nations of Latin America to deal with recurring problems in the region in a more civil and constructive way than has been done in the past.

First, I will discuss the causes. The contours of the whirlpool are shaped by two different currents that meet in the Caribbean Basin. Each current represents a different conception of security, with the United States trying to exclude foreign rivals, and Latin America trying to contain U.S. power. The current from the north has been confident and dominant; from the south, defensive and divided. These two currents collide to create the whirlpool and pose four recurring problems: dictators, revolutions, underdevelopment, and weak or flawed democracies. When the threat passes, Washington stops fighting the problems and floats to the edge, only to return to the center a generation later.

For different reasons, both the United States and Latin America have spun neurotic psychological webs around each other that have made difficult problems harder to understand, let alone resolve. I have analyzed the psychology of the relationship by examining the stalemate of Puerto Rico and the contradictions of Omar Torrijos. Puerto Rico and the United States are caught in an embrace that has benefited the island economically while crippling it politically. Omar Torrijos taught some Americans the benefits of mutual respect, but he himself failed to learn the lesson that national dignity can be attained only by democracy, that self-determination means both freedom by Panama from U.S. domination and freedom by Panamanians to choose their leaders. As a result, he left a two-sided, Jekyll and Hyde legacy: visionary Panama Canal Treaties and a criminal Noriega regime.

Today, we are better positioned than ever before to escape the whirlpool because the threat of the Cold War has passed and the promises of democracy and free trade have arrived. Two competitions were subsumed under the rubric of the Cold War, one between superpowers and another between ideologies. Both contests are over, but the fear of aspiring rivals or unpleasant rogues mucking around in the neighborhood existed before the Soviet Union, and these fears could come back in another guise. It is not too far afield to imagine that a regime that tore the bonds of democratic accountability and felt threatened by the United States might seek to collaborate with "a state of concern" (formerly called a "rogue state"). Noriega, it will be recalled, was accused of consorting with Libya and such states before the U.S. invasion. The United States and Latin America should use this propitious moment when security threats are remote to plot a permanent escape from the whirlpool. That will mean negotiating the rules that can secure democracy, raising the stakes to violating the peace, and establishing mechanisms for more cooperative approaches to development and environmental problems.

The prospects for democracy are enhanced by the collapse of Marxism and the demonstrated failure of an economic strategy that relied excessively on the state. In Latin America, two of the greatest threats to democracy had been *utopianism*—the idea that Latin America's dragons of despotism, inequality, and instability could be slain by a single slash of a revolutionary's sword—and *centralism*—the idea that justice could be attained only by an all-powerful, unified state.

Democracy is not a panacea; it does not cure a nation's ills overnight. It is a process of peaceful political change, and for democracy to work, power must be divided, checked, and balanced. Unlike Marxism or any utopianism, democracy is based on the premise that truth is partial, that everyone's ideas have some validity, that no one's views should be suppressed. Because these conceptions of democracy were so alien to Latin America for so long, few analysts realized that utopianism and centralism were the real threats. Many believed that guerrillas, paramilitary groups, or the debt crisis were the problems. In fact, the debt crisis helped democracy get started in some countries, first by delegitimizing incumbent military regimes, then by impugning the old bloated state. When Moscow, the center of world communism, renounced its monopoly on truth and accepted multiparty elections, it robbed Marxists all over the world of their certainty and laid bare their false promise of instant salvation. More important, Moscow paid democracy the ultimate compliment by acknowledging that the *only* basis of legitimacy in the modern world is the consent of the governed, not the blood of revolutionaries.

The entombment of communism meant that its more powerful Latin American opposite, anticommunism, should be buried too. The consequences of the second funeral are more momentous because the forces resisting social reforms in the name of anticommunism have been stronger in the region than the revolutionaries.

An authentically balanced and mature relationship between the United States and Latin America requires a significant narrowing of the gap that separates the region's economies. This will not happen soon, but the changes in economic policy in the last few years and the movement toward freer trade are steps in the right direction. The shift from aid to trade as the main item on the international economic agenda is another positive step toward partnership. Instead of imposing conditions on Latin America in exchange for aid, the United States is negotiating trading rules with Latin America on the basis of reciprocity. In the long term, increased trade between unequal partners is likely to narrow inequalities. In a study of dozens of nations over a hundred-year period, economist William Baumol found that poorer nations that integrate with richer ones have grown faster because of the innovations they have acquired from the leaders. Thus, productivity patterns have been converging, and are likely to accelerate as technology is transferred more rapidly in a global economy.[3] In the short and medium terms, however, freer trade can exacerbate inequalities unless special measures are taken to redistribute the gains of trade.

Prospects for finding a way out of the psychological cul-de-sac that has trapped the United States and Latin America are better today than ever before for yet another reason: the growing influence and convergence of public opinion. One of democracy's dividends is the expansion of public opinion surveys throughout Latin America and the Caribbean. Democratic leaders who can follow the pulse of the people through polls tend to be more pragmatic than those who lead by reference to ideology. Politicians know that people care less about defying Washington than about raising living standards. Confirmation of this point came in a startling poll in 1991: 59 percent of Mexicans favored forming a single country with the United States if that would improve the quality of their lives.[4]

Perhaps the most important effect of public opinion surveys and of studies of perceptions is to erode myths and stereotypes of U.S.–Latin American relations. In 1989 an office in the Mexican Foreign Ministry began systematic reviews of U.S. (and world) opinion of Mexico by charting the tone of newspaper and media articles on a regular basis.[5] The office found that America's views of Mexico were not fixed and hostile; they were often positive, and they varied by events. This simple conclusion is contrary to the view that many Mexicans had of unchanging American animosity, which, in turn, had elicited an anti-American reaction.

Beginning in 1995, major newspapers in Latin America and the United States sponsored *Latinobarometer* surveys to assess public opinion throughout the Americas. They found that the United States and Latin America shared the belief that democracy was better than authoritarianism, although Americans favored democracy by 87 to 6 percent and Latin Americans by 69 to 25 percent. The differences within Latin America were more revealing: Consolidated democracies like Costa Rica, Chile, and Argentina had ratios similar to those of the United States, whereas people in the weaker democracies—Peru, Ecuador, and Paraguay—or those like Brazil, with severe income inequalities, were more equivocal about democracy's benefits. A poll taken one year later found a shared belief in a market economy, although the differences in support were also telling: 85 percent of Americans and 65 percent of Latin Americans favored it. The entire region agreed that the inter-American agenda should concentrate on the issues of drug trafficking, trade and investment, and democracy and human rights, and 73 percent of Latin Americans said they would "defend democracy if it were threatened." The surveys demonstrate that the differences on issues and values between the United States and Latin America were not as wide as many believed.[6]

Finally, the two factors that are likely to have the most impact on reducing the cultural and psychological distance separating the United States and Latin America are the increasing immigration to the United States from the region and the declining costs of transportation and communications. Both are undermining cultural stereotypes and pormoting a subtle but real convergence of value systems that are remaking hemispheric society. Electronics and mass media, according to Cuban-born writer Carlos Alberto Montaner, "give supersonic speed to what we call acculturation. Up until now, being able to discover the influence of one nation on another was a magical feat. Now it is a matter of opening your eyes."[7] And what we are seeing is a merging and modernizing of cultures within the United States and between the continents. By the end of the twentieth century, salsa had replaced ketchup as the most frequently used condiment in the United States, and the most common name of newborn babies in California was "Jose."[8]

Immigration to the United States is the glue that is beginning to bind the nations of the hemisphere. Until 1960, more than 80 percent of all immigrants to the United States came from Europe. Since 1970, roughly half of all immigrants have come from Latin America, most of them from Mexico and the Caribbean Basin. As the century turned, the Hispanic population in the United States was about 32 million people or 11.7 percent of the total population. Two-thirds were of Mexican origin, and if illegal or temporary migrants are included, that figure approaches 75 percent.[9] The ties connecting the new migrants with their homes, although not necessarily with Mexico, remain strong. Surveys suggest that anywhere from 38 to 50 percent of the 100 million people of Mexico have close relatives living in the United States.[10] This movement of people may explain Mexico's increasing support for freer trade and economic integration.

Some Americans have begun to worry about the increasing "Mexicanization" of the Southwest, a mirror image of Mexico's long-standing fear of "Americanization." However, these fears tell just one part of the story. The other part describes the way that the United States has grown in absorbing a new and vigorous culture, and the way the new immigration has made it easier for Latin America to relate to the United States. With Spanish becoming the second language of the United States, Latin Americans can now travel to the four most populous states—California, Texas, Florida, and New York—and shop, go to the movies, get their cars fixed, and even go to school without ever speaking English. In the movie *El Norte,* a Guatemalan flees to a Mexican barrio in east Los Angeles. After several weeks of puzzlement, the man turns to a friend and asks: "Where are the gringos?"

Instead of complaining about the imperial visage of North America, Latin Americans can now see their own faces in the United States. At the same time, instead of griping about the Latin American *mañana* mentality, North Americans now negotiate with Latins who have doctorates from the best U.S. universities. The prospect of merging is not so unsettling anymore.

Three scholars from the United States, Mexico, and Canada analyzed public attitudes in the three countries and found that they are not only similar, they are converging in a way that makes further integration feasible. These analysts surveyed attitudes toward government and other institutions in the three countries in 1981 and in 1990.[11] In all three, the basic values are converging in support of political liberalization, a market-based (but *not* laissez-faire) economic policy, and a higher priority for autonomy and self-expression in all spheres of life. Even more important was the convergence in values that parents are trying to impart to their children. When asked which of seventeen qualities people would like to instill in their children, respondents from all three countries chose the same qualities and even ranked them similarly.

The authors of the survey believe that the main cause of the convergence in value systems is that young people in all three countries are much better educated and more affected by global communications. Although the survey does not include the rest of Latin America, the reaction in those countries to the proposal for a free trade agreement suggests that the convergence in values probably extends beyond North America. Indeed, the authors argue that the changes in the three countries are due more to global effects on attitudes in each nation: "A narrow nationalism that had been dominant since the nineteenth century is gradually giving way to a more cosmopolitan sense of identity."[12]

There is also an important convergence in trade patterns. From World War II until 1980, the United States and Latin America diversified their economic relations; trade with the United States as a percentage of Latin America's total trade dropped from 50 to 30 percent. But since 1980, that figure has increased to 40 percent, and the fastest-growing market for both the United States and Latin America has become each other.[13] In the 1990s, virtually all of the subregional trade agreements in the hemisphere deepened, and exports among the countries of the hemisphere grew at an annual rate of 11 percent, more than twice the rate of growth of their exports to the rest of the world.[14] An economic and geographic logic is pressing the Americas toward increased integration, and that growing interest might overcome security as the principal motive for Washington's interest in the region and Latin America's positive response.

All these factors—the end of the Cold War, the fading of Marxism, the opening and joining of the region's economies, the trend toward democracy, the power of public opinion, the impact of immigration, the convergence of value systems and trading patterns, and the new pragmatism—

suggest that the hemisphere is on the verge of a transformation. Even before these changes took root, some, like the late Gabriel Lewis, Panama's intrepid ambassador to Washington during the Canal Treaty debate, believed that Latin America could influence the United States if it used the tactics and strategies that work in Washington. That lesson seems obvious to Americans, but it was alien to most Latin Americans, who had long viewed the U.S. policy process as impenetrable. It took Mexicans more than a decade to learn that lesson and mobilize their friends to persuade the U.S. Congress of the benefits of NAFTA. A decade later, the Colombian government learned the same lesson, and worked with the Clinton administration to persuade Congress to approve $1.3 billion in aid. Torrijos's lesson for the United States—that it can be more effective in Latin America if it shows respect rather than bravado—has also been learned by some, although hardly all, in Washington.

A Hemispheric Community: Beyond the Summit

An effective hemispheric strategy for the twenty-first century must begin with a clearer understanding of the region's new economic and political geography. The population of the Americas is about 800 million people, with roughly half in the three countries of North America, and the other half in South and Central America and the Caribbean (see Table 14.1). In South America, Brazil has nearly half the population and gross product. Its President Fernando Henrique Cardoso tamed hyperinflation, redesigned the Brazilian state, played an important role in settling the dispute between Ecuador and Peru, and kept Paraguay in the family of democratic nations. On September 1, 2000, Brazil hosted the first summit of presidents of South America to coordinate strategies of free trade, democracy, and development.

Argentina viewed itself as the natural rival of the United States from the turn of the century until the last decade. During that time, Brazil deemed itself a close partner, but those times passed, and now Brazil views itself as the center of the South, with good reason. Of the four Mercosur countries, Brazil has about three-quarters of the population and nearly two-thirds of the gross product. If an inter-American initiative is to prosper, the United States will have to reach an understanding first with Brazil. This relationship was neglected in the last two decades of the twentieth century; it needs to be nurtured in the first decade of the twenty-first.

TABLE 14.1 The Americas—Basic Indicators

Group or Country	*Population (millions) 1998*	*GDP*		*Exports*		*Imports*	
		1980	*1998*	*1983*	*1998*	*1983*	*1998*
North America	396	3,198.5	9,202.7 (85% of all)	371	1,287.20	401.3	1,478.8
United States	270.0 (68.2)	2,709.0 (84.7)	8,210.6 (89.2)	256.7 (69.2)	914.9 (71.1)	309.5 (77.1)	1,097.0 (74.2)
Canada	30.0 (7.6)	266.0 (8.3)	598.9 (6.5)	85.0 (22.9)	243.6 (18.9)	76.6 (19.1)	241.0 (16.3)
Mexico	96.0 (24.2)	223.5 (7.0)	393.2 (4.3)	29.3 (7.9)	128.7 (10.0)	15.2 (3.8)	140.7 (9.5)
Mercosur	202	356.9	1,238.0 (11% of all)	39.9	111	34	148.9
Brazil	166.0 (73.8)	234.9 (65.8)	778.3 (62.9)	23.5 (59.0)	57.8 (52.0)	20.5 (60.4)	78.6 (52.8)
Argentina	36	77.0	344.4	9.2	28.2	6.5	37.5
Paraguay	5	4.6	8.6	0.4	1	0.7	3
Uruguay	3	10.1	20.2	1.3	4.3	1.2	4.7
Andean Community	109	138.0	289.3 (2.7% of all)	26	46.5	21.4	62
Venezuela	23.0 (21.2)	69.4 (50.3)	105.8 (36.6)	15.0 (57.7)	18.5 (39.7)	9.0 (42.2)	20.8 (33.6)
Colombia	41	33.4	91.1	3.8	14.9	6.2	20
Peru	25	20.6	64.1	3.7	7	3.4	12.2
Ecuador	12	11.7	19.8	2.6	4.8	2	6.6
Bolivia	8	2.8	8.6	0.8	1.3	0.8	2.4
CARICOM[1]	14.1	4.1	9.4	1.4	2.9	2.3	4.8
Haiti	8	1.5	2.8	0.2	0.1	0.4	0.6
Jamaica	3	2.6	6.6	1.2	2.8	1.9	4.2

(continues)

TABLE 14.1 The Americas—Basic Indicators *(continued)*

Group or Country	*Population (millions)*	*GDP*		*Exports*		*Imports*	
	1998	*1980*	*1998*	*1983*	*1998*	*1983*	*1998*
CACM	32	21.0	48.4	4.4	12.8	5.6	19.1
Guatemala	11.0 (34.3)	7.9 (34.3)	19.3 (39.9)	1.2 (27.2)	3.1 (24.1)	1.4 (24.4)	5.2 (27.5)
El Salvador	6	3.6	12.1	0.9	1.5	1.1	3.5
Costa Rica	4	4.8	10.2	1.1	5.6	1.2	5.8
Honduras	6	2.6	4.7	0.8	1.9	1	2.8
Nicaragua	5	2.1	2.0	0.5	0.7	0.9	1.8
The Americas[2]	790	3,726.1	10,803.9	444.4	1,464.3	467.60	1,721.1

[1]CARICOM export and import data was only available for Haiti and Jamaica.

[2]Chile, Dominican Republic, and Panama are included in the numbers for The Americas, but Cuba as well as some members of CARICOM are not because World Bank statistics did not include them.

SOURCE: of GDP, Exports, and Imports: *World Bank, World Development Report 1999/2000: Entering the 21st Century*, pp.252-3 and 268-9.

Source of Population Figures: *World Bank, World Development Indicators 2000*, Table 1.1, p.13.

Still, one must place Brazil's power in its proper context. The gross product of all of the Americas in 1998 was roughly $10.8 trillion, of which the United States accounted for $8.2 trillion or 76 percent. Canada and Mexico add another 9 percent to the total, giving NAFTA 85 percent of the market of the Americas. Brazil is the second largest economy in the Americas, but it constitutes only 7 percent of the hemispheric market, and its exports are less than 4 percent of the hemisphere's total exports. In other words, NAFTA plus Brazil constitute about 92 percent of the entire market of the Americas, but Brazil's value-added is only 7 percent.

Perhaps the most relevant point is to compare the international trajectory of Brazil with that of Mexico. In 1989, the exports of Brazil and Mexico were roughly the same—about $35 billion each—but together they accounted for 55 percent of Latin America's exports. By 1998, partly due to NAFTA, but mostly owing to a more open economy, Mexico's exports were $128.7 billion, more than twice Brazil's ($57.8 billion), and after the peso crisis of 1994, these exports fueled an annual growth rate of over 5 percent in Mexico.[15] Mexico's decision to lock into the U.S. market has internationalized its economy.

The U.S. perspective is, as one would expect, a global one. Although its first and second most important trading partners are Canada and Mexico, not only is the U.S. economy the largest in the world, it is also the largest importer and exporter of goods and services. During the past two decades, however, the amount of trade among the three countries of North America as a percentage of their total trade has climbed from less than one-third to more than one-half. Industry within North America has reorganized and become continental, and the fastest-growing market for the United States is in the hemisphere.

In the new global era, there are three pan-regional economies: North America, the European Union (EU), and a less coherent East Asia. The three areas together constitute more than three-quarters of the world's product and 80 percent of the world's trade (see Figure 14.1). As the EU enlarges to incorporate Eastern Europe, the obvious market for the United States is in South America. In brief, there is a natural and common interest beckoning all the nations of the Americas toward a new and deeper relationship.

The Summits of the Americas offer the region's leaders a perfect opportunity to try to reach a meeting of the minds on a few key issues in the Americas but also to develop a strategy to relate the region to the

FIGURE 14.1 The World's Three Main Regions—Product and Trade

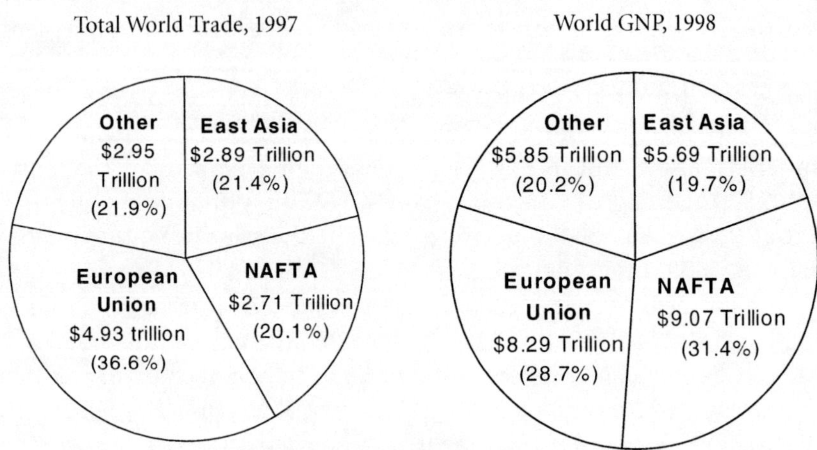

SOURCE: World Bank, *World Development Indicators 2000*. Washington, D.C.

NOTES: Total trade is total of exports and imports of goods and services. *North America:* Canada, Mexico, United States. *European Union*: Austria, Belgium, Denmark, Finland, France, Germany, Greece, Ireland, Italy, Luxembourg, Netherlands, Portugal, Spain, Sweden, United Kingdom. *East Asia*: ASEAN, China, Taiwan, Japan, republic of Korea.

world. It would not serve any nation in the hemisphere—least of all its two strongest economies—to try to shield the region from the world. On the contrary, the unquestioned economic lesson of the last decades is that trade is the engine of economic growth, and although the hemisphere is a fast-growing market, the European and Asian markets are too large to ignore. However, it is worth recalling that the critical step toward completing the Uruguayan Round was the approval of NAFTA. Europe and Japan were only ready to make the hard decisions when they understood that the United States had a "regionalist" option. The first issue, then, on the table of the next Summit of the Americas should be the further development of a hemispheric option, but one aimed at two complementary goals: to deepen relations in the hemisphere and to provide the region with an advantage at the next round of global trade negotiations. This will require a degree of coordination of trade policies that even the three governments of North America have not yet developed, but the time has come to take this step.

As long as the United States and Canada are the only two hemispheric governments at the Group of Seven meetings, the two governments should make sure that they arrive fully briefed about the views of the other hemispheric governments and ready to convey their concerns. Similarly, as the only government in the Americas with a permanent seat on the UN Security Council, the United States should consult more intensively with hemispheric governments. One issue is whether the countries of the Americas would like to organize their peacekeeping forces as a unit.

The principal agenda for the Summit Conferences should be the hemispheric issues that most concern the governments. Several Latin American presidents and Caribbean prime ministers complained that the meetings at the two Summits of the Americas were pre-orchestrated, with too little time to exchange ideas.[16] Instead, the bureaucracies of the thirty-four governments placed before the leaders plans of action that covered the gamut of human experience. The first plan had twenty-three "initiatives," including building mutual confidence, promoting cultural values, strengthening the role of women, preventing pollution, and liberalizing capital markets. The Santiago Summit's Plan was lengthier, with even more issues of a domestic, rather than a hemispheric, nature. If one measured progress by the number of meetings that these plans spawned, then the Summits were successful, but if the criterion was solving serious inter-American problems, then the governments were, at best, running in place.

There is value in having Cabinet and sub-Cabinet officials create networks to address such a wide agenda, but that is a poor use of time for heads of government, and it's not even a good use of Cabinet time if the issues are too diffuse or cannot be addressed effectively by them. It would be better for the leaders to focus on a tighter agenda and to use the time to seek a meeting of minds on a few fundamental questions from the three sets of issues: peace and collective security; the preservation, deepening, and extension of democracy and human rights; and development and the quality of life.

Collective Security

In the Americas, since the Second World War, few conflicts have been fought between states, and they have ended quickly, often because of OAS action. The most prolonged and costly wars in the hemisphere—and globally—since 1945 have been within states, not between them. The Esquipulas Accord was revolutionary in its invitation to the OAS and the

United Nations to help mediate the region's civil wars and disarm and repatriate the guerrillas. The two organizations were successful in Nicaragua, El Salvador, and Guatemala. In Colombia, a UN representative was invited to work with the government, the guerrilla groups, numerous foreign governments, and international and nongovernmental organizations. This is a good model, but it needs constant support by the United States and other governments in the area.

A major handicap of the OAS has been the reluctance of its members to contemplate the use of military force to respond to collective security problems of any kind. In the end, this aversion relegated the OAS to a marginal role in the restoration of constitutional government in Haiti, and it limits the organization's capacity to deal with a wide range of problems, not the least of which is drug trafficking. The reason for the reluctance is well-known: The OAS was established, in part, to contain U.S. interventionism. It's not clear how successful it has been in that regard, nor is it clear that this old concern is still pertinent in the twenty-first century. Perhaps the UN Security Council should remain the principal organization charged with peacekeeping and enforcement, but that means that the United States is the only government in the Americas that will always sit at that table making the decision.

The issue is a fundamental one, and therefore should not be avoided: How should security problems be addressed in the Americas? The United States, as we have seen, will sometimes seek multilateral approval, as Carter did on Nicaragua and Clinton did on Haiti, and sometimes it will just act alone as Bush did on Panama. Brazil and Argentina each threatened force to preserve Paraguay's democracy. Their behavior raises a question: Is it better for a single power to defend democracy on its own, or would a collective decision, based on clearly defined rules, be more desirable and effective? This moment of relative peace and harmony in the hemisphere offers a chance to define those rules, adapt the policies of the stronger states, and infuse the community of the Americas with collective authority to secure peace and democracy.

This new rule-based approach could be applied to four security initiatives. The first area is the new transnational criminal agenda. This agenda is the illicit side of the positive movement toward economic integration. For every legitimate transaction that is facilitated by a reduction in barriers between states, there is a corresponding opening for an illegitimate exchange. Freer trade means that goods can cross borders more easily, but so too can illegal drugs and arms. A relaxation in capital controls permits more investment across borders but also money laundering and tax havens. More commerce means more tourism and immigration, but also more illegal migration. It is not easy to separate the positive from the dark side of integration, and certainly, one country alone cannot do it. This is the twenty-first century's principal transnational challenge: how to police collectively and effectively the illegitimate transactions across borders.

The most controversial issue from this agenda of "silent integration" has been drug trafficking. Given the vitriol that has accompanied inter-American discussions of the drug trafficking issue, the survey done by *The Wall Street Journal/Latinobarometer* in 1998 found a rather surprising consensus on the issue throughout the Americas. Ninety-one percent of Americans and 97 percent of Latin Americans agreed that illegal drug trafficking is a "very serious" problem and that it has grown worse in the last decade. Second, about 54 percent of Americans and Latin Americans blame drug producers for the problem, and only 25 percent blame consumers. And finally, 65 percent of Latin Americans favor the U.S. imposing sanctions on governments that do not cooperate. The last point is a sensitive one, but it demonstrates that Latin Americans are so concerned about the drug crisis that they are prepared to accept American unilateralism if they think it could be effective. The truth is that it can't be effective if it doesn't elicit genuine and effective cooperation from other governments. Such partnerships might need to include military advisors, and not just in Colombia.

The struggle against drug traffickers should be viewed not just as a problem or a potential source of tension, but as an opportunity to adapt the inter-American machinery to a modern cooperative approach among the governments of the Americas. The "Colombia Plan" and the U.S. approach to that country's struggle are good models for what to avoid. Because it sought support from the United States first, Colombia was criticized at the South American Summit by its neighbors, who feared "another Vietnam." Colombia's problems are South America's, and it should have sought a region-wide plan to support its efforts before turning to the United States for needed funding and equipment.

A second area in need of a hemispheric initiative encompasses the remaining territorial disputes in the hemisphere. Blood has been shed in the last decades in the Falklands, between El Salvador and Honduras, and between Ecuador and Peru.[17] Those and other disputes, including Bolivia's claims for access to the sea, are often used by the military to justify arms purchases, and the dispute between Venezuela and Colombia over rights in the Gulf of Venezuela was one of the factors precipitating an attempted coup in Caracas in February 1992.

The OAS Secretary General should build on the successful mediation between Ecuador and Peru and take the lead in calling on all the disputants to agree to arbitration within a fixed period. If all states in the hemisphere agree to this process, then it will be easier for all to accept the results at the end. The process should aim to be completed in 2005, the deadline for reaching agreement on the FTAA.

The third initiative, one that has been advanced vigorously by Oscar Arias, should be a concerted effort to reduce the purchase of arms and the size of the militaries in all of the countries of the Americas. The general principle is that scarce public resources would be better used for education. The *Latinobarometer* demonstrated overwhelming support for the idea. The leaders should all agree to reduce their expenditures for sophisticated weapons by 10 percent each year and place that amount in a special fund for education. Such an arms-reduction proposal would be easier to implement if all states participated, and if an agreement were reached among the governments that sell arms as well as those that purchase them.

To track the information, a hemispheric center, perhaps at the OAS, should be established with the authority to obtain information on all arms sales and purchases in the hemisphere and the size of the armed forces. Governments would verify the information, and each could insist on outside inspection to ensure that the information is accurate. Each government's plan would be submitted to the OAS for review and final approval. The group would then monitor the reduction. Any violations would be brought before the OAS, with the expectation that noncompliance could trigger penalties.

The fourth issue is the most awkward and difficult: Cuba. Politics on the island and U.S. policy are frozen in a tragic tableau. There may be nothing that can be done until Fidel Castro passes from the scene, but that could be a while, and the people of Cuba deserve better. If there is no reconciliation between Washington and Havana until then, the prospects of a peaceful transition would appear low. If there are riots on the island, the pressure for the United States to intervene would be very intense. The inter-American community has a responsibility to act before then and try to find an alternative path.

The hard truth for both the sympathizers and the enemies of Fidel Castro to acknowledge is that the embargo has no real effect on Cuba.

The embargo is a symbol that Fidel Castro uses to show the world that the United States is to blame for his country's poverty. It would be extremely difficult to find a single product that the United States makes that Cuba could not buy from its 153 trading partners and probably for a cheaper price. Americans cross the borders into Mexico and Canada to buy inexpensive medicines, and these two countries also happen to be Cuba's principal trading partners. The idea that the unilateral U.S. embargo is the source of Cuban scarcities is balmy. But apparently some people believe it, and each year, virtually the entire membership of the United Nations—except the United States and Israel—condemns the embargo in the most colorful terms. Without the embargo, Castro would be without excuses, but even if the president were convinced this was a fruitful path, he no longer has the discretion to make such a decision himself. The Helms-Burton law codified all the executive decisions on Cuba, meaning that only Congress can lift the embargo.

One of the reasons that Latin American governments have not publicly promoted free elections in Cuba is because many of their people view the U.S. embargo as unfair. If, however, they approached the United States and indicated that they were prepared to pursue jointly a concerted democracy strategy, provided that the United States would lift the embargo, this suggestion might occasion a serious review of U.S. policy toward Cuba. American businesses, especially farmers, have shown increasing interest in trading with Cuba, but from a practical political standpoint, Congress is likely to consider such an idea only if the Cuban-American community were comfortable that it offered greater hope for democratic change than the status quo. To convince the community of that would require real leadership.[18]

Guaranteeing Democracy and Human Rights

As we have seen, the lack of representative democracy has been one of the main causes of conflict in the hemisphere, but from its inception until 1990, the OAS was very reluctant to play any role in an area, like democracy, that could be interpreted as within the bounds of a country's internal affairs. The OAS used to send missions to observe elections in Latin America, but these were passive journeys of a day or two, and the delegates never criticized a government or condemned fraud. In the precedent-shattering case of Nicaragua, however, both the OAS and the United Nations were drawn into playing more active roles than either had initially intended. Since the election was judged a success, the OAS took a rather important step of establishing the Unit for the Promotion of Democracy, whose formal responsibilities include providing assistance to electoral authorities, observing elections, and supporting processes of national reconciliation.

As the OAS membership became democratic, they began to widen the OAS mandate in support of democracy. The "Santiago Commitment to Democracy," approved by the OAS in Chile on June 4, 1991, declared their "inescapable commitment to the defense and promotion of representative democracy and human rights in the region." The next day, the OAS approved Resolution 1080, which instructed the Secretary General to convoke immediately a meeting of the Permanent Council "in the event of any occurrences giving rise to the sudden or irregular interruption of the democratic political institutional process or of the legitimate exercise of power by the democratically elected government" of a member state. The Permanent Council would then decide to convene a Meeting of Foreign Ministers to decide on the appropriate collective response.

In December 1992, in Washington, the General Assembly of the OAS agreed to amend the Charter and insert a new article (Article 9) giving the Assembly the power to suspend from membership by a two-thirds vote any government that overthrows a democratic regime (the "Washington Protocol"). The Protocol was approved by a vote of 31–1–1, with Mexico opposing and Trinidad abstaining. The protocol went into effect on September 25, 1997, after twenty nations had signed it.

The OAS has invoked Resolution 1080 in the cases of Haiti in 1991, Peru in 1992, and Guatemala in 1993. The case of Paraguay was an ambiguous one because there wasn't a coup. On April 22, 1996, President Juan Carlos Wasmosy fired the army commander General Lino Oviedo, but he refused to resign unless the president also left office. The Brazilian, Argentine, and U.S. governments actively discouraged Wasmosy from resigning, and many international leaders, including the OAS Secretary General came to his defense together with the civil society of Paraguay. The OAS, as an institution, did not play a direct role, but Paraguay maintained its fragile grip on democracy for a couple of years, at which time the country went through another set of political crises. These were also handled in an ad hoc fashion with the help of the diplomats from neighboring democracies.[19]

The inter-American community continued wrestling with the issue of how best to support democracy, and over time, OAS electoral missions became more assertive. Indeed, in the cases of the runoffs for presidential elections in Peru on May 28, 2000, and for parliamentary elections in Haiti on June 25, 2000, the OAS Electoral Missions denounced the electoral conditions and withdrew before the election. In both cases, the Electoral Commissions were perceived as being too close to the ruling party, and the opposition, with considerable justification, did not believe that the elections could be conducted properly. In Haiti, the Commission counted the results of the elections in a manner inconsistent with the Constitution, and in Peru, the Election Commission would not permit the OAS mission to have sufficient time to verify the new software for counting the results. Since the elections went ahead regardless of the OAS actions, the inter-American community was faced with a dilemma of how to treat the incumbent. In the case of Peru, the OAS did not support its own mission or call for new elections, but it sent a high-level mission to discuss with both the government and the opposition long-term reforms to assure that future elections would be free and fair.

This was a regrettably equivocal response and an errant signal to the other Andean countries where democracy is tenuous. Fortunately, for Peru, a scandal wrenched power away from Fujimori in September 2000. He accepted new elections and promised not to run. But the conceptual and practical problems that the OAS faced at Windsor have not disappeared, and to advance the democratic agenda, the presidents of the Americas should begin with two questions: What constitutes irredeemable fraud, and what should be done to reinforce democracy?

To answer the first question, the governments should seek some consensus on what constitute the minimum conditions necessary for a free and fair election. This does not mean that they should overlook those electoral or human rights conditions that allow for the full enjoyment of a citizen's rights, only that they need to make a distinction between what is essential and what is desirable. Different policies follow from that distinction. If a government does not meet the minimal conditions necessary for a free election, the inter-American community ought to be unequivocal in condemning the election and demanding a new one. If a government does not respect the "desirable" conditions, then election observers ought to be critical and urge electoral reforms in the future, but they should not withdraw or disqualify the election.

What are the minimal conditions necessary for a free election? This is a very difficult question that deserves a longer response than is possible here, but three ingredients are essential. First, physical coercion or intimidation should not be tolerated by the authorities; the campaign and the election should take place in an open atmosphere. Second, the major parties should have an opportunity to deliver their messages to the people. And third, the people should be assured that their vote will be secret and will count.[20] If the election does not meet these minimal conditions, the OAS needs to find an appropriate way to halt the process until the conditions can be met. If the results are tainted, the OAS Secretary General should be authorized to call an emergency meeting of foreign ministers to consider appropriate action. This is what occurred after Jimmy Carter denounced the election fraud in Panama in May 1989. The OAS sent a three-person delegation to try to mediate the political crisis. The mediation failed because the OAS could not decide on its objective—whether to accept or annul the previous election or negotiate political reforms—or the means—what additional steps it should take after Noriega rejected the delegation's entreaties. It is clear that the existing machinery in the OAS is inadequate for both of these tasks at this time.

Few democrats in the hemisphere would consider the three conditions sufficient to assure a minimally decent election. Most would point to the need for a free and impartial press, a fair system for financing campaigns, the clear separation of the incumbent party from the tools and resources of the state, and the necessity of ensuring that the office responsible for conducting the election and counting the results be impartial and competent, and its activities transparent. Many would argue that if one accepted anything less than these conditions, one would be applying "double standards" to judge different elections, and this is the very antithesis of democracy.

It is very hard to respond to this argument at the level of principle, but elections occur in the real world, and ultimately, the people in a country are the judge of both their leaders and the process. In a country with little or no experience in free elections, the international community has a responsibility to reinforce a process by which the people can choose their leaders in a secret ballot. The electoral conditions in Nicaragua in 1990, in Guyana in 1992, and even in Mexico in 2000 were far from ideal. In each of these countries, the incumbent government used the resources of the state on behalf of its party, and some people were afraid, and yet in all of these cases, the people chose to vote powerful incumbent parties out of office. If the international community had insisted on "first world" democratic standards, the people would not have had the opportunity to choose their leaders. Indeed, in many ways, these three cases are the defining ones. As long as the conditions in a country are no worse than they were in these countries, the international community should encourage the elections to be held.

At the same time, the international community has a responsibility of explaining to the public where the process falls short and to do so in a manner that will encourage electoral reforms to improve the process for the next election. One should be very careful before disqualifying an election, and a key guide should be the views of the opposition. Identifying a "successful election" is no easy matter, and international observers have long debated the conditions, circumstances, and criteria by which to make such a judgment. Although some would prefer a "checklist" of conditions, I would argue that a successful election is one in which the opposition freely accepts and respects the electoral process and the results.[21] To some incumbent governments, this definition gives too much weight to the opposition, but a genuinely democratic process means that the principal parties should feel that they have a stake in the process.

For the "first" or "second" elections, some international monitors or mediators might be needed to help the parties acquire their stake and assure them that the process is fair or denounce it if it is not. If the OAS could play that role, that would be desirable; if not, nongovernmental organizations might need to play it.[22] As a general rule, all governments should formally accept international observers. It is not necessary to observe all elections, but an international group, not a government, should make the choice, and that group should have full and unrestricted access to each stage of the electoral process. If it lacks such assurances, as was apparently the case with the OAS Electoral Mission in Peru, then it should not even enter the country.

What role should the international community play if the minimum conditions are not met? In the case of Guyana, the Election Commission was prepared to hold elections in 1991 before the registration list was completed or verifiable. At that time, in a private but effective manner, the international monitors brought the weight of the international community to bear on the government, which agreed to delay the election until the registration list was completed.[23] The cases of Peru and Haiti in 2000 suggest that either the negotiations to urge a postponement or clarification of election and counting procedures were ineffectual, or an ad hoc process is no longer satisfactory for dealing with this kind of problem. What is necessary is for the inter-American community to establish clear rules as to the minimum conditions necessary for free elections and severe penalties for a government or an Election Commission that chooses to ignore those conditions.

What more should the OAS do to fulfill its mission to defend democracy? It must recognize that coups do not occur in a political vacuum, and thus the restoration and consolidation of democracy requires a two-track process aimed at applying escalating international pressure to intensive internal negotiations. The OAS Secretary General should seek all of the outside help considered necessary to resolve the internal disputes that precipitated the coup and to forge a new political consensus or pact.

Cases differ, of course, and policy should respond to the differences. When Eric Gairy was overthrown in Grenada in 1979, for example, no one called for his return. But the island's Caribbean neighbors made a mistake in recognizing the regime before receiving a date for the elections and an assurance that they would be held under international supervision. Had the Caribbean nations insisted on that condition, the United States, Canada, Great Britain, and many other nations would have supported efforts to enforce it, and the region would have been saved the tragedy that followed.

Collective actions against coups or tainted elections are a necessary part of the hemispheric determination to secure democracy. But these actions are not sufficient. A positive web of relationships must be woven among the industrialized nations and Latin America's fragile new democracies. Spain and Italy were imaginative in negotiating advantageous economic agreements with Argentina that are contingent on the maintenance of democracy there,[24] and subsequently, the Mercosur countries introduced a "democracy clause" in their pact that would exclude any member that turned away from democracy. In 2000, Mexico also accepted a "political" provision in its free trade agreement with the European Union that permitted all parties to comment on matters that previous governments would have considered their "internal affairs." At the Brasilia Summit of South American Presidents in September 2000, the twelve leaders stretched their commitment. The Communiqué declares that "the Presidents agreed that maintenance of the rule of law and strict respect for the democratic system in each of the twelve countries of the region are at once *a goal and a shared commitment,* and are henceforth *a condition for participation* in future South American meetings" (emphasis added). The language would have been far more reassuring if Alberto Fujimori had not signed it because there was ample reason to doubt his sincerity, or if the other presidents had criticized his abuse of power. Perhaps the Brazilians wanted all the countries to join the group *before* deciding the procedures for exclusion.

The basic premise underlying these agreements could be extended to other countries and adapted to other issues, such as the free trade regime or territorial disputes. Great Britain, for example, could negotiate an agreement to demilitarize or lease the Falkland Islands to Argentina contingent on the maintenance of democracy. (If confidence were built over the course of a long lease, the two governments might formally transfer sovereignty.) The civilian presidents of other governments with territorial disputes might explore similar arrangements to settle their problems. Such agreements would benefit Latin American democracies in three ways: Democratic governments could take credit for ending these disputes, militaries would lose a justification for their large budgets and roles in politics, and coups would become unpatriotic and costly in economic as well as in political terms.

Democracy cannot be less than free elections, but most believe it should be more. At an institutional level, the courts and the legislature should act independently and with integrity; the press should be autonomous; and the army and police should be subordinate to elected officials. Here again, it is not always easy to identify the moment or the event when the erosion of one of these institutions sets in motion a process that leads to the dismantling of democracy. One way to step into the chain of events and prevent democracy's breakdown would be for the presidents of the Americas to ask inter-American and nongovernmental institutions to monitor and report developments so that the leaders could act before a problem became a crisis. For example, the presidents could call on the Inter-American Court to establish a hemispheric association of former judges who could monitor the courts in all the countries and issue urgent warnings, alerts, or routine reports on the state of the courts. Similarly, the Inter-American Defense Board could be directed by the OAS Secretary General to report on the status of civil-military relations in the region and to alert the Secretary General of cases in which the military acts autonomously from elected leaders. The Inter-American Press Association, working with the OAS Special Rapporteur, could play a similar role. An Inter-American Parliamentary Association could develop networks that would reinforce threatened legislatures. Each of these transnational arrangements could function as a democratic safety net, alerting presidents at critical moments to take action. It would be even more desirable if the presidents could agree in principle before a problem becomes a crisis as to what steps they would take. In addition to responding to crises, the presidents ought to fashion a plan for assisting these institutions to improve their capacity to support the rule of law.

Democracy should be a collective norm but also a means for the hemispheric community to solve other issues. There is no subject more important for the leaders of the governments of the Americas to come to an understanding about than "democracy": What are the minimal conditions, and what should the inter-American system do to protect it? If it is too difficult to reach a consensus in the OAS, then groups of democratic nations should look for alternative mechanisms. A Free Trade Area of the Americas should also have a "democracy clause" that bars nondemocratic nations from being members.

Development and the Quality of Life

The value of one's home increases as the neighborhood improves. That is another way of saying that the United States has a direct interest in Latin America's development. A second reason is that as trade and investment barriers declined, Latin America became the fastest-growing market for U.S. goods and services. A third reason why it is in America's interest that the gap in income between the two continents be narrowed is that U.S.–Latin American relations will only achieve a constructive and steady-state equilibrium when the region has greater economic weight.

We have seen dramatic progress in closing the democratic gap in the last three decades, and over the course of the twentieth century, Latin America made remarkable social progress. The rate of illiteracy declined from 71 percent in 1900 to less than 10 percent one hundred years later, life expectancy climbed from 29 to 68 years, and the population soared from 70 to 500 million. Much of this growth occurred after the Second World War. Despite the seven-fold increase in population, the per capita income was five times higher at the end than at the beginning of the century. The bad news is that the income gap that separated the region from the United States and the developed world did not narrow. Average per capita income of Latin America was 14 percent that of the United States in 1900 and 13 percent at the end of the twentieth century.[25]

Still, the reforms undertaken since the mid-1980s represent, in the words of Barbara Stallings and Wilson Peres, two senior economists, "the most significant transformation of economic policy since World War II." The question, which they pose, is what impact these reforms have had on growth, equity, and employment in the region. Their tentative conclusions, based on econometric analyses, are that the reforms have had a small positive effect on investment and growth and a small negative impact on employment and income distribution. But they probe deeper and find that the effect is only discernible when the countries are clustered according to how serious they were in implementing the full range of reforms (tariff reductions, liberalization of domestic financial system, fiscal balance, privatization, tax reform). The economies of the "aggressive reformers," including Argentina, Bolivia, Chile, and Peru, performed the best, but they undertook the deepest reforms in large part because they inherited the worst inflation and economic problems. Brazil, Colombia, Costa Rica, Jamaica, and Mexico were more cautious in their reforms because their economies were not in such bad shape when they embarked on the new approach. Their results were also more modest than those of the aggressive reformers. All the governments reduced inequalities when they increased social expenditures in the 1990s.[26] Although Latin America was successful in curbing inflation in the 1990s, it was still hampered by the world's worst income distribution, continued volatility that discouraged investment, a comparatively low savings rate, a poor educational system, and inadequate institutional structures to regulate the banking system or property rights. National governments and the multilateral development banks will have to address these issues.

From the hemispheric perspective, the pivotal issue is integration, specifically, how to facilitate the integration of the Americas in a manner that will reduce both the disparities within countries and among them. The European Union (EU) is the only regional entity that has tackled this problem explicitly in its "regional and cohesion policies," and it has had some success. In one decade, from 1986 to 1996, the four poorest countries in the EU raised their per capita income from 66 percent of the EU average to 74 percent. The differences are even more graphic if one disaggregates. For example, the per capita income of Ireland rose from roughly 50 percent of the EU average in 1973 to 90 percent in 1995. Greece had the least progress, and Spain and Portugal were in the middle. The point is that the single market and the resources transferred from the EU (2–5 percent of the GDP of the receiving country) helped considerably, but the decisive factor separating the modest progress of Iberia from the astonishing success of Ireland was national policy.[27]

Both NAFTA and Mercosur, the two most highly developed regional trading agreements in the Americas, have experienced substantial progress in trade and investment in a short time, but they also were jolted by financial crises. The problem of volatility might very well be exacerbated with such trading arrangements because the weaker economies tend to do much better during boom times or much worse during recessions than the stronger economies. If measures are not taken to dampen the volatility—for example, by a unified currency or capital controls that discourage rapid withdrawal of capital—and other steps are not taken to reduce inequalities, regional trade areas might not be sustainable.

The U.S. president needs to secure approval from Congress for fast-track negotiating authority to deepen NAFTA and to widen it, first, to include the Caribbean Basin, and then eventually to extend it into a FTAA. Brazil would evidently prefer to negotiate a South American Free Trade Area first and then negotiate on the basis of greater balance with North America. This would not pose insurmountable problems, provided that Brazil is serious about wanting to move forward on free trade.

The United States and Latin America retain vital stakes in the global trading system, and neither would benefit from an exclusive trading bloc. The European Community is undergoing an extremely difficult transition toward enlargement, and it is finding it difficult to reduce its protectionism at the same time. The "American option" remains a potent tool for reminding Europe that it will pay a price for protectionism, and it remains a powerful incentive to opening the world trading system.

The Transcendental Task

Franklin D. Roosevelt urged Americans to stop imposing their way of life on Latin Americans and become again a model that Latin Americans would want to emulate voluntarily. That is the kind of advice Americans need to hear at least once a generation. One of the ways to escape the whirlpool is to internalize the "double-standard test," to think hard about how a decision or a statement looks or sounds from the other end.

Today, the United States is on the rim of the Latin American whirlpool, certain—as it was in the past—that it has definitively escaped. It has not. Despite the passing of the Soviet Union, the imbalance in power between the United States and Latin America continues to permeate the relationship. In the *Latinobarometer* surveys that have shown a convergence between the United States and Latin America on so many issues and values, there was also a revealing question about U.S. motives. When asked whether the United States usually plays a constructive role in world affairs or tries to dominate the world, 69 percent of Americans said its role was constructive while 61 percent of Latin Americans said it tries to dominate the world.[28] With such a gap in power and perceptions, the prospect for returning to an unproductive relationship is ever-present, particularly because the United States is as averse to limiting its freedom of action as any Latin American government. But the best time to negotiate new rules is when security concerns are distant.

The OAS has been stymied for much of its existence by an inherent contradiction between its two core principles, representative democracy and nonintervention. Almost every major crisis in the hemisphere—civil wars, fraudulent elections, human rights abuses—has involved a clash of these principles, and the OAS has been left with its hands tied as these problems festered or the United States intervened—"the most unacceptable of results," in the words of former Venezuelan President Pérez.[29] The time has come for the hemisphere to contemplate less unacceptable actions, such as collective intervention. In conjunction with a definitive U.S. pledge not to intervene unilaterally, the hemispheric community should agree to intervene multilaterally as the last resort in the face of genuine threats to democracy. Why?

It is not the end of the Cold War that makes the recurring questions on dictators and revolutionaries less relevant; it is the movement toward democracy and freer trade. Outside rivalries like the Cold War troubled the hemisphere because of internal conflicts.

If structures are built that guarantee democracy, and if an environment is created that permits growth with equity, then—and only then—will those two questions of dictators and revolutions become academic. The end of the Cold War does not provide the exit from the whirlpool; democracy does. If all parties accept a process of peaceful change, then none will need to invite arms from outsiders. Democracy also promotes peace because democratic states prefer to sheathe the weapons of war rather than to fight each other.

What a tragedy it would be if the pendulum were to swing back to dictatorship. To prevent that and secure democracy, the democratic nations of the Americas should establish a proactive, collaborative mechanism for the leaders of the region to help each other through difficult moments and hard decisions.

Democracy, security, development, and the new transnational environmental and social issues all pose the same awkward questions for the hemisphere. Will nations continue to pursue these goals solely within the bounds of their sovereignty, even at the cost of chronic failure, or will they define a new system of collective obligations and responsibilities? The purpose is not a merging of states—a "world without borders"—but cooperation across borders in pursuit of universal values and goals.

The United States is the most powerful nation in the hemisphere, but it too responds to nationalistic impulses and is as reluctant as any nation to give up sovereign powers. What is needed is leadership to explain that power is not being relinquished; it is enhanced by a new approach.

Since World War II, Latin America has languished on the margins of U.S. priorities. Europe and Asia were central to U.S. interests, and with the decline of the Soviet Union, those two economic blocs are even more important. But to compete with them today, Washington needs to enlist the cooperation of Latin America and the Caribbean in building a hemispheric market and a democratic community. In some ways, the beginning of the twenty-first century resembles the 1930s, when, for different reasons, the United States and Latin America withdrew from the rest of the world and forged a new relationship on trade and security that became the basis for the post-World War II order. The difference is that global withdrawal is undesirable and impossible in the twenty-first century; what is feasible, however, is a regional emphasis as a device for developing a global competitive edge.

The new hemispheric community should not be a fortress but rather a laboratory to develop economic formulas for the global trading system, a lever to help the World Trading Organization remain open, and an inspiration for guaranteeing democracy, assimilating minorities, and righting inequities. The goal is not just an improvement in the quality of life for all people but a narrowing of the gap that separates rich and poor within the nations of the hemisphere and between them. The Americas are on the threshold of forging a democratic community of nations with sturdier identities and more permeable frontiers. If the region's democratic leaders act boldly, they can establish a model that all industrialized and developing countries will seek to emulate. If they succeed, the twenty-first will truly be the century of all the Americas.

Notes

1. Albert Fishlow, *The Mature Neighbor Policy: A New United States Economic Policy for Latin America* (Berkeley: Institute of International Studies, University of California, Policy Paper no. 3, 1977), p. 32.

2. "*Fifth Report to the Secretary-General by the United Nations Observer Mission To Verify the Electoral Process in Nicaragua,* UN General Assembly, March 30, 1990, A/44/927, p. 8. I was there in 1990 and 1991.

3. For a summary of his views, see William J. Baumol, "America's Productivity 'Crisis': A Modest Decline Isn't All That Bad," *The New York Times,* February 15, 1987, p. 2.

4. "El Ocaso de los Nacionalismos?" *Este País* 1 (April 1991): 7. The editors wrote that "this dramatic statistic suggests that Mexican nationalism is declining" and that one of the reasons is the economic crisis.

5. Interview with Mexican Foreign Minister Fernando Solana, July 20, 1990, and members of the office—Unidad de Monitoreo de Medios Internacionales—that prepares the reviews, "Imagen de Mexico en el Mundo," on a weekly and biannual basis.

6. Edward Schumacher, "A Meeting of Minds, From Peoria to Patagonia," *Wall Street Journal,* April 16, 1998. This was a summary of the first survey, taken January–March 1998. The *Wall Street Journal* printed in a separate paper the results of that survey, as well as a second one from December 1998–January 1999, and a third one on the information age in September 1999.

7. Carlos Alberto Montaner, *Two Hundred Years of Gringos* (Lanham, Md.: University Press of America, 1983), p. 6.

8. Jorge Dominguez, ed., *The Future of Inter-American Relations* (New York: Routledge, 2000), p. 7.

9. Roberto R. Ramirez, *The Hispanic Population in the United States: Population Characteristics* (Washington, D.C.: U.S. Department of Commerce, Bureau of the Census, February 2000), p. 1.

10. A *New York Times* poll in October–November 1986 found that half of those interviewed in Mexico said they had a close relative who had lived in Mexico and was then living in the United States. William Stockton, "Mexicans, in Poll, Call U.S. a Friend," *The New York Times,* November 17, 1986, p. 6. A *Los Angeles Times* poll in August 1989 found that 38 percent of those interviewed had

close relatives living in the United States. *Los Angeles Times Poll* no. 192, August 1989, mimeo, p. 17.

11. Ronald Inglehart, Neil Nevitte, and Miguel Basañez, *The North American Trajectory: Cultural, Economic, and Political Ties among the United States, Canada, and Mexico* (New York: Aldine de Gruyter, 1996).

12. Ibid., p. 1.

13. International Monetary Fund, *Direction of Trade Statistics,* 1986–1991; J. F. Hornbeck, *Latin American Trade: Recent Trends* (Washington, D.C.: Congressional Research Service, Library of Congress, March 2000).

14. Inter-American Development Bank, *Integration and Trade in the Americas* (Washington, D.C., October 1999), Annex A.

15. Data from the Inter-American Development Bank website, 2000, www.iadb.org.

16. This was confirmed by Richard Feinberg, who referred to how "the summit was choreographed" and how Clinton "moved the conversation along according to the script." Feinberg, *Summitry in the Americas* (Washington, D.C.: Institute for International Economics, 1987), pp. 154–155.

17. For a good study of the Ecuador-Peru settlement and a list of the outstanding territorial disputes, see Beth A. Simmons, *Territorial Disputes and Their Resolution: The Case of Ecuador and Peru* (Washington, D.C.: U.S. Institute of Peace, Peaceworks 27, April 1999).

18. For a full development of this proposal, see Robert A. Pastor, "The Paradox of the Double Triangle: Pre-empting the Next Crises in Taiwan and Cuba," *World Policy Journal* (Spring 2000): pp. 19–30.

19. For an excellent case study, see Arturo Valenzuela, "The Collective Defense of Democracy: Lessons from the Paraguayan Crisis of 1996," *A Report to the Carnegie Commission on Preventing Deadly Conflict* (New York: Carnegie Corporation, December 1999).

20. For an analysis of these questions, see Robert A. Pastor, "The Role of Electoral Administration in Democratic Transitions: Implications for Policy and Research," *Democratization* 6, no. 4 (Winter 1999).

21. For the contrasting answers to this question, see Jorgen Elklit and Palle Svensson, "What Makes Elections Free and Fair?" *Journal of Democracy* 8 (July 1997); and Robert A. Pastor, "Mediating Elections," *Journal of Democracy* 9 (January 1998).

22. The United Nations acknowledged this point in its report on elections: "Because of their nature, those [non-governmental] organizations are often able to make a contribution in areas where the United Nations, for political or other reasons, lacks the capacity to be effective." UN Secretary General, *Enhanc-*

ing the Effectiveness of the Principle of Periodic and Genuine Elections, November 19, 1991, p. 22.

23. As the director of the Carter Center delegation, I mediated this case. See Robert Pastor and David Carroll, "Moderating Ethnic Tensions by Electoral Mediation: The Case of Guyana," *Security Dialogue,* 24, no. 2 (June 1993).

24. "Argentina and Spain Sign US $3 Billion Cooperation Deal: Treaty Is Similar to the Recent Accord with Italy," *Latin America Weekly Report,* February 11, 1988, p. 10. For the text of the protocol, see "Cooperation Agreement with Spain Signed," *FBIS,* February 5, 1988, pp. 32–33.

25. For these data and an analysis of the region's economic development, see Rosemary Thorp, *Progress, Poverty, and Exclusion: An Economic History of Latin America in the 20th Century* (Washington, D.C.: Inter-American Development Bank, 1998), chaps. 1, 3. John Coatsworth agrees that the gap in per capita income did not narrow, although he estimates that Latin America's product was 27 percent of the United States at the beginning and at the end of the century. See Coatsworth and Alan Taylor, eds., *Latin America and the World Economy Since 1800* (Cambridge: Harvard University Press, 1998), p. 26. They also estimated that the mean GDP per capita for Latin America was 128 percent of the United States in 1700 and 66 percent in 1800, suggesting a consistent secular decline.

26. Barbara Stallings and Wilson Peres, *Growth, Employment, and Equity: The Impact of the Economic Reforms in Latin America and the Caribbean: A Summary* (Washington, D.C.: U.N. Economic Commission for Latin America and the Caribbean, 2000).

27. European Union, *The European Union: Cohesion and Disparities* (Brussels, June 1997), pp. 4–5. See also Robert A. Pastor, *Lessons from the Old World for the New: The European Union and NAFTA* (Washington, D.C.: Institute for International Economics, forthcoming).

28. Ivan Rothkegel, "Travails of a Rocky Romance: The U.S. Continues to Inspire Both Attraction and Distrust," *Wall Street Journal/Americas,* December 1998–January 1999, p. 2.

29. Address to the OAS, April 27, 1990.

INDEX